RAILROADS AND THE
AMERICAN PEOPLE

Railroads Past & Present

GEORGE M. SMERK, EDITOR

A list of books in the series appears at the end of this volume.

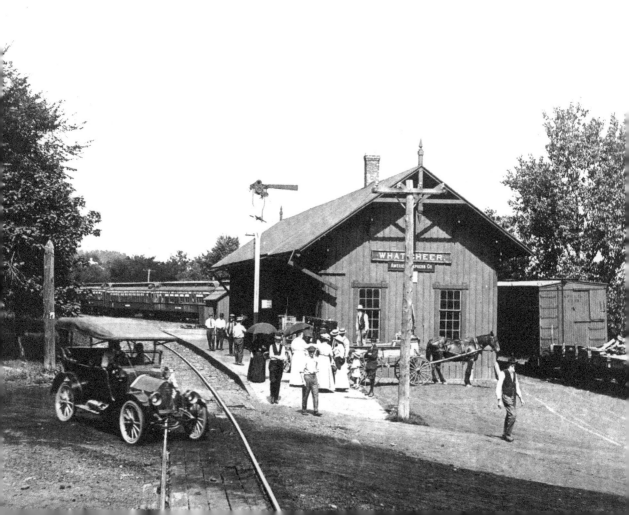

H. ROGER GRANT

RAILROADS

AND THE

AMERICAN

PEOPLE

INDIANA UNIVERSITY PRESS

Bloomington & Indianapolis

This book is a publication of

Indiana University Press
Office of Scholarly Publishing
Herman B Wells Library 350
1320 East 10th Street
Bloomington, Indiana 47405 USA

iupress.indiana.edu

First paperback edition 2017
© 2012 by H. Roger Grant

Manufactured in the
United States of America

The Library of Congress has cataloged
the original edition as follows:

Grant, H. Roger, [date]
  Railroads and the American
people / H. Roger Grant.
    p. cm. – (Railroads past and present)
  Includes bibliographical
references and index.
  ISBN 978-0-253-00633-2 (cl : alk.
paper) – ISBN 978-0-253-00637-0 (eb) 1.
Railroads – United States – History – 19th
century. 2. Railroads – United
States – History – 20th century. 3. Railroad
travel – United States – History – 19th
century. 4. Railroad travel – United
States – History – 20th century. I. Title.
  TF23.G677 2012
  385.0973 – dc23
                                    2012008227
1 2 3 4 5   22 21 20 19 18 17

ISBN 978-0-253-02379-7 (pbk.)

FOR MY FATHER,

HARRY R. GRANT (1900–1944)

CONTENTS

Acknowledgments ix

Prologue xi

1 **TRAINS** 1

2 **STATIONS** 95

3 **COMMUNITIES** 165

4 **LEGACY** 248

Sources and Suggestions for Further Reading 291

Index 297

ACKNOWLEDGMENTS

NEARLY TWENTY YEARS AGO AN EDITOR AT A NEW YORK CITY publishing house suggested that I write a social history of American railroads. The idea appealed to me, and a contract and advance were forthcoming. Yet I could not rapidly deliver a manuscript, not because I had lost interest, but because I changed jobs, leaving the University of Akron to chair the Department of History at Clemson University.

In the intervening years I continued to write articles, books, and essays on American railroad history, especially after I relinquished my administrative duties. In the process I gathered additional materials that dealt with what I saw as the four key components of a social history of railroads study: trains, stations, communities, and legacy. Indeed, I employed this basic structure to prepare an extended essay, "A Social History of American Railroads," for the *Encyclopedia of North American Railroads,* published by Indiana University Press in 2007.

It is impossible to acknowledge all of the individuals and institutions that have made this work possible. My long-standing connections with members of the Lexington Group in Transportation History, including Keith Bryant, Don Hofsommer, William Howes, Maury Klein, the late Albro Martin, the late Richard "Dick" Overton, Carlos Schwantes, the late John F. Stover, and James Ward, greatly enhanced my knowledge of railroading. Serving as editor of *Railroad History,* the semiannual publication of the Railway & Locomotive Historical Society, for eleven years provided me with additional insights. During my tenure I considered a wide variety of submissions, including some that I would likely never have read under any other circumstance. And as the sources noted on the illustrations reveal, a number of individuals and institutions graciously assisted. I should also mention that during my academic career I have written more than twenty books on various aspects of the railroad enterprise, ranging from company histories to stations and technology. In the process literally scores of public and private research collections have been examined and documentation assembled and individuals formally interviewed and informally consulted.

I am grateful to the staff of Indiana University Press, especially Linda Oblack, sponsoring editor, to ensure that this study made its way into print. Finally, I would like to thank my wife, Martha Farrington Grant, for her assistance in preparing still another book manuscript. I am certain that she knows that the research and writing process will not end in the foreseeable future.

PROLOGUE

FOR MORE THAN 150 YEARS RAILROADS HAVE EXERTED A pronounced influence on the American people. The iron horse literally became the engine for development and general well-being. By routinizing movements of raw materials, goods, and people, railroads orchestrated the growth of the national economy. In *The House of Seven Gables* (1851) Nathaniel Hawthorne said it well: "Railroads are positively the greatest blessing that the ages have wrought out for us. They give us wings; they annihilate the toil and dust of pilgrimage; they spiritualize travel!" President Warren G. Harding, a man not remembered for his insightful comments, sensed the value of improved transportation. "For the whole problem of civilization," he told a crowd assembled for the formal dedication of the government-built Alaska Railroad in July 1923, "the development of resources and the awaking of communities lies in transportation." It can be reasonably argued that if any area explains American greatness, it has been transportation.

By the end of the nineteenth century the "Railway Age" had matured in the United States. Yet line construction continued, especially on the Great Plains. In 1880 national mileage stood at 92,147; a decade later, after a frenzy of construction, it soared to 163,359, and in 1916 it peaked at 254,251, creating enough route miles to circle the earth ten times. By World War I states such as Illinois, Iowa, and Ohio claimed mileage that was so dense that small communities might have two or more carriers. Then the abandonment process began, particularly among the weakest shortlines, centered initially in the Midwest and South.

The expectations of pioneer "rail road" proponents mostly materialized. When on October 1, 1833, Elias Horry, president of the South-Carolina Canal & Rail-Road Company, addressed a Charleston audience about the impact of the opening of his 136-mile road between that city and Hamburg on the fall line of the Savannah River opposite Augusta,

Georgia, he hardly exaggerated the importance of the railroad of that day or much later. "Our citizens immediately, and correctly saw, that every benefit arising from the system [of railroads] could be extended to every City and Town in the United States, and particularly to those near the Atlantic." Horry, it seemed, possessed clairvoyant abilities.

> That by establishing Rail-Roads, so located as to pass into the interior of the several States, every agricultural, commercial, or saleable production could be brought down from remote parts of the Country to these Cities and Towns; and from them, such returns, as the wants of the inhabitants of the interior required, could be forwarded with great dispatch and economy, thereby forming a perfect system of mercantile exchanges, effected in the shortest possible time, and giving life to a most advantageous Commerce.

Over the following decades the words of Horry, the prophet, rang true. So much of the movement of goods and people depended on the iron horse. After the railroad map had apparently jelled about 1900, actions by scores of communities during the twilight period of construction indicated that steel rails and flanged wheels were still expected to ensure future prosperity. When the "inland" county-seat town of Ava, Missouri, located in the transportation-starved Ozarks, at last joined the national railroad grid in February 1910, residents cherished that moment. "At half past nine o'clock last Sunday night the old Ava died and the new Ava was born," crowed the editor of the *Douglas County Herald*.

> The welcome "toot" of a locomotive whistle was heard as the first train of the Kansas City, Ozark & Southern Railway came slowly down the hill from the John A. Spurlok homestead, and stopped in the midst of a cheering crowd at the depot. And from a gondola car at the rear end of the train stepped a cold, tired, but very happy man, a man who, in the face of abuse and discouragement had plugged away until he had made his dream come true. J. B. Quigley, almost blind, had accomplished what Ava had been hoping for and scheming for twenty years to secure – he had completed a practical railroad connecting Ava with the outside world.

The impact of railroads upon the personal lives of Americans can been seen in multiple ways. This study explores four fundamental topics: Trains, Stations, Communities, and Legacy. These units are designed collectively to capture the essence of the nation's railroad experience.

Travel by rail left lasting memories, both positive and negative. The luxury of a fast, all-Pullman train brought great pleasure, while a local with vintage equipment, frequent stops, and slow transit times did not. All types of individuals took to the rails, whether hoboes, immigrants, shoppers, salesmen, or vacationers. If a trip was not taken, the sight of a passing train could conjure up thoughts about exciting people and far-off places. On June 29, 1904, XIT Ranch cowboy William Tanner penned in his diary: "Sitting on top of wind mill tower watching an old [Fort Worth &] Denver train go toward Fort Worth. Wish it was taking me."

The railroad station once served as the focus of community life, something that knew no geographical bounds. These comments made by a woman who recalled her childhood typify memories of station life: "It was a great deal to us, watching the trains come in. Everybody in town did it, every single day. Mama showed us where to stand, and we'd go down there every afternoon after school and watch all the people and activities around the depot." Individuals directly associated with the "deepo" were important to nearly everyone. This was especially true in smaller towns where agents served as the personal link between the public and the world.

The railroad long affected communities, and its presence gave birth to thousands of places. Whether they were railroad created or not, the iron horse shaped their physical appearance. Often that included location of streets, transit lines, commercial buildings, and residential housing. From coast to coast America also had its "railroad towns" where carriers dominated local economies with their operating and repair facilities and their activities shaped the rhythms of daily life.

Then there is the legacy. Whether in language, memorials, artwork, or personal memory, this historic transport form has had a lasting impact on people and society. No other type of transportation, not even automobiles or airplanes, has left so much. Still many Americans are unaware of the diversity and extent of their rich railroad heritage.

The contents of the four units are hardly encyclopedic, yet an effort has been made to provide coverage in text and illustrations of the wide-ranging connection between people and the rails. Since the Midwest emerged as the heartland of railroads – after all, Chicago developed into America's railroad Mecca – this region has received much attention. As for the time period, most of the material involves the one hundred years between 1830 and 1930, the "Golden Age" of railroading, although the narrative also includes more recent happenings.

The story of people and railroads is vast and complicated. Yet the topic is worthy of scholarly attention, offering an opportunity to describe and explain the social components of American railroading. Nevertheless *Railroads and the American People* is mostly *social* rather than *cultural* history. The popular-culture impact of railroads covers much, ranging from pulp-fiction books to Hollywood motion pictures, and deserves to be a study in itself. For practical reasons, however, the legacy unit includes some cultural aspects. Also the subject of the social dimensions of commuter rail, whether steam or electric, has generally been avoided, and like cultural history should be explored separately.

Unlike traditional scholarly monographs, this volume has limited documentation. A listing of source books and standard works is included, offering the basic framework of materials consulted. Much of the ideas and examples represent more than forty years (even a lifetime) of my personal involvement with railroads.

H. Roger Grant
Clemson University
Clemson, South Carolina

RAILROADS AND THE AMERICAN PEOPLE

TRAINS

1

OPERATING TRAINS

From the time that the first train in America turned a wheel, the railroad generated excitement. Powered by its captivating steam locomotive, the moving train was much more than an instrument of progress; it was a true wonder. In his 1876 "To a Locomotive in Winter" poet Walt Whitman captured the essence of the attraction for this mechanical marvel: "The black cylindric body golden brass. Type of the modern-emblem of motion and power – pulse of the continent." An early patron of the Boston & Worcester Rail Road expressed similar thoughts, but in a nonpoetic fashion. "What an object of wonder! How marvelous it is in every particular! It appears like a thing of life. I cannot describe the strange sensations produced on seeing the train of cars come up. And when I started for Boston, it seemed like a dream." In a larger sense "the railroad, animated by its powerful locomotive, appears to be the characteristic personification of the American," concluded Guillaume Poussin, a Frenchman who visited the New World in 1851. "The one seems to hear and understand the other – to have been made for the other – to be indispensable to the other." Even in the recent past the National Railroad Passenger Corporation (Amtrak) engaged jazz musician Lou Rawls to record a commercial that had as its theme "There's something about a train that's magic."

People not only wanted to ride on trains, they also wanted to work on trains. "Trains got in my blood," was a reason frequently repeated by young men who entered road service, "and that's why I went 'railroadin.'" A veteran locomotive engineer explained his love affair with the iron horse:

> The first sounds that registered on my ears were the whistles of the New York Central trains hooting for a crossing. They drifted over the hill to the farm, calling me to follow the iron pike. When I was old and sturdy enough to walk six miles to the railroad, I sat on an embankment above the tracks and watched the trains go by, waved to the lordly creatures leaning out of the cab windows, and made up my mind that I too was going to run one of those snorting engines.

I

A career in railroading offered much. There was daily stimulation in the workplace. Every run provided different experiences, including train volume, track speed, mechanical conditions, weather, and personalities. "The unpredictable happened every day in railroading," said one engineman. Then there existed the sheer excitement, especially the potential for danger before the widespread use of air brakes, automatic couplers, and other safety appliances. There was also prestige and respect: the engineer perched on his thronelike seat with his head leaning out of the locomotive cab as a passenger train glided into a station, and the conductor with his uniform, first consisting of a top coat and silk hat and later a dark uniform with shiny buttons that bore the initials of the railroad company, and a matching cap with a bright brass or polished nickel badge that proclaimed CONDUCTOR. "He is an important personage," commented a Gilded Age traveler, an understatement indeed. Brakemen or trainmen also wore smart uniforms, and they had their positions duly noted on their cap badges. Even crewmen assigned to freight trains were individuals on the move. Like their passenger train brethren, they carried keys, lanterns, company-approved pocket watches, and other tools of their trade. Every trainman understood that his work was vital for national life, and the public sensed that fact as well.

For the one-hundred-plus years of the Railway Age men who ran the trains had similar duties, whether assigned to freight or passenger runs. It would not be until near the end of the twentieth century that the composition of crews changed dramatically, particularly for those railroaders operating freights. Carriers curtailed "featherbedding" practices, unproductive jobs in the day of diesel-electric locomotives that were based on antiquated steam-era work rules. (Today freight crews consist of an engineer and conductor, lacking the traditional firemen and two or more brakemen.) Historically the numbers of train personnel were impressive. Approximately 40 percent of all railroad employees, totaling more than a million by 1900, worked in train service, and that figure grew until after World War I.

Even a small child recognized the locomotive engineer. He was the man in the cab who controlled the mighty locomotive. Although the youngster would never refer to the engineer as a "labor aristocrat," which he was, he might announce that when he grew up, he wanted to become an engineer or "hogger," the common nickname. Many boys did, especially those who were raised on the farms and ranches. In the nineteenth century and somewhat later a disproportionate number of engineers came from rural backgrounds. They were farm fresh, so to speak. Prestige, compensation, and a fascination for things mechanical influenced that career choice. Then there was the drudgery of agricultural life that made young men crave excitement and travel. Said one engineer: "I sought to escape the monotony and the wretched routine of a drab life." As with all railroaders, there might be a desire to break loose from the watchful eyes of parents, particularly for those young men who would otherwise remain on the family farm. Other hiring patterns came into play. Nepotism, a long-standing feature of railroader recruitment, explains why sons of engineers and others in train service joined the running trades; railroading became a family affair.

Firemen were far less glamorous, in fact unheralded. They were the men on the steam locomotive "deck," heaving cord wood and later scooping coal, or "black diamonds," into the always hungry, demonic firebox. This was backbreaking work. (In the era of wood-burning locomotives, the fireman might receive assistance from a "wood passer," who also helped to replenish the locomotive tender at fuel stops.) "[The fireman] shoveled scoopful after scoopful of coal into the roaring hot firebox, and the glare from the fire would reflect on his hot, red face, and the heat from the open door would start the smoke curling up off his overalls," observed an apprentice fireman. "After closing the door he would step to the gangway between the tank and the engine-cab to one side and lean out to get a breath of fresh air and also to let the draft that sucked through the gangway cool his heated body for a few moments." Another fireman recalled: "It was very hard work then, coal was used and shoveled into the firebox by hand; I have shoveled 15 tons into a firebox on one trip of 12 to 15 hours." Even after the introduction of mechanical coal stokers, the job remained difficult, taking much effort to ensure the steady flow of coal and to prevent and repair equipment breakdowns. Only with the advent of oil-fired steam locomotives, which after the turn of the twentieth century started to appear in the West, did the work of a fireman lessen considerably. Most adults could identify with the rigors associated with hand-firing a boiler; after all, they attended to their domestic fireplaces, wood or coal stoves, or coal furnaces during the heating season. A railroad fireman took pride in his skills to create and maintain a hot, even-burning fire that effectively kept up the required steam pressure.

When not attending to his principal job, a fireman would take his seat on the left-hand side of the cab to assist the engineer with matters of safety, keeping a watchful eye for obstacles on the track, misaligned switches, and other potential dangers. As technologies advanced, he "called signals" and performed other duties.

The fireman and the general public knew that in time he would likely move to the right-hand seat, although some firemen preferred to keep their jobs. And there were those men who never acquired the necessary skills or gained the required seniority to be promoted. If the "fire boy" was a person of color, there was virtually no chance for advancement. After a run – prior to electric and diesel-electric locomotives – firemen were usually covered from head to toe with soot, oil, and grease.

While passenger conductors had a "clean" job (cab crewmen sometimes called them "prissy"), they encountered their own set of tasks and headaches. During the "Demonstration Period" of the 1830s and 1840s newly opened railroads frequently turned to stagecoach drivers to serve as "captains" of their trains. This was a logical decision. It was assumed that these former drivers possessed practical judgment and were fully literate. After all, these men had participated in a transportation system, making certain that equipment functioned properly, attempting to maintain schedules, collecting fares, handling paperwork, and dealing with travelers and company personnel at stops. "Good Whips," in fact, had been an important source of conductors or "guards" on early British passenger trains. Conductors normally gained their position by having been brakemen in passenger service or conductors and brakemen on freight trains.

As the railroad enterprise matured, the passenger train conductor (if there were sleeping cars, the Pullman Company provided its own conductor) found his duties varied. There was that predictable routine: "lifting" and selling tickets, seating passengers, answering questions, calling out stops, assisting passengers to detrain (and at the right station), and turning in cash fares and completing paperwork at the end of the trip. He checked the cleanliness of the cars, made certain that needed supplies for the toilets and other amenities were provided, adjusted lighting and attended to matters of heating and ventilation. The conductor needed to guard against the fraudulent use of passes, tickets, and counterfeit currency, watch out for hoboes and any other nonpaying riders, and keep a lookout for confidence men, including the card shark. He also had to quiet or expel disruptive passengers, usually those under the influence of alcohol. "Maintain good order among the passengers, and not permit rudeness or profanity," demanded the Pennsylvania Railroad. But much more was required. Remarked a conductor in the 1870s: "He should see that no time is lost at stations, have a thorough understanding of his time-card, and all the rules and regulations affecting the duties of employees, an eye to the condition of the track, trestles, bridges, culverts, and embankments." And he added, "He should frequently examine the brakes, couplings, and bell-ropes of his cars; inspect his train before starting; that his watch is in accordance with the railroad standard time; that all the necessary articles for emergencies are on board."

Travelers most of all associated the conductor with announcing the departure of the passenger train. "The most romantic call in America still was 'Booo-ard!'" observed an historian of the Atchison, Topeka & Santa Fe Railway (Santa Fe) in the 1940s. "It was sung every day by a thousand conductors, re-echoed by half a million passengers. It was almost the oldest call in the country and to most people it still meant adventure and hope and new horizons."

Occasionally, the unexpected occurred. It might be a cloudburst, blizzard, prairie or forest fire, mechanical breakdown, livestock on the tracks, derailment, or some other happening that slowed or stopped the train. Or it might be an unruly individual or group of passengers or that rare troop of bandits or desperados. The conductor needed to respond quickly and effectively. In 1913 when a boxcar of apples derailed in Malvern, Iowa, the eastern terminus of the Tabor & Northern Railroad, an 11-mile Hawkeye State shortline, the "ever resourceful conductor" handled the situation with dispatch. His train was about to depart for Tabor, but the coach combine was blocked by the apple car. Fortunately the locomotive was positioned correctly, and as a journalist reported: "The conductor just coupled his engine to a box car filled with nice straw, loaded the mail, baggage, passengers, et cetera, all in, a la scrambled eggs fashion, and hit out for Tabor."

Not everyone was overly impressed with conductors, however. "An American conductor is a nondescript being, half clerk, half guard, with a dash of the gentlemen," wrote a grumpy English visitor in the 1850s. "One thing is remarkable about him – you do not get a sight of him till the train is in motion, and when it stops he disappears. I can account for this mysterious feature in his character, only by supposing, that as soon as he touches *terra firma*, he removes from the front of his hat the word blazoned in metal, which indicates his office; and so all at once becomes an ordinary human being." When the conductor reappeared, this commentator expressed disdain. "All he says is 'Ticket!' and he utters the word in a dry, callous tone, as if it would cost something to be cheerful."

Disputes might erupt between a passenger and a conductor. One such case was described in 1857 by Anna Calhoun Clemson, daughter of the late South Carolina politician John C. Calhoun. She reported that a South Carolina Rail Road conductor "from some unaccountable whim" had refused to allow two passengers to detrain at Penn's Platform near the Clemsons' Low Country plantation. After an unpleasant exchange, he ordered these friends from Washington, D.C., to get off at the depot. The unhappy couple sought to hire a "vehicle, & negro driver" to reach their destination. When that took them only partway because of a swollen river, they had to walk the remaining distance and in the process became "muddied up to their knees." The conductor was in command, even if his decisions might create unintended consequences that hardly enhanced the image of his position or his railroad.

Yet there were highly respected, even beloved, conductors (and other crewmen as well). More likely bonds of affection developed when there was frequent contact, especially on local, branch line, and commuter trains. One such individual was a conductor who worked for the Pennsylvania Railroad in northern New Jersey. A favorite patron was financier Pierre Lorillard. In appreciation for the attention paid Lorillard, the conductor received from him a Tiffany-made filigreed, solid gold conductor's badge for his uniform cap. But this prized gift remained in the conductor's bureau drawer; Pennsylvania officials forbade the wearing of this ornamental insignia, calling it "irregular." And for years during the Christmas season, members of the communitarian Amana colonies in Iowa expressed their esteem to the Chicago, Milwaukee & St. Paul (Milwaukee Road) passenger train conductor and his colleagues "with savory hams, delicious wines and gifts."

The conductor received assistance from "trainmen" – brakemen and flagmen – although the size and nature of the crew varied from train to train, from railroad to railroad, and at times from state to state. Trainmen were apprentice conductors, and their duties ran the gamut from directly assisting the conductor in collecting tickets to calling station stops. Passenger trainmen, though, did not face the rugged and dangerous assignments of their brethren on freight trains, where before air brakes and the limited braking power of locomotives trainmen scrambled over the tops of cars to set and release brakes with their brute strength. Although passenger personnel had braking duties prior to the advent of air brakes, they had only to turn brake wheels on the platforms of the several cars. Similarly, trainmen on "varnish" (passenger) runs were spared the excessive coupling and uncoupling of cars, especially daunting (and dangerous to fingers and hands) in the era of link and pin couplers. Their counterparts on freight trains repeatedly needed to open and close switches, having many more opportunities to "bend the iron."

Coach passengers had contact with conductors and trainmen, and they recognized the presence of engineers and firemen, yet they probably encountered other onboard employees. The tendency of American railroads to lack rigid class accommodations led most travelers to make their trips in a "day coach." Inevitably they became familiar with a young vender, the "news butcher" or "news butch." This entrepreneurial lad, who was not a railroad employee but rather self-employed or representing a commercial news agency, offered passengers reading materials, particularly newspapers, and oddments that included candy, fruit, and cigars. "A great personage on an American train is the newsboy," observed Robert Louis Stevenson, the Scottish writer, in his 1892 book, *Across the Plains*. "He sells books (such books!), papers, fruit, lollipops, and cigars; and on emigrant journeys, soap, towels, tin washing dishes, tin coffee pitchers, coffee, tea, sugar, and tinned eatables, mostly hash or beans and bacon." Tom L. Johnson, the wealthy industrialist and traction magnate and later

reform mayor of Cleveland, Ohio, recalled that he became a news butcher at the tender age of eleven after striking up a friendship with a conductor on the Chesapeake & Ohio Railroad in his hometown of Staunton, Virginia. "One day he [conductor] said to me, 'How would you like to sell papers, Tom? I could bring 'em in for you on my train and I wouldn't carry any for anybody else, so you could charge whatever you pleased.'" Explained Johnson:

> The exciting events attending to the end of the [Civil] war naturally created a brisk demand for news and I eagerly seized the opportunity to get into business. The Richmond and Petersburg papers I retailed at fifteen cents each and for "picture papers," the illustrated weeklies, I got twenty-five cents each. My monopoly lasted five weeks. Then it was abruptly ended by a change in the management of the railroad which meant also a change of conductors.

Travelers usually appreciated a Tom Johnson coming down coach aisles, but they might have complaints. Their most common concerns involved prices that they considered too high or the quality too low, and the seller was also affected. Roy Disney, brother of Walt Disney and a youthful entrepreneur, was duped by the Van Voy News Service of Kansas City; the company repeatedly provided him with rotten fruit. Failing to make a reasonable profit because of disgruntled consumers, Disney quit.

On some railroads the news butcher had a predecessor, the water boy, who provided this refreshing liquid before mechanical water dispensers. "Every half-hour or so a boy passes through the car with a can of iced water, out of which you can have a drink for nothing," an English visitor

They're ready to serve. About 1920 Pullman Company personnel assigned to the Baltimore & Ohio's all-Pullman *Capitol Limited* assemble in Grand Central Station in Chicago. The white Pullman conductor stands on the right and the white barber on the left. Six of the seven people of color are porters, and the seventh, attired in white, is either a bus boy or a lounge attendant.

William Howes Jr. coll.

observed in 1862. But there was a negative, a perceived health risk: "[You drink] out of the public glass." The water boy might also peddle various sundries. He and the news butcher yielded to the sandwich man, who sold sandwiches, usually ham and cheese, and coffee or tea. As with the news butcher and the water boy this vender ballyhooed his offerings.

Coach passengers might have contact with the train porter, usually a person of color. This non–Pullman Company employee assisted the conductor and trainmen, announced stations, and performed janitorial chores. He customarily provided complimentary or rental pillows, popular on overnight or extended daytime journeys. Unlike the Pullman porter, this onboard worker was not likely to receive much in tips and depended mostly on his low-wage railroad salary.

But after the Civil War much better (and more expensive) amenities became available to travelers: namely dining, parlor, and sleeping cars. These improvements increased the size of the onboard staff, for each car had especially assigned employees. The Pullman Company, which by 1900 monopolized the sleeping-car business, not only provided its own conductor, but also had a porter, nearly always black, assigned to each car. The porter made up berths and performed various additional services, including shining shoes, brushing clothes, and assisting his boss, the always-white Pullman conductor. On most trains the Pullman Company maintained the parlor car that was likely attached to the rear of the "limited" express or luxury train. (Locals, including those that operated over main lines, lacked such equipment.) The attendant, again usually a person of color, offered refreshments and reading materials, provided pillows, and watched over operations. During the golden age of passenger service, crack trains included a bar car where drinks (except during national prohibition or in accordance with state laws) and light meals were offered, and it was once more staffed by porters or attendants.

On the all-Pullman Chicago–Los Angeles Super Chief, pride of the Atchison, Topeka & Santa Fe Railway, the Fred Harvey Company oversaw the cocktail lounge. In 1937 two employees work their bartending magic, the year this classy train made its debut.

William Howes Jr. coll.

On the finest trains where "passengers were guests" additional personnel served travelers. During the 1920s, decade of the greatest number of long-distance passenger trains, the swank New York Central all-Pullman *Twentieth Century Limited* employed a men's barber, a ladies' maid, and a stenographer. As the train sped along the 960-mile "Water Level Route" between New York City and Chicago, its skilled staff pampered passengers, resembling crews found on the best transatlantic liners. Its foremost rival, the *Broadway Limited,* provided similar attentive onboard personnel, helping to make for the most pleasant journey possible. "There is leisure here, of body and spirit, leisure and charm and quiet thoughtful comfort," enthused a rider on this all-Pullman Pennsylvania train. Another commentator simply said: "These trains were luxury ships on steel wheels."

While frugal-minded and short-distance passengers avoided sleeping and parlor cars, they might splurge on a meal in the diner. This brought them into contact with the well-dressed and well-trained steward and waiters. Possibly these passengers gazed upon the behind-the-scenes cooks who toiled in a tiny, but efficiently arranged, galley kitchen. Until the post–World War II era the steward, who supervised dining-car operations, was white; the remainder of his crew were African American men or occasionally Filipinos or other nationalities.

Largely unseen, except when the train made station stops, were the men who worked in Railway Post Office (RPO) and baggage/express cars, equipment located immediately behind the tender or later the electric or diesel locomotive. The RPO car usually had several clerks who sorted the mail and orchestrated their deliveries to on-line post offices and connecting RPO routes. Some trains had both a company-employed baggage handler and an express agent. The latter worked for the private firm (Adams, American, Southern, Wells Fargo, or others) that held a contract with the railroad. Then after 1917 the federally controlled American Railway Express operated this business, and following 1929 the industry-owned Railway Express Agency took charge. The express agent, perhaps with assistants, managed packages and protected against robberies of high-valued shipments – gold, coins, currency, and securities.

RIDING TRAINS

When the architects of the first American railroads contemplated what would be the results of their handiwork, they expected that their transport form would focus on passengers and not freight. If the latter was handled, the haulage would be lightweight goods. "Railroads could not carry heavy freight," remarked a commentator on the evolving Railroad Age. "That must be left to canals." Such an assessment quickly proved to be wrong, and freight carriage dramatically changed commercial transportation. Still, as everyone had initially surmised, the passenger business became critical to carriers.

From the first primitive passenger trains that plied the rickety tracks of the Baltimore & Ohio (B&O) in the late 1820s to today's flagship Acela trains operated by Amtrak over the heavy steel rails along the Northeast Corridor, a ride on flanged wheels has provided varied experiences, good or bad.

Early on there was the novelty of the railroad trip, although even today many first-time riders have this feeling. Diaries, letters, newspapers, and other sources contain abundant evidence that a train journey was memorable. In October 1832 a passenger on the pioneer New Castle & Frenchtown Rail Road in Pennsylvania expressed the excitement of most contemporaries: "Not an incident happened to break the spell of the enchantment which we all felt in cutting the air at this rate – the houses and trees all seemed to be rapidly passing us, and sometimes a bird would, when we were descending, look to the eye as if its wings were of no use to it." For this traveler the railroad offered a true sensory experience.

A few years later the *Wilmington Gazette* made much of the initial run over the Wilmington & Susquehanna Railroad between Wilmington, Delaware, and Elkton, Maryland. "This was the first trip of the cars over the road, and there was some little anxiety, and apprehension, entertained by many of the company as the result of the experiment, and the chances of some accident or catastrophy, where as yet, the locomotive, cars, engineer and road, had not become very well acquainted with each other." Not only did hundreds of curious well-wishers flock to the several stations and the right-of-way, but this journey provided a bit of excitement. "A sturdy oak, that had not been sufficiently looked to, by the workmen and engineers, and which seemed rather to dispute a passage for *The Yankee* [locomotive] and his train, extended a branch some distance into the road which swept the sides and tops of the cars, breaking some twenty or thirty panes of glass, and scattering the pieces with violence enough to draw blood from half a dozen noses, that were too prominent to escape a collision." Yet no serious injuries occurred. "After adjusting the difficulties from this accident, and bestowing proper attention to the wounded, by laughing them into a pleasant countenance again, we continued our course." The return went without incident and those on board were amazed at the "lightning speed" of their journey.

It was exhilarating for railroad passengers to experience the fastest form of conveyance in their lives, and there were other perceived advantages. "One of the happiest effects of traveling on railroads is the freedom it gives you from the impertinence and impositions of porters, cartmen, *et omne id genus* [and things of that kind] who infest common steamboat landings," opined a traveler on the B&O in 1834.

> A long and solitary row of carriages [passenger coaches] was standing on the shore awaiting our arrival; not a shout was heard, scarcely anything was seen to move except the locomotive, and the arms of the man who caught the rope from our boat. The passengers were filed off along a planked walk to the carriages through one gangway, while their luggage, which had already been stowed safely away, was rolled on shore by another, in two light wagons; and almost without speaking a word, the seats were occupied, the wagons attached behind, the half-locomotive began to snort, and the whole retinue was on the way with as little ado and as little loss of time as I have been guilty of in telling the story.

Passengers repeatedly noted the amazing physical aspects of the railroad corridor, particularly during the earlier years. In 1836 Freeman Hunt, editor of the influential *Hunt's Merchant Magazine*, marveled at the span that the Rensselaer & Saratoga Rail Road had erected over the mighty Hudson River.

> The railroad bridge, over which the cars cross the Hudson from Troy to Green Island, on their route to the Springs, is certainly a noble, substantial specimen of this kind of architecture. It is 1,512 feet in length, 34 feet in width, and 17 feet

Rolling stock, especially passenger cars, likewise made an impression. After the novelty of rail travel wore off, negative comments began to flow. The first pieces of equipment were anything but homey and might remain in service for decades, having been sold from the original owner to newer or poorer roads. They lacked the comfort of the modern replacement equipment that wealthier carriers acquired.

A good example involves the Northern Cross Rail Road of Illinois (original component of the Wabash Railroad) that opened in 1839 between Jacksonville, Meredosia, and the Illinois River. The public had the choice of two Spartan eight-wheeled "pleasure" cars. "The seats ran along each side, like those of the omnibus, and [they] were equally destitute of any and every other appliance for the comfort or conveyance of the traveler, other than to sit down and 'hang-on' – if he could. [A] sudden lurch of the coach would often slide a sitter half the length of the coach and land

The crew assigned to the Baltimore & Ohio's *Martha Washington* dining car reveals the division by race (the steward is white) and the labor-intensive nature of this service. This particular car, built in 1923, claimed the distinction of being the first B&O diner to be air-conditioned, that occurring in 1930.

William Howes Jr. coll.

to the eaves. It is supported by stone abutments and piers. The sides are double lattice work, covered with boards on the outside. The floors of plank, and the roof shingled. It has thirty-two skylights or scuttles. The roof is supported in the centre by a tier of pillars.

him, or her, with a gruesome bump in the middle of the floor." But a trip over the iron strap-rails of the Northern Cross was more dependable than the stagecoach alternative, and it was faster and cheaper, too.

About the same time a similar story involved a ride on Boston & Providence Rail Road. Samuel Beck, an elderly Bostonian, found a trip on his hometown carrier to be anything but pleasant.

This morning at nine o'clock I took passage in a railroad car for Providence. Five or six other cars were attached to the locomotive, and uglier boxes I do not wish to travel in. They were made to stow away some thirty human beings, who sit cheek by jowl as best they can. The poor fellows who were not much in the habit of making their toilet squeezed me into a corner, while the hot sun drew from their garments a villainous compound of smells made up of salt fish, tar, and molasses.

Concluded the crusty Breck: "The rich and the poor, the educated and the ignorant, the polite and the vulgar, all herded together in this modern improvement of travelling."

Yet progress in creating creature comforts took place. "Yankee ingenuity is rarely more pleasantly exemplified then in the luxurious arrangements for railroad traveling, of which we have now in Rochester [New York], a magnificent specimen – in the service of the sovereign people, on the Auburn and Rochester Railroad," enthused the *American Railroad Journal* in 1842. "There are six cars, designed to form two trains. The cars are each 28 feet long and 8 feet wide. The seats are well stuffed and admirably arranged – with arms for each chair, and changeable backs that will allow the passenger to change 'front to rear' by a maneuver unknown in military tactics. The size of the cars forms a pleasant room, handsomely painted, with floor matting, with windows secured from jarring, and with curtains to shield from the blazing sun." There was more. "These cars are so hung on springs, and are of such large size, that they are freed from most of the jar, and especially from the swinging motion so disagreeable to most railroads. On the whole it would be difficult to imagine any improvements that could be desired."

Travelers from abroad provided revealing insights about early railroad journeys. After all, they had a frame of comparison, first the British in the 1820s and then the Belgians and the Germans and later other nationalities. Charles Dickens did extensive train riding, and his comments appeared in his well-received *American Notes for General Circulation* that a London publisher released in 1842. This most famous of all English travelers was struck by the "classlessness" of American trains. "There are no first and second class carriages as with us, but [in America] there is a gentlemen's car and a ladies' car. The main distinction between which is that in the first, everybody smokes; and in the second, nobody does." Dickens did not encounter the Auburn & Rochester or other roads with state-of-the-art equipment, caring little for much of the American rolling stock that he rode. He was noticeably displeased with what he found on the Boston & Lowell Railroad. "The cars are like shabby omnibuses, but larger, holding thirty, forty, fifty people. The seats, instead of stretching from end to end, are placed crosswise. Each seat holds two people. There is a long row of them of each side of the caravan, a narrow passage up the middle, and a

BREAKFAST.

Fruit	Berries and Cream 20c
	Assorted Fresh Fruit 20c
	Orange Marmalade 15c Sliced Oranges 15c
Cereals	Shredded Wheat Biscuits with Cream 20c
	Oatmeal with Cream 20c Grape Nuts with Cream 20c
Coffee, Tea and Cocoa	Coffee, Pot for One 15c, for Two 25c, Cup, 10c
	Assorted Tea Drawn to Order, Pot for One 10c, for Two 20c
	Milk, per Glass, 10c Cocoa 15c Cream, per Glass, 20c
Hot and Cold Bread Etc.	Hot Rolls, Corn Bread or Plain Bread, 10c
	Dry Toast 10c Milk Toast 20c Cream Toast 30c
Fish	Broiled or Fried Fresh Fish 40c
	Broiled or Boiled Salt Mackerel 35c
Eggs and Omelets	Eggs (3) Boiled, Fried or Scrambled, 20c
	Plain Omelet 25c Jelly or Ham Omelet 30c
Hash	Corned Beef Hash, with Poached Egg, 40c
Steaks, Chops, Etc.	Small Steak 50c Sirloin Steak 70c
	Porterhouse Steak for One $1.25, for Two $1.50
	Mushrooms 25c Extra
	Mutton Chops (2) 40c, (3) 50c
	Rasher of Bacon Served with Broiled Orders 10c Extra
	Veal Cutlet, Plain or Breaded, 45c, Tomato Sauce 10c extra
	Ham or Bacon, Broiled or Fried. 40c, with Two Fried Eggs 50c
	Spring Chicken on Toast, half 50c, whole 90c
Vegetables	Potatoes Saute, 10c; Stewed in Cream, 15c
Hot Cakes	Wheat Cakes, with Maple Syrup, 20c

Bread, Butter and Saute Potatoes Served Free with all Hot Meat or Fish Orders.
Bread and Butter Free with all Cold Meats or Salads.
No Order less than 25c to Each Person.
Service by Waiter Outside of Dining Car 25c Extra to each Person Served.

A CHARGE OF 25c IS MADE FOR EACH EXTRA PERSON SERVED FROM A SINGLE ORDER.

door at each end." He followed with more negative commentary. "In the centre of the carriage there is usually a stove, fed with charcoal or anthracite coal, which is for the most part red-hot. It is insufferably close, and you see the hot air fluttering between yourself and any other object you may happen to look at, like the ghost of smoke."

Nevertheless, Americans defended their railroads from criticisms of foreign travelers. "A friend of ours, says the *Portland* [Maine] *Advertiser* [in November 1846], who has spent the last two years in travelling through Europe, assures us that the idea so generally entertained, of the great superiority of the European over the Americans railroads, is entirely erroneous, so far as the railroads of New England are concerned." This proud American observed that "the track is in general in no better condition than ours. There is much more of confusion and hurly burly at the stations, and the trains are not so exact to the time." Then there was the matter of the three classes of English cars. "The third are mere boxes, without any cover or protection from the weather, and the price in them averages two cents per mile. The second class have a cover, with wooden benches for seats, without stuffing or covers, and are made as uncomfortable as possible, to prevent people from riding in them. The first class cars are fine, [but] the average rate of fare in them is about seven cents per mile, or nearly three times as much as it is in New England."

Foreigner or not, the consensus developed that on some roads train operations were dreadful. They could be agonizingly slow, although they were generally safe because of low speeds. In the 1840s a northern Episcopal clergyman, Bishop Henry Benjamin Whipple, spent considerable time in the South and made frequent trips by rail. His journey over a portion of the Central Rail Road and Banking Company of Georgia (later Central of Georgia Railroad) especially annoyed him. "We left Macon at 8 o'clock and I may safely say on the worst railroad ever invented. The passengers are amused on this road by the running off the track, sending [strap] rails up through the bottom of the cars and other amusements of the kind calculated to make one's hair stand on end. We only ran off the track once and that was in running backwards." He recorded more thoughts about this trip. "I never have seen so wretched management. At one of the stations we were detrained 25 minutes for the men to chop wood for the engine. This is the first railroad I have ever seen where the cars were stopped to cut fuel. We were only seven & a half hours running from Macon to Barnsville [*sic*], a distance of forty miles – at the enormous rate of five miles per hour. Bah! Stage coaches can well laugh at such railroads."

Another, albeit more common complaint was that coaches lacked proper care, especially cleanliness. "The ceiling was as black as the back of a kitchen chimney, the glasses of the windows so foul we could not see through them," fussed a passenger who rode a train of the South Carolina Rail Road. "And the only covering to the naked floor was shells, orange peel, apple skins, interspersed here and there with generous puddles of tobacco spit, with huge quids moored in them, like islands in the ocean," conditions that also spoiled many a depot waiting room and platform.

Nearly universal criticisms about train travel included unhappiness with dust and dirt along with cinders and sparks. Travelers expected these annoyances before lessened somewhat when steam locomotives burned anthracite coal or fuel oil. (Advent of electric and diesel motive power diminished these concerns.) A trip could become most unpleasant. In this antebellum commentary the writer described widely encountered travel experiences: "Upon all roads in dry weather, the cars become so charged with it [dust and dirt], that the passenger lives in a sort of haze or twilight of dust, so dense, that he can hardly see from one end of the car to the other. This is the atmosphere which he must breathe." If a person were to take an extended journey, the impact on health (and comfort) could be significant.

From the dawn of railroad travel, some riders worried about their personal well-being, exclusive of the possibility of an accident that might bring injury or death. Before advances in medical sciences, there existed the belief that a lengthy train trip could cause "American Nervousness," a particular malaise common to the United States. The argument went: "It would seem that the molecular disturbance caused by traveling long distances, would have an unfavorable influence on the nervous system." While this was nonsense, contagious diseases, including influenza, small-pox, and tuberculosis, were spread in confined spaces. At that time the germ theory was not fully known, but later in the century the public understood better how and where illnesses were caused. Being in close proximity to a coughing, sneezing, or obviously sick passenger troubled many and at times led to a passenger not being permitted to begin or continue a journey.

Another worry of sorts was sleep deprivation. In the late 1830s the sleeping car made its debut, and this novel piece of rolling stock offered hope for relaxation on overnight journeys. "If you travel in the night you go to rest in a pleasant berth, sleep as soundly as in your own bed at home," raved the *Baltimore Chronicle* in October 1838 about a sleeping car that entered service between Baltimore and Philadelphia. Yet it would take decades before truly comfortable sleepers and reclining coach seats became available. Chances of having a relaxing overnight journey were highly problematic. "We arrived [from Cumberland, Maryland, on the B&O] at the little dingy, dull city of Wheeling, in Western Virginia before daylight on Sunday morning and found that we could get no further until Monday. [A]nd hastened to our beds to snatch the sleep which is next to impossible to win, or even to woo, in the hot, frowsy, uncomfortable railway car, containing from fifty to sixty people and a demoniacal furnace burning anthracite coal," wrote Charles Mackay in his *Sketches of a Tour in the United States and Canada* (1859). "Without a proper place to stow away one's hat; with no convenience even to repose the head or back except to

GREAT SOUTHERN AND WESTERN
EXPRESS
RAIL ROAD LINE.

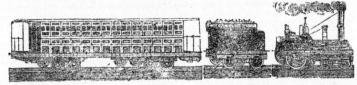

RUTLAND AND WASHINGTON
RAIL ROAD

In Connection with Rutland & Burlington, Troy &
Boston, Troy & Schenectady, and H. River Rail Roads.

Via Eagle Bridge.

THREE TRAINS EACH DAY, BURLINGTON TO TROY.

FARE FROM			FARE FROM		
From Burlington to	Troy,	- $3,00	Burlington to	New York,	$4,50
"	"	Utica, - 5,06	"	Syracuse, -	6,12
"	"	Rochester, 8,10	"	Buffalo, - -	9,60

Cars leave Burlington **7.30** A. M., **10.45** A. M., and **5.00** P. M.,
CONNECTING AT RUTLAND.

ACCOMMODATION TRAIN:

10.20 A. M. { Arriving at Troy 1.30; leave for New York and Buffalo 3.20 P. M.   Dine at Troy.

MAIL TRAIN:

2.00 P. M. { Arrive at Troy 5 P. M.; one hour for Tea, and leave for N. Y. and Buffalo 6 P. M, arriving at N. Y. 10.30 P. M., Buffalo 5 A. M., next day.

EXPRESS TRAIN:

7.30 P. M. { Lodge at Troy; leave 6.30 next morning, arriving at New York 11 A. M., and Buffalo 5 P. M., in time for Steamers to Detroit.

THROUGH TICKETS TO
TROY & NEW YORK,
SCHENECTADY, UTICA,
SYRACUSE, ROCHESTER AND BUFFALO,
☞ALSO CHECKS FOR BAGGAGE,☜

To be procured at Rutland and Burlington R. R. Office, and of the Agents.
☞ BE SURE YOUR BAGGAGE IS CHECKED THROUGH BY EAGLE BRIDGE ROUTE.☜

A. M. HERRIMAN, Ogdensburgh, }
H. BARNES, Montreal. } **A. R. FLANAGAN, Agent,**
Burlington, Vt.

1852

In 1852 the Rutland
& Washington Rail
Road, a future compo-
nent of the Delaware
& Hudson Railroad,
distributed a broad-
side extolling the
"Great Southern and
Western Express."
Although a shortline,
the company arranged
for connecting pas-
senger service. The job
printer, who probably
lacked a "cut" of a con-
temporary passenger
train, used a drawing
from the earliest
days of railroading.

Author's coll.

the ordinary height of a chair; with a current of cold outer air continually streaming in, and rendered necessary by the sulphurous heat of the furnace; and with the constant slamming of the doors at either end of the car, as the conductor goes in or out, or some weary passenger steps on to the platform to have a smoke, the passenger must, indeed, be 'dead beat' who can sleep or even doze in a railway car in America." Mackay added, "For these reasons right glad were we to reach Wheeling, and for these reasons we postponed the pleasure of making any more intimate acquaintance with it than sheets and pillows would afford until the hour of noon."

Shabby, ancient coaches, which deprived passengers of comfortable trips, including restful sleep, remained in service as railroads juggled equipment. Only when the federal government outlawed unsafe rolling stock with the Safety Appliance Act of 1893 did the worst specimens begin to disappear. Even after formation of Amtrak in 1971 older, functional equipment accommodated passengers; these "heritage" cars remained in consists long after this quasi-public corporation began operations.

Historically the worse pieces of vintage equipment spent their remaining life on branch lines and shortlines and were used for racial segregation in the South with the advent of Jim Crow codes. Also there were some non–common carriers, usually logging and mining roads, that provided the barest of accommodations. In the 1920s the Appalachian Lumber Company, which operated about 20 miles of rickety track between Pickens, South Carolina, where it connected with the slightly more elegant Pickens Railroad (a common carrier), and lumber camps in the timber-rich Eastatoe Valley, provided only an open car equipped with wooden benches. "The cinders and smoke from the Shay engine were a disaster to a lady's hairdo," remembered not-so-fondly a rider about her trips in this modified gondola.

A rider surprisingly might prefer the old and uncomfortable to the new and luxurious. Members of the Society of Friends (Quakers), for example, frequently opted for the simple. It was once common for Friends to inquire among themselves as to their mode of travel to religious gatherings. "'Did thee come Woolman or Pullman?'" wrote railroad historian Frank P. Donovan Jr. about Friends traveling to the Yearly Meeting held at their denominational William Penn College in Oskaloosa, Iowa. "As a word of explanation it may be added that 'Woolman' referred to one John Woolman, a revered eighteenth-century Quaker preacher who practiced and expounded the virtues of thrift and plain living. Therefore if the reply was 'Woolman,' it meant day coach with the inference of Spartan simplicity and minimum of comfort."

For years ratty equipment did not bother (or deter) college students in Columbia, Missouri. With the coeducational University of Missouri and two private women's junior colleges, Stephens and Christian,

opportunities for romantic encounters were plentiful. Some "late date" couples enjoyed riding the mixed train on the Missouri-Kansas-Texas Railway (Katy), with its ancient coach or combine, down and back from Columbia to the main line at McBaine, a distance of 9 miles. This accommodation left Columbia at 1:10 AM and returned at 2:30 AM, if on time. "The experience gives to routine necking parties a special homespun flavor."

On trunk routes some carriers employed their oldest coaches or constructed inexpensive ones to handle immigrants on their way to new homes, primarily in the West. In the latter part of the nineteenth century Robert Louis Stevenson had his fill of immigrant cars on the Union Pacific Railroad. "Those [coaches] destined for emigrants on the Union Pacific are only remarkable for their extreme plainness, nothing but wood entering in any part into their constitution, and for the usual inefficiency of the lamps, which often went out and shed but a dying glimmer even while they burned." He had more complaints. "The benches are too short for anything but a young child. Where there is scarce elbow-room for two to sit, there will not be space enough for one to lie." Yet Stevenson expressed surprise and real joy when he boarded an immigrant car of the connecting Central Pacific Railroad at Ogden, Utah Territory.

In 1951, under the watchful eye of the un-uniformed conductor, a woman passenger detrains from a spartan combine coach in New London, Ohio. This mixed (freight and passenger) train of the Akron, Canton & Youngstown Railroad operated on a leisurely schedule between Akron and Delphos, Ohio, a distance of 162 miles.

John F. Humeston photograph, Author's coll.

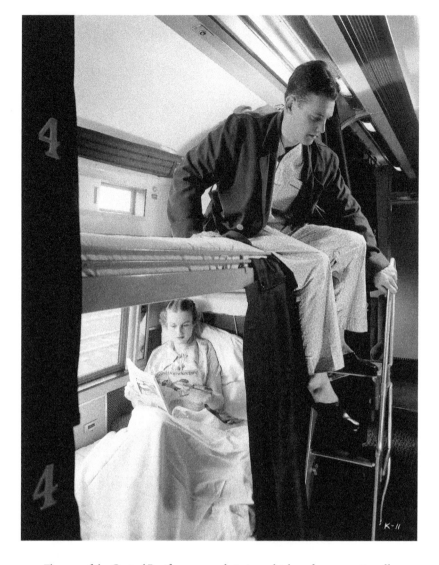

With the advent of sleeping cars, no one was likely to suffer severe sleep deprivation on most intercity passenger trains. Travelers, including this couple on board a Union Pacific train in the 1930s, gladly paid for Pullman berths if their personal budgets permitted.

Author's coll.

The cars of the Central Pacific were nearly twice as high, and so proportionally airier; they were freshly varnished, which gave us all a sense of cleanliness as though we had bathed; the seat drew out and joined in the centre, so that there was no more need for bed-boards [which news butchers rented on the Union Pacific]; and there was an upper tier of berths which could be closed by day and opened at night. Thus in every way the accommodation was more cheerful and comfortable, and every one might have a bed to lie on if he pleased.

Concluded Stevenson, "The company deserved our thanks. It was the first sign I could observe of any kindly purpose towards the emigrant."

Most immigrants had limited financial resources for their travels, but others, especially the rich, had no such constraints. As equipment improved dramatically after the Civil War and companies sought to exploit the luxury market, a passenger train might offer much more than basic transportation and limited services. On the best trains an impressive array of creature comforts could be expected. When Elizabeth Chester Fisk

traveled with her family to Montana Territory in October 1869 – partially by rail – she raved in a letter to her mother about "our sanctum" in a new and pleasant Pullman Palace Car. "Baby's head comfortably pillowed for nap on one seat, Rob and I occupying the other, while on various well-arranged hooks hang overcoat, shawls, bonnets and hat." But this train lacked a dining car, and apparently Fisk did not wish to patronize station lunchrooms. Hunger, though, would not be a concern. "Our picnic baskets contain a pair of chickens, a duck, sandwiches, apple pies, cake, cheese, pickles, &c, &c."

During the Gilded Age major carriers introduced and upgraded their principal passenger trains. It would be in 1887 that the Pennsylvania Railroad originated the first true luxury train, the *Pennsylvania Limited*. This crack flyer (and predecessor of one of the crown jewels of American travel,

While women who rode the B&O's overnight Washington to Chicago coach train, the *Columbian*, in the 1940s, did not have the option of sleeping accommodations, their coach seats provided ample leg room. Moreover, they had access to the stewardess-nurse (right), a service begun in 1937 to attract women and families.

William Howes Jr. coll.

the all-Pullman *Broadway Limited*), which operated between New York City and Chicago, offered patrons quality service, including Pullman vestibuled cars, fine dining, and attentive onboard personnel. In the words of the Pennsylvania, which soon immodestly branded itself as the "Standard Railroad of the World": "You pay for exclusive privileges and get them. You pay for strictly first-class accommodations and get them. You pay for first-class meals and get them. You pay for and receive the best service the Pullman Company and the Pennsylvania Lines can give." The railroad made much of the safety aspects of its flagship train. "Five cars connected with vestibuled platforms impervious to weather changes. In case of accident it is impossible for telescoping [of cars] to occur." And the train was advertised as an ideal choice for women. "Ladies could never before travel in such comfort. For their convenience a waiting-maid is assigned to each train, whose duty it is to serve as ladies' maid in all that the term implies. Ladies without escort, ladies with children, and invalids, are the particular objects of their care." The company pointed out that the observation car was an attractive venue. "The latter half of it is a large open sitting-room furnished with easy chairs. Broad plate windows admit a wide expanse of light, and the broad platform at the rear makes a pleasant open-air observatory in fair weather."

While most Americans only dreamed of a luxury trip by rail, they had the opportunity to read about the wondrous ride that Florence Leslie, wife of the wealthy publisher of *Frank Leslie's Illustrated Newspaper,* made ten years earlier from "Gotham to the Golden Gate." When her party reached Chicago, Leslie encountered the elegant "hotel car" that George Pullman had exhibited at the Centennial Exposition in Philadelphia. "We are greeted on entering by two superb pyramids of flowers, one from Mr. Potter Palmer [Chicago hotelier], and the other with compliments of the Pullman Car Co," wrote Leslie. "First, we were impressed with the smooth and delightful motion, and proceed to explore the internal resources of our kingdom. We find everything closely resembling our late home, except that one end of the car is partitioned off and fitted up as a kitchen, storeroom, scullery – reminding one, in their compactness and variety, of the little Parisian *cuisines,* where every inch of space is utilized, and where such a modicum of wood and charcoal provides such marvelous results." There was more. "At six the tables are laid for two each, with dainty linen, and the finest of glass and china, and we presently sit down to dinner. Our *entrees,* roast meat and vegetables, followed by the conventional dessert and the essential spoonful of black coffee." Unlike riders in a contemporary day coach, Florence Leslie benefitted from relaxing sleep.

Female members of the Leslie party did not need to worry about rowdy males; these women traveled in their own fully controlled hotel-car cocoon. But for most of the nineteenth century and somewhat later, women who boarded trains had mixed feelings about such experiences. The earliest cars carried men and women together, and a female passenger, imbued with the outlook of a proper Victorian, resented the coarseness and possibly provocative actions posed by male travelers. Moral uncertainty and social danger seemed ever present.

Railroads commonly responded to the matter of the "protection of ladies" by designating a certain car or space for females and their traveling companions. The concept of separate space for the sexes was hardly novel; for years river, lake, and coastal steamboats had customarily offered a ladies' cabin, which was often richly furnished. At the dawn of railroading the Lexington & Frankfort Rail Road (L&F), whose first passenger cars were patterned after stagecoaches, offered double-decker contraptions that required women and children to ride on the lower level and men the upper. Such arrangements on the L&F and carriers that provided what became conventional coaches generally worked well, keeping women and "gentlemen" away from boisterous, profane, and tobacco-using males. Roads might include a smoking car, allowing males freedom to indulge their habit, but at the same time not annoying "ladies and persons to whom it might be disagreeable or injurious." For that reason a writer in the 1840s (as did others later) argued, "There should be found in every train a clean, comfortable and sound car, or compartment of a car – for the use of smokers."

No one really doubted the widespread obnoxiousness of some male passengers. In one trip taken in the 1870s a female traveler had this to say about what were common annoyances: "They had drunk their flasks empty and were playing cards spitting at random in all directions and dropping oaths freely." The problem was ongoing. "The rowdy is a nuisance everywhere, and shows no partiality in his selection of a railroad car he is to patronize," editorialized the *Washington Post* in 1903. "The occupants of the day coach on nearly every train in the country are daily subjected to annoyance, and frequently to insult and abuse by the rowdy traveler." Continued the writer, "One drunken ruffian is sufficient to disturb the peace and comfort of a car load of women and children, and other passengers are usually powerless to protect themselves, unless some overt act is committed."

It was expected that trainmen should provide supervision. Companies frequently posted rules for female protection, and they were to be enforced. In the 1880s this announcement appeared in sleeping cars of the Chicago, St. Paul, Minneapolis & Omaha Railway (Omaha Road): NO SMOKING WILL BE PERMITTED IN ANY PART OF SLEEPING CARS, WHETHER LADIES ARE PRESENT OR NOT. A SMOKING CAR IS PROVIDED FORWARD. ANY PASSENGER WHO MAY HAVE CAUSE TO COMPLAIN OF ANY VIOLATION OR OF ANNOYANCE OR WANT

The Chicago & Alton, the principal passenger route between Chicago and St. Louis, maintained and repeatedly upgraded its rolling stock, which made it a popular road. In its March 1889 public timetable the company advertised its "Ladies Palace Day Cars" and its "New Smoking Cars," allowing for the pleasant separation of the sexes.

Author's coll.

OF ATTENTION OR OF COMFORT IN THESE CARS, WILL PLEASE MAKE IT KNOWN TO THE CONDUCTOR.

Yet employee oversight was not always possible. The cars might be crowded and the crew kept busy with duties other than looking after the comfort and protection of female passengers. Or trainmen might be wholly disinterested. It was also expected that proper males should demonstrate concern. Whether a ruffian was on board or not, it was assumed during the Victorian Age that honorable souls should show deference toward the "weaker sex," surrendering their seats to women and children and expressing other acts of chivalry. Women, too, had certain responsibilities. Anna Calhoun Clemson gave her daughter Floride these pieces of advice when riding a train: "do be prudent, & careful, & behave with dignity, & propriety. No giggling, loud talking, &c &c." But these dictates might be difficult to follow; after all, there was that sociability induced by train travel.

By the twentieth century significant cultural changes had taken place. No longer did most railroads segregate the sexes on trains; "Jane Crow" cars had mostly disappeared. "It is generally considered perfectly safe for a lady to travel alone over any of our railroads," concluded a contemporary observer, "and especially those that are thronged with passengers." Onboard personnel assigned to day coaches pressured males who exhibited bad behavior to act more gentlemanly. Usually they succeeded, making for a pleasurable trip. Then there were more and better trains. Some believed that the widespread use of Pullmans, with their interior beauty, "would have a civilizing influence upon even the roughest of customers." Better passenger equipment allowed middle- and upper-middle-class females to have semi-protected space, including sleeping and parlor cars. Troublesome males were less likely to be close by, traveling instead in a chair or smoking car. There was this twist. "This new type of gender separation offered men protection from the seemingly endless demands of women – an escape from the codes of deference and chivalry that had defined Victorian gender relations," observed historian Amy Richter. Yet elements of the Victorian past persisted. Male passengers might defer to female riders, just as they would accommodate the needs of the elderly and handicapped. Nevertheless resentment developed – largely among males – about the travel habits of some females. A guide book, published in 1919, for transcontinental passengers offered this commentary: "It is not customary, it is not polite, it is not right or just for a lady to occupy one whole seat with her flounces and herself, and another with her satchel, parasol, big box, little box, and bundle." The crowded trains that operated during the years of the Great War prompted this statement.

When women began winning their voting rights and gaining employment outside the home, and Victorian conventions began fading, the mixing of sexes, young and old, became "normal" occurrences. The environment of the passenger train itself pointed to this modernity: Gilded Age passenger cars with their excessive decoration gave way to simpler interiors, a marked (and refreshing) contrast to the elaborate decor of former years.

Although white female passengers may have fretted about riding trains or experienced annoying males, people of color long encountered demeaning and occasionally hostile situations. Even prior to the Civil War numerous railroad companies practiced racial segregation, and this became most pronounced in the South with the rise and strict enforcement of state-enacted Jim Crow legislation during and after the Gilded Age.

For decades the Mason–Dixon Line did not divide public racism. An Austrian civil engineer, Franz Anton von Gerstner, who visited much of the nation's networks of canals and railroads between 1838 and 1840, observed that blacks in the North were often forced to ride in separate cars. In his published commentary von Gerstner also mentioned a somewhat surprising practice that he encountered in Dixie. These were "half-fare compartments" that featured simple wooden benches located in baggage cars for people of color, yet these passengers could travel at full fare in nonsegregated coaches. When separation of the races in the antebellum North was not enforced, whites often objected to sitting with blacks. Massachusetts, a hotbed of abolitionism, was the only state that abolished race-based seating on trains prior to 1861, taking this progressive action in 1843. In legal cases in the North, racial segregation was mostly condoned. In 1867 the Supreme Court of Pennsylvania in *West Chester and Philadelphia Railroad Company v. Miles* agreed that the carrier was within its rights to remove a black woman from a train when she refused to sit in a designated section. The judges argued, according to legal historian James W. Ely, Jr. "that the company's regulation promoted the comfort and order of passengers."

The states of the Deep South firmly endorsed separation of the races on trains (and in depots) as the era of Jim Crow unfolded. Yet railroads were usually unhappy with these legislative statutes, realizing that they would need to add another coach for "the coloreds" or to have a special Jim Crow car built that featured a partition dividing the races. More cars, of course, increased haulage, switching, and repair costs. No wonder Jim Crow cars were often poorly maintained, both mechanically and custodially. And there might be an unbalanced mix in the number of white and black passengers, requiring additional equipment or another arrangement. Railroads also were not especially keen on demanding that their employees enforce the racial codes, and they fussed about having to put up mandatory signage and other trappings of segregation. But in the landmark 1896 case of *Plessy v. Ferguson*, which rejected the notion that segregation violated the due process and equal protection clauses of the Fourteenth Amendment, the U. S. Supreme Court ruled that the "separate but equal" doctrine must prevail. "If one race be inferior to the other socially, the Constitution of the United States cannot put them on the same plane."

During a rail journey blacks felt the sting of racial segregation, and their experiences were often long remembered. Historian John Hope Franklin vividly recalled an emotionally painful trip taken in the early 1920s on a Katy local in Oklahoma; he was only six years old.

> On our way to Checotah, we flagged down as usual the southbound Katy train. As it moved away, we sat down in the coach where we had boarded. When the conductor came through, he observed that we were sitting in a white coach and ordered us to the Negro coach. My mother, as firmly as she could, refused to do so, observing that she would not take two small children from one coach to another in a moving train. She pointed out that it was not her fault that the train had stopped where she could not board the so-called Negro coach.

Soon the unpleasantness occurred. "The conductor then stopped the train, not to let us move to the segregated coach but to 'teach us a lesson' by ejecting us from the train altogether. We trudged back to Rentiesville [the Franklin home] through the woods." Commenting on the event nearly eighty-five years later, Franklin wrote: "The uselessness of my mother's reasonable refusal to endanger her children, the arbitrary injustice of the conductor's behavior, the clear pointlessness of any objection on our part, and the acquiescence if not approval of the other passengers to our removal brought home to me at that young age the racial divide separating me from white America." He added: "As I cried, my mother promptly reminded me that while the law required us to be kept separated from whites and usually placed in inferior accommodations, there was not a white person on that train or anywhere else who was any better than I was. She admonished me not to waste my energy by fretting, but to save it in order to prove that I was as good as any of them."

Segregation remained part of the black experience in the South until the triumphs integrationists made during the Civil Rights movement of the 1960s. But major legal progress had occurred somewhat earlier. In 1950 the U.S. Supreme Court ruled in *Henderson v. United States* that dining car service could not be denied to a black person when seats were available at tables reserved for whites. Four years later the high court extended the principle of equality in its watershed decision of *Brown v. Board of Education of Topeka,* and in 1955 it applied the *Brown* logic to interstate public transportation in *Sarah Keys v. Carolina Coach Company.* Still, legal victories for equal rights did not mean that people of color always received equal treatment. As historian Theodore Kornweibel Jr. has pointed out, "there were still ways to wiggle around it." The Central of

In post–World War II America segregation remained in the South. For dining-car patrons on the Florida East Coast Railway in the 1950s whites sat together in one section and blacks another, with a heavy curtain separating the races.

William Howes Jr. coll.

Georgia Railroad resisted the law of the land, continuing to discriminate against black passengers into the 1960s. Being an intrastate carrier, the company could more easily maintain the racial status quo.

In his assessment of passenger train segregation Kornweibel concluded that "Despite the court's assertion in *Plessy*, it could never be benign, because it was grounded in dehumanizing African Americans." Moreover, separation of the races could be wholly illogical. "Virginia's Jim Crow law was so rigid that a white policeman escorting a black prisoner was prohibited by the train's conductor from riding together with him. At an opportune moment, the prisoner leapt from the car window and escaped," an example mentioned by Kornweibel. He added another: "On a number of occasions black passengers with very light complexions were ordered to ride in cars occupied by whites." In the latter situation, the conductor made the final judgment as to a passenger's race.

For many travelers a train ride was something special, and irrespective of class, gender, or race it was long customary for passengers to dress appropriately. That inevitably meant wearing their best clothing, even though a steam locomotive might rain soot and sparks, being common

when car windows were open. "Mother felt that her children ought to be presentable if they were going on the cars," recalled historian Bruce Catton in his account of his boyhood in Michigan. "[S]o the night before we all had to take baths, even though it was not Saturday night – a gross violation of custom that led us to make vain protests – and when we got dressed on the morning of departure we had to put on our Sunday suits, so that the special quality of the event had already been impressed on us. But when we reached the station platform the reality of the whole business came home to us."

It would not be necessary to "dress up" if an individual had the opportunity for a "cab ride," especially in the days of steam. Major railroads were reluctant to grant this opportunity, but politicians (including President Theodore Roosevelt), journalists, and others could possibly get the "ride of a lifetime." Smaller carriers, particularly shortlines, might not fuss much about nonemployees riding in their locomotives. Irrespective

People of color did not experience segregation on trains in the North. In 1960 black passengers mingle with whites on the *Day Cape Codder*, the New York to Cape Cod, Massachusetts, service of the New York, New Haven & Hartford Railroad.

William Howes Jr. photograph

**In the 1920s the
intercity passenger
business boomed.**
Railroads, including
some smaller carriers,
spent lavishly on ad-
vertising, touting the
frequency and quality
of their trains. The
Jersey Central (Central
Railroad of New Jersey)
told potential custom-
ers that it provided
fast, hourly service
between New York
City and Philadelphia.

Author's coll.

COMFORT

FIRST OF ALL IS THE CHIEF
FEATURE IN TRAVELING

ON THE

New Jersey Central

One Travels with
COMFORT, SAFETY and SPEED

TRAIN EVERY HOUR ON THE HOUR
TO PHILADELPHIA

EVERY TRAIN
A TWO-HOUR TRAIN

MANHATTAN STATIONS:
West 23d St. and Liberty St.

of the situation, such a potentially thrilling event would be remembered
and perhaps written about in some format.

In 1928 the public relations office of the New York Central hired nov-
elist-essayist-poet Christopher Morley to convey graphically "head-end"
riding and at the same time to glorify its all-Pullman *Twentieth Century
Limited.* His comments soon appeared in an attractive pamphlet that the

Dependable

New All-Steel
BANNER LIMITED
The Crack 6½-Hour Train to
ST. LOUIS

Leaves Chicago .... 11.30 a.m.
Arrives St. Louis (Delmar Ave.)........ 6.00 p.m.
Arrives St. Louis (Union Station)...... 6.15 p.m.
This is the day train to St. Louis, the Southwest and Mexico that seasoned travelers prefer. Observation and parlor car, diner service and other details contributing to travel comfort are unexcelled.

Leaving Chicago at a convenient hour in the morning and arriving at St. Louis in time for dinner or with ample time in which to make connections for the Southwest, the Banner Limited is indeed a train of preference. Through tickets are sold and direct connections are made at St. Louis or San Antonio, thence to Laredo and the National Railways of Mexico to Mexican points. *Afternoon tea served.*
RETURN SERVICE
Leaves St. Louis .... 12.20 p.m.
Arrives Chicago .... 6.50 p.m.
No Extra Fare

New All-Steel
MIDNIGHT LIMITED
to ST. LOUIS

Leaves Chicago... 2.15 p.m. 9.30 p.m. 11.45 p.m.
Arrives St. Louis..10.25 p.m. 7.03 a.m. 7.41 a.m.

Men who use the WABASH speak enthusiastically of the feeling of fitness with which they arrive at their destinations. The courteous, unruffled service, the club car accommodations and the luxury of a good night's sleep while rolling over the rock-ballasted roadbed and all-steel trains have made WABASH synonymous with comfort, among men who travel.

The early morning arrival (7.41 a.m.) and the luxurious style with which midnight lunch and breakfast are served in the club car cause business men to acclaim this the best, quickest and most comfortable way.

2.00 p.m. train operates through drawing-room parlor car.
RETURN SERVICE
Leaves St. Louis.. 8.30 a.m. 9.30 p.m. 11.40 p.m.
Arrives Chicago... 4.45 p.m. 6.50 a.m. 7.50 a.m.

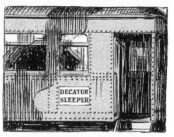

to Decatur
Local Sleeper

WABASH service considers every traveler's need. This service is typified by the local sleeper to Decatur, carried by the Midnight Limited every night at 11.45. Arriving in Decatur at 4.25 a.m. the car is switched out and may be occupied until 8.00 a.m.

Courteous attendants, the WABASH rock-ballasted roadbed and all-steel equipment are additional reasons why business men, Decatur-bound, choose the
RETURN SERVICE
Leaves Decatur............ 1.15 a.m.
Arrives Chicago .... 6.50 a.m.
Sleeper ready for occupancy at 9.30 p.m.
ADDITIONAL TRAINS
Leaves Chicago..11.30 a.m. 2.15 p.m. 9.30 p.m.
Arrives Decatur.. 3.12 p.m. 7.10 p.m. 2.55 a.m.
RETURN
Leaves Decatur.. 3.05 a.m. 11.25 a.m. 3.00 p.m.
Arrives Chicago . 7.50 a.m. 4.45 p.m. 6.50 p.m.

company distributed to passengers and anyone interested in the "World's Best Train." Wrote Morley:

> Astonishing how soon one adjusts one's judgements. Leaning from the cab window, watching the flash of her great pistons, watching the 1,000-ton train come careening along so obediently behind us. One soon began to think anything less than sixty mere loitering. All the imaginations that the cab might be uncomfortable riding are bosh. There is hardly – at any rate in those heavy 5200s – any more sway or movement than in the Pullmans themselves. The one thing a constant automobile driver finds disconcerting is the lack of steering. As you come rocketing toward a curve you wonder why the devil George [the engineer] doesn't turn a wheel to prevent her going clean off. And then you see her great gorgeous body meet the arc in that queer straight way – a constantly shifting tangent – and – well, you wish you could lay your hand on her somehow so she'd know how you feel. When George began to let her out a bit, beyond Beacon [New York], I just had to go over and yell at him that I thought this 5217 of his was a good girl. With the grave pleasure of the expert he said, "They're right there when you need 'em." He let me blow the whistle, which makes one feel an absolute part of her.

While few could sense the exhilaration of a high-speed, main-line ride in a locomotive cab, it was not unknown for passengers to experience train "races." These occurred when two railroads paralleled one another (a not uncommon occurrence), and engineers felt the urge to outpace a passenger train on an adjoining line. One such contest repeatedly took place in north-central Pennsylvania between the Reading and Pennsylvania railroads. The son of a Pennsylvania engineer recalled races between trains of these competing roads, which were both scheduled to arrive

The Wabash, a much larger road, announced its outstanding service between Chicago, Decatur, and St. Louis.

Author's coll.

in Williamsport about 10:30 in the evening. "The engineers would wait eagerly for each other at Montgomery station and then race side by side to Muncy, while passengers in the coaches would lay wagers on the outcome." He added, "As a rule, the Reading ten-wheelers were able to get under way before the Pennsy's Atlantic-type engines could hit their stride. Shenanigans of this kind violated company rules, but brass hats are said to have winked at racing as long as their own trains did not fare too badly." Fortunately these spontaneous events were far less dangerous than had been the famed steamboat races on the lower Mississippi River.

RIDING ON SUNDAYS

A railroad policy, which affected every passenger, involved train operations on Sundays. In the antebellum period foreign visitors were surprised, perhaps shocked, that passenger service in large parts of America was either curtailed or nonexistent on the Christian Sabbath. Only limited variations in timetables for Sunday operations on the Continent were standard. In fact, Sunday was often when business spiked and expanded service occurred; fair-weather Sundays had an especially magnetic attraction for riders. In the Great Britain, though, there were religious objections to Sabbath-day running, and the norm was less frequent operations.

Early on debate erupted about train service on Sundays. Some carriers, sensitive to the strong public demand to honor the Almighty with a day of rest, never dispatched runs on Sunday, although they might move the U.S. mail or special cargoes. If at times they allowed such movements, board approval might be required. At the November 16, 1835, directors meeting of the South-Carolina Canal & Rail-Road Company, the body considered a request to provide a Sunday train for legislators headed to the state general assembly, but decided that "the matter be left to the discretion of the President." Sabbatarians continually pressured carriers, especially in New England and the South, to keep trains out of service on Sundays, complaining even about the transport of the mails. And they marshaled various arguments. Foremost was the need to have a day to honor God and contemplate matters of faith. Not doing so would have negative consequences. "In a country where the Sabbath is as universally observed, as in the United States, it cannot be desecrated without the loss of self-respect, and consequent demoralization of those who violate it." If a railroader or anyone else did not attend church, the absence of train service would still allow an individual the opportunity to be at home, resting for the forthcoming workweek. Said one advocate: "At least one day in seven is required to repair the waste of six days of toil, and to allow the mind and body to recover a healthy and normal tone." These defenders of trainless Sundays believed "that by requiring Sabbath labor the Company at once excludes from its service the most conscientious and reliable employees. Men of piety and a high grade of moral principle will not consent systematically to break God's commandments." They also suggested that morally inclined investors would avoid securities of carriers that operated on the Sabbath and that patrons who opposed Sabbath-breaking would travel less on carriers that violated the holy day. It was suggested that the mere sound of a locomotive whistle on Sundays would distract citizens, making them want to visit the station or to contemplate worldly affairs rather than go to church or remain at home and read Bibles and religious literature. "We have now nearly 18,000 miles of railroads in the United States," observed a supporter of the suspension of Sunday schedules in 1854. "Railroad companies should not only not forget that their interest requires the proper observance of the Sabbath, but that they owe a duty to society to set a proper example. What a tremendous power all these roads can exert for good or evil. "

A summation of the anti–Sunday train perspective appeared in an essay, "Railroads and the Sabbath," that the *American Railroad Journal* published in 1856. "Sunday trains are the harbingers of evil to whatever town and village they enter. The peace and quiet which has prevailed from time immemorial, dies before the shriek of the locomotive, and in their stead comes the clatter of the train, the hurrying and rush of porters, passengers, omnibuses, cake and apple venders, and the confluence of village idlers." The writer made this point: "Ministers and congregations who have hitherto enjoyed the privilege of worshiping God unmolested, can no longer do so."

Yet opposition developed. One fight that erupted over Sunday operations took place on the newly organized Pennsylvania Railroad. In 1849 the company decided to suspend all service on the Sabbath. "There will be no locomotion by [the] railroad on the first day of the week, whatever the sacrifice to those interested, or whatever the urgency, for reasons public or private, for travel and the transmission of information through the community." But soon a backlash occurred. Proponents of Sunday trains responded, and in 1850 they distributed a pamphlet, *Prohibition of Sunday Travelling on the Pennsylvania Rail Road*. They refused to see Sunday train travel as "Sabbath desecration," arguing that such a restriction both was unjust and violated freedom of religion.

Because some are conscientiously scrupulous against travelling on Sunday, and whom no one has a right or wish to compel to travel against their convictions, have these a right to insist that others who have no such convictions, who many have observed with the utmost strictness of their own Sabbath [Jews and Seventh-Day Baptists], to compel them to stay at home when wishing to be there, no matter how urgent the necessity, be it occasion of business, or of sickness, or of death? It is in this compulsion that the injustice and tyranny is felt as a grievous invasion of the inherent right of the citizen of free locomotion for all lawful purposes.

The tract had more to say, mentioning that the workingman suffered from the lack of Sunday trains. "That the laboring classes, who cannot travel on other days, may with thankful hearts enjoy the venue of the country and the pure breezes of heaven at least one day in the week." Eventually this reasoning prevailed, and by the time of the Civil War the Pennsylvania dispatched both freight and passenger trains on Sundays, at least on its main arteries.

Sabbatarians' repeated use of moral suasion and their occasional political victories at extending Sunday "blue laws" to train travel gave railroads pause. Most carriers before the Civil War (and some later on) seriously considered these sentiments and decided not to operate or to provide reduced service. "In none of the New England States are Sunday trains run," reported a trade publication in 1854. "Several reach Boston early Sunday morning from New York, but none leave it, or any other New England city, on that day. Throughout all these States there is one day in seven, when even the locomotive reposes quietly in its stall, and the senseless machine pays it homage to a law ordained for the good of man alone."

Yet this commentary about New England operations was not wholly accurate. An important exception existed. Some roads operated mail trains on Sundays, and they might add a coach. Still, the State of Massachusetts, beginning in 1850 and lasting until the outbreak of the Civil War, imposed the hefty fine of ten dollars if the passenger was not journeying to church or some other religious function. On July 14, 1850, the Boston & Maine issued a circular about "Sunday Trains" that instructed employees and the public about proper practices: "Tickets will be sold on week days only. Persons purchasing tickets will be required to sign a writing, pledging themselves that they will use the tickets for no other purpose than attending church, and to such other requirements as are deemed necessary. No person will be admitted to the cars unless provided with a ticket." At one time during the antebellum period a railroad in Vermont required its conductors to read Scripture to passengers who traveled on Sundays.

Financial reasons, however, came into play, and managers torn between the sectarian and the secular opted for bolstering the bottom line. Income came from passenger trains on Sundays; many riders wanted to take to the cars, and there was mail and express to move. And Sabbatarianism had to be shunted aside during the Civil War in both the North and South because of critical train movements. Admittedly scores of carriers long embraced the "Daily Except Sundays" policy. This occurred no so much because of anti-Sabbath-breaking views, but because ridership demands did not warrant the expense. Yet Sunday was when numerous roads accommodated cash-paying travelers who were headed to a special event or some recreational location.

The absence of Sunday service on some roads continued into the twentieth century, largely for operating considerations. Still religious principles might come into play. In a bizarre twist to the debate over Sunday operations, a legal case developed in 1908 about Sabbath service on the Winona Inter-Urban Railway, an electric road in Indiana that served a popular religious camp, the Winona Assembly and Summer School Association. The principal owners of the railroad, H. J. Heinz, the condiment magnate, and J. M. Studebaker, the wagon and automobile manufacturer, were ardent Sabbatarians, and these men ordered that cars run only on weekdays. But the property was so unprofitable that it could not earn interest on its debt, in part because it served a lightly populated territory. If Sunday operations occurred, the financial situation would improve. The average summer attendance at the Assembly, it was reported, reached 250,000. The major creditor, a Chicago contractor, who had accepted $425,000 in Winona first-mortgage bonds, filed suit to force the railroad to operate on Sundays. Fearing receivership, the owners relented, and in March 1909 service began on a daily basis, being especially heavy on the Sabbath. But the road's general manager was so opposed to this decision that he resigned. Passengers, including many who attended religious programming at the Assembly, nevertheless found Sunday train service a refreshing change.

While it was highly unlikely that any patrons of the Winona Assembly who journeyed by rail on Sundays (or any other day) consumed alcohol and became unruly, some felt that Sunday service spawned bad behavior. Sabbatarians and prohibitionists continually warned about such improprieties. In the 1890s Lewistown, Illinois, took pride in being a "dry town," while Havana, located to the south on the Illinois River, was anything but dry. During the summer months an area shortline did a brisk business on the Sabbath, satisfying the drinking desires of some Lewistonians and others along the route. "Much to Lewistown's resentment, her bibulously inclined citizens used the Sunday trains as a convenient entree into the rivertown," noted a local historian. "These arid pilgrims, together with many others from the towns up and down the road, thronged the trains on their Sabbath journey to Havana, and disported themselves hilariously at the emporiums and bars of the terminal city. From contemporary accounts, it is evident that conditions on the returning trains called for more than mere ticket and fare collecting by the conductors in charge."

There was, of course, that other side of the Sunday coin. Devout Christians, especially those pious souls who traveled annually to the numerous summer religious gatherings, such as the Winona Assembly, found that Sunday rail service enhanced their religious experiences. In August 1878 a correspondent for the *Washington Post* offered a lengthy commentary titled "Gaithersburg [Maryland] Grove: How Sunday Was Spent in the Methodist Camp." Special trains on the B&O assisted this popular encampment. "The day opened bright and beautiful. At 5 o'clock the camp began to be in motion, and by 7 o'clock breakfast was over, and the people ready to receive the crowd which was expected from the city [Washington, D.C.] and the surrounding country. At 8:30 the scream of the locomotive announced the coming train, and the crowd broke for the depot. Soon the iron horse, like a thing of life, came thundering up, and deposited upon the switch six car-loads of people." More railroad action followed. "These had scarcely passed into the encampment before another train was heard, and then another, until about three thousand persons were added to the company upon the grounds. Another train came down from Frederick, Md., with a large company, and there is now, as I write, about eight thousand upon the encampment." Sunday trains, in this case, were hardly Satan's handmaidens.

TRAVELING TO POPULAR DESTINATIONS

Railroad companies long depended heavily on passenger revenues. While freight was critical, cargoes continued to travel by water – rivers, lakes, coastal waterways and canals, or they moved by a combination of these modes. Carriers relied extensively on both local and through movement of passengers, especially salesmen and other businessmen. And to enhance revenues, officials, led by general passenger agents and their associates, constantly sought to maximize traffic, attempting to fill every possible seat or berth. One strategy was to publicize a special destination, targeting families on holiday, the newly married, or visitors from abroad. By the early twentieth century carriers such as the New York Central & Hudson River would ballyhoo a trip to Niagara Falls; the Chicago, Milwaukee & St. Paul did the same for the "North Woods" of Wisconsin; the Chicago, Indianapolis & Louisville (Monon Route) pushed French Lick Springs, Indiana; the St. Louis, Iron Mountain & Southern, Hot Springs, Arkansas; the Santa Fe, the Grand Canyon; the Great Northern, Glacier National Park; and the Northern Pacific, Yellowstone National Park. In 1885 Charles Fee, general passenger agent for the Northern Pacific, envisioned the West as a land for personal discovery. "Beyond the Great Lakes, far from the hum of New England factories, far from the busy throngs of Broadway, from the smoke and grime of iron cities, and the dull, prosaic life of many another Eastern towns, lies a region which may justly be designated the Wonderland of the World." A trip to Yellowstone or some other attraction in the West would be memorable, but so might a shorter jaunt. "When we were married back in 1891, we took a train from Grand Central Depot [in New York City] on the [New York] Central to Niagara Falls – as did so many other newly weds that we knew. Riding in a sleeping car was nearly as exciting as our stay at the Falls." These special-destination riders recounted their trip in letters, postcards, and diaries, and often such written records were cherished and handed down from generation to generation. Or there might be a family oral tradition, with highlights remembered.

Even small railroads promoted trips to special destinations, if such places were on or near their lines or if they served as a connecting link. In 1891 W. A. Rich, manager of the 29-mile Phillips & Rangeley Railroad, a 2-foot gauge railroad in Maine, extolled Rangeley Lake and surrounding areas as a pleasant summer destination. Although designed to exploit extensive stands of spruce, the little pike sensed the possibilities of profitable, seasonal passenger traffic.

> There comes a time in the every-day existence of *ye citie man* when, oppressed with the cares and perplexities of the business grind, and irritated by the cease-less round of metropolitan music (?) [*sic*], – the roar of the street, the passing throng, the alarm of the fire-bell, the clang of the street-cars, and that ilk; when, with Falstaff, he "babbles o' green fields," and, looking beyond the present, in fancy sees the rippling waves of Northern Maine lakes, and hears the voices of the forest where Nature is as wild and as primitive as the aboriginal names of her forest-bordered waters.

Rich continued with his florid prose by emphasizing the attractiveness of greater Rangeley. "The route of the Phillips & Rangeley Railroad penetrates forest aisles lately hewn for its passage, through mountain scenery the finest which Maine affords. From the Rangeley Lake House it is but a stone's throw to the shore of the lake, the first of the chain. Numerous ponds surround the CITY, each affording fine trout-fishing. Teams, boats and guides can be obtained." Over the years thousands of tourists, mostly from Boston and other places in the Northeast, ventured by rail into the Rangeley outback, and surely endorsed that positive commentary made by manager Rich.

As with the Maine woods, the out-of-doors often offered a clarion call. "Flowers and also fossils fascinate me, and I favor collecting them both. Everybody was so happy with these activities." This testimonial made about 1910 explains the popularity of "Wildflower – Granite Canyon Trip" sponsored by the Colorado Midland Railway (Midland). For a decade or so this Colorado Springs to Grand Junction standard-gauge road operated from June through August a daily passenger train that served both local

During the post–Civil War era, various railroads united to promote long-distance passenger service. In the latter part of the nineteenth century, several Midwestern and Southern carriers, including the Queen and Cresent; the East Tennessee, Virginia & Georgia; and the Memphis & Charleston, joined to promote the "Cumberland Route" that operated through Brunswick, Georgia, and served Jacksonville, Florida.

Author's coll.

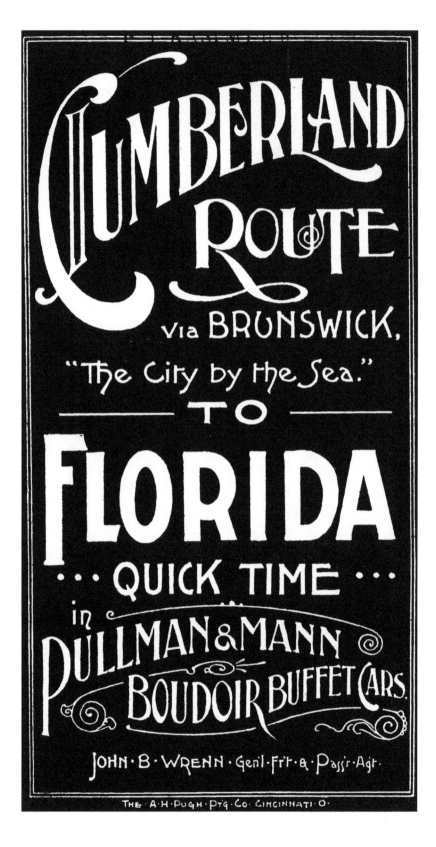

CLEAR LAKE

...IOWA...

Your Nearest Vacation Land

The Saratoga of the West

Reduced Round-Trip Fares and Summer Schedules

1925 — SEASON — 1925

ISSUED BY

The CHICAGO GREAT WESTERN

Always an aggressive carrier, the 1,500-mile Chicago Great Western Railroad strove to generate ridership. The company ardently promoted trips to Clear Lake, Iowa, which it immodestly called the "Saratoga of the West." Said this 1925 brochure: "Get away from the sweltering heat, the grind and noise of the city. Come to Clear Lake where you can breathe pure invigorating air–plunge into cool, crystal waters–loll upon sandy beaches, yes and enjoy some mighty good fishing too."

Author's coll.

travelers between Colorado Springs and Idlewild Park and those who wished to pick columbines, Indian pinks, and other seasonal flowers. The Midland made several stops to accommodate these flower fanciers. The train also halted at a tiny station, Fossil Beds, for another purpose. "Flowers, birds, fish, insects, and many other strange forms of plant and animal life of the Miocene period are perfectly preserved in volcanic shale rock, deposited in layers, which readily split apart, revealing the specimens just as they are buried during the volcanic eruptions, in prodigious numbers," announced a company brochure. "The railway owns a large deposit on its right-of-way, to which patrons may have free access, and at which stop is made." There was no question about the richness of the paleoentomological and paleobotanical specimens contained in these famous Florissant Fossil deposits. The nearly 100-mile round-trip journey on the Midland gladdened those who treasured the beauty of flowers and the mystery of fossils.

Budding environmentalists may have frowned on picking flowers and gathering fossils, yet these protectors of the earth did not complain much about the appearance of the iron horse (and people) in special natural attractions, especially the emerging national parks in the West. "When I first heard of the Santa Fe trains running to the edge of the Grand Canon of Arizona, I was troubled with thoughts of the disenchantment likely to follow," wrote the ardent conservationist John Muir in the November 1902 issue of *Century Magazine*. "But last winter, when I saw those trains crawling along through the pines of the Coconino Forest and close up to the brink of the chasm at Bright Angel, I was glad to discover that in the presence of such stupendous scenery they are nothing. The locomotives and trains are mere beetles and caterpillars, and the noise they make is as little disturbing as the hooting of an owl in the lonely woods."

RIDING EXCURSIONS AND SPECIALS

"We will charter a train at the top of a hat," proclaimed a railroad manager in 1912, and this policy statement persisted throughout the Railway Age. Excursion and special trains were ubiquitous; every common carrier became involved with these movements, even if it had to borrow equipment. Such runs began during the Demonstration Period and continued into the era of Amtrak. "The fashion of making 'excursions,' is one of the novelties introduced by the modern facilities in travelling; for by the old ways of journeying, this amusement, as it may now fairly be styled, would have been impossible," explained an industry writer in the 1840s. "Five or ten stage coaches would have cost five or ten times as much as one, and a jaunt of 30 to 100 miles and back again in one, would have been no joke. Now-a-days, it costs but little more to draw five or ten cars with a locomotive, than it costs to draw one; and the fatigue of a trip of one hundred miles is but little more than the ennui from want of employment."

The excursion train served a variety of purposes in addition to enhancing corporate coffers. Riders boarded such trains for holiday celebrations, fairs, sporting and musical events, political rallies, fraternal gatherings, military reunions, and more. Early on they provided opportunities to experience a train ride at a reasonable cost. In 1846 a Fourth of July special over the Long Island Railroad attracted hundreds. "The low price brought together a large number of passengers, and among them we saw one at least, who, although over eighty years of age, and residing within 12 miles of the city of New York, had never ventured into Gotham. It is not improbable that many persons were present who had never been twenty miles from their homes, and who now for the first time made a journey of nearly two hundred miles in one day." In the late nineteenth century the Mason & Oceana Railroad, a shortline in Michigan, ran a popular special train on Saturday nights "to bring the lumberjacks to town [Buttersville] to engage in drinking, shooting and other wholesome forms of recreation." About the same time another illustration of a less common reason for a special occurred. "Almost every farm between Norwich and Paris Hill [New York] had a hop yard, some of them close to the tracks. Whole families from Utica and Binghamton and the villages along the Chenango [River] swarmed into the district, camped in the farmers' improvised dormitories, ate the farmers' good hog meat and vegetables and fattened the children on fresh milk with the foam still on it," recounted a New York Central engineer. "Sometimes the Lackawanna put on special trains to handle the crowds, and almost every passenger [train] that scooted by us had an extra coach on its tail." Usually these specials were packed with revenue-producing riders, although carriers nearly always discounted ticket prices or offered package deals. Private entrepreneurs also rented trains, hoping to turn a profit. Organizations likewise made arrangements for a special or assigned equipment to a regular consist, again revenue makers for the carrier if not for the chartering party.

Railroads used a variety of equipment for their excursions. While their finest rolling stock, including sleepers, might be employed, carriers commonly selected their oldest cars, wishing to retain their better equipment for scheduled trains and also not wanting damage caused by rowdy passengers. One circus special in Illinois required that some riders take the "Poland China Pullmans," namely livestock cars with clean straw, and others to board flatcars that were equipped with plank seats and with canopy protection from soot and summer sun. Usually excursions trips were not especially long, often less than 50 miles one way. Patrons probably did not care much about the quality of the ride; the trip was an adventure with anticipation going and satisfaction returning.

BOSTON AND WORCESTER RAIL ROAD.

THE HAYMAKERS,

AN OPERATIC CANTATA,

WILL BE PERFORMED BY A SELECT COMPANY OF LADIES AND GENTLEMEN

AT TREMONT TEMPLE, BOSTON,

WITH APPROPRIATE SCENERY, COSTUME, AND ACTION,

On Friday Evening, April 1st, 1859.

The Solo Talent will consist of

MRS. J. H. LONG,	MR. C. R. ADAMS,
MISS S. E. WHITEHOUSE,	MR. P. H. POWERS,
MISS D. D. PEARSON,	MR. G. GOVE,
MR. J. F. BARTLETT.	

AN EXTRA TRAIN

From MILFORD will be run for the occasion.

Leave Milford	at	5.15 and 7.00 P.M.
Framingham		6.03 and 7.40
Natick		6.13
W. Needham		6.21
Grantville		6.25
Reach Boston		7.00 and 8.25

RETURNING---Leave Boston at 10.30.

☞FARE FOR THE TRIP, HALF PRICE.☜

E. B. PHILLIPS, Supt.

BOSTON, MARCH 29, 1859.

For generations the great American holiday was the Fourth of July, and carriers responded appropriately, weekdays or not. In a small broadside, issued on July 3, 1848, by W. M. Parker, superintendent of the Boston & Worcester Rail Road, the public received this message: "**Fourth of July.** All every day trains will be run as usual on the Fourth of July, and will besides leave Boston for Worcester and Way Stations – Millbury, Milford, Saxonville, Lower Falls and Brookline, after the Fireworks in the evening." Social events were popular on the Fourth, and "picnic groves," parks, and other gathering spots attracted flocks of celebrators by rail.

Rivaling Fourth of July observances were fairs. Virtually every railroad that served the city hosting a state fair operated special trains with discounted tickets or did the same for scheduled trips. It might be the New York State Fair in Syracuse, the Missouri State Fair in Sedalia, the Texas State Fair in Dallas, or the California State Fair in Sacramento. The

Special Excursion Rates
—TO—
SCRANTON, PA.
BY THE

N. Y., ONT. & W. RY.
ON
Monday, Aug. 10th, 1903.

Residents along the Scranton, Pennsylvania, branch of the New York, Ontario & Western Railway who wished to shop and see attractions in Scranton at an attractive price could do so on August 10, 1903. This excursion was somewhat unusual, being scheduled for a weekday rather than a Saturday or Sunday.

Author's coll.

Rates and Time of Trains, as follows:

STATIONS LEAVE	TRAIN TIME A. M.	Fare	STATIONS LEAVE	TRAIN TIME A. M.	Fare
Norwich, N. Y.	6.20	$2.50	Walton, N. Y.	8.02	$1.50
Oxford, "	6.36	$2.25	Beerston, "	8.10	"
Guilford, "	6.49	"	Rock Rift, "	8.15	"
Parker, "	6.52	"	Apex, "	8.22	"
Sidney, "	7.10	$2.00	Cadosia, "	8.40	$1.00
S. Unadilla "	7.16	"	Hancock, "	8.45	"
Youngs, "	7.19	"	Starlight, Pa.	8.58	"
Maywood, "	7.27	$1.75	Preston Park, "	9.05	"
Franklin, "	7.35	"	Winwood "	9.12	"
Northfield, "	7.42	"	Poyntelle, "	9.20	"
Delhi, "	7.20	"	Orson, "	9.25	"
Delancey, "	7.35	"	Pleasant Mount	9.35	75 cts
Hamden, "	7.39	"	Uniondale, "	9.38	"
Hawley. "	7.42	"	Forest City, "	9.48	"
Colchester, "	7.52	"	Arrive at Scranton at 10:40 a. m.		

☞ Returning Train will leave Scranton at 4 P. M.

Don't fail to take advantage of these low rates of fare and visit the Electric City of Pennsylvania and its big stores, fine buildings, parks, and attractive Wyoming Valley scenes on every hand.

☞ For further particulars apply to agents, or address

J. C. ANDERSON, G. P. A.,   G. A. PAGE, T. P. A..   J. E. WELSH, T. P. A.,
56 Beaver St., New York.   Oneida, N. Y.   Scranton, Pa.

B 1937 7-31-5m   Sanders Printing Company, Scranton, Pa.

Minneapolis & St. Louis Railroad (M&STL), whose lines laced sections of the Hawkeye State, counted on the popular Iowa State Fair in Des Moines for passenger income. Between August 25 and September 2, 1910, the road daily dispatched a special over its Des Moines and Alberta Lea & Southern divisions from Estherville to the Capital City that left at 7:10 AM for a 2:50 PM arrival, and allowed fairgoers to return on any train. To attract patrons there were the customary LOW RATES for round trips.

The Minneapolis &
St. Louis Railroad
took advantage of the
annual Iowa State Fair
in Des Moines. Other
Hawkeye state carriers
also offered reduced
fares on special trains
or regular runs so that
Iowans could attend
this educational
and entertainment
extravaganza.

Don L. Hofsommer coll.

THE MINNEAPOLIS & ST. LOUIS RAILROAD CO.

ALBERT LEA ROUTE

Low Rates

TO

DES MOINES

ACCOUNT

IOWA STATE FAIR

August 25 to September 2

	TIME OF TRAIN	ROUND TRIP FARES
Leave Estherville	7.10 AM	$5.40
" Raleigh	7.30 AM	5.15
" Terril	7.42 AM	4.95
" Langdon	7.58 AM	4.70
" Spencer	8.10 AM	4.55
" Ruthven	8.55 AM	4.15
" Ayrshire	9.14 AM	3.90
" Curlew	9.30 AM	3.70
" Mallard	9.42 AM	3.60
" Plover	9.55 AM	3.45
" Rolfe	10.10 AM	3.25
" Gilmore	10.29 AM	3.05
" Pioneer	10.43 AM	2.85
" Clare	10.56 AM	2.70
Arrive DES MOINES	2.50 PM	

RETURNING, Regular Train leaves Des Moines 12.50 noon,
(daily except Sunday).

Excursion tickets will be on sale August 25th to
September 2d, inclusive; good to return on all trains
up to and including September 5th, 1910.

For further particulars consult agents or address

W. K. ADAMS, District Passenger Agent,
512 Walnut Street, Des Moines, Iowa.

Or the fair might be an annual local event, yet still popular. "The Coshocton County Fair was held in the first week of October," recalled a resident of this central Ohio county. "And the old Walhonding Flyer [a Pennsylvania Railroad branch-line train] became an excursion train with twelve or fourteen of those old wooden coaches. And they would haul as many as a thousand people to and from the fair only." These trips generated memories galore. "I rode it many of times and it was really something. On the return trip, drunks were numerous, lots of fights you know, and I recall distinctly once when my mother took a pin from her hat, caught a drunk in the seat of his britches to keep him from falling into the seat on top of us."

The possibilities for special trips were infinite. The financially strapped Georgia & Florida Railroad (G&F) was as aggressive as any carrier with its special and excursion business. Between its opening in 1907 and the outbreak of World War II, the road offered numerous special excursions with attractive fares and also discounted rates on scheduled runs. Many of these were trips to Augusta, the largest city on the road, including one that ran on July 12, 1926, and cost $3.50 round trip from Douglas, Georgia, a distance of 160 miles. GO TO AUGUSTA AND VISIT THE CONEY ISLAND OF THE SOUTH. EXTRA COACHES FOR WHITE & COLORED PEOPLE. PLENTY OF ROOM. AMUSEMENTS FOR WHITE PEOPLE: VISIT DEANS BRIDGE. FOR COLORED PEOPLE: BIG BALL GAME BETWEEN SWAINSBORO TIGERS–AUGUSTA WHITE SOX. In conjunction with the Southern Railway through the Augusta interchange, the G&F in 1913 promoted THE BEAUTIFUL ISLE OF PALMS (for "Whites Only") outside Charleston where "the Surf Bathing is unsurpassable. The beach without an undertow. No flies, mosquitoes or other insects on the Island." That same year the G&F again teamed up with the Southern to offer SPECIAL LOW RATES TO CHATTANOOGA, TENN. AND RETURN. The railroad sought to attract attendees from south Georgia and north Florida to the Confederate Veterans' Reunion. The G&F advertised a special round trip rate of $8.70 from Madison, Florida, to the conclave via a connection with the Southern at Hazlehurst, Georgia. Then there was a special that reflected the times. In October 1923 the Douglas chapter of the Ku Klux Klan chartered a G&F train that carried about one hundred members and their families to a Klan initiation in Valdosta. "The local lodge marched from their meeting place to the train, all masked, and made quite an impression on the onlookers," and "hot refreshments was served on [the] special train from Douglas."

The G&F and other carriers did their best to increase ridership during the Great Depression, at times reducing fares to two cents or less per

Western carriers spent heavily to promote leisure travel. Even a small carrier such as the Denver, Northwestern & Pacific Railroad, which operated a 214-mile line between Denver and Steamboat Springs, Colorado, publicized in 1911 "Its marvelous scenery and unequaled one day trips."

Author' coll.

mile. Specials that could be organized meant more passenger revenues, although the rate per mile might be only a penny. As hard times deepened, the G&F boomed the "Special Prosperity Train Excursion" that on September 11, 1932, ran round trip between Valdosta and Augusta. "Conditions Are Getting Better, Cotton Keeps Jumping – Prosperity Is Coming." The ticket price: "$1 Round Trip for Everybody." Although the promotional prediction was dead wrong, this extra turned out to be a smashing success: 1,300 passengers crowded coaches "in the grand old excursion style." The event prompted a newspaper feature writer to buy a ticket and to report his experiences. "In addition to the fifteen passenger coaches, the train carried an extra service car, placed in the train so as to be immediately between the white and colored sections. In this service car was everything one needed to eat or drink, hot or cold. Great quarters of Lowndes county cows, and fat South Georgia hogs, barbecued tender and brown, with plenty of hot coffee, with milk and sugar to go into it." He noted, "One could eat and drink at the long service table in the car, or take the food and drink into the coaches – the colored people being served at one end of the car, and the white, at the other."

A round trip between Valdosta and Augusta involved only several hundred miles, but other patrons might take rail journeys that were much longer. In the late nineteenth century travel firms appeared that promoted personally conducted tours, and often they made arrangements to have several cars, including sleepers, assigned for their needs. These group tours became the latest thing in leisure travel. Likely inspired by the popular Thomas Cook Company of London, American firms, led by Boston-based Raymond & Whitcomb Company, attracted thousands of upper- and middle-class tourists to the rails.

In 1898 conductors from the Pennsylvania Railroad and their wives joined such a tour, making a coast-to-coast trip in a consist that operated both as a separate train and as part of a series of scheduled movements. Participants believed that this trip was so memorable that they asked a fellow conductor, M. M. Shaw, to create a permanent narration. His handiwork led to a privately printed book, *Nine Thousand Miles on a Pullman Train: An Account of a Tour of Railroad Conductors from Philadelphia to the Pacific Coast and Return*. Much was said of the journey through the Rocky Mountains.

Railroads hosted a seemingly infinite number of groups, including school-children. Even in the twilight of privately operated intercity rail service, youngsters, accompanied by their teachers or chaperons, took rail outings, as did these students who were boarding a North Western train in Wisconsin.

Author's coll.

We are now approaching Tennessee Pass [Colorado], and our engines are working hard as they climb the steep ascent. Our progress is slow, but so much the better, as it gives us an opportunity to contemplate and enjoy the indescribable beauty of this famous mountain scenery. We reach the pass shortly after four o'clock, at an altitude of 10,418 feet, the highest point on the main line of the Denver and Rio Grande Railroad. Here we again cross the Great Continental Divide and enter the Atlantic slope. Mr. Hopper [a trainman] calls our attention to a tiny stream of water flowing near the track, remarking as he does so, "That is the headwaters of the Arkansas River. We follow it for a number of miles and it will be interesting to notice it gradually increasing in size and volume as we proceed."

Conductor Shaw continued:

Leaving Malta, we pass through a fertile valley, through which flows the Arkansas River, that we notice is rapidly growing larger and more turbulent. We are still running parallel with the Colorado Midland Railroad, which for miles is within fifty feet of the Denver and Rio Grande. We notice a severe storm raging on a mountain not far away, and it seems to be snowing hard at the summit.

What may be the best remembered special involved a colorful figure of the Old West, "Death Valley Scotty." In 1905 Walter Scott, an eccentric mine owner who had a passion for speed, paid the Santa Fe $5,500 [$135,000 in 2010 dollars] to race over its rails on a special train between Los Angeles and Chicago. He wanted the trip to take just forty-five hours, establishing a record time. While the payment was hardly inconsequential, the company seized the opportunity to grab national headlines, demonstrating that it operated a top-notch speedway. The special consisted of a locomotive, baggage car, diner, and Pullman-observation car; Scotty dubbed this train the *Coyote Special*. But he did not make this trip alone, being accompanied by his wife and a newspaper reporter. In addition to the train crew, there was an onboard service staff that included a skilled Fred Harvey Company chef. At the stroke of one o'clock on the afternoon of Sunday, July 9, the *Coyote Special* began its sprint to the Windy City, steaming out of the La Grande Station in Los Angeles amid the cheers of an estimated twenty thousand onlookers. A series of locomotives and crews "scorched the ballast," bringing the train into Dearborn Station at 11:54 AM on July 11, taking just forty-four hours, forty-five minutes, to cover the 2,267 miles. At times the *Coyote* reached breathtaking speeds, clocking 106 miles per hour between the Illinois communities of Cameron and Surry. Scott learned that his blazing cross-country trip was more than seven hours faster than the previous record. Death Valley Scotty, the Santa Fe, and the nation took delight in the success of this unusual run. Interestingly, as Stephen Fried, historian of the Fred Harvey Company, noted, "Death Valley Scotty ended up becoming more famous for the record than for the gold mine he used to pay for it – which turned out be a fraud, and the train ride an attempt to distract his investors."

One enduring type of special involved passenger extras that served sports enthusiasts, especially football fans once intercollegiate rivalries developed. After World War I scores of railroads provided trains to carry the faithful to the big games. And fans came in great numbers, usually garbed in university colors and carrying pennants and homemade signs. Games that pitted such collegiate rivalries as Alabama and Auburn, Clemson and the University of South Carolina, Army and Navy, Harvard and Yale, Indiana and Purdue, Lafayette and Lehigh, Kansas and Missouri, Michigan and Ohio State, and Stanford and the University of California yearly drew thousands to the rails.

In 1911 a Clemson College student noted the excitement of the trip that led to the annual gridiron battle with the University of South Carolina. "What a glorious sight on Fort Hill [the campus], to behold over six hundred neatly clad soldier boys [this male-only land grant school had a corps of cadets], full of mirth and happy anticipation!" The description went on: "The Regiment was divided and the first half was immediately marched to the train and there boarded the first section of 'Our Special,' soon to be followed by the remainder of the Regiment, Band and Staff, which boarded the second section. Each company, as well as the Band and Staff, occupied a separate car, each of which was beautifully draped in the famous old gold and purple of Clemson." Then there was the rail journey. "The sections ran about thirty minutes apart, and as they neared each station, sudden bursts of yells and songs pealed out from the cadets. At every station there were crowds down to see us: mothers came to see sons; sisters came to see brothers; girls came to see sweethearts; and others came too." Victory came to the Clemson footballers; "the game closed with a score of 24 to 0 for the Tigers."

Even small colleges requested special trains or at least an extra car to transport the team, students, alumni, and others to a pigskin match. Simpson College, a Methodist-related school in Indianola, Iowa, engaged the Chicago, Rock Island & Pacific Railroad (Rock Island) to spot a coach or two near the science building for trips to battle gridiron foes in Des Moines, Ames, and elsewhere. "Cars of these special game trains were always filled with Simpsonians in the mood to fight Drake or confront the agricultural college."

Railroads customarily provided a string of coaches (often older cars) and perhaps a baggage car. The latter might be placed in the middle of the train, allowing for easy access to whatever services or amenities the alumni groups, businesses, or other sponsors provided: food, drinks, souvenirs, and the like. Usually the railroad could find a siding that was

within walking distance of the stadium and then store the equipment nearby.

The popularity of football specials was easily explained. Fans loved these outings. "I always looked forward to the Clemson–Carolina game every fall and when it was in Columbia taking the Southern special and with the band there, and that in itself was a big part of all the fun," recalled a Clemson cadet years later, echoing comments made about that 1911 trip. Moreover, railroads benefited from the extra revenues and favorable publicity. As for the latter, the superintendent of the Ann Arbor Railroad, an affiliate of the Wabash, sent this message to employees involved in handling fan specials from Columbus, Ohio, to Ann Arbor, Michigan, for the contest in 1959 between Ohio State and Michigan:

> This movement [of trains] is of much greater importance to the Ann Arbor Railroad than merely the movement of a number of passengers to a football game. As many of you know, the Ann Arbor derives a great deal of freight business from areas east and south of Toledo, and many of the people who are on these specials are business people and we want them to feel that they are welcome guests of the Ann Arbor Railroad and to know from the manner in which the movement is handled that the Ann Arbor Railroad is the road over which they should move, not only in coming to a football game but in the routing of their freight shipments as well.

Such an event, it was thought, provided a marquee value.

TICKETLESS TRAVEL

It is not known exactly when individuals began to board trains, freight and passenger, without paying fares or showing valid passes. Likely the

process started with the earliest carriers. Slaves were known to have stolen rides in order to escape from their masters and to seek freedom in the North or Canada. But after the Civil War and lasting through the Great Depression, countless poor, penniless men, black and white – and some women and children, too – hopped freight and passenger trains throughout the land.

Reasons varied for traveling without tickets. It appears that hard times became a crude barometer for such travel; individuals who were down on their luck sought out work, often seeking nonexistent jobs. Their ranks swelled, especially during the cataclysmic depression of 1893–1897 and the Great Depression of the 1930s. Some riders expected to find seasonal employment, whether harvesting wheat on the Great Plains, picking fruit in the Pacific Northwest, or cutting sugar cane in the South. During good times the majority of these individuals were part of America's much-needed migratory labor force, but during hard times the story was different. "Most of them [hoboes] at one time had jobs, homes, and families, and probably were upstanding individuals in their societies," reflected a Pennsylvania Railroad employee in the 1930s, "but when the economy collapsed many lost all they had. Consequently they started roaming aimlessly, to the warmer climates of the South or Far West during the colder months, returning to the northern areas in the summer. Some worked if they could find odd jobs or seasonal employment, others just bummed and begged for food, and none stayed at any one location for long."

Then there were those individuals infected with wanderlust who sought adventure: "riding the side-door Pullman" was a practical way to see America, especially the West. "The winter passes, and the warm winds of May made me long to wander again," recounted a veteran hobo. "The whistling of a locomotive on a still night had a lure, unexplainable, yet

strong, like the light which leads a moth to destruction." Another traveler aptly explained why he hopped trains. "When I was pulled through the door of the boxcar, I was pulled into another world, a world of adventure and hardship. I felt that my past life had been shut out. I was no longer a plodding farmhand. I had stepped outside the law, into the realm where men lived by their wits. If we were caught it meant prison, but the idea filled me with an elation hard to describe." For some it was the way to escape the claustrophobic nature of rural and small-town life. And for others taking to the rails was an exciting rite of passage, traveling before finding that steady job and establishing a family. Such riders generally can be correctly classified as hoboes or "boes," transients who were willing to work. Their opposites, "tramps," felt entitled to handouts or obligated to steal to avoid taking day or short-term jobs. Frequently confused with hoboes and tramps, "bums" resembled the latter, but they were not men in motion.

Still more reasons existed for "hitting the road." There were runaways, mostly teenage boys who had an unhappy home life or were simply riding away from problems. Any destination was desirable. Others sought to reach a particular place, but they were not transient workers. They might have meager financial resources, maybe enough to buy food but not money for train fare.

Extensive firsthand accounts of free rail journeys repeatedly describe the excitement but reveal the negative dimensions. Riding in, under, or on top of a freight car or on the blind [blocked doorway] of a baggage, express, or mail car or another piece of equipment was frequently dirty, uncomfortable, and dangerous.

One such saga involved a poor yet ambitious teenager who, during the midst of the Great Depression, undertook a freight train trip from his home in Idaho to enter college in North Dakota. This adventure involved hundreds of miles and two northern transcontinental railroads, Milwaukee Road and Northern Pacific. The lad did not travel alone, receiving assistance from an older brother, a seminarian in St. Paul and an experienced rider of freights.

While there had been some minor discomforts and setbacks for these two determined travelers, real hardships developed in central North Dakota.

> Earlier in the day we had seen heavy clouds in the east. They were moving across the state from the northwest. We had hoped the belt of clouds, dark and foreboding, would have dissipated before we reached them, but for once our luck failed us. Our position [on top of a boxcar], exposed and uncomfortable, became a living nightmare. Clothes and blankets quickly became soaked. The rain captured soot and smoke and dumped the mess on us. In the dark we could barely see each other or anything else through slitted lids. The rain and wind combined to make me wish I had never begun this mad trip. Even forgoing a college education seemed little enough price to pay to have escaped this torture.

Then conditions improved somewhat.

> About thirty miles east of Bismarck we ran out of the rain. The clouds must have passed to the southeast. One less torment, but we were thoroughly soaked and sodden. We couldn't discuss this blessed phenomenon. There had been very little conversation since Glendive [Montana] – shouting was exhausting and, besides, we had little need, desire, or strength to do so. We simply toughed it out. The end of the tunnel, so to speak, couldn't come soon enough for either of us.

Finally the journey ended safely.

In a similar narration, a bo found that stealing a ride on a passenger train was hardly a better arrangement than riding atop a freight car. "I crouch here in this doorway of the blind baggage [car]. For five hours I have huddled here in the freezing cold. My feet dangle down beneath the car. The wind whistles underneath and swings them back and forth. Up in front of me the engine rode through the blackness, that is blacker than the night." There was more misery. "The smoke and the fire belch into the sky and scatter into scorching sparks that burn my back and neck. I do not feel the wind that swings my legs. They are frozen. I have no feeling in them. I slink far back in this door and put my hands over my face. Great God, but I am miserable."

Then there were the serious risks. Some vagabonds robbed, even murdered, fellow hoboes. Those "knights of the road" who had earned harvest money were at risk; the lowlife "yeggs" literally harvested the harvesters. Railroad trainmen might also treat unauthorized riders badly, extracting illicit "bo money" or abusing them physically. Railroad police, termed "bulls" or "cinder dicks," too, could be ruthless. And their numbers might be significant. "Some roads, like the Pennsylvania railroad, used to have a 'Bull' for every mile!" observed "Hobo Bensson," the later so-called Official King of the Hoboes. "The Pennsylvania railroad was sure a hostile road." Similar behavior was common among town and city police, and some municipalities gained fame for the nastiness of their constabulary.

In the late 1890s two young Midwestern teenagers set out from Chicago for the wheat harvest in North Dakota. One of the two, Charles P. Brown, "Brownie," later in his autobiography wrote of their experiences, revealing the meanness of a freight-train brakeman.

> Well, Pat and I walked across the [Mississippi] river [at La Crosse, Wisconsin] on a wagon bridge and waited for a train on the west side (as the C. M. & St. P. [Milwaukee Road] crossed the river there over into Minnesota, where it followed the west bank of the river up to St. Paul), for it was easier to catch a train over there, as the yard bulls were inclined to be hostile to the hoboes in the railroad yards of La Crosse. And the railroad shacks [brakemen] were out for the money, and if they caught you hiding on their trains it was either dig up or unload (meaning pay or get off). So that evening a little after dark, a long freight train made up of empty boxcars came across the river and headed for St. Paul, the next division point north of there, so Pat and I grabbed her and climbed into an empty boxcar with several hoboes.
>
> I remember that Pat and I were setting over in one corner of the car trying to get some shut eye, when one of the brakemen stuck his lantern in through the small end door, and when he saw us in there he climbed through the door and dropped down inside the car (and he was one of them tough, hard-boiled babies too, believe me). So he held his lantern above his head (which railroad men do, as they can see much better in a dark boxcar) and says to us men, where all you bums goin' and what are you ridin' on, and some sap over in a far corner of the car makes a wise crack that is ridin' on this here boxcar, and that crack sorts of riled the old boomer brakeman, so he walked over and took a look at the wiseacre, and says, say listen bo, don't try to get funny with me, cause I am bad medicine myself. Then he turns around and says to the rest of us, come on all of you yeggs and line up here, I wanta see whatha got. So we all went over to where he was, and he says to the yegg that he had bawled out, what have ya got, and the guy told him that he did not have anything, so the shack says, you will stand a frisk and the fellow said no, then the shack told him to stand over by the door, so he sifted us out and the fellows that gave him some money, let them ride, but the rest of us that did not dig up had to unload.
>
> Well, as the train was not going very fast it was easy to get back on again, which we did, for it is hard to keep men off a long drag of empties after night where it is dark, so after playing hide and seek with the train crew all night, Pat and I rode the train into the St. Paul yards the next morning.

A "shakedown" by crewmen was common, as told throughout the writings of Brownie and by other boes who chronicled their travels. The railroad trade press also told of such happenings. "After leaving the division the beats are asked to produce 'stuff,'" noted *Railway Age* in 1887. "They are generally prepared to do this. All kinds of fares are demanded, and in case of a lack of finances, jewelry or clothing is taken." Added the publication, "These fares revert to the pockets of the brakemen, and are regarded as perquisites. No record of these fares appears upon the books of the company. As a rule, the money thus collected is usually equally divided between the conductor and brakemen. These fares usually cover all the incidental expenses of the average railroad man working in the train service department. The amounts thus collected [produce] large sums during the course of a month's time." Shakedowns aided crewmen, but they diverted revenues from carriers, and that bothered *Railway Age* and railroad managers.

Although there was no physical abuse perpetrated by the Milwaukee Road brakeman against Brownie and his traveling companion, countless acts of violence took place. Some railroaders were truly sadistic. A bo might take passage (and hopefully undetected) on a freight or passenger car by "riding the rods." The person used a wooden plank – his "ticket" – that contained groves permitting the board to slip onto the supporting metal trusses that once were found underneath most rolling stock. Jack London, who described his train travels in *The Road,* said much about the savagery of crews, including this description of how a bo might be injured or killed while riding the rods of a passenger car. "The shack takes a coupling-pin and a length of bell-cord to the platform in front of the truck in which the tramp is riding. The shack fastens the coupling-pin to the bell-cord, drops the former down between the platforms, and plays out the latter." Then the trouble began. "The coupling-pin strikes the ties between the rails, rebounds against the bottom of the car, and again strikes the ties. The shack plays it back and forth, now to this side, now to the other, lets it out a bit and hauls it in a bit, giving his weapon opportunity for every variety of impact and rebound. Every blow of that flying coupling-pin is freighted with death, and at sixty miles an hour it beats a veritable tattoo of death."

Potentially less lethal, but nevertheless dangerous, was the use of pressure hoses found on steam locomotives to attack ticketless riders. "Bound for St. Louis on Main line Mo. Pac. RR [Missouri Pacific]. I jumped the Blind Baggage of Her in Rear of Engine and when we got under good Headway the Engineer and Fireman saw me and took the Hose and Began throwing water on me," wrote a roving Bill Aspinwall early in the twentieth century. "I had to take it as I could not get off the train going at the rate of 60 miles an Hour. I was soaking wet and it was tolerable cold and I was shivering. I got off the first stop and went and got on the next car in Rear where they could not get at me with their water and went with the train into St. Louis."

Mean engine crews employed other tricks. "A tramp boarded the train at Cheyenne, climbed to the top of the coach and enjoyed hugely his elegant and rapid manner of making his journey until Sherman [Hill] was reached," noted a private detective. "At that point the engineer got a

In the early 1930s four boys, one of whom was very young, surely experienced a thrill as they rode the "blind" of a milk car attached to a North Western passenger local headed to Chicago.

Author's coll.

glimpse of him and he at once began throwing a heavy shower of cinders and increased the speed to the utmost power of the engine [and] the cinders burned into his clothes, cut his arms and legs and face."

Boes might take unnecessary risks. These involved boarding and leaving a moving train, walking or crawling under equipment, jumping from car to car, riding in a car where contents might shift, and chancing being trapped inside a box or refrigerator car. A practice not unknown during the Great Depression was for a bo to crawl inside a empty battery box beneath a passenger car; hunger, thirst, and asphyxiation could result.

Yet there was the excitement, even the ecstasy of a stolen ride. There was that scenery to savor. Traveling through the western mountains offered grand vistas from a boxcar or gondola. The rugged terrain of eastern Idaho in early September led a hobo to recall: "Early morning light revealed an enthralling scene. Spots and splashes of color, courtesy of a few deciduous trees flaunting their early autumn foliage, intruded into the realm of peaks and evergreens." Another bo revealed the pleasures of trips between Memphis and Little Rock. "I was riding along taking in all the scenery when all of a sudden we came into the most prehistoric mile after mile of swamps, filled with a multitude of birds of all sizes and colors, snakes large enough to swallow a full-grown chicken, and flathead catfish that were unbelievable." He added, "Before long we came to a cypress swamp about twenty-five or thirty miles long. What a sight, millions of cypress knees as far as the eye could see in any direction, except right down the center of the railroad. These knees looked like countless big ice cream cones turned upside down in the water. Over the years I went back and forth through this swamp country and I never ceased to marvel at it."

Real excitement might be experienced and long remembered. Two boes, who rode the pilot of a Santa Fe locomotive as it crossed central Kansas, thrilled to an unusual perspective of the railroad corridor. "But all we could do was to sit up there and hang on for dear life for the engine was rocking and swaying like a ship in a storm as she went tearing down that track through the night. Whitie says to me, what if we should hit a cow, and I said to him, for the love of Mike, don't talk about cows for these grasshoppers are bad enough, for oh boy, we were sure taking one exciting ride while it lasted." The description continued:

> The beam of light from the electric headlight on the engine stuck out in front of us and lit up the right-of-way for about one hundred yards ahead of the engine, and we could see jackrabbits and other small animals go scurrying off in the dark at the side of the track as the train approached them and one old jackrabbit thought that he could out-run us and went galloping down the middle of the track ahead of the engine until we overtook him and then he turned and jumped like a bolt of lightening to one side. Now the light beam from the headlight, shining on the track, made the rails look like two silver ribbons that were being unreeled out of the darkness ahead of us and swallowed up right under the pilot below us as we went sailing along through the dark night and gee, we were getting thrills and chills in turn, one after the other.

Some ticketless riders were able to avoid a freight car, blind, or locomotive pilot. More likely to be female than male, these boes employed a variety of tricks to escape payment or detection. "I beat the passenger trains by telling the conductor I lost my ticket [and] by hiding in the ladies toilet," recalled Lena Wilson, a radical socialist who once said, "The railroads rob the workers. Why shouldn't we rob the railroads?" If she was caught, the consequence was being removed from the train – hopefully at a station and not an isolated trackside location – or being turned over to the railroad or local police.

There might be an expression of real concern for a traveler without a ticket. "Box-Car Bertha," whose autobiography made the libertine Bertha Thompson famous, told of a happy ending to an unpleasant train journey. "Ena and I took an Illinois Central train, in an empty box car with four men hoboes, in bitter cold weather, and arrived in Nashville two days later. We rode the front end [blinds] of a passenger train from there [toward] Chattanooga." But during that leg of the journey the conductor caught these two women, although he did not eject them. "When the conductor found us half frozen on the blinds and asked us where we were going, we said 'Chattanooga.' He took us into the coach and let us sit down." Another act of kindness followed. "The passengers took up a collection and paid our fares, and one older woman, plainly dressed, invited us to her home in Chattanooga. We accepted, and stayed three days."

After the Great Depression the hobo and tramp largely disappeared from the rails. The military draft, good wartime paying jobs, and the growing popularly of hitchhiking along highways contributed to this decline. Yet some still hopped trains. But conditions had changed, especially with railroad rolling stock. "If there aren't any empties, which is becoming more and more the case today, you must settle for an outside ride, which may be a gondola, a flatcar, or a piggyback," opined a modern-day hobo. "The last is the smoothest ride because of the specially cushioned springs, but it can be the coldest as there's no protection from the wind." In the early 1990s a controversial book appeared (railroad officials objected strenuously to its publication). *Hopping Freight Trains in America,* where author, Duffy Littlejohn, a free-spirited lawyer, provided a 353-page handbook on how to take such illegal adventures. Littlejohn suggested that the principal reason to take to the rails was for excitement. "Riding the rails is a real kick in the pants. You get on board this huge, hulking amalgamation of metal weighting tons and tons and tons, then take off across the great American Wilderness. You get a feel of power and purpose. It's like riding the back of a giant steel dragon lumbering across the land." Recently an inveterate rider of the rails said much the same: "It is pure, unadulterated, unhomogenized America. You see everything from the seediest underbelly of industrial areas to rural places to people's backyards with laundry hanging on a line." But he admitted that "freight train riding is dying."

It was possible to ride trains legally without purchasing a ticket. One did not have to be a hobo, tramp, con artist, or adventure seeker to gain free passage. Until passage of the Hepburn Act in 1906, a wide range of individuals customarily received complimentary trip or annual passes, allowing them to ride most or all passenger trains on a particular road without cost. Office holders, lawmen, journalists, clergymen, and others obtained these much-sought-after "franks." In 1844 James Gadsden, president of the South Carolina Rail Road, wrote U.S. Senator John C. Calhoun to tell him the good news. "It affords me a high gratification to be the Organ through whom is tendered a Free Travelling Ticket for Life on the South Carolina Rail Road. Your name will be registered at the Different Depots, and the officers will receive instruction to permit you to pass free of charge, at all times and on all occasions, in any of the Travelling Trains." In 1839 that same railroad, then the South-Carolina Canal & Rail-Road, allowed "resident Clergymen going out from Charleston on

During the heyday of widely distributed annual passes, railroads customarily used these free franks to present a positive corporate image. The Western & Atlantic Rail Road selected a drawing of the impressive passenger terminal in Atlanta, Georgia; the Mississippi & Tennessee Railroad opted for fancy printing; the Rio Grande Western showed the spectacular scenery existing along its Rocky Mountain route.

Author's coll.

pastoral duties free tickets," a policy sparked by a petition from "sundry citizens of Aiken" who earlier had received authorization "that Rev. D. People, who preaches once a month at that place, might on those occasions have a free passage to and from, on the road."

Not only did a railroad garner political support with complimentary travel, but there were other reasons. "Sheriffs are given passes for somewhat the same reason that clergymen get them," explained the Iowa Railroad Commission in 1882. "The latter are encouraged to raise the standard of character through the State and the former to lay hands upon those whose standard of character is so low as to make treatment of a penal nature necessary. The railroads feel that the more the parson and the sheriff can be encouraged to travel the more safe life and property will be on their lines."

These recipients of a railroad's generosity might express their appreciation, although some took the practice as a given right. About 1900 the sheriff of Monroe County, Iowa, sent letters of gratitude to the headquarters of the Chicago, Burlington & Quincy (Burlington), Iowa Central, and Wabash railroads for "extending this kindness of an annual frank to me as the chief law enforcement officer." Even if free passes were not extended, fare reductions pleased beneficiaries. In 1858 the Pittsburgh, Pennsylvania, Conference of the Methodist Episcopal Church went on record in its official minutes with this acknowledgment: "Thanks to the railroads for passing the members and visitors of the Conference over their roads at half fare."

Yet there was a major downside to free or cut-rate travel. The number of riders who used passes was significant; for example, in 1897 railroads in North Carolina distributed approximately 100,000 passes that cost carriers more than $300,000. Even extending passage to other railroaders was an annoyance to the large, popular carriers. Officials of shortlines demanded that trunk roads "exchange" annual passes; that was good for the former but not the latter. But fortunately the cost was not excessive. No wonder industry leaders applauded the provision of federal legislation that limited passes to railroad employees, although the past policy had made them friends.

Paying passengers also fussed about passes. Why should some ride for free when they had to purchase tickets? To make riders feel better (and still use passes) Jonathan Reynolds, president of the Hot Springs Railroad in Arkansas, had passes printed to resemble two-dollar bills, "so that paying passengers would not feel discouraged." Patrons, though, may have caught on to this creative ruse.

While the public could understand why railroads extended annual or trip passes to their own employees and others on "foreign" roads, these "free rides" usually came with restrictions. Workers discovered that they could not usually ride "crack" trains, whether the *Broadway Limited, Crescent Limited, Empire Builder,* or some other first-class or luxury train. At times carriers imposed severe limitations on the use of their passes. Family members of a Southern Pacific track worker, who had been reassigned from Shoshone, Nevada, to Westwood, California, in the 1930s, learned that their passes came with major drawbacks; they were eligible to ride only on a single train, and that train would pick them up at Shoshone just one day a week.

If persons did not receive complimentary passes, there were still ways of rightly riding without cost. Merchants who sought out-of-town clientele might refund the price of a round-trip ticket if the person bought an expensive item. At the turn of the twentieth century, several clothiers in Cleveland paid either the full or partial cost of railroad transportation *if* the fashion-conscious customer bought a suit of clothes or made a purchase of a specified amount or more. About the same time, a Kansas City retailer offered free transportation to everyone who lived within 100 miles who bought five dollars' worth of merchandise. Small-town merchants often howled at the practice, not wanting to lose out on business, or they matched with similar offers or discounts.

Other concerns and individuals offered free tickets. It might be a construction firm that sought workers, promising complimentary transportation. Or it might be a real-estate company representative that sought out potential buyers. In a common ploy a representative of the Midwestern reality firm of C. A. Elmen & Company in 1912 promoted land sales in south Texas and made this offer: "I have chartered a special sleeper for our excursion on Tuesday, October 15th, and will make a rate of 50 cents per night for sleeping accommodations and special low rates for round trip tickets. Those buying land will get **FREE TICKETS THERE AND BACK.**" In 1879 the *St. Paul Pioneer Press* told of two young women who had been brought to the city from Chicago "to enter a house of ill-fame." When they became disenchanted with their employment, the "proprietress, Kate Campbell, objected to their return because she had advanced the money to pay the cost of their wretched journey here." Fortunately, a friend in Chicago arranged for train fare home.

Another example of free transportation involved "drover specials." For decades railroads in the West and Midwest operated seasonal stock trains. These runs took range cattle to the feedlots in the Corn Belt, and later, when the cattle were fattened, trains delivered these animals to slaughter houses in such places as Chicago, Kansas City, and Omaha. Similarly, carriers transported other animals, including horses, mules, sheep, and hogs. Cattlemen and their cowboy employees commonly received complimentary accommodations as they accompanied their livestock, but they hardly traveled in luxury. Some railroads owned "drover" cabooses.

These cars were longer than the standard equipment and provided bunk beds and cooking facilities. Carriers wanted this livestock business, but the downside was that these riders might become too frisky. Alcohol and boredom might prompt them to discharge their firearms, taking aim at telegraph insulators, switch lamps, and other railroad property.

Reports circulated of individuals who, while not riding for free, concocted clever, even bizarre, schemes for bargain travel. In February 1914 a headline that surely caught the attention of newspaper readers was this: "Shipped Son as a Hog." In an article that originated in the *Stock Yards Daily Journal*, published in St. Joseph, Missouri, a reporter told of a recent shipment of household goods on the Chicago & North Western Railway (North Western) from Bertrand, Iowa, to Burke, South Dakota. Included in the waybill was "one hog valued at $10." Since this involved an interstate shipment of livestock, inspection by a veterinarian at the destination was required. But when the veterinarian checked the boxcar for the hog, he could find no such animal. A more thorough search revealed "a boy, curled up in a corner of the car, none the worse for his trip." It seems that by billing the shipment as part livestock, the lad's father received an attractive rate on the household goods. "The boy was sent by the shipper as a substitute" and for much less than a coach ticket.

TROOP TRAINS

Another way to gain free or reduced charges for transportation was to be a member of the armed forces. Whether in scheduled passenger trains or in special troop movements, hundreds of thousands of Americans in uniform have had Uncle Sam pay their passage. The use of the rails during wartime began early on, dating from the Mexican War of the mid-1840s. (By coincidence, this was the same time that the Prussian Army first moved a large military contingent by rail.) Yet during this victorious conflict with Mexico the U.S. Army relied more on steamboats because of the disconnected nature of the American rail network.

But less than twenty years later the rail grid had changed dramatically. With the outbreak of the Civil War military leaders of both the North and the South understood the strategic and economic importance of the rails. "The railroads in the South," observed historian Douglas Southall Freeman, "meant more than the mountain ranges and scarcely less than the great rivers in determining the lines of advance and defense." Troop movements were ubiquitous and might be monumental. In summer 1863 Confederate General Braxton Bragg used the rails to transport nearly 30,000 soldiers from Tupelo, Mississippi, via Mobile, Alabama, to protect Chattanooga, Tennessee. A year later Union commanders rushed about 25,000 troops of the XI and XII Corps of the Army of the Potomac from Washington, D.C., to that Tennessee city.

Accommodations during these wartime moves were less than ideal. More so than in the North, a ride on a Confederate railroad was often less comfortable than a wagon journey, although somewhat faster. "We soon found that traveling on a Rebel railroad was very different from what it would be on one in our northern states," recalled a Union Army prisoner from New York, who in June 1864 rode trains with fellow captives.

> Their rolling stock was nearly worn out, the rails broken, splintered, and battered, the ties rotten, and, altogether, it was a dangerous matter to ride at all upon them, to say nothing of speed. For greater safety, their fastest trains were limited to 12 miles an hour by Act of Congress. Their stops are frequent, for their wheezy old engines use double the fuel they would if they were in good repair, and their wood and water stations are separate, thus making a stop every 4 or 5 miles.

Passengers in the South found their travel options limited or made uncomfortable by the volume of troops on the move and the poor state of their railroads. "We had orders to haul no passengers," remembered a conductor on the Charlotte & South Carolina Railroad, "but it was almost impossible to keep them off at times, as trains were so irregular, and often so crowded that all the passengers could not get on them." In October 1864 Margaret Crozier Ramsey, wife of the prominent Knoxville, Tennessee, physician J. G. M. Ramsey, recorded in her diary a memorable trip from Bristol, Virginia, to Charlotte, North Carolina:

> The cars were in a bad condition very rough traveling, left Bristol 12 o'clock at night. There was very little light no fire and it was very cold going through the mountain. When we got to Burkesville in Va. met the train from Richmond with many sick and wounded soldiers. They filled the car we were in the gentlemen with us had to stand very dark, could scarcely see to distinguish anything. There was a surgeon along who seemed to be very kind to them but had a poor chance to do anything for them – the car was so crowded.

She closed this way: "It was very unpleasant and dangerous trip. The road was not safe and the cars very shackling."

Being a passenger during the Civil War could result in much more than discomfort; death was a distinct possibility. Union and Confederate forces repeatedly attacked trains, particularly those that carried troops, adding more casualties in this four-year bloodbath. Civilians were not immune. On the morning of September 27, 1864, a group of Southern guerrillas led by Captain William "Bloody Bill" Anderson arrived in the central Missouri town of Centralia. After torching the depot of the North Missouri Rail Road, these men waited for the midday westbound

They're "On to Cuba."
The Spanish-American War had begun, and on April 20, 1898, members of an Iowa volunteer unit receive the proper send-off at the Boone station. A photographer offered this keepsake image for sale.

Author's coll.

passenger train. When it arrived at the station, the Anderson bushwhackers came aboard and forced the passengers out onto the platform, where they robbed them. On that unlucky train were twenty-five unarmed Union soldiers who were on furlough and were heading for their homes in northwestern Missouri and southwestern Iowa. Anderson questioned these men and next they were told to strip. The then naked or nearly naked soldiers were gunned down at close range. Also murdered was a German civilian who had the misfortune of wearing military-style clothing. Unable to communicate in English, he could not explain his noncombatant status. The only Union soldier to survive, though wounded, sought safety under a wooden loading dock. Anderson's men set it ablaze, believing correctly that was where he had gone. When the fire drove out the trooper, he, too, was mortally shot.

With military encounters after the Civil War, troops and civilians did not have to be concerned much about possible domestic attacks. Moreover, the quality of troop trains increased markedly. By the time of that "Splendid Little War," the Spanish-American War in 1898, and the following, albeit less splendid, Philippine Insurrection, trains were faster, roadbeds smoother, and sleeping and eating accommodations better. "We sailed right along the Union Pacific RR as we headed to our camp in San Francisco, Calif.," commented a volunteer in the 1898 conflict. "I may not have gotten the sound sleep that I usually got at home, but it was alright and the food was not bad either, better than I expected or was told."

By the time the United States entered the Great War in April 1917 more improvements had taken place to the railroad network and rolling stock. Unlike the case in the Spanish-American War, volume became heavy; more troop trains raced across the country to East Coast points of embarkation. The big rush came in September 1917, when more than 200,000 regular army troops entrained between September 5 and 9. Subsequently railroads handled about 350,000 national guardsmen ordered to mobilization camps. Chapters of the American Red Cross were kept advised of troop movements, and they tried to make these trips more pleasant. "The equipment for a single refreshment unit provides enough coffee, for instance, for 1,200 men. A meal consists of coffee, sandwiches, sausages, and cold beef, with buns or pie. In case of hot weather, iced tea is expected to take the place of coffee. Special preparations will be made for the sick and wounded."

Plenty of frightened men had their "free" wartime train experiences. "My uncle had never been much beyond the family farm [in Iowa] when he was drafted," recalled a nephew years later. "He was literally shaking when he got on the train for Camp Dodge outside of Des Moines. He went overseas, but he did return from an adventure of a life time, although somewhat shell shocked by the whole experience of World War I."

A scared serviceman, who had never strayed far from home, might have more reasons to be frightened about train travel. As during the Civil War, wrecks of troop trains took place. One of the worst occurred near Marshfield, Missouri, on September 17, 1918, killing twenty-five soldiers and injuring many more. There were even a few instances where trains encountered attacks of sorts. In September 1917 pro-German supporters allegedly fired on a troop train on the Pennsylvania Railroad as it passed through Mingo Junction, Ohio, wounding four soldiers, one seriously. "A colony of several hundred foreigners, the majority of them steel workers [presumably sympathetic to the Central Powers], resides near the place where the attack is said to have occurred." Such an event, though shocking, is understandable since the war was one of the most unpopular in American history, second only to the Vietnam Conflict.

Yet hundreds of thousands of Americans rallied to the colors. In the process the press reported an unusual tale aboard a troop train. The young wife of an Arizona solider refused to be separated. "Directly I heard that my husband was to go abroad. I tried to join the National Red Cross in

Douglas, because I wanted to be near him. They would not accept my services." But being resourceful the woman decided that she could follow her mate. "When the troop train pulled out of Douglas I was at the end of the train, and my husband was at the forward end with his company. With my hair cut short and wearing a khaki uniform and service hat, I felt confident that I would pass muster. I made myself as military as possible in my bearing." At first she succeeded, but "two days after the train started I was discovered by one of the officers and put off at some out-of-the-way station in the West and told to go back to Douglas." Her odyssey, however, did not end with an immediate return trip. "I said good-bye again to my husband, but I really didn't promise him to go back home, or I should not have got on the train again. You see, the train had to switch there for about half an hour and all the soldiers got out to run up and down after the long journey. When the cry came 'All aboard!' I jumped on the end car, where I had several friends, and they took care of me out of sympathy." At last the troop train arrived at Hoboken, New Jersey, and this determined woman then stowed away on the transport ship. After two days at sea she was discovered, but sadly she never encountered her solider-husband. After arriving in France, the woman was returned to the United States and placed on a by train back to Arizona, and all gratis transportation.

During World War I the civilian public learned that it was unpatriotic to travel too frequently. And since carriers reduced regular service to allow equipment to be employed for military purposes, it was not always possible to schedule a journey at a preferred time. By November 1917 railroads had curtailed about 10 percent of their passenger train mileage. When Washington "federalized" much of the industry in December 1917, more regulations took effect. Limitations on baggage, for one thing, were especially troubling for traveling salesmen. "The shortage of baggage cars has become so serious," reported the *New York Times* in July 1918, "that it has been necessary in some instances to attach freight cars to troop trains to take care of troop equipment. Freight cars, however, are not made to travel over twenty or twenty-five miles an hour, and their use on troop trains has resulted in delays caused by hot boxes."

In some ways events of World War I were a rehearsal for World War II. Again the federal government became intimately involved with wartime transport, not with federalization, but with controls exercised by the Office of Defense Transportation (ODT). Once more the railroads became the arteries by which troops and military-related personnel traveled. Yet World War II would be a conflict that lasted longer, required movements to both coasts, and involved far greater volumes. Although buses and airplanes transported troops, railroads moved nearly 98 percent of all military personnel. Specifically, the War Department routed 33.7 million

service men and women in organized groups of forty or more, and of these 32.9 million went by rail. Little wonder that the *Official Guide of the Railways* added a supplement to its monthly editions called "List of Military Posts and Camps in the United States, Showing Railroad Passenger Station," something missing from issues published during World War I.

As in previous wars, individuals in uniform took multiple train journeys. Service personnel during World War II, though, experienced more trips by rail than had their predecessors. The typical GI, whose compatriots exceeded 12 million by spring 1945, made five train journeys during the training process and more to the point of embarkation. Then there were the trips to the military base for "mustering out" and finally back home and return to civilian life. In all, the total of trips on MAIN (Military Authorization Identification Number) trains was approximately three times greater than during the Great War.

The war years witnessed other trains that handled war-related passengers, and they also traveled on Uncle Sam's nickel. Western railroads operated scores of "alien specials" for the War Relocation Authority. These

In July 1946 a troop train, running on the Wabash Railroad, thundered across the Grand Trunk Western Railway crossing at Ashburn, Illinois. Even though World War II had ended officially, troop movements continued. The military draft remained, and service personnel were still returning from overseas duties and moving between stateside military bases and mustering-out centers.

John F. Humeston photograph, Author's coll.

were trains that carried Japanese-Americans to interior holding sites, the American version of Russian gulags. Later a variety of roads transported German and Italian prisoners of war to detention camps. There were also hospital trains, with their medical staff and the wounded, maimed, and dying.

The railroads were able to meet the challenge. Most companies, ranging from the mighty Pennsylvania to the lowly Missouri & North Arkansas, had excess equipment. Because of the substantial drop in passenger patronage during the Great Depression, coaches, diners, sleepers, and other pieces of rolling stock stood idle on sidings and in yards. But with wartime conditions, virtually every car entered service, at times after hurriedly made repairs and alternations. Lounge, club, and tavern cars, however, might be removed from revenue service, allowing for greater train capacity, or converted for other purposes.

As during the Great War, civilians were encouraged not to take trains because of the crush of military and related movements. Initially moral suasion was employed. Railroads ran repeated advertisements in newspapers and magazines and posted notices that explained to potential riders the impact war was having on travel. Toward the end of the conflict the ODT ordered railroads to stop handling any Pullman trips that were 450

miles or less, affecting about two hundred runs nationally. This action added almost nine hundred sleeping cars to the pool available for the exclusive use of the armed forces. What became an American advertising classic – the creative work of Nelson Metcalfe Jr., a professional copywriter commissioned by the New Haven Railroad for wartime messages – said much about troop movements: "The Kid in Upper 4":

Not all service personnel slept in Pullmans or troop sleepers, as this photograph of soldiers on a Southern Pacific train attests. Rest was welcomed, but hardly refreshing.

Don L. Hofsommer coll.

It is 3:42 A M on a troop train. Men wrapped in blankets are breathing heavily. Two in every lower berth. One in every upper. This is no ordinary trip. It may be their last in the U.S.A. till the end of the war. Tomorrow they will be on the high seas. One is wide awake . . . listening . . . staring into the blackness. It is the kid in Upper 4. Tonight, he knows, he is leaving behind a lot of little things – and big ones. The taste of hamburgers and pop . . . the feel of driving a roadster over a six-lane highway . . . a dog named Shucks, or Spot, or Barnacle Bill. The pretty girl who writes so often . . . that gray-haired man, so proud and awkward at the station . . . the mother who knits the socks he'll wear soon. Tonight he's thinking them over. There's a lump in his throat. And maybe – a tear fills his eye. It doesn't matter, Kid. Nobody will see . . . it's too dark. A couple thousand miles away, where he's going, they don't know him very well. But people all over the world are waiting, praying for him to come. And he will come, this kid in Upper 4. With new hope, peace, and freedom for a tired, bleeding world.

Next time you are on the train, remember the kid in Upper 4. If you have to stand en route – it is so he may have a seat. If there is no berth for you, it is so that he may sleep. If you have to wait for a seat in the diner – it is so he . . . and

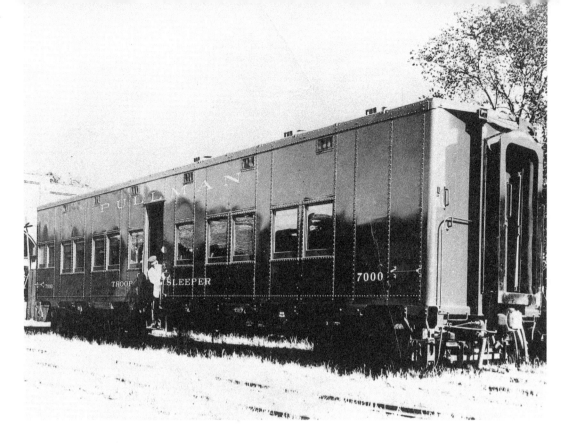

An estimated 125 million passengers traveled 98 billion miles during World War II, and service men and women accounted for a large percentage of this traffic. This crush prompted the Pullman Company, with government approval, to construct what were stripped-down sleepers. Although the ride quality was less than ideal, Pullman personnel sought to make troop travel comfortable.

William Howes Jr. coll.

thousands like him . . . may have a meal they won't forget in the days to come. For to treat him as our most honored guest is the least we can do to pay a mighty debt of gratitude.

Major carriers used their public timetables to reiterate the importance of civilians avoiding unnecessary travel, and to remind them that if they had to make a trip, they should expect crowds, delays, and other annoyances. "A word *before* you board the train" was the title of an announcement page in the May 3, 1943, Southern Pacific schedule. "Crowding can't be helped. Many of our cars usually available for civilian travel must be diverted constantly for military use. We're short of cars, and we can't buy new ones now. We're also short of locomotives. Consequently, we can't run additional trains." These comments followed: "Ever since the war began we've been making up thousands of special trains for troop and war freight movements. We've had to take popular passenger trains off regular runs to clear our tracks, and to use the equipment thus released for troops – or fill out remaining trains to absolute capacity." A contemporary Frisco timetable made the message simple and direct: "The Government has first call on all equipment for the movement of men and materiel. Your interests, whether passenger or shipper, are secondary."

Then there was the dining-car dilemma. "With several hundred passengers on a train and only one 36-seat dining car, it takes a long time to serve everyone," explained the Southern Pacific. "Compared with pre-war

1940, we're now serving nearly *three times* as many dining car meals with no additional dining cars." The company limited service to breakfast and dinner, the latter starting at 4:00 PM, a practice that other carriers commonly employed.

The Pullman Company pressed into service all of its functioning equipment. As the war continued, the company received authorization from the Defense Plant Corporation to construct troop sleepers, which resembled steel boxcars with windows and had trucks suitable for passenger train speeds. In late 1943 twelve hundred of these special cars began to enter service; a troop sleeper accommodated thirty men, each to his own bed. Later another twelve hundred became available. Triple-deck berths were arranged crosswise against one side of the car with the other side being the passing aisle. In some ways these cars were better than traditional sleepers. "A Pullman generally could carry 39 soldiers," remembered one veteran. "Two soldiers could be put on a lower bunk and one on the top." Officers, however, preferred standard equipment. "Many of the cars were compartmentalized, with about seven state rooms. These were saved for the higher ranking officers or other important people." Whether in standard or troop sleepers, the Pullman Company sought to maintain service quality, and that meant porters and fresh linens.

In ways that paralleled the tale of that World War I–era woman who "followed her man" was this remembrance of another woman during World War II. Near the close of war a young St. Louis–area school teacher fell in love with an army airman who was stationed at nearby Scott Field. When he told her that he was to leave for Salt Lake City, she was asked to drive him to Union Station. "I was delighted that I could, as I dreaded telling him goodbye." Once in the cavernous waiting area, the couple talked at length and he suggested that she bid farewell on the platform. (He was able to get a special pass since security concerns barred visitors from the trainshed.) "Upon arrival at the [Wabash] train, John asked the Conductor where the 1st stop was, and when the reply was Delmar Station, he invited me to accompany him, which I did and planned to take a taxi back to Union Station to my parked car." But the journey did not end a few miles away. "As we were enjoying the beginning of our ride together when the train pulled out of Union Station, loaded with troops except for me, John jumped up and ran to the Conductor and asked where the next stop was, and Kansas City was the answer." Happily he learned that his girlfriend could take a return train about midnight and arrive back in St. Louis in time to teach her morning classes. "Sooo-oo that was my next invitation from John! I accepted with the condition that I must call my parents at Delmar Station so they wouldn't worry about where I was. I ran down the steps at the Delmar Station stop, only to hear the Conductor call, 'All

While it was not exactly in the "unexpected" category, passengers on North Western's *Rochester Special* during the 1920s might have been surprised or at least curious about the train's custom-built hospital car. Some patients going to and from the Mayo Clinic in Rochester, Minnesota, required this service.

Author's coll.

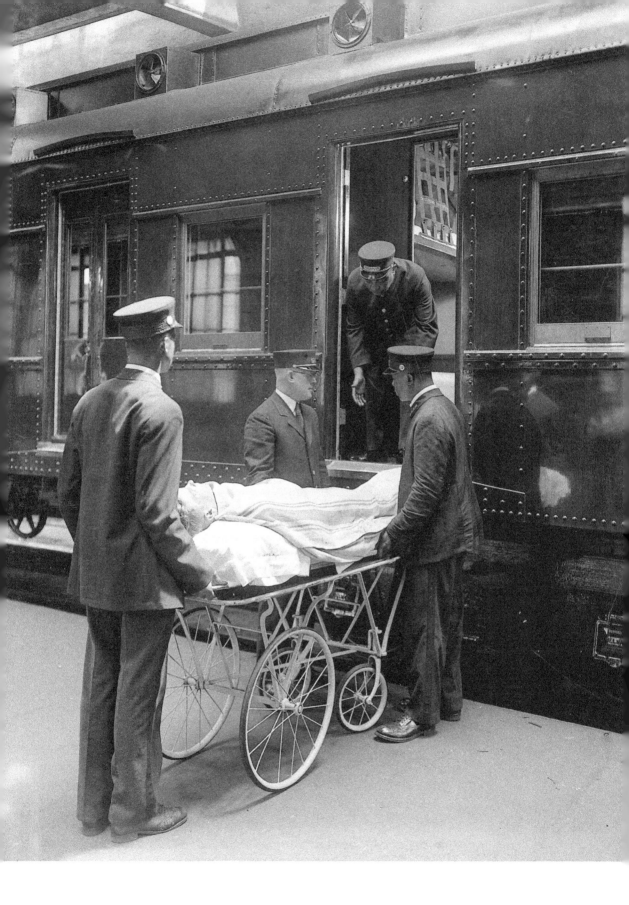

Aboard' – so I ran back up, because being with adorable John meant the most to me." The resourceful boyfriend put her mind at ease. "He could hand a telegram with money to High Hill stationmaster when the train stopped for water. The telegram to Mother and Daddy said, 'Have gone to Kansas City with John. Having a wonderful time, Love, Nellie Jane.'"

While happy stories have been told about travel on troop and scheduled passenger trains during World War II, there were also unpleasant experiences. And significantly, they later affected intercity rail travel. Frequently military personnel complained about crowding, long lines, inadequate food, and more. At the Great Northern station in Minneapolis some disgruntled (and presumably hungry) soldiers raided boxes of baked goods and other food containers that were on unattended baggage carts. As the war came to a close, nine troop trains, composed of old coaches and converted boxcar-diners and carrying more than three thousand soldiers from Camp Shanks north of New York City, did not have contented riders. "Many of the men protested to their officers over the accommodations," reported the *Washington Post.* "To emphasize their protests some of the soldiers carried seats from the coaches and, placing the seats on the station platform [at Orangeburg, New York], beat clouds of dust from them." The troop trains were more than dirty. "None of the coaches was air-conditioned. Three men were assigned to every two seats. It was understood they would have to take turns lying down."

These memories persisted. "I will never take another train," proclaimed an Illinois veteran. "If I can drive or certainly take an airplane, that's the way I travel – not on a train. Had enough during WW2!" Another displeased warrior was the future baseball writer Roger Angell, who in 1942 boarded a troop train after basic training in Atlantic City, New Jersey. His trip to the West Coast was hardly enjoyable. "Days on end, stuffed into ancient, sooty Pullman cars, we rolled and clacked westward, while we dozed, played cards, talked, laughed, got depressed, wrote letters, and read endlessly. At night, we bunked three to a section, taking turns in the upper berth (a delicious single) or squalidly doubling up, head to foot, in the lower. I still recall waking up in the middle of my first night and slowly comprehending that I was staring at the pale toes of Private Pete Hoffman."

Although it is impossible to know the impact the troop train experience had on postwar passenger travel, railroad officials sensed a threat. In 1949 a North Western passenger department employee said it well: "We have to realize that our money-making trains are made as fine as possible. We need to get the ex-GI and his family on them or the consequences will be grave." However, the degree of success for most roads was limited. Many military personnel and civilians had vivid recollections of crowded, dirty, and worn-out trains.

Most rail journeys were relatively uneventful. There might be crying babies, rambunctious children, inebriated adults, or talkative, inquisitive passengers. Perhaps there were cranky trainmen or late trains. Yet there was nothing that seemed truly out of the ordinary, and this was fine with riders.

The unexpected might occur, however, and it might involve a wide range of happenings. Until the advent of modern all-metal equipment, better motive power, stronger track structures, safety devices, and rigorous training of operating personnel, derailments and accidents were not infrequent, heightening fears among passengers. Between the Civil War and World War I newspapers routinely reported passenger-train disasters, and ran headlines with such scary words as "Dreadful Accident," "Horror," "Railway Massacre," and "Slaughter." The fact that train accidents killed more railroaders than they did passengers was little comfort to anxious travelers.

In the formative years of railroading, major accidents were few, but minor derailments were common. The iron strap metal that was attached to the wooden rails might loosen and cause the locomotive or possibly coaches to leave the track, resulting in little damage but often lengthy delays. Speeds were slow, explaining the absence of many fatalities or serious injuries. Even with the growing use of iron T-rail, speeds remained modest. Therefore when derailments occurred, they usually were merely annoyances.

As speeds rose, numbers of movements increased and the rail network mushroomed, more passenger train accidents, often of a serious nature, took place. After the Civil War at least one major tragedy occurred annually, and the frequency of accidents soared. The peak of the carnage took place in 1907, and a writer for *World's Work* sought to explain why. "Our railroads kill their thousands every month in wreck or trespass. In more than half the cases, the real truth underlying the tragedy is the fact that the train was running at forty or fifty or sixty miles an hour over tracks that were built for trains that never ran but thirty miles an hour. The people demand it. The railroads must obey." He continued, "Each year, the manufacturers of locomotives are called upon by the big lines to produce and deliver more and more engines that can haul a ten-car passenger train at sixty miles an hour. The cry is ever for more speed. The railroads take big risks. They have to. Competition grows terrible, and the railroad, like the individual, must live."

The most deadly events largely coincided with the high point of accidents, including the worst wreck in the nation's history. On July 9, 1918, two Nashville, Chattanooga & St. Louis passenger trains, running at approximately 50 miles per hour each, smashed together while operating over a piece of single track outside Nashville. One hundred and one passengers and crew members died, and 171 were injured. Among the victims were many African American laborers who were bound for jobs at a munitions plant near the Tennessee capital. Crew errors apparently caused this carnage.

Another much-talked-about passenger train disaster during this period was the "Green Mountain Train Wreck," which occurred on March 21, 1910, between the Iowa towns of Green Mountain and Gladbrook. Fifty-five passengers and trainmen died. This deadly mishap happened when two sections of a badly late Rock Island passenger train bound for St. Paul, but detouring over the rails of the Chicago Great Western (Great Western) jumped the tracks. The locomotives, each running in reverse because of the inability to turn them when the train reached Great Western rails, caused the accident. The tender of one locomotive left the rails, plunging it and the locomotive and the second tender and locomotive into the mud. The stop was sudden and total. The greatest loss of life occurred in the two wooden cars that followed the all-steel Pullman that was coupled to the second locomotive. The day coach literally disintegrated, and every person riding in it was either killed or seriously injured. The smoking car, which followed, was smashed at both ends, and few of its occupants escaped death or injury. "These two cars [day coach and smoker] were like egg shells when preceded by a heavy sleeper, and followed by heavy, steel cars and sleepers." No one sustained serious injury in the eight cars back of the smoker, and none of that equipment left the rails; the deadly telescoping involved only the first three cars.

The dead, dying, and injured littered the wreck scene. A passenger who was aboard the last Pullman car told journalists that the place reminded him of a Civil War battlefield. Another eyewitness commented, "It was a horrible scene of mangled bodies, detached legs, arms and human parts, and gore splashed everywhere. Here was a body with the head crushed into an unrecognizable mass. There another torn, mangled and bleeding, mere pulp wrapped in blood-drenched rags which had been clothing."

After the accident the site became a madhouse. Survivors aided the injured as best they could, and outside help was quickly sought. Soon medical assistance came from nearby communities. Within a few hours a relief train arrived from nearby Marshalltown and highballed back to that city with the victims. The following day the local newspaper reported that "at the station a multitude gathered white-faced and horrified waiting the coming of the special train. The cars were crowded with dead and dying and wounded. The hurry calls for wagons and conveyances brought teams on the full run thru the streets. One by one the bloodstained victims

were taken thru the windows and tenderly as might be sent away to the hospitals and the temporary morgue." No wonder passenger-train wrecks traumatized the public.

Only somewhat less frightening than a passenger train "going into the ditch" was the far less common holdup, the famed "train robbery" that pulp fiction, motion pictures, and television programs have engraved on the American mind. Just as wrecks peaked before World War I, so too did robberies. The bulk of these events occurred during the latter part of the nineteenth century and largely in the West.

While no two train robberies were identical, roaming outlaws were usually more interested in taking bullion, currency, and other valuables from baggage, express, and mail cars than in holding up passengers. Still that happened. In one of the earliest heists, which occurred near Cincinnati, Ohio, in May 1865, robbers attacked an Ohio & Mississippi passenger train, and in the process turned over the locomotive, tender, and baggage-express car. Luck was with them; they found a large amount of cash and securities. Gang members also robbed passengers – "gallantly sparing the ladies" – of their pocketbooks, watches, and rings, a practice that prompted William Sydney Porter (O. Henry) to observe: "If you want to find out what cowards the majority of men are, all you have to do is rob a passenger train."

The train robbers who gathered the most national, even international, attention (and lasting fame) belonged to the James gang, led by

On August 12, 1939, passengers who traveled on the westbound *City of San Francisco*, operating over the Southern Pacific, had their journey horribly disrupted. An apparent act of sabotage–a case never solved–wrecked this crack train as it crossed a bridge in Palisade Canyon, Nevada, killing 9 passengers and 15 crew members. Another 121 were injured, some seriously. Survivors and their luggage wait along the nearby track of the Western Pacific Railroad for a train to take them to Oakland, CA.

William Howes Jr. coll.

the romanticized Jesse James and his brother Frank. In the "Blue Cut Robbery," which occurred on September 7, 1881, these desperadoes robbed a Chicago & Alton passenger train near Kansas City, Missouri. After the outlaws stopped the locomotive and took command of the engine crew and the express messenger, they walked down the aisles and robbed the terrified passengers. Clarence Hite, a participant, offered this description in his courtroom testimony:

> Jesse said, "We had better rob the passengers." [The gang] then started through the train, beginning at the smoker and going to the rear. Wood [Hite, another gang member] carried the bag (a common meal sack). Charlie [Ford, another participant] went in front with a pistol in each hand and made the passengers deliver up their valuables and put them in the sack. I stood at the front door of each car as Charlie and Wood went through to prevent their being shot in the back. When we reached the chair car Frank [James] got on. He did not go through the car, however. Everybody was badly scared. As we were coming back through the sleeper Charlie found a bottle of wine and took a drink. We also got some cake out of a basket. We got five watches, including the expressman's. Wood took the one which I have spoken of. Charlie Ford got two, one a fine gold one and chain (English made). I got a silver one and Jesse got the conductor's nickel, open-faced, stem-winder. To go back a little. After we got through searching the passengers, Jesse came into the sleeper from the rear, and told the porter if he didn't hunt up all the money that was hid he'd kill him. The porter said he hadn't hid any, that they had gotten it all. Jesse then went to the first seat, turned it up and got about $60 and a gold watch. He then went to the brakeman and told him the same thing. The brakeman said "I gave you 50 cents – all I had." Jesse then gave him $1 or $1.50, saying: "This is principal and interest on your money." Each man's share was estimated to be worth about $140.

Passengers might be startled for reasons other than a wreck or a holdup, but soon were calmed when they understood *why* their train may have halted far from a station. Managers might direct crews to stop for a short time to honor the memory of a prominent person, often a national politician. Passengers who were aboard trains of the Wabash Railroad at 2:00 PM on September 19, 1901, would recall an unscheduled stop. Throughout the system (as well as on many carriers) the company honored William McKinley on the day of the late president's funeral in Canton, Ohio. Trainmaster J. A. Heether sent to "All Trains and All Engineers" that operated on his Moberly, Missouri–based division the following order: "'God's will not ours be done.' All trains and engines will stop for five minutes at two o'clock PM Sept 19th out of respect to memory of President McKinley."

Occasionally railroad officials received such honors by both large and small roads. One memorable event involved James J. Hill, the "Empire Builder," who passed away in May 1916. "At the hour of the funeral, 2.00 PM on May 31, every train on the Hill railroads, wherever it was, stopped for five minutes," recounted Hill biographer Albro Martin. "The passengers of a Northern Pacific train high in the Rockies, at lunch in the diner, laid down their knives and forks in embarrassed silence when the conductor told them the reason for their unscheduled stop." When Herbert Bucklen died about a year later, a somewhat similar event occurred on the St. Joseph Valley Railway (Valley Line), a 71-mile road that he had financed, built, and managed east of his hometown of Elkhart, Indiana. At the time of Bucklen's burial in January 1917 the railroad came to a complete halt for ten minutes. The tribute to the late railroad owner and president began as pallbearers lowered the casket into the grave. In an imaginative fashion a direct telephone connection was created between the burial site and the depot in La Grange, allowing the Valley Line traffic manager to use the railroad's dispatching system to notify train crews and others the exact moment when the stoppage should begin.

Another unscheduled stop for a passenger train, and for years an annual occurrence, did not honor a national leader or railroad official but rather "the Little Fellow." The event had its roots in the 1880s when a trainman on a North Western line in eastern Dakota Territory (present-day South Dakota), William "Big Bill" Chambers, struck up a friendship with the young son of a couple who cooked for laborers assigned to a work train. Although details are sketchy, the boy likely died of smallpox. His funeral, if one was held, probably took place in front of the bunk car that stood a few miles west of the hamlet of Elrod. The body was placed in a crudely built coffin and buried near the siding. "Watertown and Redfield being the only towns of any size where undertaker services could be obtained, the parents found it financially impossible to give the boy a proper burial," explained a North Western employee in the 1930s. "And the parents of the boy intimated that when they reached Redfield with this extra gang, it was their intention to go back and remove the boy's body and give it burial back East from whence they came." That did not happen. "Upon reaching Redfield with the extra gang both of the parents disappeared."

Amazingly the boy's memory remained alive. Beginning on Decoration Day 1889 and for more than forty years, Big Bill Chambers brought flowers to the grave and maintained the site. It may have been at his insistence that section men placed a rough granite stone as a permanent marker. Shortly before his death in 1931, Chambers asked the conductor on the Redfield–Watertown–Tracy (Minnesota) passenger train to continue to do "something special" on Decoration Day. The conductor agreed, and after Chambers's passing, he began the practice of stopping the train at the grave and conducting a brief memorial service. Also the section foreman kept watch over the gravesite and in late May gave it special attention.

What then may have surprised passengers not knowing about the Little Fellow – a name coined by the North Western public relations officer – was the stopping of Motor Train No. 106. No one objected.

On Memorial Day
1946 the regularly
scheduled North
Western motor
train paused at the
grave of the "Little
Fellow" near Clark,
South Dakota, to
pay tribute to this
lad who had died in
the 1880s and was
buried at trackside.

Author's coll.

Moreover, the North Western received favorable publicity for this act of remembrance, although details of why the annual occurrence evolved into more fiction than fact. After the railroad ended passenger service in 1951, area residents kept alive the trackside tradition. Even though the North Western abandoned the branch line in the 1970s, the annual ceremony continued, but accessibility to the grave became more difficult. The Little Fellow made friends for the North Western – "humanizing the railroad" – and spotlighted an unusual, if not unique, unscheduled stop of a passenger train.

It is unlikely that any other trackside grave was so remembered. Yet other burial sites dot railroad corridors. A few of these are marked, including the grave of John Hill, a construction worker who died on March 12, 1887, while blasting the Winston Tunnel in northwestern Illinois as the Minnesota & Northwestern Railroad advanced toward Chicago. Then there are unmarked graves, arguably more common. A massive site exists along "Duffy's Cut," west of Malvern, Pennsylvania, where a communal grave dating from the 1830s contains the remains of more than fifty Irish laborers. Instead of dying directly from the construction of the Philadelphia & Columbia Rail Road, a future component of the Pennsylvania, these unknown men were probably victims of a deadly outbreak

of cholera. "They were thrown away in the 1832 equivalent of a junk pile," commented William Watson, an historian who has studied their deaths.

On May 30, 1960, the annual ceremony continued, even though passenger service had ended.

Author's coll.

While a passenger train that stopped for a trackside grave ceremony or a train rider who noticed a lone headstone along a the right-of-way collectively fit the category of the unexpected, other onboard happenings also qualify. Travelers might have been surprised (and disgusted) to learn about or actually to witness high-stakes poker, three-card monte, or related card games, not really realizing that professional gamblers haunted passenger trains, especially those that catered to businessmen and salemen. Not only did degrees of skullduggery occur, but gambling was against railroad regulations and most state and territorial laws. In its coaches the Kansas Pacific Railway posted signs, printed in heavy black type, that warned: **BEWARE OF THREE-CARD AND CONFI-DENCE MEN!** Later the Pullman Company offered this admonition: "The Pullman Company calls the attention of its patrons to the fact that 'Card Sharks' and 'Con Men' have started their winter campaign on railroad trains. Passengers can protect themselves by refusing to play with strangers."

The Victorian sensibilities of passenger were likewise shocked (and more so) when they learned that prostitutes were plying their trade in

Pullman cars. Americans had long shown preference for open-section rather than "compartment" sleepers that dominated in Europe. Indeed, the Mann Boudoir Car Company failed to make serious inroads in capturing the business of competitor Pullman; travelers felt uncomfortable with the total privacy of Mann Boudoir equipment. Eventually Pullman offered alternatives to the open-section sleepers, enhancing opportunities for immoral doings. During World War II a military policeman discovered that two women had a standing reservation for a Pullman drawing room on the *Sunshine Special,* a popular Missouri Pacific train that operated between St. Louis and Texas destinations. "Business always appeared to be good on the southbound trip," he recalled. "There was never a 'line' to this rolling brothel (which was occupied by one of these entrepreneurs each night) but, somehow, word would get forward to the other sections of the train. Consequently, at approximately half-hour intervals – a couple of GI's would pass each other in the vestibules separating the first class and chair sections of the train." "Johns" took chances. They risked sexually transmitted diseases, and they could find their wallets empty.

The unusual could happen in any environment. Traveling by train was no exception, and these events differed greatly from the actions of card sharks or women practicing the oldest profession. A young Missouri couple running away to elope believed that the woman's father was in hot pursuit, and so they asked if anyone on their train could legally marry them. They were in luck. A man of the cloth identified himself and performed the spur-of-the-moment ceremony. An accommodating passenger joined the minister in signing the marriage document. While few impromptu weddings took place on board a moving train, there were births. In September 1886 a widely reported birth took place on an express train operating on the East Tennessee, Virginia & Georgia Railroad. Apparently an unwed woman from a prominent Virginia family entered a car's "toilet room" and remained there for nearly a hour. "Suspicion was aroused, and a few moments afterward a newly born babe was seen to drop to the tracks." Then a miracle happened. "The train at once stopped and the infant recovered." Concluded the journalistic report: "The affair created great excitement and an effort is being made to hush the matter up." And there were medical crises, many more than births. Serious or fatal health events were not unknown among passengers, commonly heart attacks and strokes. Railroads established protocols for such happenings. These usually involved the train being stopped at an appropriate station, a company physician called, and if a death occurred, the body removed and the coroner summoned. Passengers experiencing less severe medical problems would be attended to by a company physician, again at the nearest practical station.

Passengers on a Southern Pacific train in the 1950s may have been surprised to have had the opportunity to watch a fashion show, including a female model who wore a "pink fox, of all things," a smart evening stole.

Don L. Hofsommer coll.

The unexpected might be light and fun. In the 1950s an Allentown, Pennsylvania, department store, Hess Brothers, may have surprised afternoon riders on the Lehigh Valley's *Black Diamond* passenger train between Allentown and Wilkes-Barre. The reason: a women's fashion show. On several separate occasions models, with "gorgeous smiles," sought to stimulate interest in the latest autumn fashions. And likely they did.

An adult living seventy-five years ago had experienced a revolution in passenger rolling stock just as an adult today can recall the spectacular advances in personal technologies. There had been major improvements from the Demonstration Period through the Gilded Age in rail travel, including better seating, lighting, and heating, and more dramatic improvements were forthcoming. "Twenty years ago, the passenger would enter one of those old-style platform cars, with uncomfortable low back seats; lighted with smokey, leaky coal oil lamps; heated by a struggling but overtaxed coal stove with the dirty coal box in the corner and arctic temperature in the middle and opposite end of the car," observed writer I. M. Brown in 1930. But by then there were these wonderful changes. "The up-to-date traveler sits in a comfortable coach with high-back seats, electrically lighted and heated with a steam heating system, electrically controlled and cooled, when necessary, by the latest type fans." There was more to savor:

> The modern traveler, desiring more exclusive accommodations than afforded in the coaches, is afforded luxury and attentive service in the modern steel Pullman cars, where real diplomats – Pullman conductors and porters – furnish everything within the law that the passenger may want, from card tables, paper hat bags and bottle openers, to towels, soap and matches. In the observation Pullman, the traveler can get a better general view of the scenery, or tiring of this, he can turn to latest copies of popular magazines and pass his time as he is carried swiftly to his journey's end.

If Brown had written his comments a few years later, the unconventional appointments found on the southbound run of the *Florida Special,* operated by the Florida East Coast Railway between Jacksonville and Miami, would surely have amazed him. "The club car is equipped with a small bathing pool, mechanical horses, a punching bag and other equipment for the entertainment of passengers who want to exercise."

There were those train riders who wished for a time freeze of sorts in overnight accommodations. The Pullman Company made changes, introducing in the 1930s, for example, its Simple Occupancy Section or "S. O. S." compartments for the cost-conscious and travel-wise. "For me the Pullman Company will never improve on its classic design of upper and lower berth," opined essayist E. B. White in the early 1940s. "In my eyes it is a perfect thing, perfect in conception and execution, this small green hole in the dark moving night, this soft warren in a hard world." But not everyone would endorse the White perspective.

Not long after I. M. Brown made his observations, substantial improvements in creature comforts delighted passengers. Riders enthusiastically applauded air-conditioned equipment. It would be in the early

1930s that several carriers, led by the B & O, installed mechanical refrigeration, or what some called "manufactured weather." Not only could blistering summer temperatures be reduced in coaches, sleepers, and diners, but these systems controlled air purity. No longer would passengers have to decide between open widows with moving air but with soot and dirt, from time to time obnoxious smells, and always the noise of travel, or closed windows with cleaner, quieter conditions but with stifling, clammy heat. "Our sleeping car was not air-conditioned," related an overnight traveler in the 1930s.

> So I sweltered in a berth where a sheet stretched across wide open windows kept out the cinders and most of the air, but let in all the noises as we crashed through small towns past jangling crossing-bells, and all the odors of stock-pens as we swept alongside miles of freight trains that carried protesting live stock of every description out of the drought area. But at some indefinite hour in the night, I felt a refreshing breeze struggling with the sheet, and despite the noises and sickening smells, I dozed.

When equipment was duly updated, pure, clean air was now always possible, "thermostatically warmed or cooled, according to the season." Said a passenger on the *Twentieth Century Limited*, "Air-conditioning on this train is one of its many pleasures. I like it much more than having freshly-cut flowers in the diner or a manicurist."

But dwarfing air-conditioned in heavyweight rolling stock came the lighter, polished-aluminum and stainless-steel streamliners. (They, too, were climate-controlled.) The most famous was the *Zephyr* or *Pioneer Zephyr*, built by the Edward G. Budd Manufacturing Company of Philadelphia for the Burlington. This three-car trainset appealed to management because of its low operating and maintenance costs. Then there was the public appeal, becoming in May 1934 a national sensation when it set a record time in its dawn-to-dusk sprint from Denver to Chicago. Welcoming this trail-breaking streamliner, passengers raved about the attractive, quiet, and sleek accommodations. Their only complaint, albeit not made by many, was inadequate leg room and close quarters. A few years later that changed when Budd built a prototype passenger car for the Santa Fe that featured additional space between the reclining seats and added dressing rooms at either end of the car. As the "Age of the Streamliner" became reality, more of these cars entered service,. The traveling public could enjoy such swanky trains on a number of railroads, ranging from the Boston & Maine to the Southern Pacific.

Publications – newspapers, magazines, travel folders, and books – contained repeated testimonials about the glories of taking passage on board diesel-powered streamliners. In 1937 when the Santa Fe introduced its smart all-Pullman *Super Chief-2* between Chicago and Los Angeles, one passenger penned these comments:

The train itself is chastely beautiful and, in the tempered light of early evening, soft shadows sift across the satin sheen of its stainless steel sides. Nothing obtrudes to mar the smooth perspective from the tailored rear of the observation lounge, where shaded lights and mellow colors invite to cozy hours, to the locomotive whose apron pilot and bluntly rounded front somehow resemble the long-visored cap [of] the engineer, who even now gives expert ear to the drone of the Diesels as he tests their responses to his power-throttle.

This particular streamliner became an instant sensation, being the classiest and fastest train between the Midwest and West Coast and a favorite of Hollywood stars, politicians, and other VIPs. Soon "chief" had a new usage, becoming a verb, as in "I just chiefed in from LA."

In the post–World War II years long-distance passengers seemed most impressed with dome cars, which made their debut on the Burlington. The concept involved observatory space that resembled caboose cupolas, allowing passengers to gain a panoramic view of the railroad corridor and

beyond. A modified streamlined car No. 4714, renamed the *Silver Dome,*
entered revenue service on July 23, 1945, between Chicago and St. Paul–
Minneapolis on the *Twin Zephyrs.* Within a few years specially designed
dome cars appeared on various streamliners, including additional ones on
the Burlington and such roads as the B&O, Denver & Rio Grande Western,
and Union Pacific. Most were on western railroads, because of their more
generous track clearances and spectacular scenery. Passenger comments
were consistently positive: "I feel like I'm riding in an airplane and the
view is beautiful and resting." "Wonderful view, sold comfort even from
sun rays, freedom from wheel and track noises." "A traveler's dream by
rail realized." The dome car also delighted railroad enthusiasts: "A dome
permits you to breathe down the engineer's neck, examine the train from
stem to stern, see *all* the railroad from signal bridges to switch shanties,
and stay clean and cool in the process."

Although various railroads bet on a strong long-distance passenger
market, the decade or so after World War II was to be an Indian summer
of sorts. Americans increasingly flocked to the highways, made more attractive by turnpikes and interstates (after 1956), better automobiles and
cheap gasoline, and improved roadside accommodations. They also took
to the skies, especially with introduction of more powerful piston-driven
airplanes and then in the late 1950s with jet aircraft. Still, some rail carriers
attempted to add new equipment (or at least maintain their rolling stock)
and to pamper patrons.

Modern rolling stock did not always please potential passengers or
prevent automobiles and airliners from luring away long-distance traffic.
In the 1950s several carriers, including the New York Central, New York,
New Haven & Hartford, and Rock Island, believed that low-center-of-
gravity trains would attract riders. Much hoopla came with introduction
of such "futuristic" or "gee-whiz" trains as the *Talgo, Xplorer,* and *Train X.*
But these low-slung, ultra-lightweight designs resulted in a series of em-
barrassing (and expensive) failures.

The Rock Island's *Talgo,* no-so-affectionately described as "the train
that looks like a half-used toothpaste tube," demonstrates that "progress"
in passenger equipment might not produce the intended results. In the
July 1954 issue of *Rock Island News Digest,* the company magazine, there
was excitement about this train, dubbed the *Jet Rocket,* that would operate
the 161 miles between Chicago and Peoria. "Rock Island has scooped the
railroad industry by scoring another 'first' with the announcement of a
completely new and revolutionary type of passenger train, the *Jet Rocket,*"
extolled the publication. "In announcing this addition to the fleet of *Rockets,* Mr. [president John D.] Farrington expressed a hopeful outlook for
the future of railroad passenger business. Alertness of management, he
said, constantly to seek out new technological improvements in passenger

service not only makes the picture much brighter, but should certainly lessen concern over competition from other sources."

On February 11, 1956, with considerable fanfare, the *Jet Rocket* made its inaugural trip. Yet it was an almost instant disappointment, and within a year and a half it would be withdrawn from the Peoria run. The train offered no measure of improved passenger comfort; riders did not care for small seats, cramped toilets, low ceilings, and excessive noise. The ride was rough, exceptionally so on the secondary line that linked Peoria with the better-maintained main line at Bureau. "I had a light meal in the diner and the service ware and dish ware, especially the cups, seemed to always be flying off the table," remembered one disgusted rider. "I thought that the parlor space was just too limited for a train of this kind, for there were less than two dozen seats, not like a regular parlor car. I didn't care either for the constant racket as I set there in the parlor." Then there was the camera. The train offered a novel closed-circuit television camera that was placed in the nose of the locomotive. "The idea was to create some excitement by giving lounge passengers a simulated cab ride," noted a student of the *Rockets*. "However, after the paying customers got a look at the repeated near-misses with pedestrians, school buses, gasoline trucks and gravel haulers at grade crossings, excitement quickly gave way to sheer terror."

Not all efforts to upgrade passenger equipment can be placed into the *Jet Rocket* category. On January 11, 1969, the Penn Central Railroad (the recently merged New York Central-Pennsylvania) introduced on the New York–Washington corridor its high-speed, electric-powered *Metroliners,* with financial assistance provided by the High Speed Ground Transportation Act of 1965. These Budd-built tubular, stainless-steel cars offered excellent accommodations. Understandably these trains received positive responses and reversed a long-term decline in ridership between these two terminals. "I like speeding in grand style along at times at more than 115 miles an hour. I can get to the City [New York] faster than I can sometimes by taking the Eastern [Airline] shuttle from National [Airport]," observed a pleased Washingtonian. Another resident liked that "we didn't have to circle around Union Station several times before coming in," again a reference to air congestion. A Long Island resident wrote to the *New York Times* these thoughts: "The designers and operators have combined in the Metroliner some of the best features of air and rail transportation without bringing along the discomforts, too. The cars have the same soundproofing, recorded background music and wall-to-wall carpeting as an airliner, but, happily, not the tiny windows and crowded quarters. The aisles are wide, you can take a stroll through the entire length of the train and there are no ominous warnings to fasten one's safety belts or stop smoking." There was more that proved satisfying. "I found the attendants and operating crew of the train courteous, and filled with pride in their

train. And as if this wasn't enough to make the ride enjoyable, we arrived in New York [from Washington], with a light snow falling, three minutes ahead of schedule."

But as *Metroliners* received kudos from patrons, most intercity riders did not have much to cheer about as the railroad industry struggled for survival. Nearly all passenger carriers pushed hard to end their remaining runs; new equipment did not replace old; car maintenance was frequently lacking, and onboard amenities declined. "Train service went straight to hell by the late sixties," lamented one traveler. "In college, I took the old New York Central from Rochester to New York City a few times, but by then the rolling stock had developed the ambience of a lavatory, with trash everywhere, and the upholstery rotting, and odoriferous men snoring across the rows of seats. There were mysterious delays all along the way." The Southern Pacific, resembling the New York Central, also offered travelers less. The *Lark,* which operated between Los Angeles and San Francisco and once had been the pride of Californians, became anything but an enjoyable travel experience. Before its discontinuance in 1968 "service

Passengers who boarded the *Capitol Limited* in Washington, D.C., in December 1964 had the chance to view a first-run movie, *The Unsinkable Molly Brown.* This recently released musical, "big, brassy, bold and freewheeling," starred Debbie Reynolds and Harve Presnell.

William Howes Jr. coll.

On May 10, 2008, an Amtrak *Acela* trainset draws attention at the annual National Train Day in Union Station in Washington, D.C.

Alex Mayes photograph

on the Lark was all but eliminated. Dinner, so-called, was served on paper placemats and was limited to four items: bacon and eggs ($1.85), ham and cheese sandwich ($1.65), hamburger ($1.50), and sirloin steak sandwich ($3.25)." As for the latter offering, the comic Sam Freberg observed, "The only thing tougher than that steak is the heart of a Southern Pacific ticket agent." No progress here, either in equipment or service. Admittedly a few roads, including the B&O, Santa Fe, and Southern, maintained standards, even introducing onboard Hollywood movies and other attractions.

With travelers turning to other means of transportation, losses soared. Then in the late 1960s the U.S. Post Office Department ended RPO routes; much-needed "head-end" revenues declined or disappeared completely and more red ink spilled. Now pundits poured out columns announcing the death of the passenger train. They were right in that the era of privately operated long-distance passenger trains was nearly over.

Railroads wanted out, and they achieved that goal on May 1, 1971, when the quasi-public National Railroad Passenger Corporation, better known as Amtrak, made its debut, taking over part of the remaining intercity rail passenger operations. Nevertheless it was premature to write the obituary of the long-distance passenger train in the United States. Since Amtrak had limited finances, the remaining trains, which operated over a greatly reduced network of freight rails, had to use existing rolling stock, some good and some not so good. In time, though, progress came with equipment that replaced the ragtag "Heritage Fleet," or "Rainbow Fleet" as others called it. Beginning in 1979 scores of bi-level cars, named

Superliners, which included coaches, sleepers, dining cars, and lounges, appeared on Amtrak trains, and four years later more bi-levels entered service. "I surely like these big roomy cars and they are much nicer than an airplane," noted one traveler. "Unlike those old Amtrak [heritage] cars, everything works, including the air-conditioning and the toilets. I hate hot trains and clogged toilets."

While the betterments, represented by the bi-levels, received positive comments, it would be introduction of *Acela Express* trains as the twenty-first century dawned that captured travelers' fancy and national attention. The name itself implied a freshness to travel in America – a union of "acceleration" and "excellence." Many believed (or hoped) that an Acela success would provide impetus for more high-speed trains and routes. These Northeast Corridor trains, built by the consortium of Bombardier Transportation of Montreal and Alstom of Paris, were inspired by recent technological development in electric-powered trainsets that served several European nations, including France and Germany. "A recent trip in the brand-new first-class car of the Acela Express from New York to Boston was spiffy and comfortable, with a good breakfast delivered to passengers' seats on china, plenty of coffee refills, lots of leg room and wide aisles to stroll along," enthused a writer for the *New York Times*. "The 231-mile journey on Dec. 29 [2000] took three and a half hours, in contrast to almost four hours on the Acela Regional, which is all-electric but uses older equipment, and four hours, 50 minutes on Northeast Direct, the conventional train." Some riders remarked that the train was unusually

Although in regular service between Washington and Boston, a car on an *Acela* train in September 2008 has plenty of empty seats.

Alex Mayes photograph

quiet and bright inside and that it did not feel as if it was going as fast as it was. There was more. Said one observer: "I think this is a very sexy train. Maybe you find a partner here. Those who don't have partners can find them on the Acela Express."

Public responses also came in somewhat unexpected ways. Just as a Waukesha, Wisconsin, brewery in the late 1930s celebrated the 400 streamliners on the North Western between Chicago and the Twin Cities (400 miles in 400 minutes) with its "Fox Head '400' Beer," designed "for those who make a fine art of living," a similar event came with the debut of the *Acela Express*. In its honor the Copley Plaza, a hotel located near Back Bay Station in Boston, added an "Acela-tini" to its popular collection of Oak Bar martinis. This high-powered drink consisted of a "dash of blue Curacao to give it a blue silver hue," reflecting the blue livery of the new trains.

Even with state-of-the-art trainsets and much fanfare, the improved Acela trains frequently disappointed patrons. Tracks and electrical systems required major upgrades; less-than-perfect track produced annoying bounces, and failures with the overhead catenary and brake problems led to delays, some of which lasted for hours. Unreliable trains caused some disgusted passengers to quip that Acela really stood for "Amtrak Customers Expect Late Arrivals." In time, track and electrical betterments and modifications to the original train-set design improved operating efficiencies and public confidence. But *Acela Express* trains were hardly equal to the French TGV (*Train a Grande Vitesse*), introduced in 1981 and repeatedly upgraded with equipment and extended to additional routes, or to the world's other high-speed trains, especially the bullet trains of Japan.

While the TGVs changed the way Europe traveled, as did other fast trains in Japan and, increasingly, China, the United States has been slow to embrace the latest passenger technologies. In the near future travelers may enjoy rail progress with such projects proposed by the California High-Speed Rail Authority and similar public agencies. "I wish that I could come home from Europe or Asia to a super fast train," opined a Chicago resident. "These trains can be built and it would be money well spent for real progress in intercity transportation. I would like this to happen in my lifetime. What a joy it would be to ride on one to St. Louis or New York City." Despite this excitement, high-speed rail in the United States likely means more higher-speed diesel-electric trains that travel at 100 to 110 miles per hour and not those electric marvels that go twice as fast. Combining slow freights and fast passenger trains on the same tracks will be a challenge, but who knows what the morrow will bring. It is certain that trains will continue to play a part in long-distance travel. "I travel by train" will be words that Americans will speak in the future.

BUILDINGS

It would be during the "Demonstration Period," roughly the 1830s and 1840s, that the railroad station evolved. At the dawn of intercity railroads, officials did not fret much about depot design or construction, instead concentrating on tracks, bridges, and other physical aspects of their new lines. Recruiting reliable workers and making plans for operations and expansion also consumed time. An upstart carrier might use or modify an existing structure convenient to its tracks to serve as a depot. When in 1830 the gestating Baltimore & Ohio Railroad (B&O) reached Ellicott's Mills (now Ellicott City), Maryland, 13 miles west of its starting point on Pratt Street in Baltimore, the company decided that passengers should wait in the nearby Patapsco Hotel. When the B&O a year later extended its original stem in Baltimore the short distance to the Inner Harbor, the Three Tuns Tavern served as the depot. Railroad officials believed that travelers could fend for themselves. This had been the experience of stagecoach riders, as operators infrequently owned station facilities; rather, proprietors of hotels, stores, and taverns provided shelter and services. Yet eventually the B&O felt the need to build a structure at Ellicott's Mills to accommodate and protect shipments of freight. Later the railroad erected a depot designed for passengers, and Baltimore likewise received enhanced passenger facilities.

Throughout the pre–Civil War period, and occasionally thereafter, railroads utilized for their station existing structures like the Patapsco Hotel and the Three Tuns Tavern. What seemed like an easy, inexpensive solution to the "depot problem," however, could have unintended consequences. Take the Housatonic Railroad, which served the Housatonic River valley in western Connecticut. When surveyors located the line in the early 1840s, the hotel proprietor, Sylvanus Merwin, and his wife, at Merwinsville (later Gaylordsville) wined and dined these men at their establishment, a handsome three-story frame building with its nine-column

A railroad, including this unidentified carrier in Pennsylvania, might select an existing building, perhaps a hotel, store, or house, for its station needs. When a company gained financial strength, it likely built its own depot or remodeled the original structure.

Author's coll.

Georgian exterior. When the company built through the area, tracks not surprisingly passed next to the hotel. After the arrival of the iron horse, the wife became the village's first agent, but apparently she lacked the requisite skills. Her inability to manage train movements led to a serious accident. The railroad fired her and sent a replacement, a decision that incensed the couple. When the new agent announced his presence, the hotel proprietor asked sarcastically, "Did you bring your depot with you?" The Housatonic had no choice but to build its own structure, albeit only a few steps from the hotel.

Carriers came to prefer control of these trackside buildings, and once their financial health improved, they could more likely erect such facilities. Yet for the short term, existing structures remained that viable option. In 1856 directors of the East Tennessee & Virginia Railroad accepted the request of Henry Johnson, resident of the Brush Creek, Tennessee, to "install a depot and water station" in his community. But before the railroad would build a depot, he needed to "furnish the necessary building

free of charge for depositing the mails, for passenger and freight." This Johnson did, providing space in his "stone house dwelling."

When railroads erected their own depots, what emerged by the 1880s was a popular design. This was the single-story combination depot that comfortably (and inexpensively) served the needs of most smaller communities. This concept provided space for an agent's office (usually located in the center with a protruding bay window that faced trackside), waiting room, and freight section.

The combination type was commonly built to a standardized plan created by railroad personnel, allowing for convenience, flexibility of construction, and reasonable cost. Sizes varied widely by road. For example, several combination depots built by the Lake Erie & Western Railroad in the late nineteenth century featured these dimensions: 57'6" × 18'6" building with a 24'-long freight room, 18'-long central office, and 15'6"–long waiting room. In 1900 the Chicago, Milwaukee & St. Paul Railway (Milwaukee Road) created for a dozen or so of its smaller stations an 18' × 36' depot that provided an 18'-long freight room, 10'-long central office and a somewhat cut-up waiting room that had an 18'-long side. The Minneapolis, St. Paul & Sault Ste. Marie Railroad (Soo Line) showed that it was easy to expand the footprint of a combination depot. The freight section of its Carrington, North Dakota, depot was twice extended to make the original 80' structure an impressive 136' in length. These additions met the needs of this growing trade center. The vast majority of these structures were built of wood, and at times with boards-and-battens exteriors,

Antebellum-era depots often possess highly individualistic qualities. In the 1850s the broad-gauge New-York & Erie Railroad erected this "run-through" structure in Susquehanna, Pennsylvania, an architectural concept developed somewhat earlier.

Author's coll.

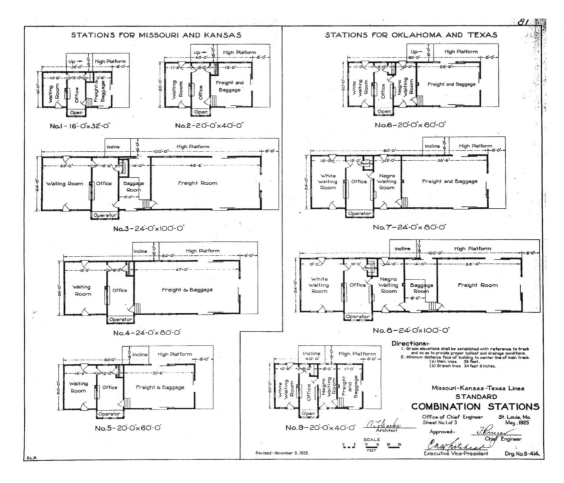

STATIONS FOR MISSOURI AND KANSAS

STATIONS FOR OKLAHOMA AND TEXAS

No.1 — 16'-0"x32'-0"

No.2 — 20'-0"x40'-0"

No.6 — 20'-0"x60'-0"

No.3 — 24'-0"x100'-0"

No.7 — 24'-0"x80'-0"

No.4 — 24'-0"x80'-0"

No.8 — 24'-0"x100'-0"

No.5 — 20'-0"x60'-0"

No.9 — 20'-0"x40'-0"

Directions:-
1. Grade elevations shall be established with reference to track and so as to provide proper ballast and drainage conditions.
2. Minimum distance face of building to center line of main track.
    (a) Main lines   29 feet.
    (b) Branch lines 24 feet 6 inches.

Missouri-Kansas-Texas Lines
STANDARD
COMBINATION STATIONS
Office of Chief Engineer   St. Louis, Mo.
Sheet No.1 of 3   May, 1925
Architect
Approved:-
Chief Engineer
Executive Vice-President   Drg. No. S-414.

Revised - November 3, 1925.

SCALE
FEET

In 1925 the Office of the Chief Engineer for the Missouri-Kansas-Texas (Katy) Railway created several standard combination plans for stations along its four-state system. The major distinction was that depots built in Oklahoma and Texas (states with Jim Crow segregation laws) required a "Negro Waiting Room," while those in Missouri and Kansas did not.

Author's coll.

further reducing costs and construction times. In his annual report for 1887 the commissioner of railroads and telegraphs for Ohio indicated that of the 2,199 depots in his state, those of wood construction totaled 2,107, typical of most states outside New England, where brick and stone were more common.

Variations in the floor plan also occurred. It was not uncommon to have a separate waiting room for women and children because of the perceived coarseness of tobacco-chewing, loud-talking, and profane males and "loafers." Female travelers had no desire to experience choking cigar smoke or to view unsightly cuspidors. Following the advent of post–Civil War Jim Crow segregation laws in Dixie, a "colored" unisex waiting room for African Americans became the norm. If a depot contained a single waiting room, people of color awaited trains on the platform or other designated places, whatever the weather, while white patrons took seats inside. A rope or curtain might divide the waiting room with a crude sign indicating THIS SIDE FOR NIGGERS. With installation of water and sewer systems, indoor restrooms replaced smelly outhouses and latrines. In colder climes, a specially insulated "warm room" protected

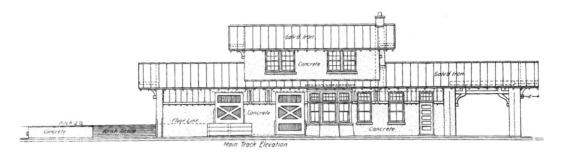

Main Track Elevation

perishable commodities that would likely freeze when outdoor temperatures plunged below zero. In larger towns and busy railroad junctions some combination depots contained lunch counters, express offices, and space for other auxiliary services.

An important variation of the combination depot, with or without multiple waiting rooms, was a structure, also commonly built to a standard plan, that provided living quarters for agents and their families. After the Civil War the concept of agents "living in the depot" became popular, largely in the trans-Chicago West. Railroads introduced this building type to rectify housing shortages in many communities, particularly raw prairie towns that had only recently appeared. An agent appreciated the availability of decent housing that was usually rent-free and included the company supplying gratis coal for heating and cooking and kerosene for lighting. There were downsides, however, namely complaints about dirt, noise, and danger.

On-site housing had its corporate benefits. The station agent was essentially on call twenty-four hours a day, seven days a week. "This would ensure the practically continuous presence of someone to receive service and emergency messages," noted a trade publication. An occupied depot meant that an agent or family member could respond quickly in a crisis, whether physically protecting the structure with a firearm (there was concern about break-ins because of cash kept in the office and valuable freight and express, including beer and whiskey before and after prohibition, stored on the premises) or reporting a fire to the volunteer brigade. If the company carried commercial fire insurance, premiums were lower for occupied structures. Railroad officials considered married agents "steady" and "reliable," and supplied housing could attract and keep these preferred employees.

Depots designed to house the agent and his family were generally of two types. One concept placed living quarters above what was usually a standard combination plan of central office, waiting room, and freight section. The Soo Line, which built scores of these "Number 2" structures in the upper Mississippi River valley and northern Great Plains, offered a simple arrangement for the second-floor layout. A narrow stairway

In 1906 the Santa Fe adopted a standard plan for its two-story depots to serve communities along the Belen Cutoff in New Mexico Territory. The upstairs apartment featured a compact kitchen, living room, two bedrooms with attached closets, hall, and pantry. Concrete construction (designed to keep these buildings cool in hot weather) and galvanized iron roofs made these depots unusual.

Author's coll.

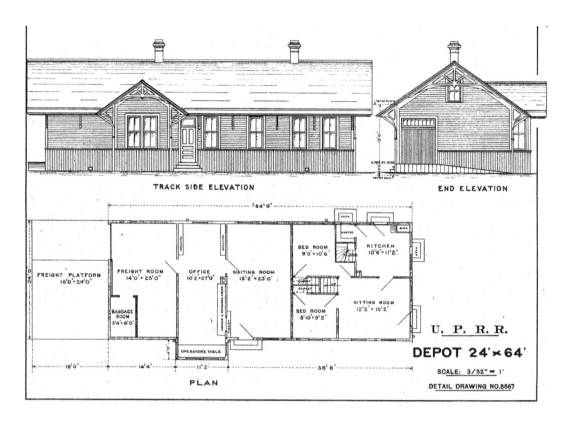

TRACK SIDE ELEVATION   END ELEVATION

FREIGHT PLATFORM
16'0" × 24'0"

FREIGHT ROOM
14'0" × 23'0"

OFFICE
10'2" × 27'0"

WAITING ROOM
13'2" × 23'0"

BAGGAGE ROOM
5'4" × 8'0"

OPERATOR'S TABLE

BED ROOM
9'0" × 10'6"

PANTRY

KITCHEN
10'6" × 11'2"

SINK

BED ROOM
8'10" × 9'2"

SITTING ROOM
12'2" × 15'2"

U. P. R. R.

DEPOT 24' × 64'

SCALE: 3/32" = 1'

DETAIL DRAWING NO.8867

PLAN

When the Union Pacific wanted to provide living quarters, a popular plan placed them on one side of the standard 24'×64' combination depot. A cozy apartment area resulted.

Author's coll.

connected the ground-floor office with the upstairs. From the top of this passageway, a hall led to a 12' × 17' living room at one corner of the front, and a small 6'6" × 13'6" bedroom occupied the other trackside corner. A 12' × 14' kitchen and a 10' × 13' bedroom extended across the back. The second floor had two tiny closets and a storage area that adjoined the kitchen. Later this depot type might be remodeled, most likely to include a bathroom.

The other design involved placing the apartment on the ground floor. While the Soo Line endorsed upstairs living quarters, the Union Pacific opted for an apartment attached to the combination depot. Company draftsmen created a 24' × 64' plan that added the four-room 475-square-foot living area on the waiting-room side and isolated these quarters from the public section. "These were simple plans," opined a company engineer. "We gave those agents only very basic housing." Specifically, the trackside sported a corner 12'2" × 15'2" "sitting room" and a 8'10" × 9'2" bedroom, and the back corner contained a 10'6" × 11'2" kitchen and a somewhat larger bedroom that measured 9' × 10'6". Resembling the Soo Line layout, Union Pacific quarters included two small closets and a food pantry. There was an inside bathroom, initially with only a tub and sink, both with primitive drains. When running water and sewer became available, a toilet was added.

A railroad might opt for *detached* housing for its agents. Early in the twentieth century when the Chicago & North Western Railway (North Western) extended a line into the developing soft-coal fields of southern Iowa, it erected depots to a carbon-copy blueprint at several locations, along with standard six-room, two-story houses. These latter structures duplicated ones utilized elsewhere on the system that accommodated track maintenance personnel. The acute shortage of housing in these rural areas promoted this building policy.

The location of the depot varied, no matter the style or type. In established communities, the structure might appear some distance from the existing town, perhaps because the community occupied a ridge or hill and the railroad needed to take advantage of an easier grade along a waterway or through a valley. It was not unusual for a settlement to spring up at trackside, being designated "Depot," "Station," or some other word affixed to the town name. Such was the case for the communities of Litchfield and Litchfield Station, Middlefield and Middlefield Center, and Washington and Washington Depot in Connecticut and Manchester and Manchester Depot in Vermont. When carriers built ahead of population, depots in these freshly established communities commonly stood at the head of the principal streets or in some other strategic places. Such might be also true for new lines that served established communities. That was the case of the Chicago Great Western Railway (Great Western), which took shape in the settled Midwest between the 1880s and the early 1900s. "The depot should be built in as close to the business center of the city as possible," argued Great Western founder A. B. Stickney. "That way the public will remember you," and he was undoubtedly correct.

If local business grew, railroads commonly replaced their modest, initial wooden depots with more substantial structures. The result might be a stylish brick passenger building and an adjoining freight house (sometimes the former depot) with its "team" tracks for loading and unloading the flow of goods. Even if the replacement or expanded structure was of frame construction, attractive details might be included. In the late 1880s the Portland & Ogdensburgh Railroad (later Boston & Maine), for example, refurbished its wooden depot in North Conway, New Hampshire. The structure received an addition with an interior of native woods "finished with oil," stained-glass windows, and a marble-top fountain in the women's waiting room.

Such upgrades received widespread public support, including praise from state railroad commissions. "A number of new station houses of unique and picturesque designs have been erected and are in pleasing contrast to many of the older ones, being of the kind that helps a town and builds up and advertises the railroad as well," observed the Ohio commissioner of railroads and telegraphs in 1892. "Handsome, comfortable and convenient depot buildings become objects of local pride and a source of increased business and traffic to the railroad." As early as the 1840s an industry spokesman agreed that beauty was important and entirely practical. "Every building may with very little if any additional outlay, be made pre-eminently an object capable of giving pleasure to a person of cultivated taste."

By the World War I era a genre of replacement buildings had widely emerged. These were the "county-seat" depots, as they were called, and for good reason they were highly prized by a community. This happened in 1904 when the Chicago, Burlington & Quincy Railroad (Burlington) opened such a depot in Red Oak, Iowa, bustling seat of Montgomery County that served the company's Chicago–Denver main stem and two intersecting branch lines. The floor plan of this brick 144' × 36' structure featured a large central waiting room with attached smoking room for men and a women's waiting room. Both the men's and women's sections had adjoining toilet facilities. The ticket office, used by the agent or operator, had the customary bay window and access to the main waiting area. At the ends of the building were the express and baggage section and a lunchroom and storeroom. The basement of this single-story depot contained additional storage, a coal-fired boiler that supplied steam heat, and a device for making carbonated water for the lunchroom. "This is a gem of a depot," crowed the *Red Oak Express,* and understandably so.

While the attractive, practical county-seat style depot elicited strong local approval, a modern urban terminal found widespread approbation from residents and travelers alike. During the Gilded Age and after, as cities grew and became the locus for a web of rails and carriers, the logic of a large terminal for an individual railroad or a union facility that some or all railroads could share became apparent. These great monuments to the Railway Age marked the landscape from coast to coast, extending from South Station in Boston to King Street Station in Seattle. Railroad termini became second only to skyscrapers as an indication of a city's importance and prosperity. Such a facility served as the modern version of the medieval city gate; civic pride in every metropolitan center demanded a fitting station. And the results impressed the public. "Without leaving the limits of the Grand Central Terminal area in New York one might lead a comfortable, active and full life, although he would *have* to leave after death to secure the services of a mortician." In many places these massive union stations became a second downtown, being more than just great transportation portals.

Large American cities often resembled London and Paris by not having just a single urban terminal. And this situation might confuse or annoy travelers. Atlanta, for one, had its Union Station and its Terminal Station,

but fortunately they were only a few blocks apart. Chicago, where rails from the East met rails from the West, developed multiple station complexes. Although the Windy City ultimately claimed a union station for its intercity trains with the debut of Amtrak in 1971, the nation's second largest population center had long had a half-dozen terminals, with their attractive headhouses (depots) and massive train sheds. Most were shared; yet travelers often learned to their dismay that there were Dearborn Station, Grand Central Depot, Union Passenger Station, and La Salle Street Station. Then there were facilities that were individually owned, notably stations operated by the Illinois Central and North Western.

In 1911 the North Western replaced its outdated 1881 Gothic-style station on Wells Street. The company took pride in this elegant state-of-the-art Beaux Arts–style terminal on West Madison Street, located near the heart of the vibrant Loop District. In addition to the well-designed main waiting room and train concourse, the facility offered a myriad of creature comforts. There were women's rooms equipped with desks and writing supplies, manicuring and hairdressing services, and a "maid in waiting." The needs of male patrons were amply accommodated, including a barber shop, shoeshine parlor, and smoking area. Available to all were an elegant dining room "with service equal to the best metropolitan cafes," telephone booths "so arranged that the opening of the door starts an electric fan and turns on the light," a drugstore, and a garage for automobiles.

While not unique, the North Western terminal created a welcoming environment for immigrants. Not long after the station opened, the

The stately Chicago & North Western Railway Terminal in Chicago, opened in 1911, cost more than $23 million, a princely sum for the time. The facility immediately became the pride of the railroad and the city.

Author's coll.

A meal could be an enduring, happy memory at the North Western Terminal in Chicago. In summer 1929 the railroad happily announced that its upscale dining room "goes Parisian with outside service."

Author's coll.

company issued *The Care and Protection Afforded the Immigrant in the New Passenger Terminal*, explaining how these travelers were assisted. This widely distributed pamphlet described the facilities and services offered these particular patrons, namely the large "Immigrant Waiting Room" with its paid attendants, bathroom for women and children, laundry room, and lunch counter. For its extra investment the railroad received high praise. "There is one station in Chicago where immigrants are well protected," concluded Alexander McCormick, president of the Immigrants' Protective League, "and that is at the new Chicago and North Western Railway Passenger Terminal." A Chicago newspaper observed that the "protection of the immigrant passing through Chicago 'from every wolf that roams the streets,' as well as the ministering to the physical comforts of the foreigners who are temporarily in the city, has been provided for by the Chicago and North Western Railway."

Then there were *true* union stations. In 1853 the first one opened in Indianapolis, designed by Thomas Armstrong Morris (1811–1904), a West Point–trained civil engineer. "The most ornamental building of its kind in the State" and located in the heart of the city, the station consisted of brick construction with a rock foundation that measured 420' × 100' and

contained five covered tracks that served eight railroads. The Hoosier capital was proud of the structure, and the *Indianapolis Morning Journal* wanted everyone to understand its significance. "Our readers have perhaps noticed that we avoid the word 'depot' when speaking of the Union Passenger Station. 'Depot' is a French word, signifying a town or place where goods are lodged for safe keeping or for re-shipment. We believe in calling things by their correct names, and we shall call it the Union Station or Union Passenger Station."

In addition to the Indianapolis terminal, a number of cities, including Cincinnati, Dallas, Jacksonville, Kansas City, Los Angeles, St. Paul, and Washington, D.C., later claimed such facilities, and nearly always they were the handiwork of a talented architect or an important architectural firm. When Union Station in Washington opened in 1907, the designers for this massive facility were headed by the renowned Chicago architect Daniel Burnham (1846–1912). It would be Burnham who captured the spirit of these transportation monuments; he ordered placed in stone over a side entrance his personal credo: MAKE NO SMALL PLANS, FOR THEY HAVE NO MAGIC TO STIR MEN'S BLOOD.

An outstanding illustration of this genre of urban union station appeared in St. Louis, for decades the nation's second-busiest passenger center. In the early 1890s the eighteen passenger-carrying railroads that served St. Louis decided that the city required a modern union depot, replacing the cramped facility that had opened in 1875. The Terminal Railroad Association of St. Louis (TRRA), the jointly owned terminal company that represented the carriers, engaged Theodore Link (1858–1923), an experienced local architect, to design a station in a practical location

One of the truly monumental union stations in America graced the downtown landscape of St. Louis. This picture postcard, mailed in 1906, shows a complex that bustled with outside activities.

Author's coll.

Early in the twentieth century Union Station in Meridian, Mississippi, began to receive patrons, and for decades remained busy. Photographs taken in 1940 and 1962 suggest the station's continued importance.

J. Parker Lamb coll.; J. Parker Lamb photograph

that would meet the needs of the fourth-largest city in America. The result would be a hefty investment for the TRRA, exceeding $6.5 million ($175 million in 2010 dollars).

Within fourteen months after the laying of the cornerstone, the public began to use the monumental Romanesque-style stone and masonry headhouse that covered two city blocks and a gigantic metal train shed that measured 700' in length and 606' in width and spanned thirty-two tracks. Although the hotel would not open immediately, travelers took advantage of the extensive array of features that Link had incorporated into the sprawling station. They could climb the grand stairway from the main entrance on Market Street to the spacious waiting room, or Grand Hall, and women could enjoy the comforts of the nearby "Waiting Room for Ladies Exclusively." Everyone could stroll along the track-level concourse, or "Midway," and take advantage of its various railroad and consumer services, ranging from travel information to a bookstore, lunch counter, and barber shop. Outside there was the tall, stately clock tower and later a magnificent fountain, "The Meeting of the Waters," designed by Swedish sculptor Carl Milles.

A fine example of the smaller version of the "grand" union station appeared in Meridian, Mississippi. In 1904 the Southern Railway, joined by three affiliates and the Mobile & Ohio Railroad, launched the jointly owned Meridian Terminal Company, and this corporate entity quickly acquired the needed land from property holders and the city for what was to be a modern union station. Two years later the terminal company opened a Spanish mission–style structure that featured a tower flanked by east and west wings. As with other stations in the South, the sexes and races occupied separate waiting rooms. This station, which came with a $200,000 ($4.8 million in 2010 dollars) price tag, was designed for future growth,

accommodating easily the needs of a city of 100,000 residents – when it
was completed, Meridian had a population of about 25,000. No one in the
self-proclaimed "Metropolis of Mississippi" complained, being delighted
to demonstrate to all that their community was no sleepy Southern town.
But the Meridian station and others were sometimes out of proportion to
the traffic potential, reflecting overly optimistic railroads or commercial
or political pressures.

Less elaborate union stations emerged. These structures typically
served two railroads, and occasionally more, at a rail crossing or junction. In Crestline, Ohio, a strategic railroad location in Crawford County
where the main line of the Cleveland, Cincinnati, Chicago & St. Louis or
Big Four Railroad (New York Central System) crossed the main stem of
the Pittsburgh, Fort Wayne & Chicago Railroad (Pennsylvania System), a
handsome union station, which cost upward of $10,000 ($145,000 in 2010
dollars), appeared shortly after the Civil War. In addition to a ticket office,
lunch counter, and newsstand, this L-shaped, three-story brick building
provided hotel space, much in the tradition of European stations. When
compared to the town's population of a few thousand residents, the size of
the Crestline depot may have surprised travelers, but the multiuse facility
nicely accommodated patrons of the Big Four and Pennsylvania.

Seemingly everyone benefited from union stations, whether in St.
Louis, Meridian, or Crestline. Railroads reduced costs by sharing expenses. If one carrier rented space to another, the overall financial

commitments might be considerably less than building and maintaining a separate depot. Those travelers who planned to transfer from railroad to railroad lauded these depots, since they would not have to walk to or to pay for transportation to the connecting station. Time, too, would be saved, especially important if an inbound train was late or the schedule called for a tight connection. In fact, state regulatory bodies consistently endorsed the concept of the union station. "To facilitate the public convenience and safety in the transmission of freight and passengers from one railway to another, and to prevent unnecessary expense and inconvenience in the accumulation of a number of stations in one place," announced the Iowa Board of Railroad Commissioners in 1888, "authority is given for any number of persons or railway companies to incorporate for the purpose of acquiring, establishing and construction and maintaining at any place in the State union depots." For obvious reasons dray and hack men and later taxicab drivers expressed less fondness for this station arrangement, relishing multiple depots. The absence of a union station in Chicago allowed Frank Parmelee, beginning in 1853, to established a lucrative depot transfer business, and the Frank Parmelee Company operated profitably into the second half of the twentieth century.

Inspired by railroads in Europe, especially in Great Britain, and for practical reasons, some depots, including union and nonunion facilities, contained hotel space or was available nearby in a separate structure that might be physically connected. As late as the 1890s that new St. Louis Union Station featured a large interior hotel. But the depot hotel was more popular during the earlier decades of railroad operations. With rapid expansion of the iron network by the mid-nineteenth century and before widespread usage of dining and sleeping cars – heralded by the 1880s as "hotels on wheels" – the need to provide travelers with more than transport seemed obvious. Thus riders could travel all day by chair car and stop at these station hotels for hot meals and comfortable overnight lodgings. Observed a writer for the *Cincinnati Enquirer* in 1857: "One of the greatest comforts and luxuries in a good railroad is a first-class hotel station where a good, well-prepared meal can be enjoyed." About the time that the Crestline depot offered hotel accommodations, the Erie Railroad, the quintessential experimenter, erected its substantial Starrucca House on its main line at Susquehanna, Pennsylvania, and affiliate Atlantic & Great Western Railway built the equally impressive McHenry House at Meadville, Pennsylvania. Over time what was considered to be a logical step in the development of railroad buildings became less important.

Not to be overlooked among depot types were the basic structures, at times not much more than wayside shelters. In places they might be a retired boxcar or passenger coach that for years served these stations. A railroad might install a bona fide depot building, with a waiting room

and freight storage area, but a separate office might be lacking. Usually the company employed a custodian on a part-time basis who opened the depot near train time and oversaw shipments of freight and express. And he (perhaps she) kept the stove fire burning during the heating season and conducted other janitorial chores. Often there would not be a telegraphic connection, but in time a company telephone might be installed.

Then there were actual shelters. These might be partially enclosed structures that gave patrons some protection from the elements while awaiting a train. Less-than-carload (LCL) freight might be left in or near the shelter for customers, with the hope that damage and thefts would not occur. Carriers in the South, most of all, found these shelters adequate to accommodate the needs of many of their rural stations. After all, early on railroads in parts of Dixie were built primarily for hauling cotton, and for decades these companies struggled financially.

Although small structures generally satisfied carriers, passengers commonly complained to railroad officials and regulatory authorities about shortcomings. It might be that the depot lacked restroom facilities or that it was closed at night, making it difficult to wait comfortably for a train. Then there was the matter of community pride. Even the smallest village expected growth, and a shelter-like structure hardly impressed

At times railroads utilized retired rolling stock to serve their station needs in smaller communities. The Missouri-Kansas-Texas (Katy) Railway selected a former gas-electric passenger car for its depot at Gould, Oklahoma.

Don L. Hofsommer photograph

outsiders. "A shack is a shack is a shack," remarked an Arkansas booster who called Narrows home. "A depot it is not."

Occasionally there were odd structures that served stations. Pragmatic carriers might use an interlocking tower for both train control and freight and passenger needs. The tower at Leipsic Junction, Ohio, where the Cincinnati, Hamilton & Dayton Railroad crossed the New York, Chicago & St. Louis Railroad (Nickel Plate), provided station services, allowing villagers and nearby farmers convenient access to each carrier. The Soo Line hastily modified a claim shanty to serve Wyndemere, North Dakota, although later the company, joined by the Northern Pacific, built a more pleasing union depot. To accommodate the crush of passengers who flocked in 1904 to the Louisiana Purchase Exhibition in St. Louis, a contractor for the Wabash erected a handsome, albeit temporary, depot near the grounds that reflected the neoclassical style of the fair buildings. As with most surrounding structures, the railroad disassembled the depot soon after the festivities ended, and laborers removed the connecting spur track.

WORKERS

Throughout the Railway Age depot personnel varied in numbers and duties. Travelers most frequently encountered the depot agent who alone staffed the station. In larger places the "official" agent was joined by additional employees, most notably clerk-telegraphers, who around the clock focused on train orders and managed related railroad business, including ticket sales. The depot might be the sole public place in a community that saw activity throughout the night, with the "third trick" operator on duty between 11:00 PM and 7:00 AM. But there might be others who labored at various tasks, including handling freight, baggage, and mail.

Who became an agent? As with all labor recruitment in the transportation sector, variations occurred, but generalizations are possible. The excitement, even the glamour, of the agent's job, and especially mastery of the cryptic Morse code, made it attractive to many a lad. The telegraph, which dated from the 1840s, was first utilized by railroads in the early 1850s for train dispatching and additional business matters; within a decade the telegraph became widely employed and then nearly universally used.

In the case of most depot agents, the prospective agent-operator came from town, for farm boys always faced daily chores and lived too far way to reach the depot conveniently. "No other labor-using institution is so well equipped to get the raw materials in labor as the railroad," opined a writer in *Railroad Men's Magazine* in 1917. "It reaches out into the villages and picks it off." A town youngster might "hang out" at the depot and, if he was

lucky, strike up a friendship with the agent. In exchange for instruction in telegraphy, bookkeeping, and the Book of Rules, or what employees called the "Company Bible," the young man performed odd jobs: fetching kindling and buckets of coal for the potbellied stoves during cold days; cleaning and filling the kerosene hand lanterns, switch lights, and signal lamps; sweeping and mopping floors; washing windows and performing other janitorial duties; helping to load and unload LCL shipments with the high-wheeled hand truck; and running errands, including delivering commercial telegraphic messages. "For many poor boys it was the break of a lifetime when they were able to learn a trade without cost and without having to live away from home while doing so," recalled an agent; "then he could step into a job in one of the most interesting industries in the world."

Since mastery of the language of dots and dashes became mandatory for any would-be station agent or operator, the determined youngster set up his own key and sounder at home, possibly connecting the equipment to a makeshift line that reached a friend's house or the residence of the local telegrapher. "I picked up a used telegraph key and car battery from an electrician, who charged the battery for a week," remembered a future agent. "I took it home, put it behind my dresser and hooked it to my key. The battery was covered with acid, which was absorbed by my overalls,

In the 1920s Burlington Railroad agent Martin Kenton is found at work in the office of the Russell, Iowa, depot. Kenton dropped out of school to become an agent, having "pestered his parents for their permission to quit school and to go to work for the railroad."

Author's coll.

causing one of the legs to fall off. As I practiced, I dreamed of building a reputation of sending 'good stuff.'" He added, "My parents didn't tell me then, but I found out later I almost drove them nuts."

It might be that the depot agent came from a railroad family. This was an industry where nepotism reigned. A father, brother, uncle, or other family member might provide the training, allowing the youngster to learn the required skills. A long-time agent for the Milwaukee Road entered the business because his station-agent father introduced him at a tender age to the profession. "In 1906 my Dad was appointed [Milwaukee Road] agent at Sioux Falls, S.D. Biggest station agent's job in S.D. 6 other railroads in town. Being of the 'old school,' my Dad thot the best way to keep a kid out of trouble was to keep him busy." This he did. "In June of 1906, at age 7, I started work at the freight office for 50c per week, working 4:10 PM (soon as I could get there after school) till 11 PM 5 days a week, 7 AM till 11 PM Saturdays and 7 AM till noon Sundays. Figured out to about 0.8c per hour – and I really worked!" This lad faced varied tasks. "I ran waybills, interchange reports, etc. over to depots and trains of the other railroads. Conductors would always hold their trains till I arrived with the bills. I crossed our Milw. R.R. bridge – was taught by my Dad how to step out on a girder if caught on bridge by a train." Later his father instructed him on how to manage additional station chores along with how to "pound brass" – sending and receiving Morse code. Recalled this agent about his background, "I am a lifelong railroader as were my Dad and Granddad before me. It never once occurred to me that I would do anything else."

The business of telegrapher was not totally a man's world. A young woman might pick up telegraphy from a relative, likely her father or brother, and become an operator or agent or eventually win promotion to the hectic and challenging duties of train dispatcher. A majority, though, found employment with a commercial telegraph company, usually Western Union or perhaps Postal Telegraph, its principal, smaller, competitor. In the early 1920s the U.S. Bureau of Labor revealed that of the 78,000 railroad telegraphers employed in the United States and Canada, 2,500, or about 3 percent, were women. Few people of color entered this profession, likely because the Order of Railway Telegraphers (ORT), the union that represented these "lightning slingers," maintained a staunch lily-white membership policy.

Another avenue to becoming a depot agent involved a person attending the popular schools of telegraphy that flourished by the late nineteenth century. These businesses, often with one or two instructors, might be found in a "railroad town," the location of division offices, and situated in a commercial building, often occupying upstairs quarters. Here with

key and sounder, the student paid to learn how to send and receive the
monotonous dots and dashes. The "professor" usually coached the student
in the other essentials of station work. After several months or longer,
graduates of these "ham factories" went to work for the various carriers,
but they might hire out to telegraph companies, joining urban offices with
their banks of instrument tables.

Most telegraph operators were employees of the hundreds of railroads with which telegraph firms had franchise contracts, an arrangement that worked well. Cheap telegraphic communications, argued the
superintendent of telegraph for the Missouri Pacific in the 1920s, "would
have not been possible without the railroad telegraph and the railroad
telegrapher. Either the capital could not have been found to construct
independent telegraph lines into the smaller and more remote places, or
the rates would have been prohibitively high."

Once an individual became qualified for agency work, having passed
tests on telegraphic skills (sending and receiving) and the Book of Rules,
knowing the ins and outs of station accounting and having obtained a
favorable medical examination conducted by a company-appointed physician, employment and seniority began. During the early decades it was
not an officer in the superintendent's office or another supervisor who usually did the hiring; rather, the president and the board of directors made
the selection, irrespective of an individual's qualifications. In September
1852 the minutes of the Memphis & Charleston Rail Road (M&C) reveal

The woman at the entrance to the Wheeling & Lake Erie Railroad depot at Robertsville, Ohio, a village in Stark County, is in all likelihood the agent-operator. Or she might be the station custodian.

Author's coll.

that James Walker was nominated by the president to serve as depot agent in Memphis, Tennessee, and the board then "declared duly elected after the ballot was counted." At the same meeting directors also elected the passenger train conductor. Apparently the M&C, like some other carriers, wanted to make certain that an employee who handled money was "morally upright." And a year later the M&C went on record that "agents shall be held responsible for all losses or damages to goods or property arising from negligence." In 1855 the neighboring East Tennessee & Virginia Railroad ordered that its agent at Knoxville post a $1,000 bond "for the faithful discharge of the duties of his office." Again there was concern about potential financial losses.

As the railroad enterprise matured, nearly always this "tin horn" agent worked the "extra board" where he (and occasionally she) served as a relief operator or took charge of a small depot. As a person advanced on the seniority list, a more attractive, full-time job might be obtained. With additional time in service, the agent could "bid in" on a better-paying station or gain protection in a current position. Yet the daily work routine was much the same at any place, at least in terms of the hours on duty. "My Dad, like all R.R. men worked endless hours, 7 days a week, 365 days a year. If they went railroading, they expected to." Only later did the eight-hour day become established, and then paid holidays and annual vacations.

Until the 1930s hundreds of "boomer-ops" were part of the station agent force. These men traveled from railroad to railroad, just as some enginemen and trainmen led nomadic careers. They were frequently young males who moved about for various reasons. Perhaps they had "itchy feet" and the desire to see the country, especially the West. Possibly they experienced unhappy domestic lives and therefore wanted to be on the go, or they might have less-than-stellar work records, needing to change jobs because of a drinking problem or other service violations. There were those boomer-ops who were outright dishonest, using an assortment of tricks to fatten their pocketbooks. A favorite tactic was to sell out of the back of the ticket book or case and pocket the money. Since the regular agent usually would check only the number on the first and last tickets sold, he would not discover the missing ones until he came to where they were supposed to be. By this time the boomer had moved on to another job, likely at another railroad.

Some carriers welcomed boomers, largely because they were willing to accept temporary employment when business exploded. The Georgia & Florida Railroad (G&F) was one such road. Management needed extra personnel (agents and trainmen) to move more and longer trains during the tobacco and watermelon rushes. And boomers could be hired more cheaply than permanent employees, a vital consideration for the always impoverished G&F. An astute observer of these wanderers, Freeman H. Hubbard, argued that "the boomer, man for man, was a more capable car hand, throttle artist, fireman, switchman, telegraph operator than the more conservative home guard." The reason for the prowess of boomers centered on their extensive experiences with hectic schedules. "The regular man, used to easy, take-your-time gait, was suddenly heaved into a madhouse of car movement," concluded Hubbard. "When work is done under unaccustomed pressure, mistakes are more likely to be made, and accidents more frequent."

Yet some regular agents did not care for boomers, even if they carried up-to-date union (ORT) cards. "A Boomer is more liberal than a Home-guard, being the tramp's next of kin," reflected an agent for the Florida East Coast, a railroad that welcomed boomer agent-operators during the citrus and vegetable rushes. "They have much in common, their expertness, wanderlust, independence. They look on the Agent as a man of low ideals, bowing down to those in authority."

The depot agent performed multiple tasks. The obvious activities, which consumed the bulk of a working day's time, involved sending and receiving railroad and public messages, selling tickets, providing travel information, and managing freight and express shipments.

Without question the hustle-bustle of station life made for many hectic moments. In 1926 the agent for the Great Western in Tripoli, Iowa, recorded some thoughts about his daily job. Although located on a branch line, the depot could become an extremely busy place. "Work can be frantic, especially when you are making switch list for local due in fifteen minutes; also fifteen to twenty waybills to make; several express shipments to prepare for passenger train, which is due to meet the local at your station, and the city telephone persistently ringing, the party on the line asking something like this: 'Did Jim or Joe get off the train?' In all probability you do not know either of them." The agent continued. "Turning around to the ticket window another party asks: 'Is there any freight for me?' without as much as telling you his name, taking it for granted that you are the local agent, you should know his name. About one minute before the passenger train is due, a traveling salesman rushes up with three trunks to check; three hundred pounds excess."

The agent in Tripoli may have needed to update the station bulletin board. Located in the waiting room or on an exterior wall that faced the tracks, this blackboard, which listed the scheduled times of passenger trains, required the agent or a helper to chalk in the status of each train. It might be "On Time" or "30 Min. Late." Passengers, especially those who needed to make a connection or an appointment, frequently kept a watchful eye on the board. Some railroads, except in bad weather, maintained a good on-time performance for their passenger runs. Such was the case of the Boston & Maine, and an agent might happily note on a daily basis: "On Time, In and Out."

Agents faced tasks that they found always annoying and occasionally troubling. Undesirable types could disrupt the demeanor of their workplace. Dissolute town idlers might harass travelers and others. Hoboes and bums might sleep on waiting-room benches, take their toilet on the premises, or seek handouts from the patrons. Being in charge of the station, the agent needed to coax the offenders to leave or request help from the local constabulary. In 1905 a newspaper in Carroll, Iowa, reported how the North Western agent, who supervised a depot that served the main line, a secondary main line, and a branch line, planned to handle the unwanted: "The agent has made the announcement that hereafter loafers will be compelled to keep away from the depot and that unless his orders are heeded some arrests will be made in the very near future." This decisive action may or may not have worked. And arrests occurred. In 1907 the Burlington agent in Red Oak, Iowa, took legal action against four individuals on a misdemeanor "public nuisance" charge. "It has been the custom of boys and young men to assemble at the depot and during the colder weather they would congregate in the smoking room, fill the seats to the exclusion of all traveling men who desired to sit in there and wait for their train, and with their tobacco and boisterousness make things generally unpleasant for all concerned." Escaping from this action were several girls. "It is not only boys who have at times proved nuisances," explained the agent, "but that some of the girls – not to give them the dignified title of young ladies – are in the same class and that the next time no distinction will be made between the sexes, but all will be compelled to answer in court."

Less extreme, but a common bother nevertheless, were passengers who did not understand the difference between "a.m." and "p.m." or who could not interpret a timetable or station bulletin board. Yet they demanded answers. In response to repeated questions about the exact time, another popular query, one frustrated agent placed the following sign under the office timepiece: "This is a clock; it is running; it is Chicago time; it is right; it is set every day at 10 o'clock. Now keep your mouths shut." With the advent of the telegraph the correct time would be sent to agents from a central office that allowed them to synchronize their depot clocks and other timepieces (later the process occurred automatically). Industry experts recognized the importance of accurate and visible station clocks. Observed John A. Droege: "It has been found by experience that the passengers are very likely to become nervous when at the windows if there is not a large clock in sight."

The goofiest questions, though, became the talk of agents and fellow railroaders. And these tales might well be embellished as they passed from employee to employee. One that agents along the Des Moines Division of the Chicago, Rock Island & Pacific Railroad (Rock Island) enjoyed involved this patron request:

> Some years ago when I was braking on the Chicago, Rock Island & Pacific, we went into a siding at Neola, Ia., to meet westbound passenger train No. 27, and we gathered in the depot office. A lady came into the waiting room. The op [agent-operator] asked if she wanted something.
>
> "Why yes," she replied. "My boy is working in the Oklahoma oil fields and I'd like to send him a brand new pair of socks by wire."
>
> "You sure can," says the operator, taking the clean socks she handed him, "but you'll have to wait a few minutes for an answer." Then he went out of sight, switched the clean socks for his dirty ones and returned with his "reply." He said the boy had received the clean socks and was sending his dirty ones to her to be washed.
>
> The woman smiled. "Yes, my boy never would change. I always have to remind him to send me his dirty socks."

Agents busied themselves in other ways, but they were not always happy with such tasks. They disliked having to move about heavy amounts of freight and express. While they might get assistance from a friendly trainman, section hand, or customer or from the youngster who was learning the business, a fifty-five-gallon barrel of oil or a metal cookstove could be a formidable obstacle, and if mishandled could cause injury. One agent complained bitterly about handling granite tombstones: "they seemed to arrive about every day!" Another fussed about shipments of wool: "Did you ever wrestle a bale of wool on a hot day? The oily wool permeates the rough burlap bag. We had no hooks so it was a free for all getting the bale out of the wagon, on a truck to the scales where we weighed it and left it for the freight crew." And pulling a loaded platform truck with its contrary iron wheels and stiff steering mechanism was always challenging, especially in snow, ice, or heavy rain.

Agents were responsible for non-depot facilities at the station. An annoyance, particularly in colder climes, involved maintenance of the water tank and its attached pump. Regularly the agent needed to check the water level, especially the cork float, which was prone to stick. If a problem developed, either the agent, a section hand, or a water-department employee made the adjustment or repair. During the winter months it was not unusual for the agent to trudge over to the pump house several times each day to keep stove fires burning in order to prevent pump mechanisms from freezing. Even when not on duty, the agent might still tend the fire.

Occasionally duties were truly monumental. In 1930 the new agent for the Wiscasset, Waterville & Farmington Railway, a faltering two-foot gauge carrier in Maine, learned that during the day he would be in charge of the terminal station at Albion, but at night he needed to be the engine watchman and "all for the princely, Lilliput stipend of $18.00 a week." As a consolation, though, the agent received a free apartment on the second floor of the depot.

Some station agents stewed over little matters. At times they resented the company demand that they don uniforms and caps. "Chicago Great Western agents," reported an Iowa newspaper in 1898, "have received notice that hereafter, while on duty, they must wear a uniformed cap and badge." Contemporary photographs suggest that Great Western agents largely complied with this directive. In 1905 an agent for the Rock Island complained repeatedly to superiors and the press that the two waiting rooms in his depot were not properly identified. "There is a tradition to the effect that the north room is for men, and the south one for women, but as neither one is so designated, the sexes and the tobacco smoke sometimes get mixed." But requests for the proper signage either were ignored or got lost, much to the aggravation of this station master. About the same time the general office of the Burlington in Chicago informed agents that they had better organize and keep control of signs posted in waiting rooms. "[Agents] must tear from the walls of stations all orders, circulars, hangers, posters, etc. Rules and regulations will be neatly framed and hung on the walls of all waiting rooms near the ticket windows," went the order. "To all advertising matter the sign will be up: POST NO BILLS." The company also wanted agents to properly maintain their depots, especially keeping waiting rooms clean and tidy. There was more. "Platforms are to be kept clean and the windows bright." Agents were told to watch out for "idle whittlers" who cut their initials on waiting-room benches and outside doors, window frames, and weather boarding.

Some employees complied, while others expressed less enthusiasm, grousing about these housekeeping demands. There were those who showed real initiative in their efforts to maintain a pleasant environment in and around their depots. An agent for the Florida East Coast did what he could to maintain a unisex toilet. "I overcame [the] nuisance by posting 'Ladies will keep this room neat. Others should.'"

Relaying orders to train crews from a country depot might become a troublesome daily task. Initially the agent placed a paper communication in the flat of his hand and then stood close enough to the moving train as it crept by the station so that a crew member could slap his palm and remove the order. The exchange might fail, prompting the agent to search for the dropped order or quickly to make a duplicate. Toward the close of the nineteenth century a more effective device appeared, the P-type bamboo train-order hoop – sometimes called a "9" because of its shape – that

SPITTING ON THE FLOOR IS FORBIDDEN

Consumption, La Grippe, Coughs, Colds and all diseases of the air passages are spread by spitting, and these maladies kill a number of people annually. It is, therefore, forbidden to spit on the floor.

It is the duty of railroad employees to warn against violating this health rule.

By the order of

W. G. BIERD, General Manager.

In the World War I era, carriers distributed thousands of signs in response to public health concerns, particularly the Spanish influenza pandemic. For years this notice probably remained posted in the station area.

Author's coll.

permitted trains to speed up through a station. Troubles still continued. If an agent used the hoop to hand up a message, he likely had to trudge along the track to retrieve it. (Without stopping the train, a crewman put his arm through the device, took off the onion-skin paper order clipped to the handle, and cast the hoop to the ground.) Finding the hoop could become an adventure when it landed in high weeds or deep snow or when it was dark. "The wood in hoops was almost the same color as the dead grass and weeds," remarked an agent. And in this case he lessened the finding problem by painting his 9s a combination of red and yellow. A prankster crewman might intentionally discard the hoop in an inconvenient spot, maybe a briar patch, or throw it into the locomotive firebox. By the 1940s the widespread use of the Y-stick ended this problem, negating the necessity of "hooping up" an order. The agent held onto the long-handled stick, and the crewman "on the fly" caught the order and the string that had kept it attached across the top of the mast.

Part of the general duties of the small-town station agent involved commercial telegraphy. Since railroads usually had a contract for such services with for-profit telegraph and cable firms, this work created its own special difficulties. While this business generated extra income for the agent, the bother might outweigh the compensation. "Invariably, somebody would show up about 20 minutes or so before you'd go off duty with a handful of death messages," explained an agent. "They expected you to accept them with graciousness and to get them out right away. All the operator made from a telegraph was 10 percent of any money he handled. If somebody came in with 5 or 6 telegrams that were to be paid for at the other end, I wouldn't get a nickel from sending any of them." He related further, "When you accepted the telegrams, you didn't know how long it was going to take to get rid of them because you had to call a relay operator and you had to wait until he was not busy. Your might sit there for 2 hours waiting for him past your time to go home." Then there were the inbound messages. "If the telegram was paid for on the other end, you never got anything out of it. If [the message] was for out in the country, and the people had no phone, and if it was an urgent message, you felt that you almost had to deliver it. If you drove out and delivered it, you never got a nickel and you never got any thanks from the people. They expected it." Lamented this agent, "There have been times when I got stuck in the snow and mud and I had to hire somebody to pull me out. It was a fine thing for the Western Union but it was a mighty poor arrangement for the agent."

Then there were the express company duties. In larger stations these firms had their own employees. No wonder the urban setting of Meredith Willson's hit musical of the late 1950s, *The Music Man*, featured the catchy song, "The Wells Fargo Wagon," which, of course, had a Wells Fargo man onboard. But for thousands of American communities the depot agent managed the express business. It was a chore, but unlike the case of commercial wire messages, the potential existed for substantial additional income. "Express could be worth as much as an agent's railroad wages," recalled an agent. "One station agent, who retired after 45 years, told me he dutifully took his railroad paycheck home to his wife after every payday. He gave her the entire check and she would dole out a small amount to him for cigars. Little did she know that he kept his [Railway Express Agency] check, which was as much as his railroad pay." That explains why some station openings triggered intense rivalries between potential holders, and the one with greatest seniority usually claimed the prized post.

A downside of express activities for the small-town agent involved the care of packages and other items. In order to deter thefts, a railroad might construct a "safe space" in the freight room, or the agent himself might fabricate such an enclosure. Following the repeal of national prohibition in 1933, the Southern Railway agent in Landrum, South Carolina, located a few miles from the North Carolina border, constructed a cage with heavy wooden slats. The reason was simple. Once again his county was wet, while neighboring counties in North Carolina remained dry. The Landrum agent used his handiwork to protect shipments of whiskey bound for the town's half-dozen liquor shops.

Agents usually took seriously the protection of railroad property. They had no desire to see acts of vandalism or thefts. To make certain that his depot was secure, Albert Burnham, the agent for the New York, New Haven & Hartford Railroad (New Haven) at Unionville, Connecticut, early in the twentieth century rigged up a primitive burglar alarm in the depot and connected it to his nearby house. One night the contraption sounded, and Burnham rushed to the station with his rifle. He found two intruders preparing to blow open the office safe. Shots were exchanged; one burglar was killed, and the other fled down the tracks.

Depot agents might be involved in activities that were not considered railroad-related or company-sanctioned. An entrepreneurial agent might sell an assortment of items to travelers. Popular oddments available at the ticket counter were spools of thread and related sewing notions. There might be much more, though. When the picture postcard craze burst upon the American scene about 1905 and lasted until World War I, images of the town, especially the station and the railroad corridor, were popular. Stationery also might be offered. If the buyer wanted a stamp, the agent usually could oblige. These sales were both a service to the public and a source of modest income for the agent. Some carriers objected, but these transactions regularly occurred.

During the Railway Age the basic units of public education were the one-room school in the country and the grammar school in town, where generations of youngsters learned their ABCs and 3-Rs. Yet not everyone possessed reading skills, perhaps having dropped out of the educational system at a tender age or having recently arrived from a non–English speaking country. The agent then served as the community's "reading man." Individuals who could not read knew that the agent could. "If any reading matter came their way," explained a long-time Milwaukee Road station master, "they usually headed for the depot to have it interpreted." And if a notary public or official witness was needed, the person in the depot office probably could assist.

Occasionally an agent offered medical assistance. One such person was S. S. McBride, who in 1882 became agent for the Denver & Rio Grande in Espanola, New Mexico Territory. Described as a "jewel of a man," McBride was both congenial and resourceful. Since it would be years before the village had a trained physician, he practiced medicine by using "Dr. Humphrey's Homeopathic Medicine Chest" and apparently with success.

Agents had their "down time" as well. While it was unlikely that any two days on duty were identical, there were gaps in the work routine. These periods allowed them to catch up on paper work, chat with railroaders and townfolks, communicate by wire with neighboring agents, and maybe do some recreational reading, perhaps newspapers, union and company publications, or copies of the *Police Gazette* or other male-oriented magazines. There were reports that agents, even at the busiest stations, did not work too hard. Early in the twentieth century a consultant, hired by the New Haven to make the property more efficient, conducted an inspection of the various operating divisions and found at least one not-so-diligent employee. "At one important station I had noticed a fine looking old gentleman, dressed apparently for a tea party, strolling around with a gold headed cane. I asked who he was and what he did, and was told that he was the station agent, and that he came down every day for an hour or two." That did not settle well with the investigator. "I put his name down as a candidate for the pension list, and then discovered that he was a brother-in-law of [investment banker] J. P. Morgan." The courtly man retained his position.

If a depot had only a few employees, productive or not, there might be food-service workers. Usually they were not on a railroad payroll, but hired by a private party that leased space. Lunch counters were common, even after railroads introduced dining cars on their better trains. While there might be a nearby "depot café" or "beanery," a food service under the depot roof was convenient and expected in larger stations, terminals, or junctions. The Minneapolis & St. Louis Railway (M&STL), for one, which provided travelers with limited dining-car opportunities, gave patrons, employees, or anyone else a chance to buy food, especially light fare, and coffee and other nonalcoholic beverages ("a bucket of hot mud and a sinker" translated to coffee and a donut) in nearly a dozen of its depots in Iowa, Minnesota, and South Dakota. M&STL employees, and compatriots elsewhere, liked that these depot lunchrooms made it possible for them to refill conveniently their "forty-eight-hour buckets," those capacious lunch pails that supplied food for an extended trip over the road. For years the company marked public timetables with an "*e*," which indicated a depot lunchroom – *e* for "*eats*." Unlike some railroads, the M&STL did not receive many complaints about these leased facilities.

A community might take pride in having a depot eatery that served exceptional food. In the 1940s writer Alvin F. Harlow fondly recalled the lunchroom in the junction depot in his hometown of North Vernon, Indiana, a station the B&O and Pennsylvania shared. He vividly remembered the oyster stew, ham sandwiches, "always made with buns," fried chicken, and the occasional fried rabbit. Then there were the pies, including custard and in season green gooseberry. "Pie was then the lunch room's chief reason for being, the traveling public's favorite belly-timber." And these were exceedingly tasty indulgences. "There was a good cook at our lunch room. 'You can't get better pie in Cincinnati,' the trainmen said, and that was praise indeed." Homemade pies also made the lunchroom in the joint Central New England and Housatonic depot in Canaan, Connecticut, popular with travelers, train crews, and townspeople. Once a resident overheard two patrons of a Parisian café discussing French pastries, and during the course of their conversation mentioning his hometown. "One man asked the other if he had ever tasted anything so delicious. His

companion replied that the pastries were excellent but 'you can't beat the apple pie at the station in Canaan, Connecticut.'"

Travelers in the West long associated lunchrooms with the Fred Harvey Company, a firm founded in 1878 by the entrepreneurial English immigrant Frederick H. Harvey. Originally these facilities served only stations on the main line of Atchison, Topeka & Santa Fe Railway (Santa Fe), and later there were "Harvey Houses" on other parts of the sprawling system and several "off-line" locations, including the Terminal Tower complex in Cleveland, Ohio.

Harvey saw the need for quality food and good service for railroad patrons and employees. Any observant train rider would agree. A guidebook for travelers in the West, published in 1869, contended that "railroad restaurants are chiefly kept by very avaricious and inhospitable persons who demand fifty cents for admission into their rooms, but manage, either by not opening their doors for several minutes after the train arrives, or by a deficiency of attendants, to deprive their customers of a fair opportunity of receiving or appropriating a fair compensation for their money in the form of viands." Continued the commentary: "Frequently, too, the food is filthy bread badly baked and unwholesome; the tea and coffee cold, or so

It has been several years since the Burlington Railroad opened its smart, brick county-seat depot in Red Oak, Iowa. Located on the east side of the building with a convenient trackside entrance, the lunchroom offered customers a variety of food and sundries, including the always popular ten-cent cigar.

Montgomery County History Center, Red Oak, Iowa

bitter and black that they are far from furnishing an agreeable repast." The assessment was not far off the mark; food and service were often abysmal, hardly hotel quality.

Yet there were also good eateries at trackside, and they existed nation-wide. The quality, though, was inconsistent and often poor, attested to by this vaudeville song that celebrated the fare of a commercial salesman:

> The old railroad sandwich, the iron-bound sandwich,
> The fly-covered sandwich that sets on the shelf,
> How oft in the days when I worked as a drummer,
> Have I at some crossing jumped off for a meal,
> And seeing the sandwich proceeded to put it
> Where the moths couldn't harm it and thieves couldn't steal.

Sensing a golden opportunity, Harvey embarked on becoming the "Civilizer of the West." He was more than a man with a good idea; he became an effective "hands-on" businessman. An attractive contract with the Santa Fe allowed him to utilize space in existing and new depots. From the start Harvey made frequent inspections of his lunchrooms and restaurants, always vigilant as to matters of food and service. He wanted to ensure that his "sky-high standards" were never compromised. This attention to details did much to explain why Harvey prospered.

The renowned members of the Harvey workforce were the "Harvey Girls." These usually young, attractive women wore black dresses with "Elsie collars" and black bows, black shoes and stockings, and heavily starched white aprons. They became living symbols of the Harvey en-terprise. These employees, who were always Euro-Americans (people of color, including Hispanics and Native Americans, worked as dishwashers, maids, and "pantry girls") usually came from "back East" and received good salaries (and tips), board and room, opportunities for advancement, railroad passes, and a sense of belonging to the "Harvey family."

Whether travelers or not, the public loved "Meals by Fred Harvey" served by skilled Harvey Girls. No one said it better than Elbert Hub-bard, guru of the American Arts and Crafts movement: "At Fred Harvey's you are always expected. The girls are ever in their best bib and tuckers, spotlessly gowned, manicured, groomed, combed, dental-flossed – bright, intelligent girls – girls that are never fly, flip nor fresh, but who give you the attention that never obtrudes, but which is hearty and heartfelt." Or as humorist Will Rogers ruminated in his popular "Daily Telegram" syn-dicated newspaper column: "Wild buffalo fed the earlier traveler in the West and for doing so they put its picture on a nickel. Well, Fred Harvey took up where the buffalo left off. For what he has done for the traveler, one of his waitress's pictures (with an arm load of delicious ham and eggs) should be placed on both sides of every dime." Rogers added, "He has kept the West in food – and wives."

Most everyone agreed with Elbert Hubbard and Will Rogers. While Harvey Houses served hot, delicious entrées, their desserts where particularly memorable. One woman, who as a youngster enjoyed Fred Harvey meals, happily recalled: "I remember that Fred Harvey ice cream sundaes as the most delicious and satisfying ice cream sundaes in the world." Even the water tasted good, perhaps having been imported from mineral springs to avoid the alkali-laden wells often found in the West.

Employees of the Fred Harvey Company also staffed several important urban stations. The St. Louis terminal, for one, had both a lunch counter and an upscale dining room operated by these talented workers. The latter facility attracted both travelers and denizens of the greater St. Louis area, being popular with the latter for Sunday dinner.

Whether a lunchroom was in the depot or in a nearby café, it was not unusual for a conductor or trainman to announce the impending opportunity for a meal. Crewmen on the North Western reminded passengers when they were about to arrive in Jewell, Iowa, that the ten-minute stop allowed them time to hurry over to the nearby J. B. O'Connor's Beanery, "Open Day & Night," "Warm Meals and Lunches at All Hours," to buy a cup of its famous bean soup. On some trains crewmen did more than make a food announcement. After learning details about how many planned to eat (and even what they wished to order), a telegram would be sent from a nearby station to inform the kitchen staff. For years the Georgia & Florida, which never provided dining-car service, instructed passenger conductors to wire the G&F Café (non–railroad owned, but adjacent to the depot and renowned for its fried chicken) in Douglas, Georgia, about the number and kind of meals requested, a service that was especially appreciated when the road carried troops during the two world wars.

Big city stations had an army of workers who performed various tasks. When the traveler entered these complexes, he encountered a "Red Cap" or some other obliging individual who took charge of personal luggage and informally provided information about train operations and travel. This smiling porter, often a person of color, did not until the New Deal era ordinarily receive a salary from the depot company, but rather relied solely on tips. This might be a good source of income if the Red Cap worked in a busy terminal like Pennsylvania Station in New York City or Union Station in Washington, D.C., but in smaller places like Augusta, Georgia, or Spokane, Washington, tipping was usually much less lucrative even with fewer competing attendants. There just were not the swarms of people and baggage. Railroad officials looked on Red Caps as licensees or concessionaires to serve travelers and not as employees, caring nothing about the generosity of the public. In some terminals, though, these men might receive a regular income based on their additional services, operating

Travelers who passed through the North Western station on Wells Street in Chicago encountered the ubiquitous "Red Cap." Although the Red Cap was usually a person of color, this 1899 folder depicts an accommodating white helper.

Author's coll.

elevators, performing janitor duties, or similar jobs. The Red Cap usually delivered the luggage to the baggage master, who, with helpers, made certain that the items found their way to the baggage car, Pullman berth, or other destination. Some Red Caps worked in the same place for years. Joe Banks, a St. Louis Union Station Red Cap who began in 1915 and was still handling luggage in 1948, received brief fame in 1931 when the syndicated "Ripley's Believe It or Not" column noted, "He estimates he has met 1,113,000 trains but never has ridden one." Seventeen years later Banks believed that he had greeted 3 million trains and he still had not taken a train trip.

After the luggage had been stored, the traveler walked to the ticket window, perhaps en route passing members of the janitorial staff, who swept floors, cleaned windows, and polished brass hardware. The public understood that the ticket seller, usually one of many, would provide detailed information, if needed, about the journey, including transfers and accommodations. Often he intimately knew the routes and schedules, but if he did not, he consulted the thick monthly edition of *The Official Guide*

Although not a union station, the Mt. Royal Station in downtown Baltimore, designed by E. Francis Baldwin and Josias Pennington and opened in 1896, provided the essential services to passengers. The facility gained fame for its comfortable waiting-room rocking chairs as shown in this ca. 1950 photograph.

William Howes Jr., coll.

of the Railways and Steam Navigation Lines of the United States, Porto Rico, Canada, Mexico and Cuba (*The Official Guide* or the *Railway Guide*) for the exact information. The sale of the ticket came next and might include an additional coupon for sleeping or parlor car space.

But that ticket seller, like his counterpart at the country station, daily faced a range of queries. In 1901 the bureau manager for the St. Louis Union Station gave fellow members of the St. Louis Railway Club ex- amples of the staggering array of questions that his personnel handled:

> "What track does the 'Banner Route' leave for Warrenton?"
> "Does the one o'clock Pennsylvania Limited stop at Caseyville?"
> "Can I get a through sleeping car on the Cannon Ball to Hot Springs?"
> "How far into Maries County does the new 'St. Louis Line' go?"
> "Give me a 'Land of the Skies' timetable."
> "Can I get a 'Commercial Traveler' train about noon?"
> "Where does the 'Continental Limited' go?"
> "Can I get dinner on the 'Knickerbocker' to-day?"
> "Do I use the 'Q' or the 'K' line from here to Quincy?"
> "Can I check a dog on the 'West India Flyer'?"

With baggage checked, itinerary known, and ticket in hand, the trav- eler might enter the main waiting room to take a seat on one of those hard wooden benches, or he might stroll off to the restroom or newsstand, tobacco shop, shoeshine parlor, barber shop, flower stall, eatery, or some other specialized facility. As with Red Caps, individuals who offered these products or services were employed by firms that leased space from the depot company, yet they were an integral part of the station population. If, for some reason, the passenger misplaced or found an item – book, eye- glasses, umbrella – there usually was a "Lost and Found" window where a station employee would assist. Finally, the traveler likely heard the un- seen "train caller," who boomed out the departure of his train, slowly announcing the railroad, name and/or number, destination and principal intermediate stops, and platform location.

The public probably noticed other individuals who were part of the daily life of urban terminals. There would be a line of hacks, later motor- ized taxicabs, with their drivers, who dropped off passengers and visi- tors or awaited outbound fares. In a conspicuous part of the station there would surely be a representative of the Travelers Aid Society. Women and children especially, in need of assistance, could obtain information, advice, guidance, and protection without charge. This organization traced its roots to 1866 when the Young Women's Christian Association in Bos- ton established a travelers' aid office in the city's railroad stations. In 1907 the New York Travelers Aid Society was incorporated, and this organiza- tion served as a model for other units, leading to formation in 1917 of the National Travelers Aid Society.

Terminals had their own police officers (or used city policemen), who kept an eagle eye open for pickpockets, purse-snatchers, confidence men, or other lawbreakers who gravitated to places with crowds and strangers. Likely located in a detached structure would be expressmen who sorted packages or who picked up and delivered them. Before Congress passed the Parcel Post Act in 1913, private concerns handled packages. Companies such as Adams, American, and Wells Fargo were well known to the population, and for good reason. Also nearby, and possibly physically connected, would be the U.S. Post Office with its army of employees. Mail could be efficiently moved to and from Railway Post Office cars and storage cars that contained "sealed" mail. The station itself provided office space for the terminal company or the owning railroad, and that meant more people in the facility. All of these workers made the general area of the railroad terminal a beehive of activities that lasted around the clock. No other place in the city rivaled the continual commotion of the urban station.

At these great railroad facilities there were personnel who were went largely unseen or unnoticed: telegraphers, white-collar workers, and kitchen staff. Even the station master usually kept a low profile, but not always. For years William Egan, who served as general station master at the sprawling Pennsylvania Station in New York City, roamed the public spaces. On one occasion he found a boy who was apparently lost. After a short conversation Egan learned that the lad had run away from his home in Cleveland, Ohio, "because he wanted to see the Atlantic Ocean." Rather than turning the youngster over to authorities, Egan put him on a Long Island Railroad train and told a subordinate to let the boy enjoy a day at the seashore. That evening the lad was sent back to Cleveland, the

The arrival of a passenger train was once a welcome occasion in small-town America. In 1912 a large crowd, onlookers and passengers alike, gather at the station of the Lexington & Eastern Railway in Hazard, Kentucky.

Bobby Davis Museum, Hazard, KY

kindly station master having notified the worried parents that their son was safely on his way home.

A PLACE FOR PEOPLE

Irrespective of the size of the depot or terminal, the station drew Americans from all walks of life. It was the place where people, goods, and information passed. By the latter half of the nineteenth century virtually everyone realized that the rails were the life blood of the nation; the American depot was very much a public place. For some it was too public. "Let the stations be closed to this swarm of idlers, hackmen, porters, school-boys, peddlers, bad women, swindlers, pick-pockets and conductors' 'friends,'" complained a post–Civil War English visitor. But unlike the situation in stations in Britain and some other nations, the public here did not need a platform ticket to enter.

In raw railroad-spawned towns, the depot early on was probably the sole place that offered "public space," and at times the building welcomed residents and others to non-railroad functions. Religious groups might hold their weekly services in the waiting room, and fraternal organizations might do the same for their meetings. There were additional uses. "The single waiting room served for weekly dances which later graduated to the Pemberton House, the new hotel in the growing town," remembered a childhood resident of the North Western depot in Canistota, South Dakota.

The most likely folks who could be found inside or on the station platform were the passengers awaiting their trains. As in the formative

C B & Q DEPOT   REPUBLICAN · NEB

years of airline travel, these individuals commonly wore their Sunday-best clothing. An almost endless array of reasons explain the objectives of those who planned to board a train: the matron who was off to a distant city to see her newborn grandchild; the student who was returning to college; the man of the cloth who was on his regular circuit of religious services; the soldier who was rejoining his unit; the vacationer who was anticipating the holiday of a life time.

In the annals of American transportation the depot was hardly unique as a central meeting place. It was a convenient location for residents and travelers to gather and chat, resembling the inns, taverns, and stores of the pre-railroad age. During the time of stagecoaches and canal packets these places were well patronized, being "the centre of life and affairs for the men folk, church committees and politicians, idlers and business men, all resorted thither, to discuss and arrange affairs together." The much later bus stations and airport terminals would be less likely to serve as community centers.

During the Railway Age nearly everyone encountered the waiting room. Hopefully, the agent, by maintaining it physically and controlling rowdies, made the place as pleasant as possible to await a train. Nothing, however, could be done about uncomfortable benches. When a family arrived at a small Northern Pacific depot in Montana, they faced a long and not-so-enjoyable wait for an extremely late passenger train. "We reached Logan about six o'clock. Bought crackers and cheese, sardines and pickles and lunched in the waiting room. And here we waited till 1:30 AM trying to find a soft place on the wooden benches, and resting place for our weary

About the same time a branch-line local steams into the Burlington Railroad station in Republican, Nebraska. The hack driver from the Eagle House hotel is ready to pick up guests and their luggage.

Author's coll.

heads, other than a pine board. Then came the whistle and our train appeared." Yet, unlike the molded chairs found in modern air, bus, and rail waiting rooms, a person might be able to stretch out on one of the long benches and catch some sleep.

A common part of the mix of passengers in the depot waiting room was the traveling salesman; "drummers," "knights of the grip," or "commercial travelers" moved from town-to-town to call on clients. Most of these men, who were "drumming up business," worked for wholesale firms whose territories the web of rails had expanded. Nationally their numbers swelled as cities grew, industrialization increased, and frontier regions blossomed. Drummers rose by a factor of six between 1880 and 1920 before the automobile dramatically reduced their presence on trains. A salesmen for a candy company, based in Minneapolis, noted that in the 1890s he averaged about 1,800 rail miles monthly, yet that distance was probably less than traveled by a majority of salesmen. It was a treat for anyone at a station to see this hustler alight from an arriving train, "a stranger who acted as if he owned the place, who was at home with the wonders of the age. He cut a splendid figure, and thought so himself." As another commentator put it: "He was a man of the world." No wonder there were teenage girls who "put on their flashiest cloths" and strolled to the depot to eyeball the young drummers who detrained.

Others waited to meet a family member, friend, or business associate or were merely curious about who in the community was arriving or leaving. Once Youngstown, Ohio, received the trains of the Cleveland & Mahoning Railroad in 1856, a local historian observed that "from that day on, anyone who had an opportunity to do so, made it a point to meet the train, note who got on and who disembarked, then hurrying homeward to report the goings and comings of his neighbors." In 1883 a resident of Helena, Montana Territory, expressed excitement about the recently opened Northern Pacific transcontinental line: "It is a goodly sight to see the train coming in here every evening and we drive down almost every day. The depot is about ¾ of a mile from our house." Early in the twentieth century there was a resident of Burke, Texas, who was not about to miss the arrival of daily Southern Pacific passenger train. Recalled an acquaintance, "I've seen him in there [a barbershop near the depot] all lathered to get a shave, and the train would blow and he would jump up with lather still on his face, because he was going to meet the train!" The memories of a woman journalist remained strong about her depot experiences. "When I recall my life in Lander, Wyoming before the First War, I have such vivid recollections of the railroad. The daily arrival and departure of the passenger train was a prized event in our lives. Mother usually allowed me to go over to the depot to see who was leaving and who was coming to town." There was more. "Maybe that train might be bringing us something of interest,

In October 1968 students from Montana State University in Bozeman are about to board Northern Pacific train No. 25, the *North Coast Limited*, that's headed to Seattle. College towns had long been an important source of passenger business, and rail service helped these schools to shape their recruitment strategies.

Philip R. Hastings photograph, Don L. Hofsommer coll.

perhaps we'd be getting a package from the express company that operated over the North Western Line." She added: "I always liked the clicking of the electric telegraph, knowing that I was hearing a message that came from Casper or even Chicago." Station visitors might take advantage of the passenger train that carried a Railway Post Office car, mailing a letter or postcard in the polished-brass mail slot or handing the item to an accommodating postal worker. The individual might be in the depot to send a telegram, pick up a freight shipment, or conduct other matters such as planning a trip. The traveler surely encountered other persons on depot business, whether a drayman or mail handler.

At most stations of any size there would be those individuals who catered to travelers' needs. One was the hack driver, adorned with a marked hat that announced his trade or with a handful of advertising cards, anxious to take a person and his luggage to a hotel or other destination. A enterprising hotel manager might employ a youngster known as a "hotel runner," who would meet trains, especially ones that came in the late afternoon or early evening, and then distribute handbills, display a signboard, or in some other way announce his employer's overnight amenities. A brisk competition, perhaps with exaggerated truths, might erupt among these purveyors of services. If there were special attractions nearby – a natural feature like a cave, mineral spring, or waterfall, or some manmade point of interest – a fairground, racetrack, or public monument – solicitors might stand on the depot platform, in the waiting room, or near the entrance to attract business. In a few places an agent for a steamboat company might generate passengers from an incoming train, who had the option of continuing (probably at a higher fare) on a connecting railroad.

On the platform, whether made of cinders, planks, or bricks, lurked other hustlers. It could be only the lad who offered the latest newspapers, repeating his shrill cry of "morning paper!" Or it might be the sellers of food or drink or other items. Perhaps it was produce. Farmers might sell fruit and vegetables to passengers or to commercial buyers. "A farmer sold a hamper of lima beans for twenty two dollars [ca. 1912] on the Delray [Florida] platform," remembered an agent, and such transactions were hardly rare. In the West it was not uncommon for Native Americans to gather near the depot to peddle their handicrafts, to pose for photographs (at a price), to perform feats of skill (also for donations), or to offer travelers for a few pennies "peeps" at their papooses, wrapped in Indian blankets.

Other non-travelers joined the hustle-bustle. It was common for a newspaper to send to the depot a reporter to gather news about and from travelers. That same person might see if the agent or other railroaders could provide interesting copy; after all, nearly always the freshest gossip could be found there. "The agent was truly our link with national events, for in those days before radio and television the telegrapher got everything first, including the weather forecast," recalled the daughter of a small-town editor. "My father haunted the depot for these forecasts as well as important world events." Before World War II, newspapers, especially those in railroad communities, frequently published railroad-oriented columns such as "Railroad News," "In Railroad Circles," "Train, Track and Shop," and "Yard Notes," replete with news and speculation. A newspaper might report numbers of hotel guests brought in by the daily trains, suggesting that these figures were a barometer of the community's economic health.

Few would disagree that there was the sheer excitement associated with depots, most of all those big-city terminals. In the 1930s a brakeman on a Rock Island passenger train told a traveler how keyed-up he became when he watched limiteds about to depart. "Ever stand in the Union Station at Cincinnati or St. Louis, or in one of the big stations at Chicago or Minneapolis," he asked, "at night maybe, when the big boys with their names on their tails are all lined up to go – the Bluebonnet, the Chief, the Corn King Limited, the Katy Flyer, the Viking, the Meteor, the F.F.V., the Flamingo, the Wolverine, the Zephyr, the Columbine, the Golden Arrow?" Their names alone exuded wonder and class.

When radio burst upon the national scene in the 1920s, from time to time a broadcaster, eager for news that would interest listeners, dispatched a reporter with his microphone and other gear to met a passenger train and to interview what seemed to be the most intriguing people. Such was the case at the recently opened Cincinnati Union Station, where for several years a local radio station conducted a fifteen-minute show called "Train Time." Even the national radio media provided live broadcasts, best represented in the "Tommy Bartlett's 'Welcome Travelers'" program that after World War II originated from Chicago and was first aired on ABC and later NBC affiliates. In the late 1930s and early 1940s a variation occurred with a radio station in Villa Grove, Illinois. An enterprising employee, using a pack shortwave set with an antenna mounted on the rear of a passenger coach, conducted man-on-the-street type interviews with riders aboard the Chicago & Eastern Illinois local, the *Egyptian Zipper,* between Villa Grove and Tuscola.

Then there were the platform loafers. While agents and other depot personnel may not have cared for them, most onlookers were harmless. Watching the comings and goings of trains, travelers, and the other activities associated with station life had its appeal, but some individuals enjoyed just the ambience of the place. "For if there is anything I like to do it is to loaf, just loaf around a country railroad station where they have about two passenger trains a day each way, with a freight coming along occasionally," admitted an unidentified writer in 1908. "Quiet and peace,

Scene on Depot St. Elburn Ill.

In 1910 loafers, perhaps joined by bona fide travelers, rest in front of the Elburn, Illinois, depot. Station loafers usually appeared when a passenger train was about to pull into the station.

Author's coll.

with nobody about and the wind ruffling idly the leaves on the trees, and the empty glistening rails stretching away mysteriously." There would also be time to nap. "When you wake up and look around to see if anything new has happened in the world since you dropped off, you see coming along the track slowly and silently a solitary figure, all the time looking down in front of him and to either side as he comes – the section boss." As the narrator went on, "After you have met him thus for two or three days, if he takes you for a man, he will tell you when the track was stone ballasted and when they put in the 90-pound rails, and if you tell him, which is true, that everything along here looks kept up in perfect order he will tell you that this section last year took the prize offered by the company for the best-kept section on the road."

The platform loafers who may have most annoyed railroad personal in the South were flocks of freed blacks who, after the Civil War, often appeared at stations, especially on Sundays. Although a few of these former slaves may have been bona fide travelers or were there to welcome family or friends, most were not. They just wanted to experience train-time, imagining perhaps a journey to a happier, more prosperous place. "As the train passes, the negroes gather in groups to gaze at it, until it disappears in the distance," noted a visitor to the South in the 1870s. "The negroes swarm day and night like bees about the trains."

136   RAILROADS AND THE AMERICAN PEOPLE

Another breed of loafers, some of whom bothered the public and might be subject to municipal vagrancy laws, were panhandlers. Usually they asked depot patrons for a few coins for train fare or more likely for food and drink. Others were less likely to irritate. One such individual was the peripatetic blind man with his hand organ, who gladly accepted donations for his musical performances.

Although not exactly loafers, but known to loiter in the larger stations, were men who sought sexual favors from other males. Parents, police, and railroad personnel might warn youngsters (others, too) to be eternally vigil for "perverts" – code name for homosexuals – who customarily frequented restrooms or remote places.

There was a time in the late nineteenth century when some passenger trains carried weather information. Working with the U.S. Signal Corps, railroads employed codes that were displayed on tin signs attached to the sides of baggage cars. This simple code consisted of red and blue circles, half moons, and stars that told watchers on depot platforms or along the right-of-way of expected higher, lower, or continuing temperatures, general rain or snow, localized rain or snow, or fair weather. "Cards explaining the signs are distributed in the various towns & villages," noted a railroader in 1888, "and the farmers along the way look out for the signs as the morning trains pass." At some stations railroads erected a "weather pole" that displayed these same symbols, updated periodically by the agent. In 1887 the Fulton County Narrow Gauge Railway attached such a pole to its Lewistown, Illinois, depot. "This innovation was hailed as a real public

The relaxed fellow seated on the far left probably realizes that train-time at the St. Joseph & Grand Island (Union Pacific System) station in Sabetha, Kansas, is somewhat different. It is not the knife-nosed McKeen Motor Car, but rather the presence of a commercial photographer.

Author's coll.

service and a valuable aid to farmers and others interested in fore knowledge of the weather for 24 or 48 hours." Accuracy was hardly guaranteed.
Although government personnel used surface analyses beginning in the
1870s, it would not be until the 1920s that meteorologists recognized the
existence of weather fronts. Yet telegraphic communications between
stations made it possible to guess on future conditions. Then there were
those who believed that they could determine approaching weather by
listening carefully to a passing train. Residents along the Tullulah Falls
Railway in Georgia and North Carolina allegedly "forecast the weather
by the sound of the locomotive whistle," which was impacted by changes
in barometric pressure and wind direction. For years engineers on trains
coming from the North into Florida whistled repeatedly to notify urban
and rural residents, particularly citrus growers, that freezing temperatures
could be expected.

It was more common for a depot to contain a large bronze or brass
bell than a weather pole. Although the routine varied from railroad to
railroad and from station to station, the agent or some designated employee rang the bell three or five minutes before a train departed and
then a few seconds before the wheels started to turn. The bell might also
be rung to announce the arrival of a train. Inspired by railways in Great
Britain, the practice was not limited to the earliest railroads in the United
States. Stations as diverse as those operated by the Atlantic Coast Line
in Wilmington, North Carolina; Elizabethtown & Somerville (Central
Railroad of New Jersey) in Elizabeth, New Jersey; New Haven in Taunton,
Massachusetts; Southern in New Orleans, Louisiana; Southern Pacific in
Sacramento, California; and Virginia & Truckee in Carson City, Nevada,
at one time had a station bell. Some railroads opted for gongs rather than
bells to announce arrivals and departures. Travelers and residents might
depend upon these soundings to learn the correct time, especially for
departures or for other preannounced moments. This practice virtually
disappeared when it ceased to meet a public need. By the late nineteenth
century watches became plentiful and relatively inexpensive, resulting in
fewer individuals who needed a bell or gong signal.

Something as mundane as getting a refreshing drink of water could
draw individuals to a depot. With the appearance of drinking fountains
or "bubblers" after World War I, stations might provide these mechanical
devices for quenching a person's thirst, either indoors or on the platforms
in above-freezing weather. Earlier there might have been a wooden barrel,
with communal cups, that supplied drinking water, having been pumped
from a station cistern or well or supplied from a city water system. In
the 1880s a huge barrel, connected to a public main, was placed on the
platform of the Norfolk & Western Railway depot in Norfolk, Virginia.
Patrons of that road and the Norfolk & Virginia Beach Railroad, which

shared the station, enjoyed cool drinks in the summer, kept that way by an employee who regularly added blocks of ice. "It was like a spring in the desert to the thirsty passengers of each road," noted one writer, "until someone found a dead cat in it."

EVENTS AT THE STATION

Posting a letter or possibly learning a weather forecast, gaining the time of day or getting a drink of water, drew people to the station, but more likely it was a special train that brought hundreds to witness an uncommon event. During the Gilded Age and into the Populist-Progressive Era of the late nineteenth and early twentieth centuries, politics played a vital part in the lives of most Americans. The electorate "voted the way they shot" in the Civil War, the press showed extreme partisanship, and adults end-lessly debated politics in depot waiting rooms, hotel lobbies, or anywhere else where people congregated. Election days were occasions for partisan dinners that were preceded by days, even weeks, of parades, rallies, and speeches. Almost instantly word spread when a politician planned to pass through a community, or certainly if he were to stop and speak from the train.

During the Railway Age, politicians, nearly always candidates seek-ing state or national office, employed trains in their quest for victory. In fact, the tradition continued for decades, albeit on a much-reduced scale. The last nationally famous "whistle stop" tours took place in 1948 in the months before President Harry Truman stunningly defeated his Repub-lican challenger, Thomas Dewey. These whistle stops played a critical role in Truman's surprise win. Dewey, too, embraced a similar, albeit less extensive, campaign strategy. Even as recently as 2008 Barak Obama made several campaign trips by rail, and in January 2009 he rode an Am-trak special between New York City and Washington, D.C., as part of his inaugural festivities.

Arguably no other office-seeker used railroads more extensively than William Jennings Bryan, "the silver orator of the Platte." This Nebraska Democrat, who unsuccessfully sought the presidency on three occasions, 1896, 1900, and 1908, repeatedly took to the rails. Although Bryan relied on trains and at times electric interurbans during his failed bids against incumbent William McKinley in 1900 and William Howard Taft in 1908, it would be his monumental campaign in that realigning presidential election of 1896 that resulted in extensive rail travel. Trains took him to parts of the East and large chunks of the Midwest, the battleground states against Republican McKinley. Bryan concluded that New Eng-land was strongly behind his opponent and that he had substantial sup-port in the South, Great Plains, and West. After all, the South was solidly

Democratic, although there were pockets of Republican strength, and as the fusion candidate with the People's Party, he would surely outperform McKinley in the trans-Missouri West.

In his efforts to bring voters his message of "free silver," Bryan made several sweeps that totaled more than 18,000 miles over numerous roads. At first he rode observation cars that belonged to the regular consists of trains, but toward the end of his hectic campaign the Democratic National Committee leased a private car with that essential rear platform, *The Idler* ("a most inappropriate name, it seemed to me," said Bryan), and happily he "was robbed of the inconvenience which necessarily attends a frequent change of cars."

Being mindful of this remarkable accomplishment of nearly overtaking McKinley and looking ahead to 1900, Bryan assembled a book-length account of his efforts to capture the White House, *The First Battle: A Story of the Campaign of 1896.* There were four distinct circuits that "the Great Commoner" undertook, including his third trip of 12,837 miles that zigzagged through Missouri, Kentucky, Tennessee, North Carolina,

Pennsylvania, New York, West Virginia, Iowa, South Dakota, Minnesota, Michigan, Ohio, Indiana, and Illinois. The most frequent stops, highlighted by "an address by Mr. Bryan," occurred in the Old Northwest, must states for success in the electoral college. Often the attendance at a station, decked out in flags, bunting, and banners, "was proportionate to the size of the town." But there were places where too many people gathered, threatening personal safety. "At Delphos, Ohio, the depot platform gave way, causing considerable fright but no injury," wrote Bryan. "This was the first experience with falling platforms, but during the campaign there were five or six other accidents of this kind."

Rival and victor William McKinley, for largely personal reasons, especially the fragile health of his wife, Ida, undertook the campaign of 1896 from the front porch of his Canton, Ohio, home. "I cannot take the stump against that man," he said. "If I took a chair car, he would ride a freight train. I might just as well put up a trapeze on my front lawn and compete with some professional athlete as go out speaking against Bryan. I have to think when I speak. I can't outdo him, and I'm not going to try." Still McKinley spoke to enthusiastic crowds, but they arrived and departed at the Canton depots on regular and special trains of the Pennsylvania, Valley, and Wheeling & Lake Erie railroads.

Folks who jammed depot platforms to see Bryan or some other politician may have sought entertainment rather than political insights. There were, however, those truly entertaining moments that interrupted daily life. A circus train that steamed into their home or neighboring community best represented such an experience, tapping a growing market for professionally organized public entertainment.

After the Civil War circuses, and somewhat later "Wild West shows," moved by rail. The latter usually had big-city destinations, but the former, depending on the size, called at places large and small. After all, there were one-ring as well as three-ring circuses. The giants in the industry, Barnum & Bailey, Cole Brothers United Shows, Forepaugh Sells/Sells Floto, and Ringling Brothers, owned their own railcars, scores of them, for the transport of animals, performers, staff, and a wide assortment of paraphernalia, including their hallmark canvas tents. In order to travel the rails, managers would have railroads provide locomotives and crews and would operate as "extras" over predetermined routes. During the zenith of the American circus, which occurred in the 1880s and 1890s, there were more than fifty companies, including the small "railroad shows." The equipment of these firms usually consisted of several cars attached to scheduled trains, and they offered entertainment to a more limited territory than their bigger brethren. An example was Bob Hunting's Great Show that toward the end of the nineteenth century toured mostly in western Pennsylvania and eastern Ohio. The company's consist included a sleeping car and several box and flat cars that held performance necessities: four horses, three ponies, a bandwagon, ticket wagon, three baggage wagons, and several tents, including the "Main Canvas."

Whether the monster Barnum & Bailey Circus or the modest Bob Hunting's Great Show, the unloading process, usually on a siding near the depot, attracted onlookers, especially throngs of youngsters. And they eagerly followed the animals and wagons, frequently organized in a circus parade led by a steam calliope, to the performance site. Even the trooping back to the awaiting train captured attention. The station agent received special notice; he knew the schedules and the arrangements for these happenings that pleasantly interrupted daily life.

Rather than providing entertainment, some other trains promoted education. While politicians long took to the rails, as did circuses and then some carnivals and amusement shows, the time of the "demonstration trains" occurred mostly from the turn of the twentieth century to World War II. And they appeared in all parts of the country, being common in the Midwest, Great Plains, Pacific Northwest, and South. Just like the candidate who stopped at the depot or the circus train that a crew "spotted" on an adjoining siding, the train of education followed a similar practice. It may have been the Great Northern Railway that inaugurated this movement for agricultural betterments, sending in the late 1890s a load of farm equipment and exhibits on a special train that called at a number of stations in Minnesota. In fact, James J. Hill, founder-president of the Great Northern, strongly advocated better livestock, seeds, and tillage practices. Agriculturalists flocked to the sites, heard lectures, and received printed materials from experts about how to increase crop yields, improve stock breeds, bolster milk production, and practice a variety of scientific farming methods. These specialists might be employees of a railroad agricultural department or "agricultural demonstration department," and they might be joined by faculty or staff members from land grant colleges and universities and representatives of the U.S. Department of Agriculture or state agricultural bodies. Their work was hard. "All hands are feeling the strain of the long trip which began at Leesville," reported a writer for the *State* newspaper in Columbia, South Carolina, about the Clemson College agricultural car winter tour. This extension train had begun its stops on January 3, 1905, and ended them at Chesterfield on February 15. "The work has been constant and has covered the entire low country."

During the heyday of demonstration trains, mostly in the 1910s and 1920s, an array of movements took place. These specials might roll over the rails of giants Southern and Southern Pacific or of the much smaller Georgia and Missouri & North Arkansas railroads. Carriers endorsed the concept, explaining why they donated equipment and personnel. Agricultural diversification and the wider application of modern farming techniques would enhance the quantity and quality of farm products, thus increasing business. Newspapers duly noted their schedules. The *Red Oak* (Iowa) *Express,* for one, did so by announcing the March 1, 1910, appearance of the "Seed Corn Special," a joint effort of the Burlington and the Iowa State Agricultural College. The paper described the tour and listed arrival and departure times: "The special train will be made up of two coaches, in which lectures will be given by eminent agricultural professors under the direction of Prof. P. G. Holden." The *Express* urged farmers to gather at the most convenient Burlington depot, indicating that the train would call at Shenandoah, Essex, Elliott, Griswold, Henderson, Carson, Randolph, and Sidney. And the paper noted, "There will be an evening lecture at Villisca after which the train will run to Creston [a division point] to lay up."

In 1911, the Wabash Railroad, whose lines stretched between Buffalo and Kansas City, teamed up with the College of Agriculture at the University of Missouri and the Missouri State Board of Agriculture, pioneers in this type of educational outreach, to send a "special lecture train" on a three-day, twenty-one-station whirlwind tour. Consisting of several baggage and passenger cars and staffed by university and state personnel, the train stopped at Wabash depots, where onboard specialists informed farmers (others might arrive at trackside, including townspeople involved

in agribusiness activities) about such topics as "corn improvement," "feeding the dairy cow," and the "College of Agriculture."

Later, in the 1920s, the Wabash gained positive recognition in agricultural circles for its poultry improvement work. The plan was to offer active and potential chicken raisers "profit building ideas." Typically such prearranged meetings included presentations by extension specialists and a variety of displays. In addition to items placed on board, the company hired a lumberyard to erect near the depot a model brooder house and engaged a hardware store to install a brooder stove. A county extension agent then maintained poultry production. The special returned to show off the young chicks and still later made another visit, "featuring on that occasion the feeding and housing of the flock for winter egg production." These stops attracted "big crowds," including farm wives who customarily raised small numbers of chickens, reminding one Wabash station agent of the "excitement and crush of circus day."

Railroads recognized specific opportunities and needs. In 1908 the Spokane & Inland Empire Railroad (an electric interurban built to steam-road standards) operated its "Fruit Special" over its 127-mile network of lines. Personnel from the University of Idaho and Washington State Agricultural College sought to nurture the established apple industry. The educational train stopped in small towns like Colfax, Freeman, and Liberty Lake, where lecturers told listeners about the best methods of producing and marketing fruit. Somewhat later carriers in the South dispatched

For decades agricultural demonstration trains plied the rails throughout the Great Plains and Pacific Northwest. Early in the century the Southern Pacific Farming Demonstration Train pauses in the Douglas County, Oregon, town of Riddle. A few years later a similar special draws a good crowd to the Great Northern station in Ephrata, Washington. And about 1920 the Montana Better Live-Stock Special calls at Glasgow, Montana.

Don L. Hofsommer coll.

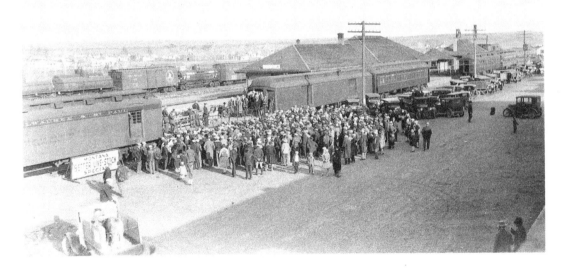

educational trains that assisted farmers with problems of insects and diseases. Bright tobacco, for example, was susceptible to the scourge of blue
mold, threatening to reduce drastically crop yields. In the 1920s and 1930s
agricultural extension agents repeatedly boarded "Blue Mold Control"
educational trains to inform tobacco growers of the most effective mold-
fighting techniques. These trains called on farmers at stations throughout
the bright tobacco belts of the Carolinas, Georgia, and Virginia.

While farmers learned about improving their methods, including
disease control, and became acquainted with better seeds and improved

Clemson Agricultural College of South Carolina was a pioneer in the deployment of agricultural demonstration trains. During a multiweek trip in the winter 1906, the consist, with its staff and exhibits, attracts visitors in the state's Low Country.

Clemson University Archives

strains of animals, they and townspeople alike came to stations to gain knowledge of how to improve their dreadful roads. The first of the "good roads" trains appeared in spring 1901 when the Illinois Central dispatched from Chicago to New Orleans a dozen-car special that included eight cars of road-building equipment. In the Crescent City crews rebuilt a suburban street, demonstrating the practicality of new approaches to an age-old problem. Other railroads followed, including the Burlington, New York Central, Norfolk & Western, and Southern. Carriers wanted better roads that would enable farmers to reach their main and secondary lines more easily and diminish their unrelenting demands for construction of costly, low-density branch lines. There was also the feeling that good roads would encourage farmers to diversify and lead to a more stable flow of agricultural traffic. (Railroad officials failed to envision the financial devastation that hard-surfaced roads and rubber-tire vehicles would ultimately have on their business.) And gestating state highway commissions sought to enhance public support, including increased taxes, for all-weather roads to lift drivers out of the seasonal mud and ruts. By World War I thousands of Americans had had personal contact with these technological-betterment trains.

And there were wars. During the Civil War troop trains for the first time operated in large numbers. Thousands of men in both blue and grey departed from railroad stations for service, and at times these movements drew large, enthusiastic crowds. Along the routes, townspeople cheered "their boys" and at stops for water, fuel, and other reasons might provide them with food and drink as they gawked at the consist. Early in the conflict a Confederate solider from Texas recalled that his unit received a warm welcome at every depot in South Carolina, where women of all ages "flocked in loaded with baskets of provisions, fruits and delicacies of every character." Similarly, a visiting British army officer, who in 1863 traveled throughout large sections of the South, made these remarks about his journey from Atlanta to Augusta on the Georgia Railroad: "At some stations, provisions for the soldiers were brought into the cars by ladies and distributed gratis. When I refused on the ground of not being a [Confederate] soldier, these ladies looked at me with great suspicion, mingled with contempt, and as their looks evidently expressed the words 'then why are you not a solider?' I was obliged to explain to them who I was." He further remarked that "I was told that Georgia was the only state in which soldiers were still so liberally treated." As for drink, folks who arrived at station stops might offer more than coffee, tea, lemonade, and water. "Women by the scores hovered around the train and supplied the men with whiskey, which they concealed under their skirts," observed a Union soldier who left for war from New York state. Some soldiers happily paid those on the platform for this forbidden drink. During the conflict the North Carolina Rail Road operated the longest train up to that time, twelve coaches crammed with Confederate soldiers bound for Virginia, and a train that made frequent station stops along its route from the Tar Heel State to the Old Dominion.

In subsequent conflicts troop trains repeatedly attracted station crowds. During the Spanish-American War, Private Henry Hackthorn, member of the 51st Iowa Volunteers, wrote his parents in Stuart, Iowa, that he had had a pleasant train trip across the country from Camp McKinley in Des Moines to Camp Merritt in San Francisco, and "at all the different towns the people came out with flowers and gifts and in California they brought fruit." Soldiers, sailors, and marines who traveled by rail during later military actions and wars shared similar experiences. When the federal government mobilized troops to capture Pancho Villa, who had orchestrated a deadly raid on the border town of Columbus, New Mexico, Company M, 2nd Infantry, of the Connecticut National Guard received orders for Texas. On June 23, 1916, the day that these soldiers left for training, more than ten thousand well-wishers flooded the New Haven station in Torrington, Connecticut. Memory of that crush of humanity promoted company officials to request that men bound for service during World War I say their farewells at home and not at the depot.

It was during World War II, with millions of troops on the move, that some station platforms became scenes of intense activities. United Service Organization (USO) units, numbering 125 by war's end, opened canteens in depots and in wooden huts on station platforms throughout the country, giving service personnel a much appreciated "touch of home." A cup of hot coffee, a homemade sandwich, and a freshly baked cookie did much to ease the homesickness that bothered many a service man and woman.

The largest and busiest USO operations involved the coming and going of passenger and troop trains at the Union Pacific station in North Platte, Nebraska, a division point on this busy east-to-west-coast rail artery. Volunteers at this patriotic outpost daily welcomed, fed, and entertained up to five thousand men and women in uniform. An estimated fifty-five thousand canteen workers from more than one hundred communities at various times assisted, handing out sandwiches, candy, cake, donuts, cookies, coffee, sodas, milk, and cigarettes. A typical daily shopping list required these items: "160–175 loaves of bread, 100 pounds of meat, 15 pounds of butter, 45 pounds of coffee, 40 quarts of cream, 500 half-pint bottles of milk and 35 dozen rolls." Every day about twenty birthday cakes were handed out to lucky celebrants. Church and service groups also came to sing gospel songs and seasonal Christmas carols. USO supervisors in North Platte estimated that by the end of the conflict more than 6 million individuals had received trackside services. "When those trains would come in and when they'd leave," remembered a canteen volunteer, "you would have a big lump in your throat because you just knew that some of them wouldn't come back." A North Platte resident described their USO station activities as "our own war industry – exporting morale."

While the figures for the USO at North Platte were astounding, statistics for the second busiest USO facility, located at the union station in Lima, Ohio, were likewise impressive. Some 4 million service personnel stopped while traveling on the B&O, Big Four, Erie, and Pennsylvania railroads, and consumed vast qualities of food and drink. Six hundred volunteers and nearly ten thousand home cooks kept the round-the-clock operation functioning. The popularity of the USO in Lima led to its ongoing, albeit greatly reduced, scope, till it finally closed in 1970.

USO canteens were also an important part of stations in major urban centers. At Cincinnati Union Station, a critical node for troop transit with thirteen trunk carriers, dedicated volunteers staffed its "Troops-in-Transit Lounge," coming mostly from area religious organizations. During the war the USO initiated scores of these lounges nationwide, established under the supervision of local Travelers Aid Societies. In five years of operation (opening on June 8, 1941, and closing on June 10, 1946), Cincinnati

hostesses served 3,340,141 military personnel, checked 2.2 million pieces of luggage, and sent out more than a million pieces of personal mail. In addition to the main lounge area, the USO in 1942 opened the "Quiet Room," proving a place for "six screened cots to care for weary GI's waiting for train connections," a facility that was later expanded. Toward the end of the conflict volunteers cared for more than 4,000 babies from military families in a special balcony lounge that featured cribs and couches. "This is the best thing the USO has ever done for me," a soldier told a *Cincinnati Enquirer* reporter. "My wife and baby and I have come all the way from New Orleans."

The practice of assisting service personnel continued after World War II, but at a greatly diminished level. USOs remained active in major terminals and at a few lesser locations during the Korean Conflict and also into the era of Viet Nam. But by the late 1960s most military personnel went on commercial and military aircraft or chartered or military buses. No longer did residents gather at the station to greet and assist those in uniform.

While purity and goodness can be rightly associated with USO personnel and troop trains, devious individuals occasionally exploited military people on the move. A hobo related this tale of woe. "I knew one guy

During World War II the accommodating USO in Cincinnati Union Station shows hospitality to a GI and his family, allowing the mother to prepare a baby bottle and the child to have a cookie.

Cincinnati Museum Center–Cincinnati Historical Society Library

who used to meet the troop trains in the depots and take up a collection from returning wounded veterans or guys that were on their way overseas with the promise to go get them some whiskey [something that the USO never provided]. As soon as he collected twenty-five or thirty dollars, he would disappear and they were out of x number of dollars and didn't get any whiskey either." Trickery by "fast buck hustlers" was difficult if not impossible to prevent.

There were few if any true war "funeral" trains; corpses, whether military or civilian, traveled in baggage and express cars. Occasionally, though, railroads handled funeral specials for prominent personages, usually politicians, and they regularly drew to stations and trackside impressive crowds. The most famous was the 1865 funeral train of martyred President Abraham Lincoln. This widely viewed train retraced Lincoln's 1,600-mile trip from Springfield, Illinois, to Washington, D.C., in 1861. The final journey back to Springfield consumed thirteen days, beginning on April 21, 1865, six days following his death. At major stops, including Philadelphia, Buffalo, Cleveland, Indianapolis, and Chicago, the coffin was unloaded from the nine-car consist and taken in a solemn procession to a public building for viewing. In Philadelphia alone an estimated 300,000 people filed past the flag-draped bier after the body had been removed at the Broad Street Station of the Philadelphia, Washington & Baltimore Railroad. Mourners ignored time and weather to pay their respects to the fallen "Rail Splitter" at trackside communities and along the route. "As we sped over the rails at night, the scene was the most pathetic ever witnessed," wrote Chauncey Depew, the New York Central & Hudson River executive who later became a prominent Republican U.S. senator from New York. "At every cross-roads the glare of innumerable torches illuminated the whole populus from age to infancy, kneeling on the ground, and their clergymen leading in prayers and hymns." When the train steamed into the station at Syracuse, New York, the locomotive engineer recalled, "the train was greeted by the most impressive demonstration I have ever seen. The train shed was covered with the national colors and black festoons. An immense, silent throng had waited hours to glimpse the cortege."

While historians place Abraham Lincoln in the top rankings of American presidents, they have been less kind to Warren Harding, listing him at or near the bottom, a "failed" chief executive. Yet at the time of Harding's sudden death on August 2, 1923, in San Francisco, there was an enormous outpouring of grief. Starting the following day the Harding cross-country funeral special transported his body to Washington, D.C., and later the special brought it for burial in his hometown of Marion, Ohio, making for a 4,000-mile journey. Along the route, especially at station stops for fuel,

water, and replacement crews, hundreds of thousands of mourners turned out to pay their respect. Fellow Masons, who donned full dress uniforms and plumaged headdresses, waited at each stopping place. When Florence Harding saw the huge crowd that had gathered around the North Western station in Cedar Rapids, Iowa, she requested that the train creep through the throng so that everyone could see her husband's casket. In Chicago a somber crowd, which numbered more than a quarter of a million, awaited the sorrowful arrival. The Southern Pacific, Union Pacific, North Western, and B&O delivered the body, which arrived in the nation's capital on August 7, but station crowds made it impossible to maintain any semblance of a schedule. Following the state funeral held the next day, the Pennsylvania and Erie handled the special to Harding's final resting place in Marion, where thousands gathered at the town's union depot.

The tradition continued of honoring deceased political leaders with funeral trains. Two trips were to be especially memorable. In April 1945 a Southern Railway special took the body of President Franklin D. Roosevelt from Warm Springs, Georgia, located near the "Little White House," to Washington, D.C., a slow-moving journey that attracted tens of thousands of onlookers who crowded scores of depot platforms, large and small. At Clemson, South Carolina, so many people gathered at the station where the train paused briefly that some cadets from Clemson College climbed the steeply pitched roof of the depot in order to gain a better view. "It seemed like a good idea at the time, but it was really dangerous

On August 8, 1923, the much-viewed Harding funeral train creeps past bystanders at the North Western station in Boone, Iowa. Men have removed their hats in respect for the twenty-ninth president of the United States. The train is headed to the nation's capital.

Author's coll.

Even within living memory the rare funeral train attracted somber crowds. Between March 31 and April 4, 1969, thousands gathered at stations between Washington, D.C., and Abilene, Kansas, to observe the ten-car Dwight D. Eisenhower funeral special. Several railroads participated; Chesapeake & Ohio, Norfolk & Western, and Union Pacific handled this somber movement. On the morning of April 1, the special moves slowly through Maysville, Kentucky (*above*), and later that day passes through North Vernon, Indiana (*facing page*).

William F. Howes coll.

considering how many of us took to that vantage point," remembered one participant. He might also agree with Thomas Reynolds, who wrote in the April 14, 1945, edition of the *Chicago Sun* that "there is something almost terrifying in the transition of a presidential train into a funeral train." In June 1968 the scene was much the same when the body of slain U.S. senator from New York and Democratic presidential contender Robert F. Kennedy traveled in a Penn Central Railroad special from New York City to the nation's capital. "Along the route of the train, Boy Scouts and firemen braced at attention; nuns, some wearing dark glasses, stood witness; housewives wept," wrote Kennedy biographer Evan Thomas. "Thousands and thousands of black people waited quietly in the heat, perhaps because they lived close to the tracks, but also because they had felt for Kennedy, and knew they would miss him." The normally four-hour trip took the Kennedy train nearly twice as long, and when the occupants detrained in Union Station they heard the sounds of U.S. Navy Band drummers. Lasting memories for all.

During the golden age of railroads other memorable trains called at depots. Both prior to and after the announced closing of the frontier in 1890, railroads dispatched extra movements or added cars to scheduled runs that brought immigrants and land seekers to points along their lines. In 1886 Josiah Strong, minister and social critic, observed, "To-day, easy

transportation makes regions populous and wealthy, which once were uninhabitable." Carriers, even smaller ones like the Burlington, Cedar Rapids & Northern and the Mississippi Central, that operated in the trans-Chicago West and the South had land departments, designed to sell real estate on public lands or obtained from land grants or to work with private promoters in encouraging agricultural settlement. Companies often induced agrarians, both from foreign lands and from settled regions of the country, to make purchases, offering attractive travel rates, perhaps selling half-price or cheaper tickets, and reducing charges for household goods, farm equipment, and livestock.

Railroads brought tens of thousands of settlers to new or developing farm lands and upstart communities. Many a station would be crowded with these newcomers detraining and overseeing their belongings. Between 1874 and 1883 the Santa Fe was instrumental in attracting to Kansas

Railroads transported thousands of settlers to the American West. The Central Pacific attached "emigrant cars" to its freight trains. Women and children occupied coaches, while male members rode in cattle cars or boxcars with their household goods, farm implements, and livestock. This photograph dates from 1886 as the train stopped at Mill City, Nevada.

Don L. Hofsommer coll.

thousands of German-Russian farmers from their eastern European homes, and with them came the hardy red "turkey" wheat that revolutionized grain production on the central plains. Wanting to settle the region quickly, the company treated these land-takers kindly, creating temporary housing for them in several towns and then transporting these industrious agrarians and their possessions to their acreages.

The experiences for other land-seekers might not have been what they expected. "Nearly forty hours after leaving Chicago, the train arrived in Ismay, [Montana,] where a crowd of husbands had been waiting for it since early afternoon," related Jonathan Raban, who examined the settlement-promotion of the Milwaukee Road on the high plains prior to World War I. "The dazed and travel-strained emigrants lifted their bags and boxes down on to the track. They had been expecting a city, with street lamps, signs, illuminated storefronts. They stood under a clear night sky, looking in perplexity at a bare scatter of buildings, their blocky shapes silvered by starlight. Ismay might as well have been Haynes, or Reeder, or McLaughlin." These flimsy prairie towns never evolved into the thriving places that their backers had intended. By the 1920s persistent drought and faltering commodity prices triggered an exodus of townspeople and farmers alike.

Land-takers could be truly hoodwinked. Allegedly a representative from a not-so-reputable real-estate firm, who had shown newcomers farms outside a Texas panhandle village, urged them to sign their purchase agreements on the depot platform before they boarded their train back to the Midwest. It so happened that adjoining the station was a nearly overflowing pond. Surely abundant rainfall had made this a land of milk and honey. But unbeknownst to the buyers, the company had arranged for tank cars of water to be drained into the recently dug pond to create this attractive, albeit deceptive, setting.

Just as real-estate agents, commercial salesmen, and other business-men took advantage of the expanding railroad network, so also did members of religious bodies: ministers, priests, and laypeople. Mostly they traveled in the trans-Chicago West following the Civil War. From Lake Superior to Puget Sound, Omaha to San Francisco, and New Orleans to San Diego men (and some women) of faith brought the Gospel to developing communities. They held their religious services in a recently erected church, or they found space in the waiting room of a newly built depot or hotel, school, or some other commercial or public structure.

In order to solve the question of how to find a suitable location and bring inspirational messages of the Bible, Jesus Christ, and the denomination more directly (and conveniently) to isolated folk, the idea developed for a specially constructed chapel car, employing a concept that had originated about 1870 in Czarist Russia when the Russian Orthodox Church introduced its "church-on-rails." The experiences of earlier religious groups, who had used the network of canals during the heyday of passenger packets, may also have been recalled.

It would be the Protestant Episcopal Church that pioneered the chapel car in America. The idea was discussed in the February 1889 issue of the denominational *Spirit of Missions*. "The Rev. Edward Abbott contributed a suggestive scheme, whereby a Missionary Bishop might make the most of his itinerary in an extended jurisdiction, where towns are springing up on the lines of railways, but where the facilities for holding services are the poorest." The writer noted that the Rev. Mr. Abbott suggested that "there are directors' cars, paymasters' cars, and construction cars, so there might be a Bishop's car in which he and his wife (he must be childless) might live and move from place to place. The car should be fitted up so that it may be readily converted into a chapel and the people in the village gathered in for worship and counsel."

The concept caught on with several religious denominations. Not only did the Episcopalians place in operation the first American chapel car, the Pullman-built *Church of the Advent: Cathedral Car of North Dakota,* constructed in 1890, but Baptists, Methodists, and Roman Catholics operated such equipment that regularly paid calls to hundreds of station sidings throughout widely scattered sections of the country. In the 1890s an Episcopal chapel car, donated by the North Western, ran extensively in the Upper Peninsula of Michigan. "Archdeacon Williams was a frequent traveler on the rails, baptizing and confirming new members to the faith along the way in such towns as Thomaston, Ballentine, Matchwood, Ewen, Bruce's Crossing, Kenton, Three Lakes, Champion, Humboldt, Eagle Mills, Munising, Wetmore and Seney," noted this commentator. "All were depots along the Duluth, South Shore and Atlantic Railway. Many were logging settlements and the railroad was helpful in arranging for the car's use."

Unlike the case with other special trains that pulled into a station, occasionally townspeople did not welcome the chapel car. In some places, especially in the South, community prejudice against Roman Catholics ran high. In the 1920s the Ku Klux Klan in one North Carolina community sought to expel a chapel car and its priest, delivering this letter:

> The Catholic [Atlantic] Coast Line Station
> The Catholic Church on Wheels
> Plymouth, N.C.
>
> Sir:
> This is notify you that your presence in this city is not desired, and I would advise that you get the 3:55 train of this date to carry you away safely. A hint to the wise is sufficient.
>
> Plymouth Klan 140

However, no ugly incident took place in Plymouth; the local Klan did nothing, and the priest went on with his duties.

More exotic than Protestant or Catholic chapel cars were the so-called orphan trains that appeared roughly between the Civil War and World War I. There actually were few trains that were filled with orphans being sent from eastern institutions to homes in the Midwest or elsewhere. Rather these "little wanderers" went alone or in small groups on scheduled passenger movements and were frequently accompanied by a representative of the orphanage or asylum. Their numbers, though, were significant. Between 1853 and 1929 the New York Children's Aid Society, for one, placed out at least 150,000 of the area's poor. Most were children whose parents had died or were physically unable to care for them or were unable to provide for their financial support. Other youngsters lacked relatives who were able or willing to take them into their households, or these children were illegitimate or mandated to a correctional facility. Operators of these founding homes and related institutions believed that their wards would flourish in a rural environment; they needed to be removed from the negative influences of urban life. Farmers, it was thought, would make ideal parents, and thus the necessity to transport these special children.

During the time of the orphan trains, various agencies used personal letters, local newspapers, and posted notices to announce the arrival of adoptable children. At the scheduled time, a crowd might assemble at the depot to receive the children, if prearranged, or to look them over and decide if they wanted any of them. The latter was more likely for teenage boys, who could go to work immediately on farms. Scenes varied, but this one typified the process: "The children were attended by nurses and must have ranged from 2 to 4 or 5 years of age," noted an eyewitness to a Sisters of Charity placement in Hays, Kansas, in 1902. "The people were lined up all around the [Union Pacific] station and the nurses brought the little ones out. All of them had tags on their clothes with the name of the person who was to adopt them and the nurses passed them out to the people who called for them."

But with the professionalization of social work and child-protection laws enacted during the Progressive Era and later, orphans no longer boarded trains in cities for stations in the hinterlands. Most everyone agreed that this was a necessary reform. "Nearly every kid I knew who had been sent to farmers from the orphanage had run away because they could not stand the treatment," said a foe of out-placements. "They're too tight to hire men – so they get orphans and work hell out of them."

At a few depots, in contrast, a thoroughly enjoyable experience for youngsters occurred, the Christmas season event of welcoming the "Santa Train." The most durable and well-known of these unusual consists began during World War II and traveled the Clinchfield Railroad. In 1942 businessmen in Kingsport, Tennessee, decided to cheer the children of the impoverished families of the dreary coal mining towns to the north, mostly isolated places in western Virginia. From the rear vestibule of the early morning southbound passenger train, which left from the Clinchfield's northern terminus in Elkhorn City, Kentucky, Santa's special sleigh chugged along the nearly 100 miles toward Kingsport. A volunteer dressed as the venerable Ol' Saint Nick tossed hard candy to throngs of children who had patiently waited on depot platforms. When passenger service ended in the mid-1950s, the company continued the popular tradition, largely because of "some behind-the-scenes pressure from major shippers."

Even in the modern era of freight-only railroads, the popularity of the Santa Claus special remains, associated with smaller "regional" and short-line carriers. In 2010 these seasonal trains, for example, spread joy along the rails of the Indiana Rail Road, the Greenville & Western Railway, and the Keokuk Junction Railway, making stops at stations (or downtowns) and at announced road crossings.

Railroad companies themselves might spark the appearance of sizable station and right-of-way crowds. During the depths of the Great

Depression when good news was not plentiful, several railroads, including the Boston & Maine, Burlington, Mobile & Ohio, and Union Pacific,
introduced breathtaking internal-combustion streamliners and provided
an appreciative public with announced showings of their new equipment.
Even after these streamliners entered revenue service, residents flocked
to stations to see these trains stop or whiz by.

It would be the Burlington that drew the greatest attention. In June
1933 the railroad ordered a "high-speed, light-weight, streamline passenger train" from the Budd Company, a Philadelphia manufacturer. Named
the *Zephyr* after the gods of the west wind by Burlington president Ralph
Budd, the train consisted of three units: a power car and two articulated
coaches. It was fabricated with state-of-the-art stainless steel and was propelled by a diesel engine recently developed by General Motors. In April
7, 1934, the Art Deco–styled *Zephyr* rolled out of the Philadelphia plant
and departed on a five-week tour of East Coast and Midwest cities. In New
York City this "new speed king of the rails," displayed at both Pennsylvania Station and Grand Central Terminal, drew enormous crowds. At the
latter, "Plans were made to exhibit it there until 9 PM. But at 5 PM the count
disclosed that 55,560 already had inspected the train, and the rush hours
brought constantly growing numbers," reported the *New York Times*. "It
was finally decided to extend the exhibition to 10 PM." The streamliner
then made a month-long journey through the West. At scores of stations
long lines of the curious inspected the silver train or watched it sail past.
Before the *Zephyr* entered regular revenue service in November 1934

between Lincoln, Omaha, and Kansas City, the train made a sensational "dawn-to-dusk" run from Denver to Chicago to celebrate the reopening of the Century of Progress Fair in the Windy City. On that record-setting journey, tracked by national radio hook-ups, the *Zephyr* and the railroad basked in the glow of public excitement and adulation. The 1,015 miles were covered in thirteen hours and five minutes at an unheard of average speed of 77.6 miles per hour, and depots and road crossings along this four-state route were packed with expectant and then admiring crowds.

It was an event to remember. An estimated 1 million people observed the fast-moving *Zephyr*. As J. S. Ford, assistant master mechanic of the Burlington, told reporters: "It seemed like the entire population was lined up at every town, city and village to cheer us along." Commented the *New York Times,* "At each station, where crowds were gathered to see the silver kind of transportation speed through, the track was guarded by local law officers, posts of the American Legion and Boy Scouts."

LIVING IN THE DEPOT

Not only were there countless people who experienced train-time or an uncommon event at the approximately eighty thousand stations in the United States, there were those hundreds of railroaders and their families who occupied these trackside premises, giving them ringside seats to the daily or special happenings. Living in the depot provided a range of experiences, positive and negative.

The availability of decent, rent-free housing in a remote community pleased the railroad agent and his family. Even if the agent possessed the financial means, there was little incentive to build a house because of the expectation that an early career assignment in some primitive locality would lead to a position in a larger, better-paying location that offered good, affordable housing. Also the stock of rental properties in villages was usually limited, unattractive, or nonexistent. If the depot stood a considerable distance from an established town, the agent faced long walks or the need to acquire his own transportation, becoming potentially unpleasant in bad weather. For the single agent a boarding or rooming house might be unavailable or unacceptable. These railroaders repeatedly complained about unsanitary conditions, especially bedbugs and rodents, and they howled about cranky proprietors and landladies, poor or no food, and bathing limitations. But depot housing, although hardly elegant, was an acceptable option. "We didn't have luxurious conditions in the depot," related a Soo Line agent who lived in several depot apartments in Upper Great Plains communities, "but we knew what to expect. My wife and I were able to create a cozy, comfortable living space."

Yet complaints occurred. It might be the lack of modern plumbing, although that varied by railroad. The Southern Pacific initially provided water, if possible, to its buildings, and later sanitary facilities. Others companies never offered these amenities. "We had a cistern under the basement which we had water hauled into," recalled a one-time resident of the M&STL depot in Madison, Minnesota. "The pump (hand pump) was in the kitchen by the sink. The water was just used for washing, and we hauled all our drinking water in glass jugs."

Plumbing-related matters may have caused concern, but there was always the inconvenience of an upstairs apartment. The stairway, often steep and narrow, might make it impossible to bring up a bulky piece of furniture, and it necessitated awkward climbs for carrying water, coal, household supplies, and other items. "On washday we had to pack the water up for mom to do the wash," recounted a child of the depot. "There was a 'coal house' across the side-track behind the depot where we went to get coal for the stove and coal oil for the lamps. There was a wood-pile next to the coal house where my dad and I chopped wood." Completing these chores required numerous up-and-down trips.

A more generalized statement about how challenging life could be came from a former inhabitant of the New York, Ontario & Western Railway depot at West Monroe, New York. Since the station was located in the thinly populated area of the state's Oneida Lake district, the company wisely offered living accommodations. But the railroad hardly created attractive accommodations. "I don't know how my mother ever endured those years, from about 1923 to 1930. The station had no electricity, no running water, and no indoor plumbing. We bathed in water collected from the roof downspouts, and water for cooking and drinking was available from a well at the nearby milk station." Heat for the living space, located on both the ground and second story, "was provided by the kitchen and office stoves." Even communications were modest: "We were connected to the outside world by the telegraph in the office and a hand-cranked phone that was shared with about twelve other people."

Then there was the noise of such close proximity to trains. A regular visitor to the Burlington depot in Berwyn, Nebraska, found it "very strange to live that close to the tracks," and it was "quite an experience when the trains went past – the noise and the place kind of shook." The coming and going of passenger trains annoyed inhabitants, too. "I never really got used to all of that noise," recounted the daughter of a station agent in South Dakota. "The piercing cry of the whistle, the clanging bell, the squeaking wheels and the monster locomotive itself would give you a good startle in the middle of the night and might keep you awake." She added, "A stopping passenger train always seemed to be especially loud, with the mail, baggage and express being worked and the passengers coming and going. There weren't any 'Please Be Quiet' signs on the platform!" Actually, some residents might be affected by the *lack* of noise. The wife of a Southern Pacific agent at Goleta, California, recalled that "it was the silence caused by the train that did not arrive on time that was most likely to wake one up from a sound sleep."

Dangers at stations were obvious, especially for children. "Locomotives could sneak up on even an adult," remarked a veteran station agent. "They weren't always that loud." A former depot resident recalled that his mother hated the depot. "She worried about me and my brother and sister. The platform and the tracks were our playground, and the trains on the main line provided a frequent, serious threat." His mother's concerns were real. "Youngsters were easily injured falling when running across the tracks. I once tripped with my toes on one rail and made a one-point landing on my jaw against the other rail. My jaw wasn't broken, but I was in pain and couldn't eat for awhile." Added this commentator: "Years later, when I wanted to reminisce, my mother would not discuss our days in depots. She never overcame the dread of tracks and trains." Such a feeling lingered among many a station mother. "And how many times did the mothers have to start thinking about where everyone was playing when she heard the first 'toot' from the approaching steamer?" recalled the wife of an agent who long inhabited the depot in Snyder, Nebraska.

A personal mishap or the potential for one added an element of excitement to depot living. It was the passing of people through the depot, whether passengers or greeters, senders or seekers of freight, express, or telegraphic messages, who collectively made for a fascinating environment. "The folks there at the railroad station were the center of town life. We kids were really proud that our father was the agent and telegraph operator there. He was important and so we thought that we were too!" If there were circus specials, trains with politicians or troops or chapel cars, those who lived in the depot likely were the first locally to learn about the upcoming event. "My dad knew when the circus was coming to town long before the posters went up on the fences and other places around town." Children of the depot had the opportunity to see what was happening firsthand, peering perhaps from windows of their trackside home.

THE HIGHLY PERSONAL

While a train with intriguing or uncommon travelers remained fixed in the collective memories of Americans, there were those highly personalized experiences, which took place at stations, large and small, that made the railroad experience unforgettable. It would be impossible to comprehend fully the flood of memories; virtually everyone had some memorable contact at depots during the Railway Age and even past the heyday of passenger travel.

Some remembrances smacked of the humorous. Shortly before a refurbished Union Station in St. Louis opened as an urban shopping mall and hotel in the mid-1980s, the developer asked the public to share their memories. Here was one of the more amusing: "In 1925, when I was ten years old, our family of six arrived from a small town of 500 in Arkansas to live," related a resident of St. Louis County. "I had never seen a large city. The station was beautiful and seemed huge. I was turning around and around staring up wide eyed in amazement as it all seemed to glitter with lights. I hollered out, 'So this is St. Louis,' thinking the station *was* St. Louis in my childhood mind. My eighteen year old sister suddenly slapped me across the face saying, 'Everyone is staring at us, stop acting like a hick.'"

There were some troubling, even horrendous, events that took place at a station. It could be fisticuffs between individuals or groups. It might involve a group of rival immigrants, drunken coal miners, or rowdy cowhands. No wonder municipal and railroad police kept an eye out for possible trouble at the depot, especially larger facilities. A widely remembered happening of this sort involved a president of the United States. On the morning of July 2, 1881, James A. Garfield, who had taken the presidential oath of office only four months earlier, was about to board at train at the Baltimore & Potomac station in Washington, D.C. As Garfield and his personal secretary walked through the women's waiting room toward the door of the main waiting room, a disturbed, disgruntled office seeker, Charles Guiteau, fired two shots at the president, inflicting mortal wounds that would take the president's life eighty days later. After the tragic event, and for years to come, the curious flocked to this station to see where one of the most dastardly events in American history had occurred.

On the lighter side would be the memory of a special animal associated with a depot. Although it was against company rules, agents, operators, baggagemen, and other station personnel might keep a dog or cat or possibly a more exotic animal. One depot pet was Roxie, the "railroad dog," who became a mascot of sorts for agents and other employees of the Long Island Railroad (LIRR). On a summer day in 1901 a young woman traveling on the LIRR asked the baggageman at the Long Island City terminal to place her puppy in the baggage car and said that she would retrieve the dog at Roslyn, located on the Oyster Bay branch 24 miles distant. But the anxious canine liked neither the baggage car nor separation from his owner, breaking away at the Floral Park station and climbing onto a train headed back to Long Island City. The dog wandered up and down the line searching for his mistress and often spent nights in the Garden City depot. For more than a dozen years Roxie rode Long Island trains, and spent time in various depots, including Pennsylvania Station in New York City. But one day the dog died in his sleep at the Merrick depot; he was honored with burial on the station grounds. A tombstone, initially the pet's water bowl, marked the site, and animal lovers still leave flowers.

Most memories that people associate with a station involved something far less dramatic than the assassination of a president or more mundane than a roaming canine. Certainly wartime experiences were plentiful and indelible. From the Civil War through the Korean Conflict, millions of Americans used the rails to go off to and hopefully return from military service. Just as the Great Depression etched countless memories into the minds of adults and children, the experiences of World War II, which followed, did much the same. Railroads were busy, pressed to their limits. When it came to people, trains moved 98 percent of all military personnel, and passenger volume, expressed in revenue passenger miles, soared from 23 billion in 1940 to 95 billion in 1944, a peak figure never again attained. That year at St. Louis Union Station, for example, 71,744 trains, which carried more than 24 million passengers, used that facility.

While not all greetings and partings were emotional or long remembered, some were. As poignant as any were the memories of a Missouri woman who recalled events at an often-crowded St. Louis Union Station. There was the excitement of the arrival:

> On a morning in 1945, my small daughter and I were eagerly on our way to Union Station to meet my husband. He was due home on a delay in route from Louisiana prior to shipping out to the Pacific. He had been gone four months, and we missed him so much. We just knew we would be able to see him the minute he got off of the train. What we didn't realize was how many soldiers there were also en route from so many places headed for the same place we were. We thought, of course, that he was the only one, wasn't he ours? Wasn't he special? We got there in plenty of time, actually very early, but when the time came, several trains came at about the same time, and soldiers in khaki just poured off of them by the thousands. We couldn't find him. We had lost him. He didn't make it. They changed his plans. We would never see him again. All of a sudden he was there, couldn't see him for the duffel bag he carried. But we cried, we hugged and although there were so many people there it was almost unbelievable, the crowd just seemed to fade away. He was home.

Then there was the departure:

> When we had spent the time he had at home, all too soon it was time for him to pack that bag again and leave. We knew this time it would be a long wait. My father took us down again to Union Station, but what a difference. The time it was very late at night, small clusters of people were telling their guys goodbye, and looking as sad as we felt. When it came time for my husband to board his

train and it pulled away in the almost deserted terminal, my girl and I just stared out at it through the doorway and watched until we couldn't see the red lights on the end car of the train anymore. What a lonely cold feeling it was, all the joy we had felt a week before just seemed to vanish with those red lights.

We were to go to Union Station many times, but that memory will live with me for all times.

Whether in a vibrant metropolis or a sleepy village, "train-time" meant much to the public. "The depot is always a beehive of activity," as a commercial traveler put it in 1903. "The hustle-bustle, which is America, can be found there." For generations the station served as community gateway and window on the world, being an intimate part of daily life. For some the setting became nearly sacred space, notwithstanding the joys and sorrows and maybe the noise and crush of humanity. "My memories of the big North Western terminal are similar to some that I associate with my church," related a Chicagoan. "It was very special for me."

QUEST FOR RAILS

When railroads made their debut, there were Americans who seemed uncertain about this exotic transportation form, failing to foresee that rail lines would rapidly become the nation's economic arteries. Individuals occasionally expressed real hostility. "If God had designed that His intelligent creatures should travel at the frightful speed of 15 miles an hour by steam, He would clearly have foretold it through His holy prophets," charged a resident of Lancaster, Ohio, in 1838. "It is a device of Satan to lead immortal souls down to hell."

Then there were those individuals, even with a more enlightened view of religion, who had philosophical differences with railroad promoters and worried about the implications of a potential sea change in domestic transportation. In the late 1830s Andrew Johnson, a future president of the United States, blasted the internal improvement program in his native Tennessee. Like fellow Jacksonians he considered charters granted to railroad companies to be unconstitutional because they created monopolies and perpetuities. Johnson also believed that a railroad would destroy much of the business of wayside taverns, throw out of work those men who depended on the "six-horse teams," introduce fatal diseases, and "violate the laws of nature" by pulling down hills and filling up valleys.

And the loss or destruction of place troubled many. "The laborers commenced work on the depot grounds, in the rear of Pleasant St. on Monday week; and they have made sad havoc with the pleasant places, where 'many a time and oft a weary pilgrim' has reclined his tired limbs, of a summer's afternoon, under shade of an old tree," reflected the *Northampton* [Massachusetts] *Gazette* in 1845. "The aged are filled with sadness to see the places of their childhood so changed by the 'hand of improvement.'"

If citizens lived on a navigable body of water – ocean, lake, or river – they still might not have been enthusiastic about this little-understood and experimental technology. Those individuals who had gained access to canals, including the strategic and profitable Erie Canal, which was the harbinger of the national canal craze, were mostly satisfied with their "artificial rivers." Probably they did not want the iron horse to damage either public or private investments.

But the widespread realization emerged that canals, navigable or "canalized" streams, deep-water lakes, and coastal waterways could never effectively shatter the isolation of various regions, particularly more localized sections. That explains why in the 1820s and 1830s lawmakers in several states funded roads or "turnpikes" in districts that were to be bypassed by state-sponsored canals, usually because these "ditches" were impossible or too expensive to build. Waterways, moreover, were repeatedly affected adversely by weather; ice, snow, fog, drought, heavy rains, and high winds wreaked havoc on the movements of goods and people.

Furthermore there appeared no good reason for travelers to rely on roads. It would not be until the twentieth century that the national network of roadways became passable. For decades roads were poor or nonexistent. The experiences of an Ohio woman, related to a friend in New Hampshire, captured overland travel in the nineteenth century: "At five o'clock we took stage for Elyria, which is ten miles from Oberlin – road very bad from ruts and mud. We were in constant danger of overturning. Once when we came to a ditch in the road the gentlemen got out and took down a fence, so that we could turn aside into the adjoining field and ride around the obstacle." Efforts to construct turnpikes (usually toll roads), plank roads, and other improved thoroughfares met with only scattered success. Governmental units showed little interest in expending public revenues, leaving travelers to use trails made by wild animals and Native Americans or some other roadway. A notable exception was the famed National Road, the "Great Western Road" or "Grand Portage" from the Atlantic seaboard to the trans-Allegheny West. What emerged by 1817 was a modern road extending from Cumberland, Maryland, to Wheeling, Virginia (West Virginia), strategically situated on the Ohio River. By the 1840s the National Road sliced through Ohio and Indiana, but sputtered out in Illinois. Its projected goal of St. Louis, Missouri, was made less pressing with expansion of rail lines into the region.

If Americans were uncertain about any radical changes in intercity transportation, a deep curiosity existed about the steam locomotive and how this machine might overcome the tyranny of distance. Newspapers, word-of-mouth, and public demonstrations spread the idea that steam power could be successfully employed for land transport. In the summer of 1831 residents of several Ohio River valley towns were treated to an "important exhibition" of what its Kentucky promoter called his "Locomotive or Steam Carriage, Drawing a Car on a Miniature Rail-Road." Advertised extensively, this showing became a popular attraction, even though the exhibitor charged admission. Readers of the *Madison* (Indiana) *Republican* of July 14, 1831, saw this advertisement:

> This exhibition is to be held at the Madison Masonic Hall from 9 A M till 9 P M, will be a rich treat to the friends of State or National Internal Improvement. The Locomotive works with great celerity and precision, drawing a splendid miniature CAR, in which two persons may ride at the same time. Both the Locomotive and Car are constructed on the most improved principle, by Mr. A. Bruen of Lexington, and the workmanship may be safely pronounced of the very first order. The novelty of this machine has never failed to exit the admiration and curiosity of all who have seen it. Admittance 25 cents [$5.00 in 2010 dollars]; children half price.

There was something wonderful about a mechanical contraption that spewed smoke and steam and made strange clanking sounds. This transportation marvel left a profound impression on observers; after all, the pioneer locomotive of the 1830s resembled an oversize barrel thrown on its side, with a tall smokestack, two sets of wheels, and an assortment of pipes and valves.

Just as canal fever had swept over portions of the Mid-Atlantic, Old Northwest, and South, the expectation that flanged wheels could solve nagging transportation problems triggered a clamor for railroads. As time passed, the canal, once extolled as an indispensable artery of commerce, gradually fell into disuse, vanquished by the iron horse. The railroad represented the quintessential national urge to conquer time and space. And it was thought that railroads would help make the United States of America a more perfect union. At the opening of the Eastern Rail Road between Boston and Salem, Massachusetts, on August 27, 1838, the Rev. Dr. Flint expressed the hope of the emerging Railway Age: "Railroads – the strong clamps which are destined to bind together with ribs of steel the whole of this great country; may they be multiplied and extended till they shall have cemented this Union beyond the possibility of severance."

By mid-century much had been written about the superiority of the railroad over the canal. "A canal may be a useful agent for the transportation of the coarsest kind of luggage [cargoes], but the only influence it exerts are to be found in its material results," reflected a writer in 1850. "It belongs to the past and has no sympathy with modern ideas. The rail is the great agent of social life – the great instrument of social intercourse which is the necessary condition of all civilization. The influence of a canal ceases when it delivers the barrel of flour it undertakes to carry. In estimating the influence of a railroad this only function of the canal is hardly taken into account. It serves equally well, and better, the material wants of man, and in addition it gives the highest condition of social enjoyment and intellectual progress." Concluded this philosophical observer, "The opening of a canal may stimulate the growth of towns, by the increased facilities it gives to business, but none are attracted to it except as a mere instrument of transportation. But every person wishes to get within a reach of a railroad, because he feels himself in reach of everything connected with it. It brings him into the world, in immediate connection with all that is best worth seeing and hearing, which he may visit and enjoy at will."

The feeling grew that rail lines, unlike canals, offered the financially able the chance to escape unpleasant urban environments – the same argument that streetcar and interurban promoters would later extol. "People will not be willing to endure the stenches and insalubrity of a great city when one-half hour will place fifteen miles between their residence and the hundreds of crowded warehouses and houses that make up the city itself," suggested a journalist in 1852.

> It will now be possible with ease and at comparatively trifling expense to live in the country and daily transact business in New York, Boston or Philadelphia, by means of the railroads which are among the most important instruments of that commerce, the principal cause of the wealth and growth of those cities. The person doing business in the city has a large choice of pleasant towns and villages, where living is cheap, and all the concomitants that make up life, eminently pleasant.

While not every American community expressed a burning desire for a railroad, hundreds, if not thousands, of places did. The iron horse gave a town an opportunity to gain urban prominence. Perhaps it had been bypassed by earlier internal improvement schemes or had lost the initial round of county-seat fights or had missed out on state or territorial institutions – those ubiquitous political plums. The wish was for access to a trunk line, linking the community with important commercial emporiums. Other places were willing to settle for *any* rail outlet.

The needs were obvious. "Before the coming of railways corn could not be sold or even given away in many sections and it literally rotted in cribs," observed a mid-nineteenth-century writer. "Some sold at eight cents per bushel. It then took two bushels of corn to purchase one pound of cut nails." In 1853 the *Selma* (Alabama) *Sentinel* reported that "another large lot of pine spars have been brought down from Shelby and Bibb counties by the Alabama and Tennessee Railroad. This is an evidence of the value of railroads. This Timber is brought from a section of the country, four years ago impenetrable, and these trees as they then stood were worthless." Similar tales were widely circulated and remembered. In 1869 the editor of the *Cedar Falls* (Iowa) *Gazette* expressed these thoughts: "Iowa needs for her proper development, an east and west line of [rail] road through each tier of counties, and these connected at intervals of every 40 miles by lines running north and south. Until she is thus gridironed she cannot have too many roads, and until then the projection and agitation of new railroad enterprises will not and ought not to cease."

Communities who won a railroad always seemed to want another. As early as 1852 citizens of Fond du Lac, Wisconsin, already served by the iron horse, hoped that they were about to welcome the recently organized Milwaukee & Fond du Lac Railroad. "With two railroads," prophesied a resident, "this city will be *some* among small fish."

Americans sensed that the railroad could make their lives more comfortable and pleasurable. It meant that prized anthracite coal for home heating and cooking became more obtainable and at better prices. It meant that affordable, finished lumber was readily available, a boon for those settlers who had established themselves on the largely treeless prairies and who wanted to abandon their dugouts, "soddies," or tarpaper shanties for "real" houses. It meant that residents of inland communities who had developed a taste for Chesapeake Bay oysters could order a barrel of these delicacies, packed in ice, and enjoy them in season. The iron horse sparked and sustained what became rampant consumerism.

The development of the railroad prompted Americans to reflect on the impact of steam power on regional, national, and even world transport. At the end of the 1830s S. D. Jacobs, president of the Hiwassee Rail Road, offered at a directors' meeting what became oft-repeated arguments for building these iron roadways. "By the construction of our railway alone our state [Tennessee] no longer is an isolated community. The mountain barriers which have so long and so effectively hemmed us in have been broken down, the vast mineral wealth which is possible, but which now is buried in the earth, will be speedily and extensively developed, our agriculture and manufacturing resources will be brot [*sic*] into more action and profitable use." He added that "a passage may be transported to the seaboard in 2 days and expense of transportation will be reduced to about one third the present cost." A decade later the editor of the *American Railroad Journal* mused in his essay "The Past and Future" "By steam power all the various products of the earth are rapidly, and with trifling expense, centered in the same spot. Under these influences the old relations of society are rapidly disappearing, and new ones are taking their place. Tradition is fast losing its power over the minds of man."

Every state had places that eagerly sought the "steamcar civilization," beginning in the 1830s and lasting for nearly a century. Early on, citizens of the prosperous farming area of Edgefield District (County), South Carolina, wanted a rail link to the recently opened 136-mile Charleston-to-Hamburg line of the South-Carolina Canal & Rail-Road, then the longest railroad in the world. Meetings were held, but sufficient capital was not raised, although a private firm, the Hamburg & Edgefield Plank Road Company, built a short-lived and money-losing wooden roadway to the railroad's western terminus. It was erroneously believed that plank roads were "sure to be extensively introduced wherever there is timber suitable for them – and they are sure to become extensive and useful feeders to railroads." Notwithstanding the road's failure, residents of the district and the courthouse settlement of Edgefield still pursued their railroad dreams. Merchants and planters in and about Edgefield Court House twice won state charters, but their railroad projects failed, remaining "paper" entities. In 1853 a subscription of $30,000 to construct a branch of the Greenville & Columbia Rail Road also fizzled. It would not be until after the Civil War that the Edgefield, Trenton & Aiken Railroad, a 6-mile stub of what later became part of the Southern Railway, reached Edgefield from nearby Trenton. Finally in 1929, with the last major railroad construction project in the state, the Georgia & Florida Railroad crossed the county on a north–south axis, providing a direct connection for Edgefield and its environs to the north at Greenwood and to the south at Augusta. For more than ninety years agitation had persisted in Edgefield for a railroad or improved railroad service.

As the web of rails expanded after 1830, not every American community found the railroad network to its liking. Because of geography, funding, politics, personal whims, or just bad luck, places were bypassed. Trackage usually needed to follow the contours of the land; excessive grading, bridging, and tunneling escalated construction costs. Railroad leaders might decide that such expenditures were warranted, but more often they opted for the least expensive route. Established communities would be missed, forcing citizens to consider these options: accepting the status quo, relocating physically, or constructing their own rail connection.

A map of any state reveals communities that missed out on the railroad. They might exist along a navigable river, canal, or other body of water or perhaps along an early trace, trail, or road, or more likely they were interior settlements in an agricultural or mountainous area. Places like Buffalo, South Dakota; Highlands, North Carolina; Kilmarnock, Virginia; Ozona, Texas; and Waynesville, Missouri, never saw a railroad. Their residents dreamed of having the iron horse in their midst, but that was not to be.

By the start of the twentieth century some American communities feared that the railroad map had finally jelled. Often the only viable financial option for many places would be a steam shortline. This is what happened in Page County, Iowa, located in the rolling "Bluegrass Country" of the Hawkeye State. The hope for one town, College Springs, was to obtain the iron horse; for another, Clarinda, it was to break a rail monopoly that meant poor service and high rates. By 1910 these desires had reached a fevered pitch. Residents of College Springs (1900 population of 693) did not relish the fact that their town was allegedly the largest place in Iowa without a railroad. Their pride, the struggling Amity College, wanted improved travel opportunities, expecting that a railroad would attract and retain more students from the region. And nearby farmers sought better, dependable transport since they were "compelled to haul their products and supplies miles to the nearest railroad." Stated the editor of the local *Current Press*, "College Springs never needed a Rail Road worse." Citizens of the Page County seat, Clarinda (1900 population of 3,822), had several lines of the Chicago, Burlington & Quincy Railroad (Burlington), but passenger accommodations were modest and poorly coordinated, and the company appeared uninterested in serving patrons, refusing, for example, to install a telephone in its freight house. There were also strong, recurrent demands for lower freight charges. Adding to these concerns was this statement made by an officer of the Clarinda Commercial Club: "We came to a realization of the fact that without competition in railway facilities it was useless for us to try to get factories to come here."

Eventually a brighter day dawned for Page Countians. Instigated by civic-minded businessmen and farmers, residents organized the Iowa & Southwestern Railway, popularly called the "Ikey." The company built a 17-mile railroad from Blanchard, a town 6 miles southwest of College Springs and located on the Omaha line of the Wabash Railroad, through College Springs, to Clarinda, opening for revenue service in 1912. Unfortunately, a few years later a poorly built and equipped road, inept management, and a hostile Burlington forced the Ikey into bankruptcy. Two reorganizations failed to save the property, which was junked at the end of World War I.

While the Ikey used steam motive power, some localities after the Spanish-American War got a last chance when "traction fever" became widespread. Near the end of interurban building the Oregon farming villages of Mulino and Robbins, for example, finally received rail service with the arrival of the electric Willamette Valley Southern Railway.

Then there were numerable town relocations. From the start, it seems, communities either reoriented themselves or moved themselves to the railroads. By the mid-nineteenth century the nexus of some colonial-era places – Scarsdale and Tuckahoe, New York, are examples – had shifted to the rails. When the Northern Pacific Railroad extended a branch line through McLean County, North Dakota, in 1904, the village of Turtle Lake was left 4 miles beyond the end-of-track, and so inhabitants removed themselves to a newly created townsite. Somewhat earlier the Northern Pacific had built through Foster County, North Dakota, but its tracks missed Newport, dealing that settlement a fatal blow. Villagers therefore left for Melville, a trackside town platted on a nearby section of land. In 1889 citizens of at least one hamlet in what became Cook County, Georgia, did not bother to wait for grading, tie, and rail gangs to research their neighborhood as the Georgia Southern & Florida Railroad built south from Macon toward Florida. As soon as surveyors pounded in their right-of-way stakes, "the citizenry moved their stores on sleds and wagons from Puddleville to the marked railroad depot site." It was often practical for buildings, usually of modest wood construction, to be placed on skids or rollers and pulled by animal teams or later by steam-traction engines to a railroad location.

Citizens of Emmitsburg, Maryland, faced the curse of forever being an "inland" town. The community, which dated back to colonial times, had benefited from a long-distance public road that extended from Baltimore to Pittsburgh. But this artery was poorly maintained, and when railroads entered the area, freight and stagecoach operators either quit or relocated. Soon after the Civil War the Western Maryland Railroad decided to extend its end-of-tracks from Union Bridge, Maryland, westward to Hagerstown, Maryland, a distance of 40 miles, and in the process considered three routes across this mountainous section. Ultimately, the company decided to run its line through the settlement of Rocky Ridge, south of Emmitsburg. Explained John Lee Chapman, Western Maryland president, "[The line] will pass through Middleburg and within five miles of Taneytown, Johnsville and Woodsborough, within six miles of Emmittsburg [sic], and within two miles of Creagerstown, through Graceham and Mechanicstown, and within three miles of Catoctin Furnace, and then passing up Owings Creek Valley, passing through Harbaugh Valley it reaches the summit of the Blue Ridge, which it crosses within one mile of Monterey Springs, and within six miles of Waynesboro." Chapman continued, "It then passes down Germantown Valley, taking the West side of Mount Misery, through Smithsburg and Cavetown to Hagerstown."

The population of Emmitsburg hardly took solace that the Western Maryland would also miss other communities. Instead they, like civic boosters in Page County, Iowa, took action. "The business people of Emmitsburg," observed a local historian, "decided at a town meeting that the community needed a railroad connection to carry products to and from markets if the town was to stay in existence." A major proponent of the road was Father John McCloskey, who wished to promote the town's Roman Catholic girl's school, Mount Saint Mary's College, which dated back to 1810. He knew that a rail connection would benefit students, teachers, and visitors alike. In March 1868 backers of the Emmitsburg Railroad received incorporation papers, and they forged ahead to create a dependable link to the outside world. Optimism reigned. "The road will be seven miles, the grades and curvature exceedingly easy, and the entire cost of the road when ready for the locomotive, will be about $110,000" – so went a contemporary report. But it would take another seven years before the little pike opened, slowed by some rough topography, the need to erect a 100-foot span over Tom's Creek, and inadequate funding. Finally, on November 22, 1875, the first train rumbled over the line. Eventually the Western Maryland gained control of this independent carrier and upgraded the trackage and rolling stock, making the "Emmitsburg Branch" more secure and useful. Yet the pride of building *their* railroad remained strong among townspeople.

Occasionally a routing decision stemmed from sheer spite or whim. Not long after the Civil War Dr. E. D. Standiford, president of the Louisville & Nashville Railroad (L&N), arrived in the railroad-starved town of Danville, Kentucky. His personal appearance was hardly that of a senior executive, being dressed in the clothing of a surveyor who had been out in muddy conditions. When Standiford asked the innkeeper at the Gilcher House for an overnight room, he was directed to a primitive attic loft with its shuck-filled mattress bed and a candle or two. Standiford, who had failed to identify himself as a railroad official, asked for better accommodations. The clerk refused, saying "That room is plenty good for the looks of you." Thereupon this angry guest wrote across the open page of the hotel register: "Surveyors: locate the road just far enough away from Danville so its citizens can barely hear the whistles blow." Standiford signed the edict with his name and title, and that's what happened. Only much later did the municipally financed Cincinnati Southern Railway build through Danville. If anyone wished to use the L&N for their freight or travel needs, they faced an inconvenient journey to the remote depot.

A similar tale explained why the county-seat village of Boonesboro, Iowa, failed to gain railroad service. In 1865 the Cedar Rapids & Missouri River Rail Road (CR&MR) was extending its line across central Iowa and within a few years would reach Council Bluffs and a connection with the expanding Union Pacific. Two ranking officials of the CR&MR, John I. Blair and W. W. Walker, attended a "railroad meeting" in Boonesboro, and initially they were pleased with events, including financial commitments to their project. But as Walker spoke, he noticed that someone had apparently taken a package of papers from the pocket of his overcoat that hung on a backroom chair. "Cutting his remarks short, [Walker] at once picked up his coat and beckoning Mr. Blair, they walked out of the building," recounted an eyewitness. (Later it was revealed that the thief had taken right-of-way maps and town plats.) "Before showing up again they purchased lands a mile or more east of the courthouse and subsequently located the depot almost a mile and one-half northeast of the public square in Boonesboro, and located the town of Boone on lands purchased for that purpose."

Blair and Walker wished to punish Boonesboro by barely missing the community. Their actions caused Boonesboro to fade rapidly, attesting to the ability of a railroad to be either a maker or breaker of existing settlements.

TRIUMPH

Some places lucky enough to be on the verge of gaining the iron horse celebrated the *start* of construction. At the dawn of the Railway Age citizens of Columbia, South Carolina, knew about the success of the South-Carolina Canal & Rail-Road Company (SCC&RR), and they were eager to forge a connection. City fathers of Columbia, the capital and the largest interior city in the state, wanted to extend their economic ties over a wider area. Their hope-of-hopes, though, was to see the Louisville, Cincinnati & Charleston Rail Road (LC&C), a corporate entity then separate from the SCC&RR, become a transmontane carrier that would ultimately reach the Ohio River. On March 21, 1838, a grand celebration took place to commemorate the initial 62-mile phase of construction, featuring a parade, artillery fire, and inspirational speeches. Everyone seemed involved. As the *Columbia Times* told it:

> Yesterday was a proud day for Columbia, and for the State. The first ground has been broken in the great enterprise of the Louisville, Cincinnati and Charleston Rail Road! Agreeably to the public notice a Procession was formed at 10 o'clock in front of the State House, under the direction of Col. R. H. Goodwyn, as Marshall of the day, in the following order:
>
> 1. Uniform companies of the Town.
> 2. City Guard.
> 3. Governor of the State and suite.
> 4. President, Directors and Engineers of the Company.
> 5. Clergy and Theological Students.
> 6. Stockholders of the Company.
> 7. Intendant, Wardens and Officers of the Town.
> 8. Judges, Officers and Jurors of the District Court.
> 9. Officers and Students of the South Carolina College.
> 10. Teachers and Students of the Male Schools.
> 11. Citizens of the Town and Country.
> 12. Committee of Arrangements.
> 13. Cavalry of Richland District.
>
> The whole was followed by a large number of carriages and citizen cavalry. On arriving at the ground, the Richland Corps formed a hollow square around the staging erected for the Orator, and after the invocation of the blessing of Providence upon the work by the Rev. Dr. Leland, the President of the Company, Robert Y. Hayne, Esq. addressed the meeting in an appropriate and patriotic speech prepared for the occasion. After the address the President set the example of throwing up a shovel full of ground, which was followed by all who were near enough to partake of that honor. The assemblage was altogether the largest one we have ever witnessed on any occasion in Columbia, and comprised all the beauty, patriotism, talent and wealth of the surrounding country.

It would not be until 1842 that rails reached Columbia from the Branch-ville connection and at last denizens of the Capital City had an easy connection to the sea and to other parts of the Southeast. A through ocean-to-river route would have to wait until after the Civil War; the LC&C built only about 10 percent of its projected mileage before dissolving.

Once a rail line opened, citizens felt confident about the future. The rail connection, it was popularly assumed, guaranteed permanence, prosperity, and growth. No place of consequence could possibly exist beyond the sound of a screeching locomotive whistle. No wonder the editor of the first newspaper published in Oklahoma Territory, the *Guthrie Get Up,* proclaimed in the inaugural issue of April 29, 1889: "WANTED – MORE RAILROADS." He inserted these heartfelt words under the front-page masthead; no one could miss this sentiment.

The response might be personal. When the Burlington & Missouri River Railroad reached Jefferson County, Iowa, on the eve of the Civil War, a Batavia resident wrote his brother in Lane County, Oregon, about the wonderful impact of having easy access to rails. "Our railroad is now Completed and the Cars are roling a Long in Splendor and not only the Looks, But all heavy freight Such as Salt & Iron or any other heavy Articles is much Cheaper than formerly & in fact our groceries & everything we have to buy is Cheaper, generally Speaking. And if we have anything to Sell it brings the Cash right at home." He continued with his flawed prose. "But this is a Progressive age for Little did you & me think that we could here the Iron Horse come snorting along when we Located in Iowa, but such are the facts and that beyond dispute."

Excitement is in the air as the first Chicago & North Western Railway passenger train enters Lander, Wyoming. In 1906 the company reached this rail-starved section of the state. Although the line never advanced further west, officials contemplated an extension to the Pacific Ocean, perhaps the Oregon coast.

Author's coll.

For many Americans receiving rails it was a time for community re-joicing. Throughout the construction years, this jubilation never disap-peared, albeit some places "went all out" to celebrate. These commemora-tions occurred widely; no section missed out on these joyous occasions.

Just as residents of Columbia, South Carolina, had celebrated the commencement of construction on their rail outlet, they did not miss the opportunity to cheer the arrival of the first steam cars. "A splendid barbe-cue was given at Columbia on the 28th of June to welcome the arrival of Charleston at Columbia by the opening of the rail road between these two cities," reported the *Niles' Register* in a communication of July 30, 1842. "Upon landing from the cars, the citizens of our town, with the rifle corps, the dragoons and the Charleston light infantry, were filed off to receive our city guests (the city officials of Charleston, the president and directors of the railroad companies, and citizens of Charleston generally)." Follow-ing a spate of prayers and speeches, the visiting dignitaries got the royal treatment. "The volunteer companies received and escorted [them] to the table, where a temperate and earnest discussion took place on Congaree mutton, Berkshire pigs, and Durham veal. A variety of wines and liquors were spread upon the board. In the evening many social private parties were given. The number of persons present on this occasion is estimated at between 4,000 and 5,000."

Opening festivities often involved more than one community, just as Charlestonians participated in the Columbia celebration. When the Western Rail Road of Massachusetts completed its line between Bos-ton and Albany, New York, Albany boosters invited Boston "fathers" to celebrate the event. On December 27, 1841, the Bostonians and guests from Springfield and several other communities along the route rode a special train to Albany, where their hosts met and escorted them to their overnight lodgings. The following day these out-of-towners received a formal welcome at City Hall and enjoyed a festive dinner at Stanwix Hall. "Congratulatory speeches were made but amongst them was a letter read by Governor [William] Seward, written in 1662 in which the Governor of New York proposed to the Governor of Massachusetts the establishing of a monthly post rider service between Boston and New York (state)." Not to be outdone, the Boston delegation extended an invitation to the Old Bay State. Two days later, another special train carried about 250 Albany "gentlemen" to Boston, where they toured the city and celebrated with dignitaries at a grand banquet held in the United States Hotel. "Boston outdid herself for it was not until the last day of the year that the western delegates returned to Albany" and probably somewhat worse for wear.

An all-so-familiar celebration took place on May 18, 1854, in the Wisconsin capital of Madison. With the official opening of the Milwau-kee & Mississippi Railroad scheduled for the following day, hordes of

Madisonians and those from Milwaukee and other locales flocked to the city. "We should judge that at least two thousand people from the country were about the Depot, and at the end of the bridge where the railroad crosses the bay. Bright colored parasols ranged in groups along the shore lent liveliness to the scene," reported the *Wisconsin State Journal*. "At length the unmistakable whistle of the engine was heard, and the long train with two locomotives at its head swept grandly into sight – thirty-two cars, crowded with people. At the rear of the train were several racks occupied by the Milwaukee Fire Companies in their gay red uniforms with their glistening engines. A fine band of music attended them, and, at intervals as they slowly moved across the bridge, the piece of artillery brought along by the firemen was discharged."

County histories, popular during the Gilded Age and after, regularly contained a chapter on railroads, and this formulaic approach related memorable events that involved the arrival of the steam car. When William W. Davis wrote his *History of Whiteside County, Illinois,* published in 1908, he covered the arrival in July 1855 at Sterling of the self-proclaimed Dixon Air Line (later Chicago & North Western Railway). The monster gala was surely long remembered, and the account likely rekindled pleasant memories.

Residents of Sterling, a village situated on the expansive prairies of western Illinois, decided to make the "welkin ring." Explained Davis: "Simeon Coe furnished a three-year old ox, which was roasted on a primitive arrangement of forked sticks, and then borne in triumph, bedecked with flags and oranges, to an immense arbor of branches near the present Central school." There was more: "After the banquet B. F. Taylor, the poet, made a flowery address. The lion of the day was [U.S. Senator] Stephen A. Douglas, who talked to the masses in his own earnest style. Estimates of the multitude ran as high as five thousand." Special and regularly scheduled trains disgorged hundreds of visitors, who came from surrounding towns and villages; some made the journey from Chicago, 110 miles to the east. The railroad spurred growth, and within less than two years Sterling won incorporation as a municipality.

Also likely to occur, particularly during the antebellum decades, were celebrations that commemorated special betterments. Examples often took place during the Demonstration Period, when excitement about any new railroad or railroad improvement captured public attention and adulation. On October 3, 1839, residents of New York City expressed their joy when the New York & Harlem Railroad, a horse-powered (later steam) carrier that had opened eight years earlier, completed the double-tracking of its line "from the centre of the city, to the extent of their limits – Harlem river." At a municipal park on the Harlem River, food, drink, and speeches from an assortment of dignitaries drew the citizenry. One toast went this way: "The New York and Harlem railroad – Uniting the extremes of the city of New York into one common ward; equalizing property over the whole island; affecting healthful abodes to the industrious and frugal, in place of miserable habitations in the narrow and impure streets of the lower wards." The pronouncement closed with these words: "It is at once the poor man's carriage and the working man's hackney coach."

A community, though, might not have a "blow-out." Still, a jubilant pronouncement in the press inevitably appeared. In October 1866 rails of the westward advancing Burlington & Missouri River Railroad reached the transportation-starved seat of Monroe County, Iowa, Albia, and the town's newspaper, the *Union,* commented about the arrival of the first locomotive. "On Monday the construction train of the B. & M. R. R. came into town. This is the advent so long and so patiently looked for by our citizens, and we are almost tempted, in our enthusiasm to exclaim, 'Now let thy servant depart in peace, for we have beheld the glory of the Iron Horse.'" The editor added tongue-in-cheek, "We are now connected with the Atlantic sea-board by rail, and we congratulate the cities of Boston and New York, on their fortune in having communications with the growing city of Albia."

Three years after Albians welcomed the iron horse, the most remembered of all railroad completion celebrations took place. On the remote, high desert at Promontory, Utah Territory, the entire country rejoiced with the wedding of the rails of the "Great Pacific Road." At that parched, windswept location, which potentially could have become a permanent settlement, a cheery crowd of onlookers gathered on the morning of May 10, 1869, to watch the final ties, rails, and spikes placed on the dirt grade, commemorating the nation's first transcontinental railroad. The Union Pacific Railroad, which began at Council Bluffs, Iowa, on the east bank of Missouri River opposite Omaha, Nebraska, had built the eastern section, and the Central Pacific Railroad, which started in Sacramento, California, on the Sacramento River, had completed the shorter, albeit more challenging, western portion.

The marriage of the East with the West involved much that was memorable. There were the two polished American-standard (4-4-0) locomotives, the No. 60, *Jupiter,* owned by the Central Pacific, and No. 119, the iron horse of the Union Pacific. Chief among railroad dignitaries were Leland Stanford, one of the "Big Four" organizers of the Central Pacific, and Dr. Thomas Clark Durant, a leading force behind the Union Pacific. There were others, including a variety of railroad directors and builders; A. J. Russell, official photographer for the Union Pacific; members of the Ogden, Utah, Tenth Ward Band; soldiers of the 21st U.S. Infantry and its regimental band; and various federal, state, territorial, and municipal officials. Not to be overlooked were scores of veteran Chinese laborers from the Central Pacific, who had endured the dangers and hardships of building through the Sierra Nevada Mountains, and hard-callused Irish construction workers from the Union Pacific. These Irishmen and their compatriots were known for their rowdiness in their rough-and-tumble work camps that adjoined those infamous "Hell-on-Wheels" end-of-tracks saloons, brothels, and gambling joints. And they surely appreciated that at the Promontory ceremony "oratory and whisky flowed in almost equal measure." Then there were the cherished mementoes, including a ceremonial tie that bore a silver identification plate and the several famed spikes. One spike contained eighteen ounces of pure gold and bore this inscription: "May God continue the unity of our Country as this Railroad unites the two great Oceans of the World." Another spike, which consisted of iron, silver, and gold, came with this proclamation by the governor of Arizona Territory: "Ribbed with iron, clad in silver and crowned with gold, Arizona presents her offering to the enterprise that has spanned the Continent and dictated the pathway to commerce."

Countless Americans eagerly awaited news of the ceremony. After all, there existed the widespread belief that this engineering feat exceeded any human enterprise since the building of the Egyptian pyramids. And the public was able to celebrate at the exact time of the glorious union. Arrangements had been made for the telegraph to announce almost instantly when the spiking occurred. A telegraph wire to the east over the Union Pacific and beyond had been wrapped around the last spike, and another wire, connected to the Central Pacific's telegraph line, had been attached to the silver maul that Stanford would use. The telegraph was so configured that in every city with fire-alarm telegraphs the driving of the much-anticipated spike would be "heard." Residents of such places as Boston, Chicago, New Orleans, New York, Omaha, Philadelphia, and Washington, D.C., were ready to cheer when the fire-alarm bells rang. Thousands also assembled at Western Union offices to wait for their gongs to sound. If they wanted the message; it was amazingly simple: "Done," the word sent by W. N. Shilling, the Western Union telegrapher. While admittedly held in an isolated location, the "golden spike" event became truly public; Americans throughout the land participated.

There would be other community-celebrated spike-driving events, and they involved both large and small projects. In most cases where a last-spike ceremony occurred, the union took place far beyond corporate limits. Still the event excited residents in nearby places and drew the attention of others, especially those associated with the triumphant railroad. Such was the case of the meeting of the rails for the last northern transcontinental road, the Chicago, Milwaukee & St. Paul Railway (Milwaukee Road), which occurred on May 19, 1909, near the western Montana hamlet of Garrison.

Early in the twentieth century, leaders of the sprawling, financially robust Milwaukee Road decided that their company could profitably tap the traffic to and from the Pacific Northwest by extending a line from South Dakota to Washington state and could compete successfully with the Great Northern and Northern Pacific, the other two northern transcontinentals. In 1905 the Milwaukee Road incorporated subsidiaries in the states to be served by its "Pacific Coast Extension," and three years later recast them into a larger satellite firm, the Chicago, Milwaukee & Puget Sound Railway.

At a distance of more than 1,400 miles and at a cost that exceeded $225 million [$5.5 billion in 2010 dollars], the rails were completed, and a spiking event took place. "The scene of this interesting incident was just a mile and a half east of the historic sport where the golden spike of the Northern Pacific was driven a quarter century ago," reported a Missoula, Montana, newspaperman. "There was not, however, the formal ceremony attendant upon yesterday's affair that characterized the event which Henry Villard made so dramatic when the Northern Pacific was completed." But notwithstanding the unexpected death of a leading Milwaukee Road investor, recent floods, and the strategy of building the new transcontinental in sections rather than from one or both ends, the railroad recognized its impressive accomplishment. On a warm mid-May

day a special train, whose onboard passengers included railroad officials, civic leaders, and journalists, journeyed out of Missoula toward the designated spot, approximately 70 miles to the east. Unlike events at Promontory, there were no prolonged, organized activities. "The last rail lay on the ties, ready to be swung into place," wrote an onlooker. "There was no time lost. Roadmaster Nick gave the word to the track foreman; the rail was pushed into place at 2:06 and was quickly spiked to the ties. At 2:21 the last spike was handled by Division Superintendent to Nick." After he swung the hammer five times – missing once – the spike was securely in place. Later that day construction workers, who included both American and Japanese laborers, celebrated, and the more than 12,000 residents of Missoula basked in the limelight of a nationally, indeed internationally, reported event.

The same year that the Milwaukee Road completed its Pacific Coast Extension, the opening of the 14-mile Hooppole, Yorktown & Tampico Railroad led to an end-of-track gala in Hooppole, Illinois, that featured food, drink, and a spike-driving. Residents of the heretofore isolated farming communities of Hooppole and Yorktown were exuberant about achieving a rail connection with the Burlington at Tampico. "The program called for a gold spike to be driven by [Mayor] John Daley of Hooppole," noted a writer in 1940. "Thrifty tillers of the soil resented the use

A big celebration it is not, but nonetheless significant. The event is the driving of the last spike in the construction of the Great Northern Railway between Lake Superior and Puget Sound. This action occurred on January 6, 1893, in the western Cascade country.

Don L. Hofsommer Coll.

of a trinket so costly as a gold spike and when the celebration began, they were vastly relieved to find it was only a bit of rusty iron covered with gilt." But a "golden spike" it was for farmers and villagers; at last these folks had a railroad.

A celebratory event might not find its way into a county history or another historical publication, but newspapers, local and at times from a distance, inevitably described how a community welcomed the iron horse. The Promontory model was not always followed, taking place in only a small minority of line completions. Yet a recognition of some sort nearly always occurred.

In the year following the joining of the Union Pacific and Central Pacific, which had triggered so much national excitement, another public welcoming took place in Los Angeles, California, sans prayers, speeches, and special spikes. Citizens of the little adobe town and their neighbors took delight in having the first railroad in their part of the Golden State. On October 26, 1870, the tiny Los Angeles & San Pedro Railroad, which extended from the deepwater port at Upper San Pedro Bay (Wilmington) to the intersection of Alameda and Commercial streets in Los Angeles, was ready, and so promoters invited the public to take a complimentary trip. Many did. "It was a hot dusty, bumpy ride, because the company had to use just about all the rolling stock it had, but no one minded, and the fifteen hundred excursionists had a fine time." When the riders returned to Los Angeles, the new depot was the setting for a "victory" ball, and "everyone stampeded for the affair." A few days later the railroad officially opened for regular freight and passenger operations, continuing to please residents.

A decade later a variation of the Los Angeles celebration took place in Cincinnati, Ohio, with activities tied to the completion of the Cincinnati Southern Railway, the nation's foremost municipally sponsored railroad. In order to enhance the economic powers of the "Queen City of the West," mostly to capture trade lost to other Ohio River cities, particularly Louisville, Kentucky, businessmen and politicians used public funds to construct a 336-mile road that stretched southward from Cincinnati to Chattanooga, Tennessee, itself a growing railroad center. The building process proved to be massive, requiring 27 tunnels and 105 bridges that included the road's signature structure, a 5,100-foot-long span over the Ohio River.

In early 1880, following six years of construction, the Cincinnati Southern was finally finished, and Cincinnatians were ready to celebrate. On March 18, 1880, "the largest banquet ever spread in the United States, up to that date was given by the citizens of Cincinnati at the Music Hall." While prominent residents gathered at the food-laden tables, "not less than seventeen hundred and seventy-six Southern men, leading merchants, manufacturers, politicians, governors and other invited guests sat down to this magnificent feast." Speeches and toasts followed. In a lengthy presentation E. A. Ferguson, a Cincinnati attorney who played a pivotal role in creating the southern link, proudly told attendees, "You have seen its graceful trestles, easy curves, nowhere a single reverse one, its low grades and substantial permanent way – this marvel of the engineer's skill in linking nature to civilization. The road has been made, and it will stand." Ferguson was correct, and the Cincinnati Southern bolstered the area economy and made money for city coffers, being leased to other carriers and ultimately entering the orbit of the Norfolk Southern Railroad.

A version of the Cincinnati happenings took place with completion of the Atlantic Northern & Southern Railway (AN&S), a dramatically smaller and far less successful achievement. In December 1910 townspeople of Grant, Iowa, at last had a railroad. The freshly built, 54-mile AN&S gave residents connections with two east–west trunk carriers. At Atlantic, on the north, it interchanged with the Chicago, Rock Island & Pacific Railroad (Rock Island) and at Villisca, on the south, with the Burlington. It was on Christmas Day 1910 that a construction gang of 200 men reached Grant from the north. "The good people of the town conceived and executed the idea of giving them a 'big feed' in the Masonic Hall. There were 250 at the banquet spread most of whom were railroad men who enjoyed good appetites and showed their appreciation in more ways than one for the hospitality of Grant." Two days later another crew, which had been building north from Villisca, arrived in Grant and "another spread was given in the hall when fully 400 participated in the feasting, 200 being railroad men." Then something special happened. "At the close of the banquet C. A. Ross, one of the promoters and the consulting engineer of the road, presented to the city of Grant, on behalf of the crew and in appreciation of the hospitality and the loyalty of the town, a beautiful silver loving cup, about a foot in height and bearing an inscription as follows: 'From the south end construction crew to the citizens of Grant, in memory of the loyalty in the completion of the A. N. & S. Ry., Atlantic to Villisca, Dec. 27, 1910.'" This cup, "the pride of all Grant people," soon received a place of prominence, decorating the window of the Carey Drug Store on Main Street.

The railroad made Grant a happy place. "It was apparent from all indications that Grant was in the throes of a magnificent joy-fest," opined a visiting journalist. "Everyone was whistling, or singing a song, and good spirits were unanimous." That unabated cheerfulness, however, soon disappeared; the AN&S was doomed to a mayfly existence. The road quickly fell into a court-ordered receivership, a reorganization as the Atlantic

Southern Railway failed, and within a few years workers removed the rails, ties, and others salvageable materials and the right-of-way either reverted to the adjoining property owners or was sold.

Several decades after the Atlantic, Northern & Southern reached Grant, residents of Colorado and elsewhere learned of the festivities associated with the completion of the Dotsero Cutoff, a major private-sector betterment during the Great Depression. What took place at Bond, Colorado, a railroad junction and service center 129 miles west of Denver, was the celebration of the 37-mile mountainous cutoff that reduced the rail distance between Denver and Salt Lake City by nearly 175 miles, creating the strategic "Moffat Tunnel Route." Construction, which began in November 1932, was completed in June 1934.

The Denver & Rio Grande Western Railroad (D&RGW), the builder, rightly wished to mark this important addition to the railroad map. Special trains brought hundreds of guests to this scenic, albeit remote spot, including the acclaimed diesel-powered *Zephyr* packed with well-wishers from the connecting Burlington. In keeping with established traditions, food was served, in this case a noon barbecue that featured "tender young Colorado beef," and speeches made. Unlike long-winded orators of the past, the presenters, who included two governors, two mayors, and several railroad presidents, kept their remarks brief, averaging about five minutes each. Instead of dignitaries driving the final spikes, a train run-by took place, featuring a muscular D&RGW freight locomotive and a short string of shiny box cars. Reflecting modern technology, CBS and NBC broadcasters provided live coverage, and newsreel cameramen captured the event for movie audiences. Print journalists attended, and their reports appeared that evening or the following morning. This was positive news, and not another troubling story involving hard times or scary international events.

While they were not celebrations marking completion of a railroad artery, there were occasions when communities rejoiced at the regauging of the rails. Such an undertaking might involve changing the thousands of miles of antebellum 5-foot gauge to the standard gauge of 4'8½", as it did throughout much of the South in the 1880s, or it might focus on standardizing narrow-gauge lines, usually 3 feet in width. Between 1871 and 1883 a boom produced approximately 12,000 miles of narrow-gauge trackage. Notwithstanding the alleged advantages of these slim pikes, the feeling grew that the best service and rates could be achieved with standardized trackage linking a community to the larger railroad network.

In the late 1870s and early 1880s a major narrow-gauge road, Connotton Valley Railroad (later Cleveland & Canton Railroad), connected Cleveland, Ohio, with the towns of Coschocton and Sherrodsville to the south. Although the Connotton Valley possessed a competitive route, with a good entrance into Cleveland, and a better-than-average physical plant for a narrow-gauge road, financial difficulties and the need to interchange physically with standard-gauge carriers led management to abandon the narrow width. On November 22, 1888, residents of the growing industrial city of Canton honored the accomplishment. A fancy, printed program, *The Cleveland & Canton Railroad Co. NARROW GAUGE NO MORE!*, listed a host of scheduled events, including an "Industrial Parade, Balloon Ascension and Parachute Jump" and noontime dinners at the Barnett House and Hurford House. The honored guest was Hiram Blood, the Boston financier who controlled the company and the individual, according to the *Canton Evening Repository,* "to whose indefatigable enterprise and energy the change of the road from narrow to standard gauge is to be credited." Before an assembled group at Schaefer's Opera House in the afternoon, Blood thanked the 1,500 laborers who "last Sunday made the change in gauge," and lauded the prospects of his reconfigured road. It was a day for Cantonians to remember. "The business houses and blocks were profusely decorated with flags and bright colored bunting and the city generally was arranged in a holiday attire. Many business houses were closed, the school children were granted a half-holiday, shops generally shut down and excursion trains brought in hundreds of visitors, over one hundred coming from Cleveland alone."

Long after the railroad map had been completed and gauges had been made standard, and with line abandonments ongoing, celebrations that commemorated much earlier events gained public attention. During and immediately after World War II railroads prospered, and the industry demonstrated an optimistic frame of mind. This widespread confidence manifested itself in various ways, most notably when leading passenger carriers ordered diesel-electric locomotives and hundreds of streamlined cars with the expectation that they could regain traffic lost to automobiles and generate new business. Some companies took advantage of discretionary funds to recognize an important anniversary. These were usually roads that traced their origins to the mid-nineteenth century, when the railroad network began its first major wave of expansion. Perhaps there might have been a notable achievement or something else in the past that seemed worthy of publicizing.

The idea of a railroad-sponsored history celebration was hardly new. Industry veterans recalled how the Baltimore & Ohio Railroad (B&O) had commemorated its claim as "the pioneer railroad of the country" with a year-long one-hundredth anniversary party held outside Baltimore in 1927. The Fair of the Iron Horse – officially the Centenary Exhibition and Pageant of the Baltimore & Ohio Railroad – attracted more than 1.3 million visitors. The public applauded the grounds, exhibits, and pageant performances that as many as 12,000 attendees viewed daily from the 800-foot-long grandstand. A highlight for many was the assemblage of the historic steam locomotives *Atlantic, William Mason,* and *Thatcher Perkins,* showing the evolution of motive power during the previous century. It was a grand birthday party.

In the post–World War II era, some railroads that lacked a specific event to commemorate joined with the Chicago & North Western Railway (North Western) to mark the centennial of the arrival of the iron horse in Chicago. The Chicago Railroad Fair of 1948–1949, spearheaded by the publicity department of the North Western, allowed the company to bring attention to the first railroad in the Windy City and its train powered by the tiny *Pioneer,* a locomotive owned by predecessor Galena & Chicago Union Rail Road (now displayed at the Chicago History Museum). The North Western and thirty-five other participating railroads produced a well-orchestrated event. The fair exceeded all expectations; more than 2.5 million visitors flocked to the site along Lake Michigan. The resounding success led to a continuation of the celebration the following summer, and once again large crowds enjoyed displays, programs, and other attractions.

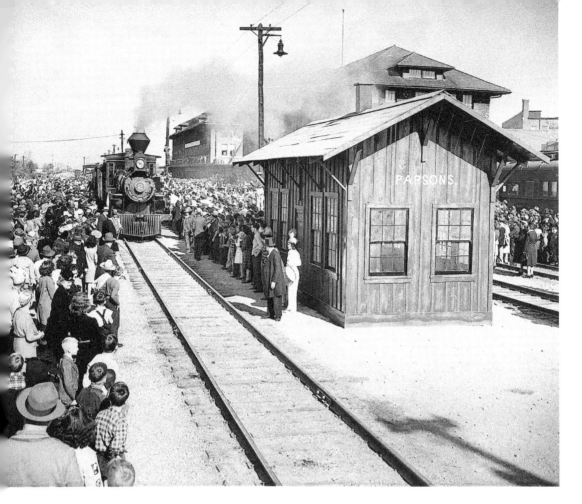

Much different from what the B&O and the North Western did with their respective "railroad fairs," the Erie celebrated the opening in 1851 of its original, core New-York & Erie Railroad "Ocean to the Lakes" artery by dispatching a special train to retrace the historic 446-mile route and staging on-line community events. This first rail connection between the Atlantic Ocean and the Great Lakes (Lake Erie) was ballyhooed as "A Milestone in American History," and no one challenged that claim.

On the morning of May 14, 1951, "four beautiful young damsels all clad in the most voluminous hoop-skirts of gay colors, vogue in the year 1851" met several hundred guests of the Erie who gathered at Manhattan's Pier 20 on the Hudson River. After a boat journey upriver to Piermont, the initial eastern terminus, a large crowd gathered in an open area near the depot to hear actors dramatize the historic nature of the occasion. Then the entourage departed Piermont for Elmira, New York. For part of the trip the train consisted of an assortment of equipment, including the *Thatcher Perkins,* borrowed from the B&O and mounted on a flatcar, and another flatcar with a rocking chair for the "Mr. Webster" impersonator. (On that celebratory trip a century before, Secretary of State Daniel Webster had demanded a rocker so that he might comfortably view, without

The Missouri-Kansas-Texas (Katy) Railway wished to publicize its seventy-fifth anniversary. On May 29, 1945, the arrival in Parsons, Kansas, of "old No. 2," a replica of the first Katy locomotive, touched off a week-long celebration. A crowd of fifteen thousand welcomes the special as it pulls near a re-creation of the community's first depot. The brick division headquarters building stands in the background.

Author's coll.

any obstructions, the passing scenery.) During the first day of the excursion, which included stops at Spring Valley, Suffern, Middletown, Port Jervis, and Deposit, New York, and Susquehanna, Pennsylvania, excited crowds waited to greet the special. Schools and businesses closed so that everyone could experience the spectacle of speeches, reenactments, and historic and modern equipment. At the close of "that splendid day" the train tied up in Elmira, and that evening a dinner was held for the invited at the Mark Twain Hotel. "Everybody who is anybody was there."

The second day featured another busy schedule. After a breakfast for guests, the train departed from the Elmira station for the original end-of-track, Dunkirk, on the shores of Lake Erie. Before the special reached its destination, it paused at Hornell, Wellsville, Olean, and Salamanca, with large crowds and repeated orations. In Salamanca a Seneca chief initiated the Erie president into the tribe and presented him with "an Indian war bonnet complete with feathers." The assembled multitudes loved the Native American touch. But in the early evening the climax of the two-day journey began in Dunkirk. Train guests joined an assembly of residents and those from the surrounding areas, including Buffalo, estimated at

In the summers of 1948 and 1949 the largest railroad fair in American history took place. Spearheaded by the Chicago & North Western, other carriers joined the celebrations on the Chicago lakefront, including the Baltimore & Ohio. The "Wheels a-Rolling" pageant became the signature event of this well-attended affair.

Author's coll.

"Wheels a-Rolling"

A THRILLING PAGEANT of RAILROAD HISTORY

—hailed by critics throughout America as the greatest spectacle of the decade. The story of the nation's dramatic rise from an unknown wilderness to its present might—packed into 70 minutes of stirring action—every minute portraying another colorful epoch in transportation progress. Attended in 1948 by well over a million spectators from all over the country. Produced in a great outdoor theater with a cast of 240 and a stage 450 feet wide. Shows four times daily—2:00, 4:00, 7:00 and 9:00 p.m. Seats for 6,000, each performance.

Before your eyes—a Wild West stage coach hold-up.

The railroad "iron horse," Tom Thumb, again races Old Dobbin.

Ride... See... America's Most Famous Trains

more than twenty thousand, for a "real blowout," featuring speeches, music, food and a parade. Finally, about 10:00 PM, festivities ended and most guests returned to their assigned Pullman cars for the overnight return trip to New York City.

While the Erie commemorative trip across the Empire State marked a positive historical occasion and was universally lighthearted, saddened citizens might gather at stations to witness the end of passenger service or to watch the last train leave town. Usually these somber affairs were

In 1951 the Erie Railroad, flush with funds following World War II, commemorated the centennial of the opening of its core route between the Hudson River and Lake Erie. In May the well-publicized Erie special attracts large audiences in such places as Wellsville and Salamanca, New York. Actor Dallas Boyd, who portrayed Daniel Webster in the reenactment of the original celebration, is a smash hit. Onlookers, too, enjoy pieces of old and new equipment.

Author's coll.

It's a wintry day in 1945 when the last Burlington Railroad freight train leaves Van Wert, Iowa, on the mostly to-be-abandoned branch line between Humeston and Clarinda, Iowa. This photograph, taken from the rear of the caboose, shows a friendly crowd of schoolchildren waving their goodbyes.

Don Ultang photograph, State Historical Society of Iowa

unorganized, but interested persons – members of rail enthusiasts' groups, perhaps a chapter of the National Railway Historical Society, local historical societies, or history-conscious individuals – notified residents through newspapers, radio broadcasts, or personal contacts that an end-of-an-era event was about to take place. Most of these happenings were simple affairs. When the last Burlington train departed Van Wert, Iowa, on the soon-to-be-abandoned trackage between Humeston and Clarinda, Iowa, in December 1945, about twenty-five Ellston grade-school children and their teacher, joined by the depot agent, watched and waved to trainmen on their farewell trip to the West.

TOWNS

The bidders of hearty goodbyes to the crew of the last train to steam westward from Humeston, Iowa, probably did not know that several generations earlier the railroad had led to the creation of this farming community. In 1872 a satellite of the Burlington, building south from the main line at Chariton, pushed through the area on its way to St. Joseph,

Missouri, providing what a county history writer said was "the occasion of Humeston's coming into existence as a village."

For a century railroads played a phenomenal role in urban making and expansion. This was not surprising. Thousands of places had traced their origins to water arteries, whether natural or manmade. As the *American Railroad Journal* put it in 1837: "The Genius of [lakes, rivers, and canals] waved her wand, and towns, villages, and cities sprang up as by enchantment – churches and institutions of learning were reared where once stood the wigwam and the Indian." When the 308-mile Ohio & Erie Canal was built between Lake Erie and the Ohio River in the late 1820s and early 1830s, it gave rise to settlements whose names reflected their origins: Canal Fulton, Canal Dover, Millersport, and Port Washington. As with later railroad places, citizens of these canal communities held great expectations, hoping that travel would be easier and shipping costs lower.

When railroads appeared in long-settled regions, they also spawned towns, usually at important junctions or developing trade, mining, or manufacturing centers. In 1904 Henry Gassaway Davis established "not a naturally located community" at Gassaway, West Virginia, to serve as the midway division point for his newly constructed Coal & Coke Railway that stretched 175 miles between Charleston and Elkins, West Virginia. The place took hold and quickly won incorporation, but it did not fit the way that public roads ran, being designed solely for the directional orientation of Davis's mineral-hauling railroad. Earlier, in the 1870s, a writer of a promotional book for the Delaware, Lackawanna & Western Railroad

When the wreckers come to remove rails and other salvable materials, there is little community interest. Yet a lad watches as a wrecking crew lift rails of that Burlington line in Weldon, Iowa, 13 miles west of Humeston.

Author's coll.

mentioned the recently established town of Huntly, New Jersey, only 22 miles from New York City and in a region that had been settled since colonial times. "This is one of the latest creations in the shape of a town on the road. First appears a station, then a house; then some fine day the sleepy traveler opens his eyes and is astonished to find a village. A store follows, then a church; first the body then a soul."

In some ways an "accidental" legacy of railroad construction led to the establishment of a settlement, whether in a populated area or not. As building progressed along a projected route, construction camps, which popped up at intervals, were usually ephemeral. When work was completed, the tents, prefabricated structures, or bunk cars moved elsewhere, although the railroad might place at the site a piece of rolling stock for train-control or maintenance purposes. Or the place might again become vacant. Yet such a location might be appropriate for town creation.

One such example took place in 1913 as the Rock Island built a 65-mile cutoff connection between Allerton and Carlyle, Iowa. Along the marked survey the contractor selected a location in eastern Warren County for a camp to accommodate his graders, trackmen, and other workers and named the place Beech. Since there were no rival villages nearby and the site was on what emerged as the major north–south artery between Minneapolis and Kansas City, a permanent settlement took shape (with the blessings of the Rock Island). Beech served the adjoining farming area until automobiles and trucks diminished its economic viability.

Railroads also sparked expansion of existing communities, at times stimulated by their own support operations. Burlington, Iowa, the former territorial capital, was already a flourishing Mississippi River town before the rails of the Burlington arrived from Chicago in 1855. With the iron horse Burlington grew impressively, energized by the opening of a shops facility. Then in 1880 the railroad removed the complex to the western edge of the city, allowing room for much-needed expansion. The relocation sparked creation of an adjoining townsite, West Burlington, the project of the West Burlington Land Company. Following establishment of West Burlington in 1884, that community thrived. Six years later the *Railway Master Mechanic* called the place a "Model Workingmen's Village." Its population of more than one thousand included roughly three-quarters of the seven hundred men employed in the railroad shops.

In the case of DeKalb, Illinois, 60 miles west of Chicago, the appearance over time of three steam railroads, first the North Western, later the Chicago Great Western (Great Western), and finally the "Rockford Route," initially the Illinois, Iowa & Minnesota Railroad but soon reorganized as the Chicago, Milwaukee & Gary Railway, led to sustained growth. Even the last steam road to serve DeKalb, which arrived in 1904, sparked impressive economic development, including a piano factory, expansion of a wire plant, and several residential additions. "DeKalb has been growing so fast of late years," editorialized the *DeKalb Evening Chronicle*, "that people have grown to expect a whirl here all the time." Three railroads fostered public confidence by bringing tangible economic improvements.

Hundreds of railroad-spawned towns sprouted at trackside and were far more common than most Americans realized. As the English visitor Anthony Trollope put it: "With us railways run to the towns; but in the States the towns run to the railways." Although communities commonly sprang up where rails preceded settlement, being spaced at regular intervals of from 5 to 15 miles apart, they also popped up in established areas. Cardiff, Tennessee; Hamlet, North Carolina; Hope, Arkansas; Kankakee, Illinois; Miami, Florida; Port Arthur, Texas; and Texarkana, Arkansas/Texas, for example, share a railroad-birthed heritage. Once more the time period lasted for a century, continuing long after the U. S. superintendent of the census in 1893 announced the closure of the frontier and Frederick Jackson Turner speculated before fellow historians on the impact that free or inexpensive lands had on shaping the American character: democracy, individualism, materialism, nationalism, optimism, and that desire to "move about."

Town making kept railroad officials busy. As Arthur Stilwell, founder of the Kansas City Southern and the Kansas City, Mexico & Orient railroads, after whom Port Arthur, Texas, is named, recalled in an autobiographical essay, "The buying of townsites, laying them out, naming the principal streets after the directors of the road or my friends, and booming these newly found communities as desirable places for people to locate, constituted no small part of my work." Yet these men knew the importance of such activities. In 1859 Charles Lowell, head of the land department of the Burlington said it well: "We are beginning to find that he who buildeth a railroad west of the Mississippi must also find a population and build up business." About a decade later General Grenville Dodge, chief engineer of the Union Pacific, expressed a similar sentiment: "The first object in building up towns should be to bring business to the road, settlement of the adjacent lands, and the encouraging of permanent improvements in the town." He believed that "the establishment of lumber and coal yards at the best locations for towns will add vastly to the sale and settlement of our lands, especially if special rates should be given for both as the great drawback now is the want of *fuel* and *lumber*."

The excitement of new towns, including lot sales, often offered at public auction, took place over vast areas, especially in the trans-Chicago West, and for decades was ongoing. As late as the 1920s such events still occurred. The Electric Short Line Railroad, known as the Luce Line after the father-son promoters William and Erle Luce, developed several towns

There is plenty of activity at the newly established town of Libby, Montana. On May 3, 1892, rails of the Northern Pacific arrived, and it is not long thereafter that this photograph of the railroad corridor was taken.

Don L. Hofsommer coll.

as this non-interurban (but using both gasoline and steam motive power) built west from Minneapolis. Traditional lot sales, boosterism, and optimism were part of the town-development mix.

In 1923 a product of urbanization on the Luce Line happened at Cosmos, situated on the rolling wheat lands of Meeker County, Minnesota, as construction workers headed toward South Dakota from Hutchinson. On June 28, 1923, a BIG AUCTION SALE OF COSMOS TOWNSITE LOTS. THE BIG NEW TOWN ON THE ELECTRIC SHORT LINE RAILWAY EXTENSION, sponsored by the Interurban Development Company of Minneapolis, took place. This Luce-controlled firm employed a hard-sell approach. "Many will double and treble their money by buying at this sale. Investors made thousands of dollars in the early days buying lots on the west extensions of railway lines, and you will be able to do better there where money is plentiful. Don't tell your children in years to come you could have bought lots in COSMOS, but show them your profits by buying at this AUCTION SALE." The townsite company reminded readers that "Nicollet avenue land [in Minneapolis] could be bought at $40 an acre at one time; now it cannot be bought for $6,000 a running foot; same in proportion in many good Minnesota towns, with not the same chance that COSMOS has." Prospective buyers were told that "all streets have been graded and arrangements for 1,000 trees have been made to beautify the City of COSMOS." Two years later another "valuable lot" sale occurred.

"These lots are all located south of the railroad tracks on Main Street and by the school. ALL THE FREE WATERMELON YOU CAN EAT. COME EARLY AS AT 1 P.M. A VALUABLE PRIZE WILL BE GIVEN THE ONE WHO CAN EAT A LARGE MELON FIRST. Both sales went well; the village grew, and on July 21, 1925, the weekly *Cosmos News* made its debut and continued to champion the community. "Since the advent of the railroad, Cosmos has made rapid growth and the necessity for a newspaper to keep up the good work was beginning to be felt," wrote the publisher in the inaugural issue. For years Cosmos maintained a rather stable population of several hundred residents and effectively served nearby farmers and their families.

Cosmos would not be the only important Luce Line town. As Cosmos took on cosmopolitan airs, the arrival of the rails gave birth to Lake Lillian in 1923. Located on the south shore of a beautiful prairie lake, 9 miles west of Cosmos, the place benefited when the businessmen of Thorpe, a nearby inland village, relocated to Lake Lillian, leaving that settlement but a speck on the map. "Thorpe will move bodily, taking the creamery, the bank and every other business institution with them," reported an area newspaper. The Thorpe State Bank became the First State Bank of Lake Lillian, and this financial institution immediately flourished. The community saw increased public activities with the building of a school, establishment of a post office, and formation of the First Lutheran Church. Like Cosmos, Lake Lillian got its own newspaper, the *Lake Lillian Echo,* which began weekly publication in March 1926.

The Luce Line had made Lake Lillian. The remarkable growth of the community prompted the *Echo* editor to reflect: "Picture an ordinary country-side with nothing save growing grain, meadow grass, gophers and muskrats to break the monotony of nothing and you have a view of Lake Lillian's townsite a little less than three years ago. Then the railroad came, buildings were moved in, and others erected new. Boom business was conducted in a dozen and more places." The editor closed with these thoughts: "Today we have over twenty-five different business places and enterprises in our thriving village. Last Thursday, village officers were elected, as a first step in the organization of a village council. Thus it is that Lake Lillian enters upon the roll of villages."

Not all railroad-created towns succeeded, instead failing to become that "New Philadelphia" or "New Chicago" or something far less grand. Some actually disappeared almost as soon as they appeared. When rails of the Eastern Division, Union Pacific Railroad (Kansas Pacific) were extended across the vast, open Kansas prairies soon after the Civil War, there were various end-of-track shack towns. One settlement, Coyote, consisted of "canvas saloons, sheet-iron hotels, and sod dwellings, surrounded by tin cans and scattered playing cards." Its principal street, with the memorable name of "Rat Row," served in 1868 as the center of life for the rough-and-tumble track laborers. "The Pacific railways have been responsible for more and worse towns than any other single cause," asserted a writer for *Harper's New Monthly Magazine* about these ephemeral places. "Every temporary terminus of track-laying became for the time being a city, wicked, wonderful and short-lived."

Over time other railroad-birthed towns withered away as economic changes made them irrelevant. Initially there was a wave of commercial and residential building and a general feeling of optimism. Residents expected that their town would become a successful trade center and that the iron horse would remain the dominant force in transportation. However, the impact of the automobile and truck and all-weather roads after 1920 commonly had adverse consequences, creating drastically altered conditions for retailing and marketing. The years of struggle caused by the Great Depression and extensive drought also had a negative impact, as did later changes in commodity marketing and the substantial decline in the number of farms and ranches. Places like Cottonwood, South Dakota; Denton, Georgia; Gluek (nee Grace Lake), Minnesota; Le Roy, Iowa; Mildred, Montana; and Myra, Texas, nearly vanished.

A railroad itself could diminish the vitality of a town that it had spawned. The case of Van Horne, Iowa, illustrates the impact of corporate decisions. In 1881 and 1882 when the Milwaukee Road built across the Hawkeye State to reach Omaha from Chicago, a number of communities took shape. One was Van Horne, named after the supervising engineer, William Van Horne (later the Canadian Pacific Railway executive and *Sir* William), which took shape in 1883 and grew rapidly, largely because the company made it a division point. In addition to the railroad erecting a two-story wooden depot, a twenty-stall roundhouse of limestone construction, and other supporting structures, the community experienced a building boom, including a stylish three-story frame hotel. Residents admired this first-class facility with its attractive dining room and lobby on the ground level, its twenty tastefully decorated rooms on the second floor, and its spacious ballroom on the top floor. What seemed to be a bright future for this Benton County community soon changed, however. The company discovered that the water, which came from a nearby reservoir, contained high levels of lime that adversely affected locomotive boiler performance. Nine years after the founding of Van Horne, the Milwaukee Road relocated the division point to Marion, 27 miles to the east. This "twin city" of Cedar Rapids soon became a small metropolis of note. Meanwhile Van Horne sputtered and never became more than a farming village. The town's pride and joy, the hotel, was reduced to ashes from sparks of a passing locomotive, and the roundhouse, no longer needed, was torn down and the limestone crushed to improve area roads.

There were sites that became much more prosperous than Van Horne. Railroads wanted their towns to blossom, enhancing freight and passenger revenues and functioning as places for effectively organizing traffic. There were hundreds of success stories. Company officials might do their best to make certain that specific towns got a special attraction or institution or won political "plums": county seat, land-grant or normal college, insane asylum, prison, or possibly the territorial or state capital.

The Louisville & Nashville Railroad (L&N) took keen interest in Lake De Funiak (later De Funiak Springs), Florida, located on the road's Pensacola–River Junction line in the panhandle region and named after L&N official Fred De Funiak. In the mid-1880s the railroad promoted the establishment of a seasonal Chautauqua Assembly, patterned after the original Chautauqua Institution, located on Lake Chautauqua, New York, and initially designed as a Sunday-school training place for Methodists, but soon expanded into an adult-learning center. "The anticipation of a busy town with an affluent growing population and a reputation for educational progress undoubtedly was the key to the fervent support given the Chautauqua," observed an historian of De Funiak Springs. "Increased population density would lead to increased land values and heightened use of railroad lines by both passengers and freight." For several decades this Chautauqua Assembly thrived, yet De Funiak Springs never became the town the L&N and boosters expected.

While there was no conflict about establishing a Chautauqua assembly, county-seat fights, on the other hand, flared widely. They centered on where the seats of government would be for newly organized counties, or they involved growing railroad towns wishing to capture courthouses from established seats, usually smaller places that lacked rail connections or had inferior railroad service.

Representative of courthouse battles was the one that raged between 1874 and 1888 in Rush County, Kansas. Two inland communities sought the coveted prize, Walnut City and a newer settlement, La Crosse, 5 miles to the north. Although Walnut City initially claimed this honor, a developing La Crosse forced a countywide election in 1877. Voters decided to move the seat, but unfortunately for La Crosse they rejected a bond issue for a courthouse and jail. Residents of Walnut City remained determined and forced another election. This time Walnut City won, although there were charges of ballot-box irregularities. After a legal battle, county records and officers returned to Walnut City, but more law suits followed, resulting in a legal victory for La Crosse. The struggle, though, continued and quickly focused on acquiring a rail line. In 1885 pro–La Crosse county commissioners denied the petition of Walnut City residents for a vote on a railroad subsidy bond issue, but they accepted a similar request from La Crosse. Walnut City wanted to commit $15,000 to the Walnut Valley

& Colorado Railroad, affiliated with the Atchison, Topeka & Santa Fe Railway (Santa Fe). La Crosse wished to contribute much more, $120,000 for the Kansas & Colorado Railroad, a satellite of the Missouri Pacific Railway (MOP). Ultimately Walnut City won the right to vote a subsidy, and the funds went to building this Santa Fe appendage, which reached the community in September 1886. The much larger tax subsidy was also approved, supporting construction of the main line of the MOP westward from Salina, Kansas, to Colorado Springs, Colorado. Then in February 1887 La Crosse gained this trackage with the best wishes of MOP official-dom. The presence of a major trunk artery strengthened La Crosse and increased the surrounding population. Even though additional court action ensued and still another election took place, this final contest, held in August 1887, made La Crosse the permanent county seat, ending the most vitriolic courthouse conflict in Kansas history. The defeated Walnut City dwindled in population and importance.

Usually the railroad town won, but not always. In the late nineteenth century a squabble broke out in Pulaski County, Missouri, over the county seat. Waynesville, the established center of government, lacked a railroad, and Crocker, situated on the main line of the St. Louis–San Francisco Railroad (Frisco) in the northern part of the county, sought the prize. In 1890 this village of about five hundred residents offered to donate real estate, arguing that it was "the more beautiful site for the Court House than any other town in Pulaski County," and committed five thousand dollars for construction of a stylish brick courthouse. Boosters went so far as to furnish a set of architectural plans. They also launched a newspaper, *The County Seat Removal Advocate,* in which they presented arguments why Crocker should be county seat. "Why is land cheaper in Pulaski county than it is in Phelps and Laclede counties?" asked the paper. And the answer: "Our lands are just as good and as productive as theirs. The only answer is because our county seat is located off in an inaccessible place and theirs are on the railroad, where people with money stop off and look at the country and buy lands." Added the *Advocate,* "Crocker is the most central point on the railroad, and the most accessible point. No other place in the county would be so near the center of population." Even though two nearby railroad towns, Dixon and Richland, showed support, Waynesville, although half the size of its rival, thwarted this real threat to its civic prestige and economic well-being. Its residents made much of their central geographic location, gaining support from inhabitants in the county's southern section and using their considerable political clout.

The coming of one or more railroads could result in a redrawing of a state's political map. Railroad officials might play a role, but more likely it involved committed citizen participation. In older sections of the country counties generally predated the railroad era, but with new rail arteries

county seats might be relocated and counties carved from existing entities. As for the latter, early in the twentieth century Georgia dramatically altered its county boundaries. In 1904 the state constitution was amended as it related to creation of counties, and it did not take long before twenty-two developing New South railroad towns sought to take control of their own political units. One was Toccoa City, which owed its creation to the iron horse. Founded in 1873 and served by the main stem and a branch line of the Southern Railway, this community thrived, sustained by cotton and lumber, retail trade, and a furniture factory. With increased importance, the town sought to win the seat of Habersham County from Clarkesville, a remote village served only by a recently constructed shortline. When that effort failed in 1897, Toccoa Citians and their supporters decided that they should cleave themselves from the mother county. Several years later legal changes aided such a strategy, and in 1905 Toccoa City became seat of the new Stephens County. Two years later citizens took pride in construction of a forty-thousand-dollar brick courthouse that stood on the public square and within easy walking distance from the depot. And it would be in 1905 and 1906 that Ashburn, Cairo, Cordele, Fitzgerald, Hazelhurst, and Tifton joined Toccoa (residents dropped "City") in becoming seats of newly organized Georgia counties.

Coinciding with efforts to restructure local political centers was what became the most hotly contested battle for a state capital. This war of sorts broke out in South Dakota. Although the first capital of Dakota Territory

Squabbles between communities for the plum of becoming county seat erupted throughout the nation, being most pronounced in the trans-Chicago West. It took three elections to decide the permanent location for the seat of Box Butte County, Nebraska. Ultimately the railroad town of Alliance won, and in July 1899 the frame courthouse travels from Hemmingford to its resting site in Alliance. The exceptional skills of a Burlington Railroad's bridge and building foreman made this unusual move possible.

Author's collection

was located in the Missouri River town of Yankton and later moved upstream to Bismarck, statehood in 1889 failed to resolve the permanent seat of government for South Dakota. (North Dakotans seemed mostly content with Bismarck, centrally located and served by the transcontinental route of the Northern Pacific.) In summer 1889 a hard-fought electoral contest between Chamberlain, Huron, Mitchell, Pierre, Sioux Falls, and Watertown led Pierre to win by a large majority designation as temporary capital. As with Yankton and Bismarck, Pierre stood on the east bank of this navigable waterway, and like Bismarck, approximately in the geographical center of the state. But the South Dakota capital was barely more than a village, and a "final" decision had yet to be made. A year later another election was held, and this time Pierre defeated Huron, its only rival. Still, the "permanent" location remained in doubt.

When the plebiscite of 1890 took place, the North Western endorsed the outcome. After all, the railroad operated the sole rail line to Pierre, and it also served Huron, location of its Dakota Division headquarters. But early in the twentieth century the situation changed. The Milwaukee Road, which was the chief statewide rival of the North Western, fervently believed that Mitchell, site of its divisional operations, should become the seat of state government. This bickering led to the "Great Capital Fight of 1904," resulting in both railroads attempting to influence the popular referendum. The North Western and Milwaukee Road supplied free tickets to voters so that they could visit each company's choice – Pierre or Mitchell – and an estimated 100,000 persons accepted these offers. "In the last weeks of the campaign many special trains daily, loaded with good-natured men, women, and children, were carried into Mitchell and Pierre," reported a contemporary chronicler. "It was a great, continuous picnic, in which all of the people participated, and probably has not had an equal in American history." The two railroads also spent heavily on newspaper space to champion their cause. In advertisements and handbills the North Western told South Dakotans: "Pierre for Capital: 'Stand Pat.'" They did. Pierre won the election by about an 18,000 majority. But the North Western's pick was greatly aided by strong anti-Mitchell sentiment from Rapid City and the developing West River Country.

DESIGNING RAILROAD TOWNS

The configurations of railroad towns, whether successful or not, varied, but nevertheless they were shaped by the rails and nearly always had linear features. At times challenging topographic barriers forced a railroad to locate its station some distance from the core of an established place, but inevitably there would be a collection of businesses and homes that

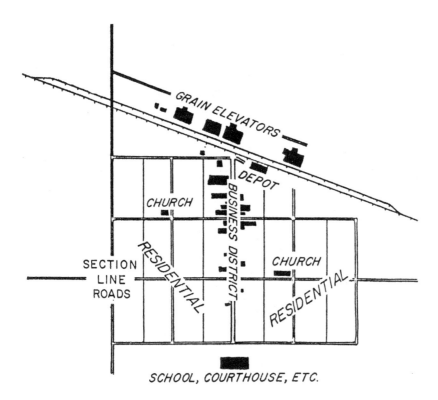

GRAIN ELEVATORS

DEPOT

CHURCH

BUSINESS DISTRICT

SECTION
LINE
ROADS

RESIDENTIAL

CHURCH

RESIDENTIAL

SCHOOL, COURTHOUSE, ETC.

Northwestern University geographer John Hudson created a drawing of a typical "T-Town," a plan commonly used on the Great Plains. Based on the actual layout of the Soo Line–spawned community of Grano, North Dakota, situated on the road's "Wheat Line," the main street runs directly from the station, making the depot the convenient commercial gateway.

John Hudson

appeared nearby. This situation might well lead to a new community, a true railroad-spawned town.

In locations where the rail line did not pass through or near an existing community, several types of development patterns emerged. In the 1850s the Illinois Central Railroad popularized what geographers call the "symmetric" pattern, likely inspired by towns fostered by canals in New York and Ohio. "There were two business streets in the symmetric railroad town, with buildings facing each other across a 300-foot railroad right-of-way designed for elevators, lumberyards, and other enterprises needing direct rail access," explained geographer John Hudson. "Land along the tracks was underused, and eventually some towns acquired a portion of it for parks."

Another common format, the "orthogonal plat," had the principal commercial street parallel the railroad. Storefronts, then, faced the tracks and the station, allowing for the centrality of the depot. Residential streets ran perpendicular to the "main drag," and the industrial section – mills, creameries, granaries, stock pens, and lumber and coal yards – stood on the "other side of the tracks." When the Atlanta & Charlotte Air Line in the early 1870s built between the two southern cities of its corporate name, numerous towns featured this street pattern, including a string of start-up villages in upstate South Carolina: Central, Calhoun (later Clemson), Seneca, and Westminster. A variation involved businesses on *both* sides of

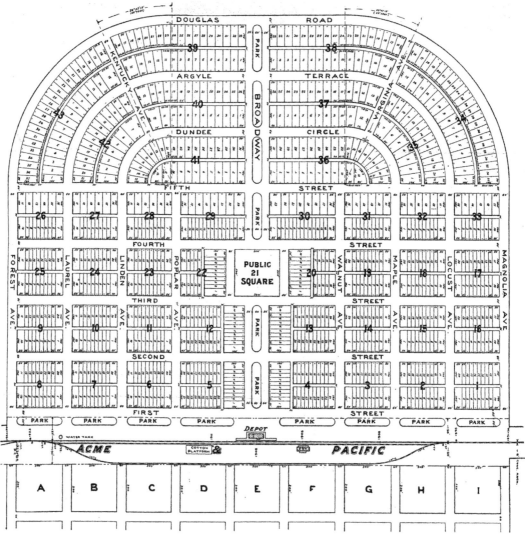

Map of the Town of Roaring Springs, Texas

An imaginative variation of the standard T-town layout is found in Roaring Springs, Texas. The townsite company argued that this station on the Quanah, Acme & Pacific Railroad is "well laid out," and surely all agreed.

Don L. Hofsommer coll.

the same street, yet still remaining parallel to the tracks. The depot usually appeared near the main street crossing. Western railroads, in particular, favored this pattern.

On the Great Plains, especially, townsite companies laid out hundreds of settlements in a cookie-cutter fashion. "Main Street began at the tracks," explained John Hudson, "creating an arrangement in which the railroad formed the bar of a T-shaped configuration." These "T-towns" meant that the principal road stopped directly at the depot's door and commercial structures appeared along the street close by. Houses, churches, and public buildings usually were constructed on the grid of right-angle streets and avenues. Some places that grew in importance, for example, Bismarck, North Dakota; Cheyenne, Wyoming; and Lincoln, Nebraska, were classic T-towns.

Usually residents did not complain much about the layouts of these railroad-spawned towns. Practicality reigned. Stations appeared on the commercial side and that ensured the safety of passengers, who did not need to cross tracks to board trains. With industrial and related business segregated from the main section, this placement pattern produced less traffic congestion; at harvest time the main street of a T-town was not likely to see a constant string of grain-laden wagons.

With both the parallel and T-configurations, a rail line might cut through a townsite on an angle and create a linear street pattern that would not be on a true north–south, east–west axis. "North was in the wrong place," lamented a resident of Carroll, Iowa. "Even after living here for years, the sun always rose and set in the wrong places, and that always has bothered me." This seat of Carroll County was laid out on an angle that paralleled the right-of-way that a predecessor of the North Western had extended through this largely empty section of western Iowa in the late 1860s.

There were town layouts that deviated from common practices, although they retained elements of popular street patterns. When the Roaring Springs Townsite Company launched Roaring Springs, Texas, in 1912, the firm bragged that the town was "well laid out," and it indeed was. In a variation of the T-town, two main streets, not one, extended from the depot of the Quanah, Acme & Pacific Railroad (Quanah) to a public square two blocks away. In a boulevard fashion, parks separated the double main street, and the boulevard, lined with building lots for retail establishments, continued beyond the public square, again with park

Roaring Springs became more than a paper plat. Not long after the sale of lots on June 19, 1913, the town quickly took shape on property that once had been part of the vast holdings of the Matador Land & Cattle Company.

Don L. Hofsommer coll.

space. Although residential lots located from First Street to Fifth Street were arranged on a standard grid, those beyond were in a semicircular or horseshoe fashion, with many lots not facing directly the cardinal points of the compass. As with other T-towns, the townsite firm placed large lots for commercial businesses, cotton gins, compress plants, lumber yards, and the like, on the opposite side of the Quanah tracks.

An urban place that owed its origins directly to the iron horse, nevertheless, might lack a neatly arranged pattern of streets. Take Atlanta, Georgia. In 1879 a writer for *Harper's New Monthly Magazine* explained succinctly how the city came into being: "The answer is found in one word – railways." After all, an earlier name for the community was "Terminus." Because several rambling turnpikes traversed the future Atlanta, later streets reflected the impact of these existing roads.

> The map of Atlanta shows a circular line representing the boundary, and having for its centre the railway station. The radius is one and a half miles. Within this circle (and somewhat also outside of it) is an array of streets so utterly irregular that you wonder how it was possible they ever could have been built up in that way. They go crooked where it would have been easier to go straight, show acute angles where a square corner could be made with less effort, and come to a sudden stop or run away into vacancy at the most unexpected points.

Atlanta was not a product of a townsite firm, yet speculation in real estate took hold once the iron horse arrived in 1842 and continued unabated as the place grew.

While a townsite company might include a park in its layout design, communities, railroad-created or already established, might claim a "depot park." Almost always located on railroad property, this public space near the depot commonly featured plantings, trees, seasonal flowers, and benches. At times the name of the town or city on a large metal or wooden sign or in large brick or cement letters (BISMARCK, JUNCTION CITY, OTTUMWA, ROCK SPRINGS) faced trackside. (Railroads referred to the latter as "welcoming signs.") When a train arrived in Akron, Ohio, some passengers did not need to watch for the signboard on the ends of the depot or to listen for the trainman call out the stop; rather they could see the huge whitewashed letters in the adjoining depot park that spelled out the name of this vibrant industrial city. "These bright, white letters are a great and positive advertisement for Akron," reflected the *Akron Beacon Journal* on the eve of World War I. This was a major change from earlier comments. "Travel is a great educator, but the man who relies for knowledge of America exclusively upon what he can see from a car window will get a false and unflattering impression of almost every town," observed the newspaper. "Certainly Akron is no exception. The greatest triumphs of scenery and architecture in which Akron abounds are not located upon the line of any of the numerous railroads that pass through this future metropolis. The traveler sees a rather humble assortment of dwellings and much unclassified junk. Hence comes the importance of making the surroundings of a passenger station as attractive as possible." To keep up a pleasing space, some railroads, including the B & O, North Western, and Union Pacific, held contests, often with financial awards, for employees who maintained the "best" depot parks. Community organizations might volunteer to keep the site tidy.

THE RAILROAD AND THE TOWN

Urban dwellers, whether they could brag of having a depot park or not, consistently agitated for attractive, practical public access to the station (or stations). This might mean the first improved streets in town – cobblestone, macadam, cinders, crushed rock, or later brick or concrete. Usually these improved roadways extended into the commercial heart of the community and beyond to public buildings or the better neighborhoods. Similarly, sidewalks to the depot might be installed. At first they were likely raised wooden affairs, designed to keep pedestrians above the water, mud, or animal waste frequently found in thoroughfares. Because of maintenance costs and the fire threat posed by these combustible walkways, bricks or concrete might be substituted, the same materials employed on adjoining main streets.

That community uplift spirit involved more than improving roads and sidewalks from the business core to the station; the first public conveyances nearly always offered connections between these two points. In the antebellum period it would be horse-drawn omnibuses that traveled over established routes and on prearranged schedules. One wag described the often jarring experience for passengers as a form of "modern martyrdom." Later, more comfortable streetcars, operating on iron rails, might provide the link. These animal cars, which began to appear widely by the 1850s, made connections to depots, whether in New York City or New Orleans, or in much smaller places such as Charleston, South Carolina, or Middletown, Ohio. In the 1870s and 1880s more expensive, but much faster and cleaner, cable cars replaced horses and mules in some large cities and in smaller places such as Lincoln, Nebraska; Providence, Rhode Island; and St. Joseph, Missouri. Still later, after 1888, the electric trolley usually meant the end to animal or cable car service, and within a few years these "juice" lines became ubiquitous. Before the triumph of electric traction, "steam dummy" street railways could be found in scattered locations. These were downsized versions of standard steam locomotives, disguised with metal sheathing as animal cars to prevent frightening horses (and hence the nickname), and they either pulled a powerless trailer or were a combined engine-coach unit. Inevitably, these steam dummies operated to the depot or terminal from the commercial or perhaps outlying residential sections. Boosters in communities of all sizes felt the need to show visitors that go-getter determination, understanding the importance of up-to-date or even experimental urban transit.

Roads, sidewalks, and street railways served an array of businesses that had a distinct railroad dependence or connection. Community after community had at least one hotel that catered to travelers, and it might be within convenient walking distance from the depot. It was hardly surprising that the two-story Commercial Hotel in Junction City, Wisconsin, stood only a few steps away from the town's small, albeit union, station that the Wisconsin Central (later Soo Line) and Milwaukee Road served. For years the latter's north- and southbound passenger trains met during the noon hour, allowing riders and crewmen the opportunity to take their luncheon in the hotel dining room. In places where Jim Crow laws segregated the races, separate railroad-oriented hotels were likely. By the 1880s in Texarkana, Arkansas, the Huckins House Hotel catered to white travelers, while the East Side Hotel, née Sherman House, served people of color, a practice that continued for decades.

Builders of the Commercial Hotel in Junction City had the railroad passenger in mind; location was hardly accidental. When in the 1890s the Santa Fe decided to construct the magnificent Castaneda Hotel in Las Vegas, New Mexico, placement was critical. When completed, the main entrance faced trackside and not the town, making passengers feel welcome, "more at home," when they alighted from their train.

Of course, hotels received noncommercial guests, but many of their patrons during the Railway Age were those ever-present businessmen or "commercial travelers." Not only did they need a place to sleep, bathe, and likely eat, but they required public spaces. The lobby was where these out-of-towners made business contracts or met friends. Often hotels offered these "men of the grip" showrooms or "sample parlors" where they could conveniently display their wares to potential customers, usually owners of hardware, jewelry, or other retail outlets. In 1913 the Foster House, located in Redfield, South Dakota, advertised: "**The best meals along the line. No. 8 stops twenty-five minutes for supper.** All trains stop long enough to get mail. Hotel 200 feet from N.W. [North Western] Depot. Spacious sample room. Free bus to Milwaukee depot." That same year the Regis Hotel in Peoria, Illinois, announced: "'Ye Home of Ye Gripmen.' Nearest Hotel to Union Depot. Hot and cold water in every room. Elegant café and Grill in connection. All car lines pass hotel. Rooms with private bath. Steam heat." And drummers who planned to stay in Clear Lake, Iowa, happily learned that the Hotel Elk offered "Good Sample Rooms, Hot and Cold Water, Electric Lights, Steam Heat."

There were alternatives to the standard hotels with their sleeping and eating accommodations. Some lodging facilities billed themselves as "Apartment Hotels" where a guest could stay for an extended time, weeks or months, and at attractive rates. These specialized hotels were usually found in medium- to large-size cities, and again they likely provided restaurants. And they were commonly located near the station or at least on a streetcar line.

Boarding houses were another place to sleep and eat. Resembling hotels and apartment hotels, but usually less expensive, boardinghouses, which were frequently within close proximity to the station, might be constructed with sleeping rooms, central bathrooms (but not always), and eating facilities. A boardinghouse might be a converted private dwelling that could take in a half dozen or so nightly, weekly, or monthly guests, and customarily offered two reasonably priced meals, breakfast and supper. "I remember I paid two dollars a week for my room and two bits [25 cents] a meal at the boarding house where I lived at there in Frankfort, [Indiana]," recounted a trainman. "Like most all boarding houses in those days [early twentieth century] it had a saloon in connection with, and the barroom was right joining the big dining room, and in the dining room there were two big long tables, where the food was put on in family style, and you could help yourself and eat all you wanted." He added, "Us boys while in off the road would loaf around in the barroom and play

Located within convenient walking distance of the St. Louis–San Francisco Railway (Frisco) station in Dixon, Missouri, a town on the main line between St. Louis and Springfield, the Frisco Hotel, opened in 1876, unmistakably demonstrates its close ties to the railroad. Although the Frisco relocated its roundhouse, maintenance facilities, and division headquarters to nearby Newburg in 1884, the hotel continued operations into the twentieth century.

Jessie McCullie Library, Dixon, MO

cards, checkers, and dominoes for little brass checks, which were good at the bar."

Then there were the infamous "flophouses." Found almost exclusively in cities, such places charged as little as fifteen cents a night for a cot or hammock. These sleeping facilities – "for men only" – were usually in either large open-air or modestly partitioned rooms. As for the latter, a railroader remembered a flophouse near Union Station in Chicago that had a "little cell-like room" with the "partitions of these little rooms were just as little higher than a man's head and the whole works was covered with heavy wire netting." Nearly always located over saloons or other "skid-row" establishments, they had minimal sanitary conditions, although some offered bathing facilities.

A slightly better quality of lodging, resembling flophouses, were the cheap hotels, popularly known as "fleabag" hotels. They might offer clean sheets and access to baths, but prostitutes, "women of the night," plied their trade throughout the building, and pool and card sharks set up shop on main floor or back rooms. In larger towns and cities these fleabag hotels were often only steps away from the station, and found customers who were both travelers and railroad employees. Men of color who felt the sting of segregation even outside the South might have no option but to patronize such places.

And there might be church missions nearby. Located in urban centers, they became somewhat commonplace by the twentieth century. While not always offering shelter, they provided food, either for free or for a donation. The quality of "vittles," though, was universally poor: "stale bread and watery soup." But many transients, hoboes and tramps, patronized them and endured the religious proselytizing.

Railroad officials did not like having their trainmen and other workers stay in boardinghouses, flophouses, or fleabag hotels that allowed easy access to alcoholic drink. Nearly every company had its "Rule G" that banned the use of intoxicants. In the latter part of the nineteenth century there appeared an attractive alternative form of lodging, facilities operated by the Railroad Division of the Young Men's Christian Association, better known as the "Railroad Y." This movement began in Cleveland, Ohio, in 1872 when several rooms in the Lake Shore & Michigan Southern Railroad station were set aside for railroaders. By the time of World War I the Railroad Y operated nearly 180 hotels nationwide, appearing in such railroad towns as Altoona, Pennsylvania; Barstow, California; Peru, Indiana; Tyler, Texas; Waterloo, Iowa; and Waycross, Georgia. The concept was to provide railroad employees with an acceptable substitute for the boardinghouse and saloon. Backers believed that if the off-work environment could be altered positively, so too could workers' behavior.

Almost always placed near the station or terminal, the Railroad Y provided members, who paid small annual dues for the use of any Y, with clean, low-cost sleeping rooms and economical, wholesome food. These Ys also offered railroaders opportunities to spend their leisure time constructively, including reading libraries, card rooms (gambling was forbidden), and occasionally indoor bowling alleys and "splash" or swimming pools. Prostitutes were banned from the premises, again different from other lodgings that railroaders patronized.

Over time dram shops, saloons, taverns, billiard parlors, drinking establishments, or whatever they were called appeared in most places (except communities that because of tradition, moral suasion, or law were dry). A traveler could usually "wet his whistle" near the depot. The location of such a "watering hole" might be on the seediest part of town where cheap bars were often concentrated. As early as the 1850s the station area in Dayton, Ohio, sported "a few dirty groggeries for the benefit of dry passengers, who cannot walk to more distant and respectable places." Before national prohibition took effect during World War I, these businesses commonly offered patrons a free or nickel lunch *if* they purchased a glass or bottle of beer. There might be gambling in the back rooms and "cribs," nearby rooms for "babes" – not babies – where prostitutes turned tricks.

There were eateries that shared a close connection with the railroad corridor and were an everyday part of urban life. As with sleeping accommodations, these places varied in quality and size, but "dingy all-night railroad restaurants" were ubiquitous. If a customer, especially a female, did not want to enter a saloon to partake of that free or nickel lunch, there were options of small nearby cafes – "hash houses" – that were not linked to a hotel or boardinghouse. In various locales these establishments might be operated by a Chinese owner, a legacy of the thousands of Chinese who worked on railroad or other construction projects. These restaurants were found mostly in the trans-Chicago West, and may have been started by individuals who had fled from the occasional virulent anti-Chinese uprisings. In a study of Asians in Texas, Chinese restaurants were noted as being common and "usually located near the railroad station," where they catered to travelers and railroaders alike.

Then, too, there might be less formal and often ephemeral food businesses that appeared near the depot. In the late nineteenth century and later, the mobile lunch wagon, especially in New England locations, was a common sight. The owner sold coffee, sandwiches, and always pies. "I loved to eat from a lunch wagon that seemed to always be outside the Central Vermont and Rutland station in Burlington [Vermont]," reminisced a longtime resident. "It sure made for good eating." Even a lemonade or soda stand might pop up. During the summer months in the early twentieth

In large cities rail-
roads, including the
Baltimore & Ohio,
often had one or
more ticket outlets.
The B&O's City Ticket
Office in Cincinnati,
Ohio, was located in
the Dixie Terminal
Building at 4th and
Walnut streets. It's
a busy place in this
ca. 1950 scene.

William Howes Jr. coll.

century Griffith (Grif) Teller, the later renowned illustrator of Pennsylvania Railroad calendars, and his brother Albert sold ice-cold lemonade
from an improvised stand close to the Erie Railroad station at Forest Hill,
New Jersey. Apparently these youngsters did so with financial success.

While a community could take pride in good restaurants or other
facilities that served the needs of travelers and the larger population, cities, including some smaller ones, applauded one or more centrally located ticket offices. Usually this specialized facility occupied ground-floor
rental space in a downtown building. This would be the place where a
traveler could acquire timetables and brochures, plan an itinerary, and
purchase the necessary ticket or tickets, including Pullman accommodations. It was not unusual for commercial clubs or similar business organizations to advertise in their promotional literature the availability of such
conveniently situated ticket offices.

Local live-wires probably ignored or at least downplayed the presence
of the "wrong side of the tracks." Most every community, even a village,
had a section located along the railroad corridor that contained an assortment of modest or substandard housing, usually unpainted frame structures with unkempt yards, and shabby commercial establishments. Some
communities had slums that rail lines physically segregated from their

"better" parts. Transients, the foreign-born, or people of color – people who were almost universally poor – lived in these places. Gary, Indiana, a planned company town started in 1906 by a unit of the United States Steel Corporation, had an adjoining area known as "the Patch." This was a sprawling collection of ramshackle houses, saloons, and other structures that sprang up south of the Wabash Railroad's tracks and beyond control of the Gary Land Company, the corporate affiliate that developed this "Magic City."

In nearby Chicago, railroads, especially the Illinois Central, which connected the city directly with states in the South, for decades brought northbound tens of thousands of people of color. Many became permanent residents of the Windy City and congregated in the bourgeoning south side ghettoes. By the 1930s white Chicagoans were known to say "blame it on the IC," explaining why these grubby and crime-infested neighborhoods, while not exactly "the Patch" of Gary, had developed in their metropolis.

Then there were the hobo "jungles." Not every locality had such a place, but virtually every railroad center or junction had at least one and maybe more. For travelers without tickets, and usually with meager resources, it was necessary to find a convenient and hopefully acceptable place to cook, sleep, and wait for the next train. There might be an assortment of cooking and eating utensils scattered about, a makeshift table or two, and primitively constructed shelters. A camp along a Rock Island line in Arkansas offered these amenities: "Many crude little make-believe houses stood near each other at the edge of the jungle. They were built out of railroad ties, and had three sides and a roof." Jungles also became sites where boes planned to meet compatriots who might be delayed or diverted elsewhere, perhaps by a stay in jail for vagrancy. "The separation of rovers is a common occurrence in tramp life," explained a bo, "and at times, owing to the uncertainty of circumstance, the most expert of drifters find it impossible to travel together." In urban centers these jungles were usually within close proximity to sprawling railroad yards, where night freights offered attractive boarding opportunities. In more rural communities jungles were also along railroad corridors and near depots or yards. At remote junctions or crossings, they might be situated in a wooded area, near a stream (for bathing and laundry), or some other practical place. If a stiff grade was nearby that caused trains to move slowly, boes took advantage of that attractive feature.

While hardly jungles, the occasional "boxcar camp" likewise did not engender much community endorsement. Most railroads stationed their maintenance-of-way personnel in so-called camp cars on a siding while they worked on track or related projects. This equipment included bunk cars, a kitchen/dining car, and other pieces of rolling stock for equipment

and tool storage. After a few weeks or months, these workers, often criticized (or feared) for their heavy drinking and rough behavior, moved on or ended their seasonal employment.

Some camps became semi-permanent. West Eola, Illinois, had such a place. The Burlington placed about twenty cars on a sidetrack to house approximately fifty Mexican laborers who toiled in the reclamation or "scrap" yard at the nearby Aurora shops. These individuals, who had arrived during the era of World War I, were ordered back to Mexico in 1934 as the Great Depression deepened. Desirous to flee the abject poverty and political strife of their homeland, these Mexicans willingly lived in ancient rolling stock that lacked running water and electricity. At West Eola, though, they made modest improvements, including porchlike additions. Moreover, the Burlington gave the camp materials for construction of a small Roman Catholic chapel. Even with their expulsion, some men managed to remain, moving to Aurora. There they found land, used pieces of abandoned equipment to build permanent houses, married, and had families, becoming part of the fabric of community life.

By the 1930s it was not unusual in an outlying area, even in the vicinity of a hobo jungle or boxcar camp, to find a golf course. A railroad or brotherhood might build and operate one, designed for the pleasure of railroaders and family members. But a railroad function in itself might become the stimulus for a nine- or eighteen-hole course with an adjoining clubhouse. Since companies required large quantities of water for

their steam locomotives, they regularly built reservoirs, and nearly always these artificial bodies were situated on a sizable acreage. Because of their often scenic beauty and expanse of land, golf enthusiasts, usually business leaders and community professionals, might lease part or most of the land from a railroad for a golf-course complex. The seasonal usage in no way interfered with a road's water supply. In fact, railroad activities were probably far removed; trackside tanks were connected by underground pipes to pumps at water-supply sites. Such was the case in the 1920s, as golf grew in popularity, when a string of county-seat towns along the main line of the Burlington in southern Iowa, including Mount Pleasant, Fairfield, Albia, Chariton, and Red Oak, witnessed the creation of these recreational facilities.

In many communities, large and small, the railroad rights-of-way emerged as public walking paths. With roadways susceptible to the vagaries of weather and rail lines connecting important points, residents found that "walking the tracks" was the preferred way to reach their destinations. Yet dangers lurked; no wonder reports of accidents appeared repeatedly. "A man was killed on the track of the Lowell railroad Friday morning, about two miles from the city, having been run over by the 11 o'clock train, going up," noted the *American Railroad Journal* in May 1845.

> The man was walking towards Lowell on the left hand track, and seeing a
> merchandise train coming down, stepped on to the other track, not perceiving
> that the passenger train was immediately behind him going up, and supposing,

as is presumed, that the bell and noise of both engines proceeded from the merchandise train. The passenger train struck him, knocked him across the rails, and ran over him, cutting his arm nearly off and his body almost in two, and of course killing him instantly.

Residents mostly showed sympathy for victims of railroad accidents, even those who deliberately trespassed. Still, there might be real resentment toward some who alighted from a train. In the central Appalachian coal fields, labor unrest frequently flared. Coal operators did not want rails bringing in men who were union organizers or pro-union workers. In the 1910s and 1920s Sheriff Donald Chafin of Logan County, West Virginia, worked closely with the companies, especially during strikes. "Chafin met every train that came into the area, grilled strangers as to the purpose of their visit, beat up union sympathizers and drove them from the county."

RAILROAD TOWNS

There is no question that the activities of railroads themselves made scores of towns. Contemporaries deemed them "magic cities" where almost overnight they appeared and grew rapidly. Indeed, the nickname for Moberly, Missouri, a community that owed its founding in the late 1860s and early existence solely to the Wabash, St. Louis & Pacific Railway, was just that: "The Magic City." Either the "direct or indirect agency of the railroad themselves" spawned these places that otherwise lacked "commercial or industrial advantages." Special urban centers resulted.

If the community was a "railroad town," with a crew-change point, division offices, shops, yards, and other facilities, additional structures might be centered near the station or along the tracks. There might be that Railroad Y, but there was surely space for company offices. While some railroads, large and small, used a depot to house divisional or corporate employees, others erected separate and at times substantial structures, and usually placed them within convenient distance of rail activities.

Division quarters commonly occupied the upper portions of a depot. The Burlington, which in 1869 platted the southwestern Iowa town of Creston on its Chicago-to-Omaha main line, immediately designated the place a division point. Later the company erected a large roundhouse and repair facility. For decades the upper floor of the three-story brick depot accommodated offices for the superintendent, clerks, and train dispatchers on the Creston Division. The attic housed dusty bundles of office records, train sheets, and other stored objects. The station was in the heart of the commercial section, with a broad parallel street on the north side and busy streets that ran in a perpendicular fashion.

Additional examples abound. The Chicago & Alton Railroad employed a similar arrangement in Bloomington, Illinois, where the upper floor of the brick depot contained the offices of division personnel and dispatchers. In a like fashion the Erie Railroad (née Atlantic & Great Western Railway) housed its divisional office personnel at Kent, Ohio, in a substantial multistory brick depot.

Small roads regularly placed their corporate headquarters in depots located in their principal towns. About the time the Atlantic Northern & Southern opened in 1910, the company erected a two-story concrete-block combination freight-passenger depot and office facility in Atlantic, Iowa, which conveniently served both its north and south lines. But there were exceptions. The headquarters of the nearby Creston, Winterset & Des Moines Railroad, a somewhat shorter carrier, were maintained in the office of the road's attorney in Creston, and the modest train operations and repair work were directed from the depot at Macksburg, the northern terminus, 21 miles away.

If a railroad were more than a small shortline, a *separate* office building, which could accommodate operating and corporate personnel, was likely. In the case of the Detroit, Bay City & Western Railroad, which between 1911 and 1917 built the 100 miles between Bay City and Port Huron, Michigan, the company owned a small brick general office building on Johnson Street in Bay City, but it was near its freight and passenger depot on Madison Street. The amount of office work, conducted by a staff of about twenty employees, required more space than a typical single-story combination depot could provide.

Then there were the truly magnificent corporate headquarters. Every trunk road owned such a building in a major on-line city or leased space in an important downtown structure. Companies, however, might maintain two central offices. For much of the twentieth century the B&O, Erie, and Union Pacific railroads, for example, had their central headquarters in Baltimore, Cleveland, and Omaha respectively. Yet each carrier felt the need to have offices in New York City, wanting executives and staff members to be within close proximity of the principal financial houses.

Representative of the grand freestanding corporate office buildings were the headquarters of the B&O in Baltimore, the Missouri Pacific in St. Louis, and the Southern Pacific (SP) in San Francisco. Since the early 1880s the B&O had taken pride in its seven-story central headquarters building at the corner of Baltimore and Calvert streets in the heart of Baltimore. The structure nicely represented the growing importance of this interregional carrier that served such cities as Chicago, Cincinnati, St. Louis, and Washington, D.C. Then disaster struck. In one of the great urban fires of the twentieth century, flames in February 1904 engulfed the structure and much of the central business district. The financial loss for the B&O was considerable, approaching $1 million plus the destruction of some irreplaceable records. But rising from the ashes came a splendid

The main entrance to the Baltimore & Ohio Railroad office building at 2 North Charles Street in Baltimore, which opened in 1904, is decorated in a patriotic mode. The event is the National Democratic Convention that in June 1912 nominated Governor Woodrow Wilson for the presidency of the United States.

E. Ray Lichty Coll.

office building, although located two blocks to the west at Baltimore and Charles streets and close to Camden Station. The replacement facility, built with structural steel and Indiana limestone, stood thirteen stories tall and was completed in 1906. Marble fireplaces and other fineries graced the building that served the company for the remainder of its corporate life.

The Missouri Pacific Railroad, which for decades was in the orbit of the Gould System and later the Alleghany holding company, had long made St. Louis its corporate home. For years the MOP, along with several other roads, rented office space in the downtown Railway Exchange Building. However, in May 1928, on the eve of the Great Depression, the company relocated to its modern Art Deco office building at 210 North 13th Street, not far from St. Louis Union Station. This twenty-two-story edifice, which cost $2.5 million, signaled to the city and the nation that the MOP was a premier carrier.

The opening of MOP headquarters excited St. Louisans. At the public reception, held on August 2, more than thirty thousand people filed through the building. "The invitations sent out for the affair announced the hours would be from 2 to 6 PM," reported the company magazine, "but long before 2 o'clock and after 6, the visitors continued to come – and to find themselves welcome." In fact, everyone had an opportunity to explore the executive suite, to meet President Lewis Warrington Baldwin, and to enjoy "bowls of icy, refreshing punch." And the Missouri Pacific Booster Band from Sedalia, Missouri, entertained the throngs at the front entrance.

Although the home offices occupied an impressive and expensive structure, the MOP soon struggled financially, beginning in 1933 a twenty-three-year period in bankruptcy. Yet the railroad continued to occupy its highly functional office building until the company joined the Union Pacific in 1983.

In the American West the premier railroad headquarters building belonged to the Southern Pacific in San Francisco. Although the deadly earthquake and fire of 1906 severely damaged the railroad's general offices, located in leased space in the downtown Flood Building, this site was reoccupied after a reconstruction. But the office situation was hardly ideal, being inadequate in size and costly in rental payments. Therefore relocation studies began in 1913, and three years later officials announced that the company would spend more than $1.8 million to erect a ten-story, E-shaped office building at 65 Market Street near its sprawling Ferry Building, allowing for water connections with the rail passenger network. For good reason Southern Pacific engineers sought to create an earthquake-proof structure. Numerous pilings, driven to a depth of 130 feet, seemed the appropriate engineering and construction procedure. When employees entered their spacious offices in September 1917, they discovered that every room faced daylight. This 280,000-square-foot masonry building, bragged the railroad, was "one of the largest office buildings west of Chicago."

Since all cities were to some degree "railroad towns," there were additional structures in these urban locales that had direct or close ties to the iron horse. Often nearly as well known as corporate office buildings were railroad hospitals. Many places claimed these facilities, some of which were massive in size and operated for decades.

Railroads had long had an association with the medical community. As early as 1834 the B&O employed a physician, an action that may have been inspired by the naval practice of ships carrying a surgeon. Just as sailing vessels journeyed far from medical assistance, railroads at times served areas that were nearly as remote as the high seas, especially in the West. By the post–Civil War years, most major roads had or would start some sort of regularized medical program; after all, the number of accidents rose as trackage expanded, freight and passenger traffic soared, and train speeds increased. Officials realized that medical help was humane, lessened the likelihood of lawsuits, and engendered goodwill among employees and the public. Although common law gave carriers little incentive to reduce the numbers of injured, most of all trespassers, roads usually accorded them medical treatment.

Railroads established hospitals in terminal cities and also in division points and shop towns. These facilities, however, were not designed as medical-care institutions for the general public, but rather to serve employees and accident victims. As early as 1869 the Central Pacific (later Southern Pacific) opened a small temporary hospital in Sacramento, claiming to be the first in the country that was established exclusively for the care of railroad personnel. A year later the company constructed a larger replacement structure with a capacity of 125 beds. Eventually the Hospital Department of the Southern Pacific operated facilities throughout its far-flung system that stretched from Louisiana to Oregon, including a tuberculosis sanatorium in Tucson, Arizona.

The Gould System was another railroad combine that launched extensive medical treatment centers. One affiliated company, the Wabash, by the 1880s operated hospitals in several communities, including Decatur, Illinois; Moberly, Missouri; and Peru, Indiana. Company officials and rank-and-file employees took pride in these facilities, especially after new or expanded hospitals became available. In 1895 the railroad built a modern hospital in Peru and closed hospitals in Danville and Springfield, Illinois, because of "inadequate accommodations." The railroad trade press called the Peru hospital "one of the most complete and best equipped hospital buildings in the country."

As with hospitals operated by the Southern Pacific, Wabash, and other major carriers, employees usually paid a small monthly fee based on their income. Yet these health-care facilities did not manage every medical condition. "Under no circumstance will treatment be given alcoholic or venereal diseases or their after-affects, [and] chronic diseases arising before the entering the Company's services," announced the Wabash Employe's Hospital Association. The organization made clear that it would not treat injuries "received in fights, brawls or any other disability arising from vicious acts." But when it came to broken limbs, eye injuries, and other work-related accidents, company surgeons and physicians attended to employees' needs. In cases of community emergencies, whether fires, storms, or train wrecks, these railroad-sponsored hospitals responded humanely.

If a community lacked a railroad hospital, a medical presence was still likely. Companies almost universally named a local general practitioner (and specialists, too) to handle medical emergencies, perform physical examinations of employees, and provide other services. These physicians received a retainer fee or payment on a case-by-case basis, and they were eligible for annual or trip passes.

Then there were noticeable patterns of workers' housing. Railroaders, especially well-paid locomotive engineers and skilled shopmen, often entered the ranks of the middle class and could afford a comfortable house, perhaps with modern plumbing and later a garage for the family automobile. Their dwellings might be situated in the better parts of town, preferably at a convenient distance from the station or other railroad facility. At a time when renting dominated, a depot agent in a small town might also boast such ownership. "When it became time for me to start school – my parents purchased a very nice home right across the street from the school," recalled the son of the Rock Island agent who then lived in Haileyville, Oklahoma. "It was one of the nicest houses in Haileyville, and believe it or not, when my folks sold it a few years later, they received a 'huge sum' of five-hundred dollars. This was in the late 1920's."

It was common for workers to live in clustered sections, likely because of their desire to be near work. If they were in train service, the "call boy" could quickly notify them of an impending run. In Emporia, Kansas, a division and repair center on the Santa Fe, homes of railwaymen became visibly segregated. The *Emporia Gazette* announced that the community had divided "into three castes – the school [normal college] and resident folk, the railroaders, and the 'niggers,'" with the men of the steel rails living in the south end of town. In Topeka, where the Santa Fe maintained its shops complex, scores of African American railroad workers lived in a nearly all black neighborhood. This area also became the Tenderloin district with saloons, gambling dens, and houses of prostitution.

Yet railroaders' housing could be widely scattered, some appearing in the nearby countryside where there was room for a cow, pig, a few chickens, and a large vegetable garden. These mini-farms supplied food for families and provided wives (usually) opportunities to sell or trade eggs, chickens, and other foodstuffs. Such was the case of the railroad town of Erwin, Tennessee, where the homes of Clinchfield Railroad employees were dispersed, including rural acreages, and were mostly modest in nature. "Only the railroad manager had a really big house in Erwin," recalled the son of a trainman, "and that was located not far from the railroad offices." For those Clinchfield workers who lacked adequate garden space, the company rented at a nominal rate tillable soil located in a large plot west of the yards, real estate that was kept for future expansion.

When compared to most urban places, railroad towns generally had a disproportionate population of male residents, possibly outnumbering females by a substantial ratio. While many railroaders married and raised children, others, including young workers and "boomers," usually lacked dependents. Irrespective of marital and family status, they were inclined to join labor unions, fraternal organizations, and other single-sex groups. The presence of buildings and meeting spaces throughout the railroad community reflected these memberships.

Since the first national labor union involved railroaders – the Brotherhood of Locomotive Engineers began in Detroit, Michigan, in 1863 – a host of railroad-labor organizations followed and covered most employment, ranging from the Order of Railway Conductors (the "Big O") to the Brotherhood of Maintenance-of-Way Employes. Such groups needed places for meetings and special events. Their activities might take place in rented or owned buildings, usually near stations or shops, or in spaces belonging to non-railroad fraternal lodges or organizations.

Over time railroad social centers also appeared, commonly called "veterans' clubs," and these usually freestanding structures had a railroad-centered location. And they were not solely male bastions. Women's auxiliaries might also have their separate places. In Wausau, Wisconsin, for example, a small, one-story frame building for decades accommodated the Wausau Chapter of the Chicago, Milwaukee & St. Paul Women's Club.

Union facilities were active places. They were the scene of regular, usually monthly meetings of their members, and more frequent ones if labor unrest was expected or a strike called. During the bitter engineers' strike against the Burlington in 1888–1889, brotherhood halls in such places as Aurora and Galesburg, Illinois; Burlington and Creston, Iowa; and Lincoln and McCook, Nebraska, were crowded daily. Non-railroad labor groups, including carpenters, plumbers, and other skilled tradesmen, might share these facilities.

Then there were social functions, designed to strengthen bonds between the union brothers and to break the monotony of life in more rural or isolated locations. On the evening of February 3, 1887, a typical social evening occurred in Huron, Dakota Territory, an operational center for the North Western. Sponsored by the trainmen's brotherhood, the festivities at a downtown railroad hall at first seemed in trouble when the band of the 11th U.S. Infantry, stationed at Fort Sulley near Pierre, canceled because of bad weather. The snow and cold also disrupted the travel plans of other out-of-town guests. But the trainmen were determined to hold their "Second Annual Ball," and they did. Apparently it was a delightful affair. "The hall was beautifully decorated," reported an attending journalist.

> Two switch stands flanked either side of the entrance door with their white and red lights; two locomotive headlights were placed at either end of the hall and shed their flashing rays upon the throng. Hundreds of lighted railway lanterns adorned the gallery circle; mottoes were "Industry," "Charity," and "Sobriety." Many banners also hung from the arch over the stage, such as "Welcome, B.L.E";

"Welcome, B.L.F"; "Welcome, O.R.C." . . . From the ventilating dome in the center of the hall was suspended a large brake wheel, encircled with different colored lights. Bunting was everywhere. And the music, well, it was a surprise to many. The new orchestra has only been organized a short time, and they have but five members, but it was wonderful how well they filled the hall with music. Caterer Eberhart served an elegant supper at 12 o'clock. Dancing was kept up till four o'clock. The boys did well.

Later in the year the Huron trainmen, like brethren in the running trades and other railroaders elsewhere, sponsored picnics, ice-cream socials, concerts, and holiday events. At times these men and their wives and girl friends invited non-railroaders to these pleasurable functions. This was more likely to happen in the more remote railroad-dominated communities of the Great Plains and West.

If they lacked their own facilities, women's auxiliaries gathered in railroad labor halls. In some places their memberships were large and their activities varied. At the turn of the twentieth century Prairie Rose #5 Chapter of the Ladies of the Locomotive Firemen and Enginemen (firemen's union) in Huron, for example, flourished. A popular event was the "Thimble Bee or Kensington," where "railroad ladies are invited to come and bring their own needlework." Railroad halls customarily complemented churches as centers for female group endeavors and get-togethers.

Railroaders joined more than brotherhoods; thousands became active members of fraternal societies, especially the Freemasons. To advance through the ranks of either the white-collar or blue-color workforce on some roads, an employee needed to be a Protestant and also a Mason in good standing. Of course, Masons enjoyed the comradeship of others and the benefits of "coffin club" life-insurance and disability protection. This nationwide organization maintained hundreds of halls, including some magnificent buildings, whether in Akron, Ohio; Fort Worth, Texas; or Watertown, New York; and they were almost always situated in a central location. Yet the Masonic order was not the only fraternal group. Take the case of employees of the Rio Grande who worked out of the Salida, Colorado, terminal. Not only did this small railroad town have an active Masonic lodge, but scores of railroaders also belonged to the Ancient Order of United Workmen, the International Order of Oddfellows, and the Order of the Knights of Phythias.

Railroad towns felt the presence of employees becoming involved in other activities, including religious and political affairs. Some railroad centers developed a distinct religious flavor, reflecting patterns of worker recruitment. Because of rampant nepotism, this particularity tended to have long-term effects. Since railroad wage earners, including agents, dispatchers, locomotive engineers, conductors, and machinists, generally enjoyed a comfortable living, they and their families could support a particular church, underwriting building and maintenance costs.

The Erie Railroad reflects the impact company workers had on the religious landscape. By the twentieth century two Erie towns, Susquehanna, Pennsylvania, and Huntington, Indiana, had diverse religious cultures. As the result of the workforce at the Susquehanna carshops, this community developed a large Roman Catholic population. Initially, German American and Irish American workers, often skilled craftsmen, dominated the Catholic population, and later immigrants from Catholic countries in southern and southeastern Europe swelled the pews, making the local St. John's Church a leading religious center. A much different situation developed in the division-point town of Huntington. Here men of the Erie, including train crews, were almost universally native-born, old-stock Protestants, with Methodists and Presbyterians being the leading faiths. Vigorous church congregations in both Susquehanna and Huntington attested to the presence of railroaders and their families.

Railroaders might take an active role in community governance. Politically these men of the rails ran the gamut from conservative to radical, reflecting the larger society. It was unlikely that a solid, local railroad bloc of voters existed; after all, the brotherhoods insisted on nonpartisanship in the political life of their members. In 1892 the editor of a Las Vegas, New Mexico, newspaper made these comments about the political inclinations of Santa Fe workers: "The railroad vote seems to be fully appreciated by all the political parties, as a county commissioner on one ticket and a legislative candidate on the other fully attest." Yet railroaders, many of whom were solidly middle-class, tended to be conventional in their political outlook. In the Midwest operating trainmen and white-collar workers often embraced the Republican Party, largely because they or their families had backed the Union during the Civil War. They approved Republican policies that favored a high protective tariff and endorsed William McKinley's "Full Dinner Pail" or Theodore Roosevelt's "Square Deal" campaign for labor. Some fretted that the pro-regulatory or socialistic tendencies of third-party organizations, particularly the People's Party, and the liberal wing of the Democracy, were political positions that could potentially damage their employer's economic well-being.

Railroaders got involved, whether casting ballots or holding public office, and their quests were likely focused on municipal rather than state or federal offices. In non-railroad communities businessmen and professionals dominated political life, but in railroad towns a strong railroader representation existed, including the office of mayor. In 1931 an industry journalist wrote an article that he called "Railroad Mayors Popular" and explained why this title rang true. "Because they are usually practical fellows, honest, industrious and congenial, railroad men make the best mayors." To this he added: "Men connected with the transportation of passengers or freight are close to the community's social and industrial life; therefore, it is only natural that many of them should be elected to the highest office which a city or town has to offer."

BETTER DEPOTS

If railroaders in a community possessed political clout, they surely joined fellow citizens to rectify any shortcomings with depot facilities. No matter the political chemistry, ambitious villages, towns, and cities expected and demanded good buildings. The annual reports of state railroad commissions, irrespective of region, repeatedly listed complaints and resolutions that involved depots, revealing that regulators gave considerable attention to such matters.

The presence of an adequate, well-maintained, convenient, and architecturally pleasing depot meant much to the citizenry of any place. After all, the building served as the gateway to the community, just as later generations would demand state-of-the-art airport terminals. Residents did not want a poorly functioning eyesore that suggested a town lacked that progressive spirit.

Examples exist of relatively cordial community efforts to achieve a better depot. Beginning in 1907 residents of Walhalla, seat of Oconee County, South Carolina, and northern terminus of the Blue Ridge Railway, launched their demand for a satisfactory building. "The matter had been put off from time to time, but in June 1909, the citizens insisted that they should be provided with a [replacement] depot," reported the Blue Ridge president to his board of directors in February 1910. If the railroad failed to comply, Walhalla threatened to lodge a formal complaint with the state railroad commission. This brought action. "After carefully investigating the matter" management authorized an expenditure for a new depot "at a cost of not exceeding $1,500." Based on board minutes, the town and the railroad seemed pleased with the outcome.

But a classic depot fight broke out in 1907 in Greenwich, Ohio, a town of nearly one thousand residents in Huron County in the north-central section of the state. Even though Greenwich benefited from excellent access to three steam railroads (Pittsburgh-to-Chicago main line of the B&O, Cleveland-to-Columbus stem of the Big Four System, and the Akron-to-Delphos, Ohio, line of the Northern Ohio), dissatisfaction erupted. The B&O and Big Four provided good depot facilities, but the Northern Ohio did not. When in 1890 the Pittsburgh, Akron & Western Railroad, a predecessor of the Northern Ohio, had built through Greenwich, it erected a modest depot in an inconvenient part of town. After the Northern Ohio emerged, it showed even less interest in Greenwich.

The railroad subsequently removed its agent and allowed the building to fall into disrepair. The Northern Ohio told patrons to use either the New London station, 7 miles to the east, or the Plymouth facility, 9 miles to the west. Residents howled. They depended upon the railroad's two-daily-except-Sunday passenger trains for personal travel, especially to the neighboring towns of Cary, Medina, New London, New Washington, and Plymouth, and for sending and receiving less-than-carload (LCL) freight, express, and mail over the road or through connections.

Greenwich residents turned to the Ohio Railroad Commission for relief. In late 1907 they charged in a formal complaint that the Northern Ohio provided "an old, dilapidated, abandoned and partly destroyed building," arguing that the structure should be replaced immediately. Seemingly unconcerned about its image, the railroad contended that Ohio regulatory statutes did not apply. Yet the law stated a carrier's public obligation: "It shall be the duty of every railroad to provide and maintain adequate depots and depot buildings at its *regular stations* for the accommodation of passengers, and said depot buildings, shall be kept clean, well lighted and warmed" (italics added). Attorneys for the Northern Ohio developed their own argument, asserting that Greenwich was "flag stop" rather than a "regular station" and that therefore this provision of the legal code did not apply.

The legal reasoning of the Northern Ohio appeared flawed. The attorney for Greenwich told commissioners that while the railroad might use the flag-stop designation in its public timetables and the *Official Guide to the Railways,* the station in reality was a bona fide regular stop. To provide his point, a postal worker, who for eight years had carried the mails to and from the depot, testified that trains *always* stopped, regardless of the proclaimed flag designation.

In March 1908 townspeople received good news. Regulators in Columbus voted in their favor, concluding that the Northern Ohio had treated the town as a regular stop. In its ruling the commission ordered that "The defendant should provide a suitable building at said station, and keep the same well lighted for the comfort and accommodation of its patrons, and that some person should be placed in charge thereof to receive and receipt for parcel freight, and that such person should take charge of incoming parcel freight and store the same in the usual and customary way until called for by the owner."

A new day dawned for Greenwich. The railroad complied; the town got its replacement depot and a full-time agent. Although indignation subsided, some residents groused about the location, even though they had won on the most pressing issues, the building and agent. Since Ohio was in the midst of interurban building, there was strong support for an electric line to serve Greenwich and nearby communities, including some that stretched along the route of the Northern Ohio. But these interurban hopes – at least for Greenwich – remained just that: unfulfilled dreams.

An earlier complaint, but with a common twist, involved residents of Sheldon, Iowa, located in the northwestern section of the Hawkeye State. As with Greenwich, Sheldon enjoyed the services of more than a single railroad. Trains of the Milwaukee Road and the Omaha Road, a North Western affiliate, provided this lively agricultural community with main-line service in all directions. In order to operate economically the railroads maintained a joint depot, a practical and popular arrangement. But in March 1887 seventy-four citizens complained in an official petition to state regulators that their depot was horribly inadequate. Their list of grievances was extensive. "There is no suitable or comfortable station house for passengers, nor any place for the protection of baggage; that the building now occupied is small, having but one room for the use of all passengers (men and women); that its dimensions are 18x20 feet; that ladies waiting for trains are compelled to stand out of doors or remain in a room with an atmosphere laden with villainous tobacco smoke, and compelled to hear profanity and obscenity." The protesters, represented by a Sheldon attorney, informed commissioners of these shortcomings; they agreed to conduct an inspection. But before that occurred, the body contacted the carriers and learned that they realized that betterments were needed. Without a formal order, the Milwaukee Road and Omaha Road made improvements, adding a waiting room and a ticket window that served both waiting areas. Moreover, the station platforms were lengthened and baggage handling capacities enhanced. The commission seemed pleased. "Exteriorly the building looked well, and while not specially pretentious was apparently adapted for the purpose much better than the average of station houses throughout the State." As for the annoyances of tobacco smoke and bad language, little was offered; these were deemed "usual" problems in a depot. Yet the body instructed station personnel to employ moral suasion, urging them to tell patrons that "the decencies of civilized life must be respected."

The spats over depots, which occurred between citizens of Greenwich and Sheldon and their hometown railroads, revealed real concerns and touches of anger. Yet a truly nasty fight erupted between two communities in Oklahoma Territory, South Enid and Pond Creek, and the Rock Island Railroad. In the 1890s the Rock Island, a corporation that was gaining a reputation for its arrogance, built depots at Pond Creek Station and North Enid, situated 19 miles apart, along its new north–south line between Herington, Kansas, and Fort Worth, Texas. While the Rock Island expected these places would become trade centers, rival communities Pond Creek and South Enid, each located about 3 miles south of the "official" stations, suggested otherwise. Unlike the Rock Island–designated stations, the two non-railroad-recognized communities grew – Pond Creek and South Enid reached a stable population of several thousand residents – and federal officials designated them as seats of Grant and Garfield counties respectively. Civic leaders understandably asked the railroad to establish depots in their hometowns. "It seemed a reasonable request," wrote William Edward Hayes, historian of the Rock Island. "Weren't the people of these towns providing a lot of new traffic for the railroad? Weren't they depending on the railroad for service?" To sweeten their requests, each town offered to donate land for a depot and to pay construction costs. But the railroad refused.

Tensions mounted. Militant residents in Pond Creek and South Enid thought that a few "harmless" shotgun blasts at passing trains might prompt Rock Island officials to change their mind. Instead the trains "hit these towns wide open, swirling the cinders and dust into a cloud with the speed of their passing." A freight train that roared through at 40 miles per hour presented a real safety concern, let alone service inadequacies. Both municipalities responded with ordinances that severely restricted train speeds within their corporate limits. Once more the Rock Island ignored public sentiments. When town marshals sought to enforce the speed restrictions, they learned that train crews carried Winchester repeating rifles and were "willing to use them."

What would be the next response? Petitions to territorial and federal offices were circulated. One strategy involved having the U.S. Congress pass legislation that would require railways that served county seats to maintain station facilities. While some progress took place in Washington, no act was forthcoming. Then a handful of citizens turned violent; on July 13, 1894, acts of consumer sabotage occurred. Irate citizens sawed through the wooden bents on a trestle over Boggy Creek outside South Enid, wrecking a fifteen-car freight train. Almost simultaneously dynamite blasts and fires destroyed track and bridges near Pond Creek. The Rock Island responded by demanding that authorities smash the "insurrection" and placing armed guards at strategic points along 25 miles of right-of-way. Federal officials then intervened, declaring marshal law in both communities and arresting the insurgents' leaders.

At last the "Great Railway War" came to an end. Although arrests had occurred, the trial in neighboring Kingfisher went nowhere for the Rock Island. A sympathetic judge dismissed the charges, and the saboteurs walked away as free men. The railroad capitulated. Shortly Pond Creek and South Enid got their depots, placed in desirable locations and with agents.

Even more bizarre acts of violence in a community's quest for a better depot occurred. One remarkable case involved residents of Urbana,

Indiana, who sought a desirable depot. Officials of the Cincinnati, Wabash & Michigan Railway, however, refused to respond positively to repeated petitions for a replacement structure, and villagers became outraged. But Urbanans responded in a forthright manner; they appointed a committee to blow up the depot. In April 1888, they did just that. "Nothing of the old building was left, except a hole in the ground." This creative strategy worked. A suitable depot later appeared in this Wabash County community.

Although Urbana residents took drastic, unlawful action, citizens of the Swedish American town of Stanton, Iowa, showed greater restraint in dealing with their hometown railroad. Yet they took direct action. Visitors to Stanton noticed an unusual characteristic of this Montgomery County community; virtually every building was painted white, providing a clean and tidy appearance. Stantonites did not object to the size, style, or location of their combination depot, but they hated the color. When the Burlington refused to repaint its weather-worn red depot white, citizens took paint and brush in hand and refurbished the building. Finally railroad officials endorsed what residents liked to call their "Little White City."

Closely related to complaints about depot structures were matters concerning agents. Repeatedly citizens voiced to regulators objections about surly personnel or the lack of adequate staffing. In 1890 the Kansas Board of Railroad Commissioners heard cries of protest from the unhappy people of Timken, a Rush County settlement located on the Chicago, Kansas & Western Railroad (CK&W), a Santa Fe affiliate. Although the railroad had built a depot and installed a siding, it had failed to provide an agent. The Santa Fe claimed that Timken generated too little revenue to justify the salary expenditure. But the commission learned from an employee of the grain elevator that "during the five month last past he had loaded nineteen cars, and could have loaded seventy-five cars if there had been a agent through whom to order cars, instead of being subject to the inconvenience and delay of ordering by letter from the nearest station, which is eight miles distant." Timken people, too, were highly annoyed that they had purchased $17,500 worth of CK&W bonds with the understanding that there would be a depot and an agent. The commission agreed that the town must have "full station facilities," and so compelled compliance.

All was not anti-railroad. State regulators, on their own, might commend a carrier for taking the initiative in constructing and maintaining an attractive and functional depot. When representatives of the Connecticut Railroad Commission early in the twentieth century inspected the Naugatuck Railroad depot at Winsted, they praised the impressive brick structure, which had been built in 1877 for about $10,000. They applauded its public space, noting the "suitable and proper conveniences for both ladies and gentlemen, so essential to the healthy and comfort of the travelers, but for gentlemen, particularly, so often neglected."

MORE COMMUNITY CONCERNS

For decades communities of all sizes expressed grave concerns about matters of railroad rates and services. There is no question that major companies faced huge fixed costs, ranging from capital betterments, such as shops and locomotives, to massive payrolls. But citizens did not fret much about corporate health. There existed a widespread belief that railroads received favorable considerations in the form of land grants, tax breaks, and a variety of public investments. Following the Civil War, railroads, it was thought, controlled legislators and public officials. Government had failed to protect the public interest against railroad lobbyists " with their pockets full of gold."

Complaints varied. Shippers did not understand why it cost more, for example, to send a carload of grain from Galva, Illinois, to Chicago than from Chicago to New York City, a distance seven times greater. Others wondered why it cost four or five cents for passengers to travel a mile rather than two or three cents.

Railroad charges for freight and passenger transport sparked community action. In the early 1870s the first major burst of public wrath against the industry occurred when the so-called Granger movement swept a large part of the nation. Spearheaded by a coalition of merchants, commercial groups, and farmers, Grangers fought to reduce charges and to end long- and short-haul rate discriminations. These reformers also agitated for state railroad commissions with powers to supervise carriers and thus to protect consumer triumphs.

Granger victories were impressive. Stringent railroad regulatory acts passed in Illinois, Iowa, Minnesota, and Wisconsin, the heartland of this reform agitation. The most controversial legislation, Wisconsin's Potter Railroad Law, which took effect in 1874, arranged freight and passenger traffic into classifications and established maximum rates for items within each category. The law generally ended the practice of carriers getting a greater rate per-ton-mile and per-passenger-mile for the shorter haul. The Potter Act also created a three-member board of railroad commissioners to implement its provisions.

Granger-era reformers could not rest on their victories. When the U.S. Supreme Court in the Wabash case of 1886 overturned the decade-earlier pro-Granger Munn decision that now limited the scope of state regulation, a public outcry occurred. This widespread unhappiness led Congress in 1887 to pass the Interstate Commerce Act that limited certain abuses, including freight rebates, and authorized creation of the Interstate Commerce Commission (ICC), the first federal-level body to regulate the business sector.

Somewhat later, following the depression of the 1890s, a massive reform crusade burst upon the American scene, the progressive movement. Similarly, politicians, frequently seismographs of public opinion, fought for additional state and especially federal controls. The Hepburn Act of 1906 made the ICC the most powerful government regulatory agency at the time, empowering it to set rates based upon complaints from shippers. Stronger still was the Mann-Elkins Act, passed four years later, that required proposed rate increases to be sanctioned by the ICC *before* going into effect. Mann-Elkins became the first federal statute to establish de facto price ceilings on a single industry during peacetime, and it came in the midst of a long-term upward trend in prices. Consumers applauded this aspect of the great national housecleaning. Reflected a cotton shipper in Valdosta, Georgia, "This town is full of happiness with what our lawmakers have done about the old railroad rate bugaboo. The politicians have been listening and doing something." But extensive federal intervention into rate-making frightened the industry, causing officials and investors to worry about their financial future.

Yet there existed an irony in the rate controversy. The maturity of railroads actually had enhanced concerns over pricing; nevertheless, this observation, made in 1913, attests to the somewhat illogical position that had gained currency: "I can remember when we were almighty glad to pay 5 cents a mile to ride in rickety little cars over a roadbed as rough as a Virginia corduroy road, 25 miles an hour, and the liver shaken out of us before we had travelled half-way to our destinations. Now we complain because we are compelled to pay 2 cents a mile to ride in cars more elegant than most of our homes, over roadbeds as smooth as a billiard table, speeding along at 50 or 60 miles an hour."

Eventually customers and railroads came to peacefully coexist. With the rise of automobiles and buses, fewer community and individual concerns were expressed to regulators about passenger rail charges. And development of trucks had that positive impact on shippers. Still, matters of rates never disappeared from the public discourse, including the years since Congress passed the Staggers Act (1980) that brought about partial freight-rate deregulation.

Service concerns regularly came to the forefront during the years of railroad domination. Railroad commission records contain frequent complaints about poorly maintained equipment, car shortages, slow delivery times, adverse switching practices, and a multitude of other grievances. In 1918 the Knox Clay Products Company of Knoxville, Iowa, backed by the town's commercial club, asked the state railroad commission to force its two railroads, Burlington and Rock Island, whose tracks ran close together, to create a physical interchange. Such an arrangement would enhance transportation options, speed delivery times, and reduce the cost of local drayage, all concerns of the clay products firm and other Knoxville business interests. The commission agreed, as other contemporary regulatory bodies tended to do.

Public concerns about railroads in their midst might be explained in a comical or silly fashion; yet, these complaints were surely based on real annoyances. Take the case of a Crosby, Minnesota, resident who in December 1936 complained to officials of the Soo Line about its noisy switch engine. "Why is it that your switch engine has to ding and dong and fizz and spit and clang and bang and hiss and grate and pant and rant and howl and yowl and grind and puff and bump and click and clank and boot and toot and crash and grunt and gasp and groan and whistle and wheeze and squawk and blow and jar and jerk and rasp and jingle and twang and smoke and smell all the doggone night long?" There is no record of whether the Soo Line responded in a community-friendly way. The annoying sounds likely continued.

Community complaints involved more than noise. From the earliest days of train operations and onward, urban residents objected, often forcefully, to the presence of locomotive and rolling stock in their streets. Indeed, the street emerged as a singularly contested environment. In Baltimore, the first American city to have tracks placed in public thoroughfares, a ruckus erupted early on. A municipal report revealed widespread unhappiness with plans by B&O management to switch from horse to steam power between the original terminus and the docks. Steam locomotives would surely frighten horses and injure their riders and also endanger pedestrians. There would be an increased risk of fires from sparks thrown out by these wood-burners, and that could lead to a conflagration or at the least to hikes in fire-insurance rates. Additional complaints developed among Baltimoreans and residents of other cities and towns. The use of soft, sulfur-laded coal meant dirty, smelly air. And collectively, the presence of a railroad, particularly in residential areas, inevitably lowered property values. Then there was this thought: "To some persons, insurmountable objection, was the encouragement offered to a monopoly interfering with the free and illimitable rights of citizens."

Objections to tracks in the streets used by steam, even animal, power prompted repeated court cases. One instance of litigation involved action taken in the late 1830s by the city government of Louisville, Kentucky, which restricted the Lexington & Ohio Railroad from using its line on Main Street between Sixth and Thirteenth streets. Backers of the ordinance made popular arguments: "The railroad obstructed the free and convenient public use of Main street; the frequent transportation of passengers in a long train of cars, propelled by steam, alarmed horses, and endangered the security of persons passing on foot, on horses, and in hacks and private carriages; diminished the value of real estate and was therefore a public nuisance." Eventually the railroad won in its suit to overturn the council, but not until after a lengthy, costly fight.

When confronted with public objections to trains operating on city streets, railroad companies did not always seek judicial regress. Some voluntarily agreed to use horses or dispatch shorter trains or trains only at night. In 1840 the editor of the *American Railroad Journal* recalled another approach to these nuisance charges. "We remember watching, with no little curiosity and amusement, the various expedients used upon the Long Island railroad, to disguise the engine in approaching Brooklyn. Among others, a sort of jacket was provided for the bright part of the works, and another for the smoke pipe; and for this or other reasons, various arrangements of the train were made, the locomotive sometimes being behind the cars." But these efforts were arguably a waste of time. "After all, it seems to us, that the horses were as little disturbed by the undisguised engine, at the head of the train, as by any other arrangement. In fact, after a while no difficulty whatever occurred, and we have seen spirited horses driven along side of the engine for some time without betraying any symptoms of fear."

More urbanites fussed about blocked crossings than about trains operating in public streets. Such annoyances usually involved switching activities that repeatedly obstructed roads, sidewalks, and other passageways. The results caused dangers and delays. People became impatient, driving around equipment or climbing over and under cars. Those who waited might arrive late at their destinations and in an aggravated mental state. Junior-high and high-school students who lived east of the active Minneapolis & St. Louis–Wabash yards in Albia, Iowa, regularly had to troop over to depot once the blockage ended and have the agent write and date a note (listing their names) to school officials, explaining that the railroad had again resulted in their morning tardiness. Maybe the students did not mind, but others – educators and parents – surely did.

Ever since the dawn of railroading, community residents repeatedly grumbled about the general appearance of the railroad corridor, especially junkyards and storage sites. Railroad facilities did not escape their wrath either. The industry press admitted that unsightly scenes existed. "Some depot yards which we have seen are not unfit theatres for the enactment of Dickens' scenes of the ghosts of stage coaches, or rather railway cars," observed a trade writer in 1846. "Old smoke stacks, broken wheels, burnt, smashed or discarded cars, heaps of cinders and or oiled rags, fill up the larger space in such places." Complaints to companies usually did little to improve the visual situation, but eventually depression-era and wartime scrap drives did much to clean up these eyesores.

While community concerns about trackside litter melted away in the 1940s, a pressing concern for many urbanites in the 1950s and later involved the loss of passenger service and then line abandonments. As private automobiles and commercial airliners drew more travelers away from trains, regulatory authorities conducted numerous railroad-instigated public hearings about "take-off" proposals. Passage of the Transportation Act of 1958 made the process somewhat easier for carriers, resulting in more communities bidding farewell to their favorite or possibly their last train.

One heated take-off case involved residents of Decatur, Illinois, a community that had enjoyed superb service provided by the Wabash Railroad. In March 1960 the company petitioned the Illinois Commerce Commission for permission to drop trains No. 117 and No. 118, *The Midnight,* its last overnight runs between Chicago and St. Louis. The Wabash claimed heavy losses and indicated that its daytime *Banner Blue* and *Blue Bird* trains would continue between these two Midwestern metropolises. But various groups and individuals from Decatur rose up in arms about the prospect of losing the overnight trains. Business people, who represented several civic groups, told the hearing examiner that their city of approximately 100,000 lacked direct access to an interstate highway, and they worried what would happen "when the weather gets ornery – when trucks bog down on snow-covered highways and planes are grounded." There were also personal objections. The most poignant came from World War I veterans and their families who worried about getting these men to the Veterans Administration facility in Chicago in time for their appointments. "They are always scheduled at eight o'clock in the morning," said one witness. "So the way the significance of this train is felt by the veteran, I think it is a crime that this train as to be removed." Decaturites lost; the Wabash received permission to terminate *The Midnight*s.

Numerous communities throughout the nation faced this pattern of dwindling railroad service: reduction in passenger train operations and then their complete elimination; consolidation or closure of depots; reduced freight traffic and line shutdowns. Apparently some places did not seem to care much about these continuing losses. Improved motor vehicles and better roadways, especially the Interstate Highway System, provided viable options; individuals could drive, take a bus, and have trucks handle most in- and outbound shipments. Still, residents in hundreds of towns fought to save their rails. This reaction dates from the era of World War I when sizable abandonments (largely shortlines) began, a process that accelerated dramatically between 1960 and 1980.

An early illustration of a town that struggled to maintain its rail link to the outside world was Belfast, Maine. In the 1860s this coastal community of 5,278 residents, situated in Waldo County, longed for the iron horse. The county was losing population, having dropped significantly over the previous twenty years, and a railroad outlet would surely energize the community. Success came in December 1870 when the first trains of the Belfast & Moosehead Lake Railroad rolled over the 33 miles of track between Belfast and a connection with the Maine Central at Burnham Junction. Investors, though, decided that it made good sense to lease their road to the Maine Central, and in April 1871 an agreement was reached. All went smoothly until 1926, when the Maine Central terminated the rental, contending that the Belfast appendage, or "Belfast branch," was no longer financially viable and claiming an annual loss of $40,000. It appeared that Belfast and the several on-line stations would forever lose railroad service. Faced with this real threat, the City of Belfast acquired most of the common stock, and the Town of Brooks took the remainder. This venture into public ownership worked well, saving service, most of all carload freight. Not unexpectedly the road stopped carrying passengers in 1960, and in recent years the line saw only intermittent freight operations. In 1991 public ownership ended. Repeated efforts by private interests to sustain freight traffic and to operate seasonal tourist excursions failed, causing a permanent shutdown in 2008.

Other communities would employ the Belfast & Moosehead Lake civic model. A more recent version is the "railroad authority," allowing threatened trackage to become publicly owned, but then leasing the property to a private for-profit operator. In 1983 the McMinnville, Tennessee, area organized the Tri-County Railroad Authority to maintain freight operations for several rail-dependant businesses on the 61-mile former Seaboard System line between Sparta and Tullahoma, trackage that had just been formally abandoned. The authority subsequently leased the trackage to the Caney Fork & Western Railroad, Inc., a unit of Ironhorse Resources, an operator of several shortlines in the South. A few years later business interests and civil leaders in Columbia, Missouri, became alarmed when Norfolk Southern Railroad announced its intention to abandon the former Wabash branch between Columbia and Centralia. These individuals quickly sprang into action. Creation of the Columbia Terminal Railroad (COLT), a division of the Water & Light Department of Columbia, permitted continuation of the movement of a variety of commodities over this 21-mile route. Later the innovative COLT offered customers transloading, warehousing, and distributing services, continuing to please the city officials and taxpayers.

A version of community sponsored shortlines is the aptly named Appanoose County Community Railroad (APNC). As with McMinnville and Columbia, Centerville, Iowa, was about to lose its rail connections; trackage that had once belonged to the Burlington and Rock Island railroads, together with one of the Midwest's last surviving electric roads, had been abandoned, but not all of the track had been removed. So in 1984 this Appanoose County seat launched a nonprofit corporation, and community fund raisers went to work. Residents chipped in $5, $10, or more in tax-deductible contributions to produce about $50,000. Businesses contributed more than twice that amount. The city government pledged $30,000 and the county $55,000. Two local banks then provided a loan of $200,000. By cobbling together sections of the former Burlington and Rock Island, a connection was forged with Norfolk Southern near Moulton, Iowa. And a few years later when Norfolk Southern abandoned its line between Moberly, Missouri, and Des Moines, Iowa, the trackage between Moulton and Albia, Iowa, was acquired, making for a 35-mile shortline. Said one area resident, "Who would have ever thought that people, businesses and local governments would have to get into the railroad business? But they did!" This was a sentiment repeated by supporters of community roads.

Not all endeavors to save rail service succeeded. In the mid-1980s Carmel, Indiana, citizens made a valiant attempt to preserve freight service on a small section of the former Monon Railroad main line between Indianapolis and Chicago. Although the owner, CSX, leased the trackage to Carmel interests and an operator, Indiana Hi-Rail Corporation, agreed to a temporary operating contract, sufficient freight revenues could not be generated. When Indiana Hi-Rail backed out in 1986, the community formed a rail authority to ensure operations. Unfortunately for rail advocates, this became another failed effort. In 1987 wreckers lifted the rails and removed ties and other salvageable materials; Carmel became an inland town again after 104 years of rail service.

A more successful approach and one endorsed by hundreds of communities involved backing newly launched *privately* owned and operated railroads. (Some states – Georgia, South Dakota, and Vermont – bought trackage and then leased it to private operators.) These arrangements meant that freight services were preserved in the wake of the major railroad bankruptcies and reorganizations of the 1970s and later when carriers eliminated routes that were poor income-producers or that did not fit their core operations. It made sense for pieces of trackage that were of greater economic value to communities than they were to their owners to become shortlines or parts of regional railroads. Upstart roads like the Dakota, Minnesota & Eastern Railroad (purchased by Canadian Pacific in 2008), Kyle Railroad, Paducah & Louisville Railroad, and San Joaquin Valley Railroad have preserved railroad connections for many places.

RHYTHM OF COMMUNITY LIFE

Irrespective of the scope of railroad operations, residents understood that the rhythms of the railroad often became the rhythms of their community. "The startings and arrivals of the cars are now the epochs in the village day," observed Henry David Thoreau. "They go and come with such regularity and precision that the farmers set their clocks by them, and thus one well-conducted institution regulates a whole country." This phenomenon became most apparent in places that had modest passenger movements, usually "double-daily" service. A morning train carried passengers who detrained and boarded, but it also brought mail, newspapers, express, and other items that were eagerly anticipated. Hearing the scream of the whistle of the approaching train as the engineer sounded warnings to protect road crossings reminded townspeople that shortly they could walk to the post office and retrieve their mail, or the coming train prompted them to call or to stroll over to the depot or express office to check on a package. Those same blasts, coming later in the day, caused citizens to contemplate a visit to the depot. "As in all American towns of the time the railroad station was a magnet that continually drew our people," reflected Sherwood Anderson about his boyhood in Clyde, Ohio. "There was a passenger train going away into the mysterious West at some twenty minutes after seven in the evenings and, as six o'clock was our universal supper hour, we all congregated at the station to see the train arrive, we boys gathering far down the station platform to gape with hungry eyes at the locomotive."

Citizens conversed about train activities to friends and others on their front porches, over back fences, or elsewhere in town. "No. 4 was late today"; "No. 9 was ahead of schedule"; or "Didn't a special come through town early this morning?" In *Main Street,* Sinclair Lewis's satirical novel about small-town Midwestern life, Gopher Prairie residents intimately understood the railroad scene. Penned Lewis, "The smallest boy or the most secluded grandame could tell you whether No 32 had a hot box last Tuesday, whether No. 7 was going to put on an extra day coach, and the name of the president of the road was familiar to every breakfast table." A parent might tell a child to come home no later then when a particular train whistled into town or make some other railroad reference.

It was common for youngsters to be more than entranced with a locomotive steaming into the station; they might also see the railroad corridor as a part of their extended playground. Using their knowledge of railroad schedules, they acted accordingly. When a train approached, daring children might place a penny on the railhead and rejoice when they retrieved the flattened piece of copper. Or they might carefully lay two pins in a cross-like fashion, and hope to find the fused metal. Realizing that a train was not expected, children, and adults too, might stroll along the tracks with their sacks or pails to pick up lumps of coal that had fallen from locomotive tenders or freight cars, reducing in this way home heating and cooking costs. Knowing the timing of railroad activities, youngsters might find pleasure in playing on idle rolling stock, a deserted turntable, or some other piece of equipment. A train might suddenly appear, or a mechanical device might start up unexpectedly. Such potentially fun-filled ventures were always fraught with danger: bruising fall, smashed finger, broken limb, or death.

The arrival and departure of scheduled trains had an impact on community life, but "railroad time" had a universal effect. In the days of dominant travel by animal power – horseback, wagon, carriage – or even by canal or steamboat, individuals easily adjusted to "God's time" or sun time (based on the sun's passage across the local meridian), setting their timepieces either ahead or behind. But with development of long-distance railroad travel a carrier nearly always maintained a single time along its route, irrespective of the position of the sun, breaking for many nature's domination or the "immutable laws of God." There would be Boston, Charleston, New York, Philadelphia, or some other "city time." Residents of a town like Aiken, South Carolina, a station near the western terminus of the South-Carolina Canal & Rail-Road Company, found that the railroad dictated local time. Citizens were free to use solar time, as were the residents of other on-line communities, but all depot clocks would be set to the railroad's "official time," namely that of Charleston, a few minutes faster.

With rapid expansion of the railroad network after the Civil War, a troubling time problem developed. The hundreds of carriers used more than seventy-five different city times, confusing the public and creating difficult situations. Did a town in New York state, with multiple railroads, employ the time used by the first or by the more or most important carrier? After all, city times established for Albany, Buffalo, and New York differed by a number of minutes. The feeling grew that time differences created chaos in daily life.

Politicians were the first to react. In January 1881 Connecticut lawmakers passed "An Act establishing a Standard of Time," and for good reason. Although the state was small, there were too many times. "East of the Connecticut River there are three standards, and two west of the river." Legislators responded largely for reasons of safety. Unsnarling the confusion over clock settings, however, required more than the action by a single legislative body.

Somewhat later efforts by railroad themselves, led by William F. Allen, a civil engineer who edited the *Railway Traveler's Official Guide,* ended confusion wrought by time setting. In April 1883 the industry's General Time Convention decided to establish four North American time zones: Eastern, Central, Mountain, and Pacific. For many communities, Sunday, November 18, 1883, became "the day of two noons." Not every place followed the convention, but within several years Standard Railway Time became nearly universally accepted, attesting to the enormous power of the railroad enterprise. Later Congress, during World War I, officially established the general structure of the railroad-created zones.

UNUSUAL HAPPENINGS

In addition to unusual train movements, whether bringing to or through a community an important personage, circus, or some other attraction, the railroad experienced another type of happening that fascinated the public: the train wreck. As speeds rose and traffic expanded, accidents increased. Although mishaps often occurred in rural or remote locations, hundreds, if not thousands, took place in or near population centers. Just as automobile and airplane disasters would attract the curious, such events involving trains, especially passenger trains, sparked excitement and concern. People walked, saddled horses, hitched up buggies and wagons, or later drove tin lizzies to the derailment. They might get carried away, interfering with relief workers and shamelessly gathering souvenirs.

How a wreck affected communities can be seen in the horrific smash-up that occurred on the evening of November 27, 1901, outside Seneca, Michigan, a village not far from the county-seat town of Adrian. It would be the deadliest mishap for the Wabash Railroad (upward of one hundred fatalities), and one of the worst accidents in American railroading. An eastbound train, No. 4, *The Continental Limited,* collided head-on with No. 13, a westbound passenger train, each crammed with Thanksgiving travelers. A train-order error led to this "cornfield meet." When the accident happened, both trains derailed, and flames consumed several wooden cars on No. 13, including two "immigrant" coaches that were packed with families from Italy bound for Kansas City, Missouri. "The immigrant cars were telescoped in such a manner that we could see within the fiery furnace, and it was awful," reported a survivor. "Men and women were pinioned in the wreckage and lay there helplessly watching the flames creeping rapidly upon them. Their groans and calls for help were heart-rending, but we could do nothing on account of the heat." Soon volunteer rescuers arrived,

and in time relief trains came from Detroit and Peru, Indiana. But "huge crowds" descended on the wreck site, coming from Adrian, Sand Creek, Seneca, and other communities and from nearby farms. Onlookers picked up pieces of melted glass and metal, bits of stained glass from the several Pullmans, and even fragments of bodies that were nearly incinerated in the conflagration. The combination of railroad workers, relief personnel, and the morbidly curious helped to destroy evidence of bodies, making a precise death count impossible.

For the next several days the wreck drew onlookers, although by this time the Wabash had posted guards to keep them at bay. "The scene of the wreck has been since visited by thousands of sightseers from all over the county," noted an Adrian editor. "Sunday last was unusually pleasant for the season, and an immense crowd to drive to the spot took the day." Added another journalist, "Nearly every person about here has visited the scene of Seneca's terrible railroad disaster; we think and talk of little else."

And commercial opportunities developed. Entrepreneurial photographers made images that they could sell as prints or picture postcards, the latter having become a national craze by the early twentieth century. Views of the Wabash wreck varied. They mostly showed the mangled wreckage of locomotives and cars, but one captured a woman taking ostrich plumes from a victim's hat.

Nearly as memorable, but lacking the powerful human drama, were staged train wrecks. Such events became popular before World War I.

HEAD ON COLLISION NEAR
PHILIP S D SEPT 6 1911

"Somewhere in the makeup of every normal person," explained Joseph "Head-On Joe" Connolly, who arranged scores of collisions, "there lurks the suppressed desire to smash things up."

Likely the only railroad-sponsored crash took place near West, Texas, on September 15, 1896, when W. G. Crush, passenger traffic manager for the Missouri-Kansas-Texas Railway (Katy), orchestrated this spectacular collision. As a ploy to bolster ridership during the awful depression of the 1890s, Crush and his associates extensively advertised the prearranged collision, arousing "public interest to a high pitch." On the day of the much-anticipated event, the Katy ran thirty-five special trains to accommodate the throng. In preparation for the crash employees gave two elderly American-standard type locomotives, renumbered nos. 999 and 1001, a festive paint job; No. 999 sported a bright green and No. 1001 showed a fiery red. Operating over a 2-mile section of special track, each locomotive pulled six empty freight cars, and the thrills began. After bringing the trains to full speed the two crews jumped to safety. Beforehand the whistles were fastened to one of the driving wheels to provide intermittent blasts, adding to the excitement. Then the collision of the two hissing monsters took place and their boilers exploded. At first the estimated crowd of thirty thousand delighted in the sights and sounds, but soon they learned of the human toll. A man perched in a tree died instantly when hit by a piece of flying metal, and a girl was killed when struck in the head by a link of chain. "It was a subdued crowd that climbed back into the excursion trains that night."

Not withstanding the tragedies at West, Texas, non-railroad sponsors hosted a number of for-profit staged wrecks, and they became "a favorite

On September 6, 1911, another enterprising photographer traveled to the site of a head-on collision between a freight and a passenger train near Philip, South Dakota, also along North Western trackage, to make an image for his "real-photo" postcards.

Author's coll.

outdoor sport." Usually these collisions were part of a fair, and they took place throughout the country, including Atlanta, Des Moines, Pittsburgh, Salt Lake City, and Tampa.

One remarkable event occurred in Sacramento at the California State Fair. Designed to "bring in a new crowd" to a faltering annual event, the proclaimed "Wreck of the Century" drew thirty thousand admission-paying attendees from all parts of the Golden State and beyond. Fortunately, the event went off without a hitch. At 4:30 PM on September 4, 1913, the action began. As with the Katy collision, two old steamers raced along a length of track toward each other at full throttle after their crews had jumped. "When the locomotives met there was a loud crash, a sort of shattering, then the ground shook, there was a tearing noise as the locomotives met," reported the *Sacramento Union*. "Cylinder boxes exploded and rolled off to the side. The driving wheels held their position pretty well, but the oilers of each locomotive moved forward and ruptured, and clouds of steam reached skyward. The cabs seemed to disintegrate before the eyes, and about all that was left were the tenders. The only thing intact were the locomotive bells which kept ringing." An elated fair board staged three more locomotive wrecks before the country entered World War I, a time when every operable steam locomotive was needed to handle the surge in freight tonnage.

An aspect of community life that created excitement, but was marked by occasional acts of violence, were labor strikes and disputes. The relationships between workers and managers in the railroad industry were generally good, much better than in mining and manufacturing. Yet turbulence erupted, most notably in 1877, 1885, 1886, 1894, and 1922–1923. Not all railroad centers were involved, although the bitter (and lengthy) shopmen's strike of 1922–1923 became widespread. This job action, which involved more than 400,000 shopmen affiliated with the Railway Employees' Department of the American Federation of Labor, protested against wage cuts and work-rule changes and affected multiple locations throughout the country, ranging from Altoona, Pennsylvania, and Decatur, Illinois, to Sacramento, California, and Waycross, Georgia.

An analysis of the shopmen's walkout supports the assessment of strikes made by labor historian Herbert Gutman. This architect of the "new labor history" contended that railroad laborers, coal miners, and iron workers often benefited from small-town milieus, finding more support in such environments than they did in major cities. It was not uncommon in these smaller places for merchants to extend credit, social and religious organizations to contribute relief funds, and law enforcement personnel to resist arresting strikers when they clashed with "scabs" and railroad police or trespassed onto railroad property.

TOO MUCH
TO PAY FOR A LITTLE SPORT

1301 Young People LOST OUT last year in this game
—TAKING CHANCES ON RAILROAD TRACKS and TRAINS

Railroad companies and railroad organizations did much to warn the public—especially youngsters—of ever-present dangers around railroad tracks and stations. This poster, which dates from the 1920's, cautions that play can turn into tragedy.

Author's coll.

Notwithstanding strong support of the shopmen in these nonurban centers, the strike fizzled out by mid-1923. Most places suffered. Strikers who returned often took pay cuts and lost seniority. Others decided to seek employment elsewhere and usually outside the industry. Commented a carman striker at a Wabash shops complex, "The railroad strike scattered the old bunch from Moberly, Mo." When former workers departed, their bills and debt obligations usually went unpaid. Those who remained struggled to catch up financially, if they could. The strike continued to haunt communities, including Moberly. Some businessmen failed in the 1920s, and those who managed to hold on were ill prepared to cope with the hard times of the 1930s. As late as 1941 the owner of the Central Coal & Supply Company in Moberly told an executive of the Pennsylvania Railroad, which controlled the Wabash, that he hoped that their affiliated property would treat his community fairly. "The town merchants of that day [1922–1923] allowed the strikers to put cards in their windows expressing sympathy for the strikers. Naturally this offended the Wabash officials. These merchants are also gone, but some of the older Wabash officials have not forgotten. If possible, we would like to start with a clean slate and cooperate in every way possible with the Pennsylvania." By this time, though, harmony had been mostly restored in Moberly and other communities affected by the unrest of the early 1920s.

While strikes injured communities, cutbacks in railroad operations had much the same effect. As the Great Depression deepened and carriers experienced sharply declining revenues, retrenchments occurred. Times were difficult in communities that depended heavily on railroad payrolls; merchants suffered, forcing some into bankruptcy. Everyone would be affected, even the youngest children. The second-grade daughter of a recently called Lutheran pastor in Oelwein, Iowa, operating and repair hub of the Great Western, remembered hearing other youngsters on the playground shout out, "The shops are closing! The shops are closing!" But having no sense of the railroad presence, she ran to her parents after school to tell them the news, believing that the "shops" were the businesses located along Frederick Avenue, the town's commercial district.

Other happenings also involved community residents. Children might stroll along the depot, freight house, lunchroom, or places along the tracks to look for the occasional small treasure, finding, if lucky, a penny or even a larger coin. Or they might collect cast-away bottles from along the right-of-way, "one cent for pint beer bottles and two cents for quart beer bottles." Later soft-drink bottles commanded higher prices. In shop towns boys might go "junking," gathering up pieces of babbit waste (also called white metal) that carmen used to protect bearings in wheel journals. They took their findings home, where they melted them, then skimmed and poured the soft metal into tobacco tins or other containers. When the babbit cooled, the lads pealed off the cans and sold the metal to a junk dealer for pocket money.

While bottle collecting and metal "junking" may not have raised eyebrows in town, another activity, often involving teenage boys, was hardly sanctioned (or it was not widely known). This involved sexual encounters in railroad yards, hobo jungles, or elsewhere along the community's railroad corridor. In his candid autobiography, *On Being Different: What It Means To Be a Homosexual*, novelist and historian Merle Miller commented on his sexual adventures in the yards in his hometown of Marshalltown, Iowa, a busy railroad center served by three main-line carriers. "There were often black boys on the freight trains, and we talked and had sex. Their stories were always sadder than anybody else's. I never

had any hangups about the color of somebody's skin." There were empty cars, abandoned rolling stock, switch shanties, and other places for male-to-male contact.

While their countless experiences were hardly noteworthy community "happenings," children and others developed a vast range of memories associated with trains. "I learned my first spelling from the names on the box cars," related one woman. "What early geography I knew I learned by asking men about the towns and cities, the names of which were chalked on the cars. I learned numbers by counting the cars on long freights."

HELPFUL RAILROADS

During the post–Civil War decades, especially, some citizens thought that railroads represented evil, committing frequent acts of corporate arrogance. Railroad officials were "robber barons" who firmly believed that the "public be damned," a statement falsely attributed to New York Central executive William K. Vanderbilt. Significantly, acts of "good" far exceeded those of "bad." Newspapers and other contemporary sources contain innumerable reports that show railroads extending much-needed (and appreciated) help. During blizzards maintenance crews fought to

While this activity was unlikely to have precipitated a childhood accident, the maker of this "real-photo" postcard of the Cleveland, Wisconsin, station, ca. 1910, caught two boys at play among items to be shipped as less-than-carload (LCL) freight. Railroads magically attracted children.

Author's coll.

clear tracks so that food and fuel could be delivered; during droughts relief trains brought in water for public drinking needs and for thirsty livestock; and during other community emergencies railroads responded.

There are numerous records of companies rushing in firefighting equipment and personnel. Smaller communities usually lacked the means to combat a conflagration, relying on ineffective volunteer bucket brigades. On July 5, 1888, flames were consuming parts of Grafton, West Virginia, prompting the B & O agent to telegraph for urgent assistance from the nearest city, Parkersburg, 104 miles distant. There was an immediate response. A special train, which consisted of "engine 738, an eight-wheeler, two flatcars holding the fire apparatus, and a coach," roared down the main line, and Grafton was saved from total destruction. In another example, a fire on January 28, 1927, fanned by high winds, seemed about to engulf the buildings and miners' houses owned by the Virginia-Harlan Coal Corporation in Balkan, Kentucky. The arrival of two locomotives of the Louisville & Nashville Railroad prevented a complete loss. Water from the engines allowed firefighters to save at least a dozen structures.

Another illustration of a railroad helping a community with a fire disaster took place in North Little Rock, Arkansas. On September 9, 1925, flames broke out in the high school, and after a valiant battle by firemen the handsome $100,000 structure became a mass of smoking, flame-charred ruins. With the opening of the fall term only a few days away, the catastrophe posed a serious question: where would students and their teachers go? The Board of Education decided that a temporary school should be built immediately to house classes until a permanent facility could be designed and constructed. Public subscriptions would be asked to reach the goal of the estimated cost of $3,000 for the temporary structure. This was when personnel of the Missouri Pacific Railroad intervened. E. F. Stroeh, superintendent of the company's sprawling North Little Rock shops, developed a plan of action. He asked members of the Missouri Pacific North Little Rock Shops Booster Club, nearly all of whom were shop employees, to assemble on a board-owned vacant lot on Third Street to build that temporary school. On the morning of Sunday, September 13, more than 350 railroaders came to the worksite. The walls and roof went up rapidly. Those who were not involved in construction contributed in other ways. Band members played a range of tunes that included "Red Hot Mama" and "It Ain't Gonna Rain No More" along with sacred music (it was Sunday). Others, including members of the women's auxiliary and their children, served a hot lunch and dinner. When darkness fell, the new structure, 48' wide, 200' long, and containing twenty classrooms, was ready, with the exception of locks on the doors, fasteners on the windows, and a few interior partitions. The following day employees paraded from the shop to the school to make the finishing touches. "An epic of civic betterment," were the apt words of the North Little Rock mayor.

Water could be as bad as fire. In July 1916, two tropical storms pounded large portions of the Southeast, with western North Carolina being especially hard hit. Torrential rains, in places approaching twenty inches, fell on already saturated soil, resulting in multiple deaths and massive property damage. Railroads did not escape; raging waters washed away track and roadbeds, destroyed bridges, blocked tunnels, and covered stations and yards. For weeks floods disrupted the flow of travel and goods. While all carriers responded to these weather-related challenges, the Southern Railway received high praise for restoring service to numerous communities throughout its devastated territory. The company rushed in emergency track and bridge crews and aided flood victims in a myriad of ways. "We can very appropriately express grateful appreciation for the Southern's help to the community while it is at the same time helping itself in the work of restoring its ruined property," editorialized the *Old Fort* [N.C.] *Sentinel* of August 10, 1916. "The assistance rendered Old Fort in rehabilitation, and the employment given hundreds of our mountain people is indeed a Godsend. And we thankfully welcome its construction forces to our town."

Historically ties between community and railroad have been strong. Yet the scope of these interactions is varied and complex. When railroads served as focal points of daily life, virtually every American experienced memorable direct or indirect contracts with them and the people who built, ran, and maintained these arteries of commerce.

4 LEGACY

 THE LEGACY OF THE RAILROAD IN AMERICAN LIFE IS ENORMOUS, extensively documented, and remembered by passing generations. In the twentieth century the automobile became the dominant form of personal transport and in the process helped to shape the national identity. Still, the railroad had a greater initial impact; after all, the iron horse represented a radical change from previous forms of intercity travel. Prior to the Railway Age transportation options involved slow-moving ships, steamboats, and canal packets and only slightly faster stagecoaches. Then there was the matter of dependability. Weather conditions – floods, snows, ice, winds, and fogs – repeatedly hampered the incumbent forms of transportation more than they did even pioneer railways. The adoption of motor cars also proved to be more *gradual* than that of passenger trains, the result of primitive technologies, high costs, and poor roads. For years citizens considered automobiles to be impractical toys, noisy and dangerous nuisances, appropriate only for tinkerers and the wealthy.

Commercial aviation likewise was slow to attract passengers. Not until nearly a half-century after the Wright brothers made their historic flight at Kitty Hawk, North Carolina, in 1903 did non-affluent and non-business travelers consider a trip by air. Only after the introduction of jet aircraft, federal deregulation, and the appearance of low-cost carriers did the masses take to the skies.

NAMES AND LANGUAGE

Unlike automobile and aircraft manufacturers, railroad companies contributed mightily to the naming of America. Admittedly the canal craze, which occurred in the several decades prior to 1850, helped to name scattered parts of America. There were places that contained "Canal," "Lock," and "Port" in their names. And there were canal towns that had "Basin," "Canal," and "Water" streets. But railroad-inspired names frequently included towns and streets, in fact, much more. Where rails did not precede settlement, fewer opportunities existed for railroad-generated or related names. Yet New England and the Mid-Atlantic states had places that included "Depot" in their town names, and streets with the same nomenclature and "Railroad," too. The South had more railroad-spawned communities and hence more places with railroad-inspired names. Branchville, South Carolina, for example, founded in the late 1830s where the Louisville, Cincinnati & Charleston Rail Road veered northward from the South-Carolina Canal & Rail-Road, received an appropriate and distinctive railroad name. "Depot" and "Railroad" streets were also common throughout Dixie.

But it was in the trans-Chicago West where the imprint of the railroad became most apparent in the naming process, involving not only towns and streets but also counties. After all, political units commonly appeared *after* the arrival of the iron horse. Take two counties in Minnesota. Pennington County honored Edmund Pennington, who headed the Minneapolis, St. Paul & Sault Ste. Marie Railway (Soo Line), and Stearns County remembered Isaac Ingalls Stearns, who directed survey work for the Northern Pacific Railroad.

Where there were more streets and places to name (sidings, junctions, villages, towns, and cities), the railroad influence (and legacy) is greater. Hundreds of communities have streets named Depot and Railroad, but also ones that honor individuals associated with the Railway Age. Dickinson, North Dakota, boasts a Villard Street, recognizing Henry Villard, who was a pivotal figure in the building of the Northern Pacific. When it comes to place names, a striking example involves a string of stations that appeared along the expanding track of the Burlington & Missouri River Railroad of Nebraska, a component of the Chicago, Burlington & Quincy Railroad (Burlington). In the 1870s the railroad's townsite arm established communities west of Lincoln, spaced about 10 miles apart, and named them mostly in alphabetical order. Crete, Dorchester, Exeter, Fairmont, Grafton, Harvard, Inland, Juniata, Kenesaw, and Lowell became these "alphabet towns." A practical explanation may have inspired this unusual naming scheme. Anyone – travelers or employees – knew their general location by merely learning the name of the nearest station, although the town of Hastings stood between Inland and Kenesaw. (Trolley companies sometimes numbered stops for the same reason.) Local boosters could claim the distinction of being an alphabet town on a major rail artery, setting their prairie villages apart from rival communities.

Usually there was no pattern in town names; the process occurred randomly. A good case can be found in eastern Washington state. Oakesdale honored Thomas F. Oakes, an officer of the Northern Pacific; Endicott and Prescott were named for William Endicott and C. H. Prescott, directors of a railroad holding company, and Starbuck venerated General

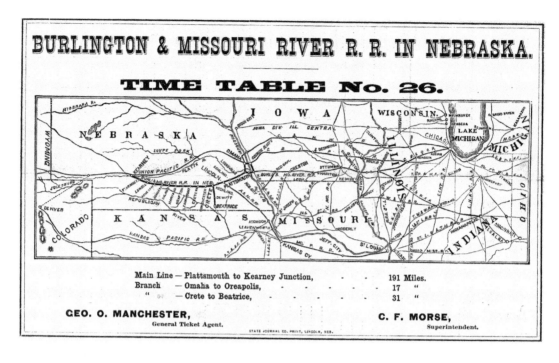

BURLINGTON & MISSOURI RIVER R. R. IN NEBRASKA.

TIME TABLE No. 26.

Main Line — Plattsmouth to Kearney Junction,   ·   191 Miles.
Branch   — Omaha to Oreapolis,   -   -   -   -   17   "
"   — Crete to Beatrice,   -   -   -   -   31   "

GEO. O. MANCHESTER,
General Ticket Agent.

C. F. MORSE,
Superintendent.

STATE JOURNAL CO. PRINT, LINCOLN, NEB.

By the early 1870s the Burlington & Missouri River Railroad in Nebraska, part of the expanding Burlington system, operated a 191-mile main stem between Plattsmouth and Kearney. Time Table No. 26, issued in August 1873, duly marks the company's string of recently established "alphabet towns."

Author's coll.

W. H. Starbuck of the Oregon River & Navigation Company, who was fondly remembered for providing his namesake community with its first church bell. In Georgia the Georgia Rail Road and Banking Company created Camak, Cumming (now Burnett), and Dearing, all named for organizers and directors. Phil Campbell, Alabama, also honored a company director, in this case an executive of the Birmingham, Sheffield & Tennessee River Railroad (née Sheffield & Birmingham Coal, Iron & Railway). Another illustration comes from Texas. Edna, Inez, and Louise, three towns along the New York, Texas & Mexican Railway and later part of the Southern Pacific, recognized the daughters of Count Joseph Telfener, an Italian nobleman and road sponsor. Billings, Montana, is the largest city that bears a railroad name, immortalizing Frederick Billings "because he was president of the Northern Pacific at the moment surveyors reached the tent city."

The naming legacy also involved the highly novel. Initially Primghar, which became seat of O'Brien County, Iowa, was an unnamed station on the Illinois Central Railroad. The town's promoter decided not to venerate himself, a family member, or a business associate, but rather he imaginatively combined the last initials of the first eight people to detrain, creating a unique name. While residents may still delight in explaining the clever origins of Primghar, those who live in another Hawkeye State community, Colo, may be reluctant to point out that their town name honors the dog of railroad official James I. Blair, whose beloved pet was crushed to death by a construction train. Probably nobody in Mobridge, South Dakota, frets much about the genesis of their hometown and its name.

In 1905 when the Chicago, Milwaukee & St. Paul Railway (Milwaukee Road) launched its Pacific Coast Extension, surveyors needed to cross the meandering Missouri River. Once they determined the precise location, they drew their construction maps and called the site "Mobridge," shorthand for Missouri River bridge. In time a thriving town grew up on the west bank, and the temporary moniker stuck.

The Mobridge name fits with the longtime philosophy of the Milwaukee Road toward town naming. H. R. Williams, a company executive, believed that the carrier should follow a rational process: a name should be short, easily spelled, dissimilar from other stations in the vicinity, and "pleasant sounding." This railroader also knew that the U. S. Post Office Department must give its stamp of approval; after all, there could not be two post offices with identical names in the same state or territory. Williams was directly responsible for naming thirty-two towns in Washington state, including Horlick – after a popular brand of powdered malted milk – and Vassar – after the elite women's college in Poughkeepsie, New York.

It was common for a carrier to create a town and town name that reflected its railroad connection. When the Burlington established a station and division point in Union County, Iowa, in the late 1860s, Creston was chosen. This was an appropriate choice; the site was on the highest point ("the crest") of its line that stretched between the Mississippi and Missouri rivers. Over time there would be a spate of "Junction" and "Junction City" town names, including Valley Junction, Iowa (renamed West Des Moines in 1938); Junction City, Louisiana; and Junction City, Ohio.

A railroad might be pressured, even forced, to use a particular name. When the Housatonic Railroad decided to establish a station 35 miles west of Bridgeport, Connecticut, the land parcel came with a stipulation. Glover Hawley, the owner, demanded that the place be named for his family; hence Hawleyville, Connecticut, came into being. By the 1870s the village served the Housatonic and three other railroads. While not coerced, the Maine Central Railroad agreed with residents of Mosquito, located deep in the Maine woods, that a name change was in order. Mosquito was surely descriptive of the settlement and the surrounding region, but hardly encouraged visits of sportsmen and summer campers. The railroad willingly placed on its depot signboard a more inviting name, Troutdale.

Less permanent than place names are the plethora of pet names or nicknames for individual railroads. While corporate consolidations, especially with the merger madness of the 1960s and more recent megamergers, have drastically reduced the number of major carriers, there are still those who recall the popular name for a particular road. It might be just one or two words: "Burlington" for Chicago, Burlington & Quincy; "Central" for New York Central; "Nickel Plate" for New York, Chicago &

St. Louis; or "Big Four" for Cleveland, Cincinnati, Chicago & St. Louis. More commonly there would be a play on the road's initials, and there are ample examples. Take two Midwestern roads, Chicago Great Western and Minneapolis & St. Louis. While the former might be called the CGW or Great Western, some wags, usually employees, referred to it as "Cinders, Grass & Weeds, "Can't Get Worse," or " Great Weedy." Often the public referred to the latter as the M&STL or the Louie, but creative folks said that the corporate initials really stood for "Misery & Short Life," "Maimed & Still Limping," or "Midnight & Still Later."

The fun with initials continued. "All Tramps & Soldiers Free" for Atchison, Topeka & Santa Fe; "Beefsteak & Onions" for Baltimore & Ohio; "Busted & Maimed" for Boston & Maine; "Dangerous & Rapidly Getting Worse" for Denver & Rio Grande Western; "Grab Baggage & Walk" for Green Bay & Western; "Hell Either Way You Take It" for Houston East & West Texas; "Jesus Wept & No Wonder" for Jamestown, Westfield & North Western; "Leave Early & Walk" for Lake Erie & Western; "Ma & Pa" for Maryland & Pennsylvania; "May Never Arrive" for Missouri & North Arkansas; "Pretty Rough County & No Water" for Pierre, Rapid City & North Western; "Tomatoes, Potatoes & Whiskey" for Toledo, Peoria & Western; and "Wobblety, Bobblety, Turnover & Stop" for Waco, Beaumont, Trinity & Sabine. Some carriers had nicknames whose meanings have been lost in time. Two "twilight"-era Iowa shortlines, which quickly failed, the Creston, Winterset & Des Moines and the Iowa & Southwestern, were known as "Crazy Willie & Dandy Molly" and the "Ikey." It might be that the initials spelled out an acrostic nickname: Missouri, Kansas & Texas became the "Katy," Kansas City Southern the "Casey," and the New York, Pennsylvania & Ohio the "Nypano." It was suggested by hoboes that the unusually large letters that the Chicago, Rock Island & Pacific once painted on its boxcar (C. R. I. & P.) meant "Come Right In & Pee."

Even the super railroads of the twenty-first century have their pet names, often products of imaginative (and at times disgruntled) employees. "Better Not Send Freight," "Big New Santa Fe," or "Buy Norfolk Southern Fast!" for Burlington Northern Santa Fe; "Nazi Southern" and "Nellie Sue" for Norfolk Southern, the latter referring to its thoroughbred horse logo; "Chicken S – t Express" and "Chessie's Still Experimenting" for CSX, and "Uncle Pete" for Union Pacific. When Union Pacific experienced difficulties amalgamating operations of the Southern Pacific into its sprawling system in the late 1990s, those within and outside the company suggested that UP really stood for "Usually Parked" or "Union Pathetic." And some irate customers and employees liked to say that "It's hard to spell STUPID without putting UP in the middle." Earlier the aborted merger between the Southern Pacific and Santa Fe promoted workers on both roads to believe that the initials of the anticipated SPSF stood for "Shouldn't Paint So Fast," referring to equipment that had been prematurely relettered.

Just as nautical and highway experiences led to words and phrases that have enhanced American English – from "shipshape" to "pedal to the metal" – the same can be said for railroad encounters. Often these enduring terms originated with workers and dealt with operations: "full head of steam," "blowing smoke" (boasting), "high ball" (full speed ahead), "pull the pin" (end or stop), "asleep at the switch," "derail," "off the rails," "train wreck," "side-tracked," "on track," "on the advertised" (on time), "to railroad," (force), "no way to run a railroad," and "tank town" and "whistle stop" (for villages and other insignificant places). Over time these words and phrases seeped into the language.

Then there are other phrases that have a direct railroad connection. Who doesn't know the phrase "wrong side of the tracks," being a reference to poorer housing stock or actual slums often found on one side of the railroad corridor. For years residents of urban milk sheds – territories that supplied dairy products to cities – might remark that someone or something was "as regular as a milk train." And there are other examples. It might be "Scott free," tied to the political clout of Pennsylvania Railroad executive Thomas Scott. Following the Civil War Scott placed a paid company representative in the Pennsylvania State House in Harrisburg who watched over legislative proposals. Hence when adjournment came, a lawmaker allegedly sighed with relief: "We're Scott free." Annoyed passengers, unhappy with delays, had their own expression: "to lie like a timetable," indicating that trains frequently ran late, at times excessively so. The public might use the self-explanatory phrase "as tight as a Pullman Window" or a politician might warn to "get on board before the train leaves the station."

Occasionally these railroad-inspired phrases sprang from a complicated and not fully understood past. Take the famous "public be damned" utterance, directly associated with a prominent "robber baron" railroader of the Gilded Age. According to conventional wisdom William Henry Vanderbilt (1821–1885), son of America's "first tycoon," Cornelius Vanderbilt (1794–1877), spoke these words in a mean-spirited way. Historian Albro Martin, who sought to explain the context of this remark, believed that Vanderbilt was asked by journalists if his New York Central System planned to introduce a passenger train comparable to the *Pennsylvania Limited*, which the rival Pennsylvania recently had placed on the competitive New York to Chicago route. Martin wrote:

> Learning that the man who knew the answer to that question was in Chicago at that very moment, two enterprising reporters rushed to the scene and brazened their way into the very car in which Vanderbilt had just sat down to dinner.

> "Will not the Central follow the Pennsylvania's lead in thus serving the public's needs for better passenger service?" [they asked], but Vanderbilt, like business executives now, did not suffer fools gladly, and Vanderbilt resented the idea that he was motivated by anything but basic principles of good business. "The public be damned," Vanderbilt spurted, "[if] we will run limited trains because the Pennsylvania runs limited trains."

Concluded Martin, "It would have been enough to make a modern public relations man collapse in tears."

Albro Martin made two points correctly. There is an association of the Commodore's most capable son with the enduring remark, and the pronouncement damaged the image of big business. But the real story is different. According to an account penned by an executive of the Chicago & North Western Railway (North Western) who was close to the event, Martin offered a flawed explanation.

Early on October 9, 1882, when William Henry Vanderbilt was aboard his private car on a special en route from New York City to Denver with a stopover in Chicago, a freelance journalist attempted to interview him. The Vanderbilt train was halted east of the Windy City and the time was about 2:00 AM. Needless to say, this member of the fourth estate, described as a "guerrilla space writer," namely a person "who picked up or invented items as he could and sold them to the newspapers," was rebuffed by the staff and was not permitted to enter the cars. Yet the young man showed tenacity; he rode on the open platform to Chicago. The journalist still hoped to gain access to Vanderbilt. "The morning was cold and rainy, and the young man had a pretty disagreeable ride, exposed to the full force of an October storm," related the North Western official. The reporter was understandably in a bad mood when he reached the station, and he went to the nearby Grand Pacific Hotel, where he "invented and wrote his memorable but utterly false interview."

The caption of the fake parley was "Vanderbilt Plans." The writer alleged that he had chatted with the prominent railroad executive at the hotel about various matters, including the Nickel Plate Road, which recently had entered the Vanderbilt orbit. Supposedly the interview went as follows:

> Mr. Vanderbilt, does your "Limited Express" pay? If not, will you abandon it, or are you running it for the benefit of the dear public?
> Look here, young man, do you know me? *The public be damned.* I don't take any stock in that twaddle about working for the good of anybody but ourselves. I continue to run the "Limited Express" because – well, because I want to. [Italics added]
> The freelancer sold the piece to an unsuspecting Chicago newspaper. Then other dailies reprinted it, and in the process more commentary appeared. The story or stories caused such a sensation that Vanderbilt ordered placards attached to his mansion in New York City that proclaimed: I NEVER SAID ANY OF THESE THINGS.

The official who attempted to set the record straight offered this commentary:

> On the afternoon of the day that Mr. Vanderbilt started west the writer of this chronicle sent for the reporter to come to the office of the North Western. When he came, he told the writer the story [as related], and freely and fully acknowledged his invention had no foundation whatever saving his own imagination, as he had neither seen nor spoken to Mr. Vanderbilt. In the Winter of 1882–83 another officer of the Chicago & North Western Railway met this reporter in Washington, D.C., to which city he had recently transferred his inventive talents, and he then openly told the story as he had told it to the writer of this record. By this time the man had become "conscience stricken" and asserted that he was very anxious that Mr. Vanderbilt should know this fact, and that he should forgive him for the pain the fraudulent story had caused.

But the damage was done. Americans had a phrase to vent whatever unhappiness they might have with railroads and their leaders. These words carried a real punch; they were easily remembered and frequently used to describe actions in the greater corporate world. During tough economic times, especially, it took little for the public to developed anger against the rich and powerful.

The Railway Age even had an apparent impact on language pronunciation. As early as 1855 a writer for a trade publication detected that the repeated movement of people on the expanding web of iron rails affected local and regional speech. "It is a well known fact that the English language is spoken with greater purity in the United States than in almost any part of Great Britain itself. We have fewer dialects, and those far less diverse from each other than are to be found in that island, and probably within even one hundred miles of London." He suggested, "By means of the railroad there is constantly going on among us, a sort of rubbing off, so to speak, [of] provincialisms, and bring instead a *universal harmony in language*" (italics in original). Continued internal migrations, facilitated in part by rail travel, and later radio and television, have further homogenized spoken English.

RAILROAD ENTHUSIASTS

While the "public be damned" statement entered the general vocabulary, railroad enthusiasts found pleasure with railroad-inspired words and phrases, keeping alive some of the nomenclature. Over the course of several generations tens of thousands of Americans have considered themselves to be railroad hobbyists. These individuals, mostly male, indulged their obsession by pursuing various activities. Perhaps they took and collected pictures of rolling stock and structures; acquired hardware, including bells, whistles, builder's plates, lanterns, cap badges, and switch keys and locks; and gathered printed matter, principally books, periodicals, timetables, name-train folders, tickets, passes, train orders, and maps. Or they found pleasure with model trains and miniature live-steam and garden railways. Countless more enjoyed watching and riding trains.

There were also those, including Alfred Hitchcock and Harry Truman, who admitted that they loved to read the *Official Guide to the Railways* ("the bible of train schedules"), imagining journeys to distant destinations or fantasizing about trips that once were possible. "Most of my travels on short lines have been vicarious, via the *Railway Guide,* in which obscure little paragraphs buried beneath the schedules of big lines announce the continued survival of the Live Oak, Perry & Gulf or the Waco, Beaumont, Trinity & Sabine River in a world that daily seems more hostile to their existence," commented railroad enthusiast Archie Robertson in 1945. "Too often the notices carry the depressing legend, 'Freight Service Only,' sometimes the words are plastered all up and down the margin, as if to forestall the eager fan from dreaming."

There could be bizarre dimensions of the hobby. In the 1940s a Harrisburg, Pennsylvania, enthusiast was reported to own a collection of odors obtained from the privies of small-town stations. "While traveling for a chemical concern he carried with him bottles containing a chemical which captured them for posterity," related an observer of the railfan. "Labeled with the name of the line and station, they now line the walls of his study."

It is not clear when the railroad enthusiast first appeared. Evidence suggests that as long ago as the 1840s an employee of the Western Rail Road of Massachusetts kept a detailed record of locomotives and other pieces of equipment, much like "train spotters" in Great Britain would later do for generations. "Many British boys (and a few girls) collected engine numbers and names, writing long freehand lists in grubby notebooks." There are other early records of individual, albeit unorganized, fan activities. "My interest in railroads and locomotives in particular dates back to my earliest recollections," recounted one train lover. "In 1886 when I was 5 years old my parents moved to Maynard, Mass. on the Marlboro Branch of the Fitchburg R. R., now the Boston & Maine R. R. Sometimes Dad and I would walk 2 miles over to South Acton on the main line of the Fitchburg R. R. and watch trains while sitting under an elm tree."

Later enthusiasts moved on to do more than train watching. "As far back as 1910 there were scattered throughout the country many men who were interested in the collection of railroad photographs and data," explained Charles E. Fisher, who in 1921 founded the first railfan organization in America, the Railway & Locomotive Historical Society (R&LHS). "Some were interested in photographs of the old-time locomotives; others preferred only the modern and, armed with cameras, took these photographs, but a few others set to work to acquire timetables, tickets, posters, notices, hat checks, etc." Added Fisher, "Most of these men exchanged prints with acquaintances. The Great War put a ban on some of this work, but after the war clouds had lifted and peace declared, many of the collectors dug out their collections and resumed work."

Organized activities did not begin until after World War I. It would be Fisher, a graduate engineer and Massachusetts resident, who shaped the R&LHS. Joined by a score or so of friends with similar interests, he created a New England–based organization that sought to attract serious students of railroad history. "Many plans were discussed. One thing we realized was that we would never receive any donations of [historic] materials unless we had a place to display them," Fisher later recalled. "The invitation of the Baker Library [at Harvard University] in 1925 solved that problem. We also realized that we must have some sort of publication to hold the membership together and, to give it a personal touch, it should represent the work and efforts of our members."

The determined Fisher forged a successful organization, and for fifty years he remained the sparkplug for the R&LHS; he was "Mr. R&LHS." Significantly, Fisher edited *The Bulletin of the Railway & Locomotive Historical Society* from its inception in 1921 until John H. White Jr., transportation curator at the Smithsonian Institution, took charge following Fisher's death in 1972. At that time the semiannual publication was renamed *Railroad History*. "Too much credit cannot be given to Charley for his unceasing efforts to preserve and disseminate railroad history," wrote a fellow enthusiast to his widow. "He did more than any other man has ever done – or the Railroad Industry as a whole has ever done."

Yet Fisher's personality caused problems, affecting the development of organized railroad activities. His monolithic management, lack of charm, and vindictiveness caused members to leave and precluded others from joining. This prompted train lovers in the 1930s and later to flock to newly formed groups, including Railroad Enthusiasts (launched in 1932 in Boston by several R&LHS directors and the prominent locomotive photographer Horace Pontin), International Locomotive Association, International Engine Picture Club, Railroadians of America, and most importantly the National Railway Historical Society (NRHS).

It would be the NRHS that rapidly became the principal enthusiasts' group. Unlike the R&LHS, the NRHS developed from two electric traction organizations, the Lancaster (Pennsylvania) Railway & Locomotive Historical Society (unrelated to the R&LHS), formed by five "juice" buffs in 1933, and the somewhat larger Interstate Trolley Club, founded a year later in Trenton, New Jersey, with members from the greater New York City and Philadelphia areas. It was on August 18, 1935, when representatives of these two bodies gathered in Baltimore for a "farewell" excursion over the

Railfans love to ride trains. On April 2, 1955, excitement builds as enthusiasts are about to depart Jersey City, New Jersey, on a Central Railroad of New Jersey special. A rare camelback steam locomotive provides the motive power.

Don Woods photograph, William Howes Jr. coll.

soon-to-be abandoned Washington, Baltimore & Annapolis Electric Railway that leaders decided to merge, creating the larger fan-based National Railway Historical Society. Soon the NRHS invited other independent clubs to join, becoming "chapters" of the parent organization. Within a year the NRHS started a magazine, and in 1938 it held its first national convention. By 1941 the organization claimed sixteen chapters that stretched from Boston to Akron, Ohio.

Members of the NRHS found much to like. Regular meetings provided comradery with fellow fans, and usually included railroad movies, refreshments, and "bull sessions." Being part of a national and professional-appearing organization helped to foster rail excursions. In 1936 a group of Akron area enthusiasts formed a "Committee" or club that a year later became the Eastern Ohio Chapter of the NRHS. "The NRHS affiliation impressed railway companies when the chapter approached them about hosting a trip," recalled a founding member. Earlier the club had discovered, much to its dismay, that steam roads either expressed hostility toward excursions or wanted too much money.

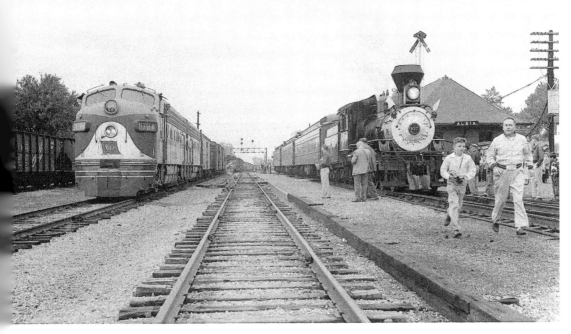

On October 14, 1956, members of the Iowa Chapter of the National Railway Historical Society and others descend on the Burlington station in Albia, Iowa. The steam-powered special, which operated on the Chicago–Denver main line between Ottumwa and Chariton, is headed to Indianola, terminus of a soon-to-be-abandoned branch line. Although the historic ten-wheeler No. 637 attracts attention, the daily Des Moines–bound Wabash freight is also an attraction.

John Humeston photograph, Author's coll.

Following the forced inactivity of the World War II years the democratic NRHS expanded impressively. It continued to attract members from a wide spectrum of society, including rich and poor, men and women, gays (who likely remained in the "closet"), and occasionally people of color. There was a membership requirement that an individual must be at least sixteen years old, and many a teenager eagerly anticipated the time when he could join. By the 1960s scores of NRHS chapters flourished from coast to coast, and even one in Hawaii. Most chapters published newsletters and organized "fan trips." Some collected rolling stock, restored old depots and other structures, or established research archives. And the national organization continued to produce a widely read (and saved) quarterly magazine, *The Bulletin,* and to hold annual conventions, highlighted by multiple trips designed to appeal to photographers and "mileage hounds." The latter were individuals who wanted to ride as much trackage as possible, especially as the number of freight-only lines soared.

Unquestionably the NRHS developed into the quintessential railroad enthusiast organization. The national and individual chapters provided ample opportunities to experience railroads up close, becoming what some called "foamer" groups. In the early 1980s this somewhat derogatory word was allegedly coined by a librarian at the California State Railroad Museum to describe a patron who "foamed at the mouth" when he examined photographs of Southern Pacific steam locomotives. Journalist James McCommons noted the foamer image when he gave an account of NRHS members who visited the headquarters complex of Burlington Northern

Santa Fe in suburban Fort Worth, Texas. "Back in the visitor's center, it was easy to tell the railroad guys [employees] and the vendors from the rail fans in their shorts, train T-shirts and ball caps weighed down with buttons." Added McCommons, "They carried plastic ditty bags with BNSF stuff. A nerdy-looking fellow (there's no other way to say it) in a red vest – a *Classic Trains* magazine logo on the back – herded the group."

The R&LHS, on the other hand, much smaller in size, traditionally attracted the "cerebral railfan." Members showed more enthusiasm in reading about railroads, especially their technical past, creating personal libraries of books and periodicals, and assembling photographs. There were annual meetings and rail outings, but not to the extent of the NRHS, although there was (and still is) overlapping membership.

Yet most, if not all, of the various monikers for typical railroad enthusiasts apply equally to members of the NRHS, R&LHS, and related organizations or to individuals who remain unaffiliated. They include: foamer, railfan, rail hobbyist, train buff, train chaser, train fanatic, train freak, train lover, train nut, and train watcher. And there are a few other terms that are less kind and politically incorrect.

While the NRHS remains the dominant enthusiast organization, a phenomenon of the post-1960s has been creation of the single railroad company historical society. Precipitated by the massive wave of corporate mergers, railfans have expressed a fondness for "fallen flag" carriers. All of the large roads, which the super carriers have absorbed, have such organizations, including publications, websites, and annual meetings. The Baltimore & Ohio Historical Society, Chicago & North Western Historical Society, Illinois Central Historical Society, Milwaukee Road Historical Association, New York Central Historical Society, Southern Pacific Historical & Technical Society, and Southern Railway Historical Society are representative. Small, even obscure roads also command interest. Fallen flags like the Denver, South Park & Pacific; New York, Ontario & Western and Rio Grande Southern have their own organizations, paralleling the activities of those that immortalize former Class I roads. Interestingly, the now-defunct Midland Continental Historical & Technical Society at its zenith in the 1980s boasted more members (85) than this former North Dakota shortline had route miles (68).

Coinciding with the single-road historical groups have been other enthusiast organizations that focus on a particular aspect of the railroad past. One example is the Railroad Station Historical Society, organized in 1968. It has sought to record the histories of individual depots, of railroads, and of regions, occasionally including those outside the United States. The organization produces a newsletter, publishes the sporadic paperback monograph, and maintains a website.

In the more recent past railroad companies themselves drew attention from the public, especially enthusiasts, with steam-powered runs. In 1977 the *Chessie Steam Special*, pulled by ex–Reading Railroad 4-8-4, No. 2101, blasts up Sand Patch Grade near Meyersdale, Pennsylvania. The Chessie System wished to commemorate the 150th anniversary of the Baltimore & Ohio Railroad. "We hope you have as much pleasure on the trip as we had planning," said Howard Skidmore, a Chessie System executive. "Remember that while this is an old-fashioned train out of the past, America's modern railroads are very much a part of the present – and the future." Railroads, including Chessie, did not want anyone to think that they were transportation dinosaurs.

William Howes coll.

Railroads remain a popular pastime. "The railroad hobby interest has more active groups than any other type of hobby," is the conclusion reached by a rail-enthusiast observer. "In 2010 there are at least 900 [fan groups] scattered over the United States plus additional groups specializing in model railroading." But with increasing usage of personal electronics, particularly for social networking, organized activities have declined. Or as Harvard University public policy professor Robert Putnam has argued, all types of "in-person social intercourse" are diminishing. Yet there are young enthusiasts. "This is an online generation who is less likely to read magazines or attend formal meetings," opined a youthful railfan, "but corresponds voraciously over the net – emailing, texting, and posting hundreds of photographs on blogs and Flickr."

While support for enthusiast organizations may have peaked, the fact remains that railroad-oriented books and magazines continue to be produced in large numbers, doing much to preserve the railroad legacy. Although scholarly and semi-scholarly railroad books have appeared for more than a century and remain part of the publishing programs of commercial, university, and private or vanity presses, distinctively railfan works have a more recent history.

During the 1930s the railroad-enthusiast book genre made its debut. The pioneer work was *Trains* by Ralph Selph Henry, which Bobbs-Merrill published in 1934. Henry, a public relations man and an accomplished amateur historian, offered a popular account of railroading that was richly illustrated, albeit with unimaginative stock publicity photographs. Four years later what some consider to be the "first real railfan book," *Along the Iron Trail*, printed on glossy, heavy-stock paper by a small Vermont publisher, appeared, the authors being two avid enthusiasts, Frederick Richardson and F. Nelson Blount. "We realize that many books have been written on railroads," explained Richardson and Blount, "but we have written still another book that is designed primarily for the thousands of railroad fans." Later Blount, who founded Blount Seafood Corporation, used his wealth to acquire vintage steam locomotives and other pieces of rolling stock, eventually creating Steamtown in Bellows Falls, Vermont. Following his death much of the collection became the nucleus of the Steamtown National Historic Site in Scranton, Pennsylvania.

But it would be Lucius Morris Beebe (1902–1965) who established himself as the "father" of the heavily illustrated railfan book. "Taken as a whole, the bibliography of my book jobs has been intended as an adult, largely pictorial aspect of Americana," Beebe told *Trains* editor David P. Morgan in 1962, "one that I am sure somebody else could do better but that nobody else seems to have wanted to do in the terms I visualized and appraised it." A graduate of Harvard College and scion of a prominent New England family that had grown wealthy in the leather trade and banking, Beebe became associated with high-brow cultural activities, especially the "café society" of New York City. By the mid-1930s his weekly writings, "This New York," had developed into a popular *New York Herald Tribune* syndicated column. (The bon vivant Beebe also favored gourmet cooking and fine wines.) Knowing that he was a lover of trains, an editor at Appleton-Century in 1935 urged him to produce a largely pictorial work on railroads. Initially Beebe refused, apparently because of the poor quality of available railroad photographs. Not to be stymied, the Appleton-Century editor suggested that Beebe take his own photographs. Beebe agreed, and in 1938 his first railroad book, *High Iron: A Book of Trains*, was released. Although the work contained historic photographs, most images came from his camera, a quality 4x5 Graflex Speed Graphic. *High Iron* sold well, even at the hefty price of $5 ($75 in 2010 dollars). Railroad enthusiasts and general readers admired his creative photography, and they enjoyed his colorful language that portrayed an enterprise rich in nostalgia. Said Beebe, "The impact of the railroad on the American imagination has been greater than that of any other industry." Three follow-up books, all published by Appleton-Century and its successor Appleton-Century-Crofts, *Highliners* (1940), *Trains in Transition* (1941), and *Highball: A Pageant of Trains* (1945), found appreciative audiences.

By the end of World War II Beebe had become a byword in the train-book field. No one criticized his abilities as a photographer, but serious students of railroads fussed about his chronic factual errors, sweeping generalizations, and doctored photographs. Even in his other writings, accuracy was not his objective. "He must have a great respect for the truth," quipped actress Tallulah Bankhead, "since he very rarely uses it." In a way Beebe redeemed himself when he joined forces with Charles "Chuck" Clegg Jr., a gifted photographer who became Beebe's lifelong professional and personal partner. Together they created what became the most popular enthusiast book ever, *Mixed Train Daily: A Book of Short Line Railroads*, published by Dutton in 1947 and later reprinted by Howell-North. Six original paintings by artist Howard Fogg further enhanced the work.

The well-received *Slow Train to Yesterday: A Last Glance at the Local* by Archie Robinson, published in 1945 and illustrated with original drawings, may have inspired Beebe to write *Mixed Train Daily*. Robertson, a man of multiple talents – teacher, newspaper reporter, and government bureaucrat (a railfan, too) – wrote well and imaginatively. "Those of you who find Beebe's prose a bit too florid or pontifical will discover that Robertson's writing goes down very well indeed," observed *Trains* contributor Fred Frailey. "He's like a favorite uncle who comes to visit, always bringing new stories to tell, and he tells them in a tone of amusement and affection toward the subjects. In this case, it is the out-of-the-way short lines of that era."

For *Mixed Train Daily* Beebe and Clegg devoted much energy to riding and photographing shortlines throughout the country, concentrating on roads in the South and West. This time Beebe conducted bona fide research, interviewing employees and tapping other sources. "By stretching beyond his standard formula," observed railroad historians Dan Cupper and Tony Reevy, "Beebe captured the feel, as well as the physical setting, of the local train and the oddball short line." Remarked one railfan, attesting to the power of *Mixed Train Daily*, "I got this book from my public library as a youngster, and I kept looking and looking at the pictures and reading and rereading the text. I even recall staring at the end sheets, with that photograph of the right-of-way of some badly maintained shortline in Pennsylvania." Never again did Beebe replicate the quality or success of *Mixed Train Daily*, although he continued to add books to the shelves of railroad enthusiasts. By the time of his death in 1965 Beebe had produced nineteen books.

Roughly corresponding with the appearance of popular railroad books were various periodicals. The first of this genre was *Railroad Man's Magazine*, which began in October 1906, and in 1932 became *Railroad Stories*. Its publishing firm, the Frank Munsey Company, was reorganized after Munsey's death in 1919, leading to a suspension of the magazine for nearly a decade. Interestingly, the longtime editor, Freeman Hubbard, did not have the railfan in mind, designing the monthly for blue-collar railroaders and filling its pulp pages with breezy railroad fiction by such authors as Frank Packard, Frank Spearman, and Cy Warman. Yet it was possible for railfans to place free advertisements that stated their interests (and addresses), usually mentioning photography or a particular road or region.

By the late 1930s *Railroad Magazine*, as *Railroad Stories* was retitled in 1937, had morphed into a fan-based publication, even sponsoring the Railroad Camera Club to encourage fans and readership. Although it continued to reprint pieces of "Railroad School" fiction, this publication blazed the trail for railroad hobbyists. "It was at an early age that I first found *Railroad Magazine*," recounted Donald Duke, who established Golden West Books, a publisher of popular railroad-related works. "I really wanted to buy it, but my folks said 'no.' They objected to the magazine's advertising which included trusses, pads for incontinence, and the sale of lessons on how to be a taxidermist." But Duke was undaunted. "However, all was not lost, as my birthday was coming up and my grandmother asked me what I wanted. I firmly answered, 'a subscription to *Railroad Magazine.*'" He received his wish. Another contemporary railroad enthusiast had a somewhat different experience. "I happened on a copy of the August [1937] issue of *Railroad Stories* magazine," recounted Cornelius W. Hauck, a Cincinnati, Ohio, financier and cofounder of the Colorado Railroad Museum, "and with that exposure I quickly developed a fascination for narrow-gauge and short-line railroads." Industry trade journals, which date back to the 1830s, brotherhood publications, which appeared decades later, and company-sponsored employee magazines (Erie Railroad produced the first one in 1905) failed to offer opportunities for hobbyists like Duke and Hauck to indulge their pleasures.

It was Al C. Kalmbach (1910–1981) who increased interest in the railroad hobby by improving the quality of railfan-oriented periodicals. His creations were the first unequivocally hobby magazines. Initially it was *The Model Railroader,* a monthly that made its debut in 1934, and then *Trains*, which was a monthly prototype magazine, six years later. Kalmbach popularized model railroading as an all-encompassing hobby. "Through the pages of *MR* he brought the pioneer model railroad hobbyists together," observed an acquaintance. "The magazine provided a

In June 2006 Cornelius (Corny) Hauck, one of America's foremost railroad enthusiasts, stands at the station of the Cumbres & Toltec Scenic Railroad in Chama, New Mexico. This popular tourist line, which is owned by the states of Colorado and New Mexico and was once part of the Denver & Rio Grande Western's sprawling narrow-gauge network, is a Hauck favorite.

Cornelius Hauck coll.

medium for the exchange of ideas. It also provided much more. It helped create a feeling of camaraderie among model railroaders. Buying the magazine was like joining a club." Sales of *Model Railroader* soared, especially after World War II, jumping from 20,000 in 1945 to 100,000 in 1950. Other entrepreneurs also entered the field, publishing by 2010 ten commercial model railroad magazines.

Al Kalmbach experienced a similar success with *Trains,* which his Kalmbach Publishing Company, based in Milwaukee, Wisconsin, immodestly proclaimed to be "The Magazine of Railroading." Unlike competitor *Railroad Magazine* and its predecessors, *Trains,* which first appeared in November 1940, did not publish stories and railroad lore, but featured nonfiction contributions. Readers kept back issues, often binding them for future reference. An annual index made finding that article or picture much easier.

Just as enthusiasts have initiated and nurtured a rich variety of railroad historical organizations and publications, there have been individuals who have done much to preserve railroad history and to bring attention to the industry and railfan. And they may or may not have been active in organized groups. Thomas T. Taber and Rogers E. M. Whitaker, known to many as "E. M. Frimbo," are two such notables. Both men represent different aspects of this celebratory hobby.

Thomas T. Taber (1899–1976) was a path-breaking railfan. While born in Brooklyn, New York, he spent most of his life in neighboring New Jersey. A high-school dropout, the bright, ambitious Taber became a long-time employee of the New York Life Insurance Company. As a teenager he started to take photographs of locomotives in and about his Montclair home. This passion continued. The perfectionist Taber wanted to capture only certain types of engines, and they had to be positioned just so, with sunlight illuminating their drivers. As a traveling representative for New York Life he began in 1921 to visit much of the country, places that often lacked active railroad shutterbugs. During the course of his photographic adventures Taber made contacts and forged friendships with others who shared his passion for railroad photography. "There were unwritten rules in the photo hobby," explained Taber's son, Thomas T. Taber III. "Prints were not sold; you traded or gave. You never copied pictures of another photographer so as to give (or sell) prints to friends." But some violated the code, copying and selling their own and others' prints.

As with so many railroad hobbyists, Taber expanded his collecting activities. Just as he was methodical with his picture-taking, so he was with his acquisition of artifacts, particularly locomotive bells, builder's plates, and railroad signals. When it came to bells, Taber sought out only representative ones. "Dad had seven bells, and again, he was not interested

in quantity, but rather a complete portrait of the evolution of design." A
similar strategy came with builder's plates, not numbers but a representative variety from the various locomotive manufacturers, including Baldwin, Grant, and Norris. In time Taber assembled a collection of several
historic railroad signals, which he installed at the end of his driveway in
Madison, New Jersey. "Dad collected only four because that was all that
was needed to show the evolution of pre-color-light signaling." The bulk
of Taber's railroadiana passed into the hands of museums or remained
with family members.

Thomas Taber did more than collect. As he grew older, his interests
broadened to the preservation of railroad passenger service in New Jersey,
and he worked to improve commuter operations. Following his death the
Erie Lackawanna Railroad recognized his contributions by renaming
the 5:30 PM *Dover Express* the *Tom Taber Express.* "The name appeared in
suburban timetables and on the Hoboken station sign track," noted his
son. "He is the only railfan to have had a train named for him."

The enthusiast activities of Rogers Whitaker (1900–1981) were strikingly different from those of Thomas Taber. Born into an upper-middle-
class family (his father was an editor of the *Journal of the American Institute
of Architects*), Whitaker attended Princeton University, but he dropped
out during his sophomore year. Going to New York City to seek his fortune, he worked initially as a fact-checker for the *New York Times.* In 1926

Although Rogers Whitaker was not able to add much new mileage in his 1980 trip over the Oak Point–Bay Ridge line of Conrail in New York City, he did pose for a photograph in front of the high-rail vehicle that became stymied by junk on the tracks. "Mr. E. M. Frimbo" stands on the left and his host, Henry Posner III, is on the right. In the middle is John Baesch, who worked with Amtrak's Northeast Corridor.

Henry Posner III

his career took a turn when he joined the staff of the *New Yorker* magazine. Over time his duties varied, including fact-checking and layout. Eventually he became an editor and wrote the much-beloved "Goings on About Town" section.

Whitaker's love, though, was train riding. When he was only nine years old, he took his first solo rail trip, and that passion never ended. Just as Thomas Taber established collecting goals, so in a way did Whitaker. He wanted to ride *every* mile of railroad in North America. By the early 1950s he had racked up more than four hundred railroads and covered some 900,000 miles of track, much of which he traveled to reach other railroads that he wished to add to his "collection." When railroad writer Alvin F. Harlow interviewed Whitaker in 1953, he described Whitaker's dogged persistence to achieve his objective. "During his vacation he really does places, and may gather in short lines by the dozen. And in emergencies – for he has friends in rail circles who tip him off to sudden, rare opportunities – he may leave his desk in mid-week and rush off somewhere."

Whitaker never tired of adding to his mileage list. In 1980 at age eighty, just a year before his death, he made arrangement with Henry Posner III, a Conrail employee, to take a ride, via a high-rail truck, between Oak Point and Bay Ridge in New York City ("new mileage for him"). But as Posner remembered, "Unfortunately we derailed on the garbage covering the line. I destroyed a tire during the re-railing attempt, the journey 20% complete." By the time of his passing Whitaker had accumulated about 2.7 million miles of rail travel, covering most of the existing mileage on the continent.

Whitaker wrote extensively about his rail journeys. Contributions to the *New Yorker,* however, did not carry his name, but rather what became his familiar pen name, E. M. Frimbo. After his death a close friend, Tony Hiss, brought out a book that he titled *All Aboard with E. M. Frimbo, World's Greatest Railroad Buff.* It was a fitting memorial to this exceptional lover of trains.

While dedicated railfans found their own ways to preserve the nation's railroad heritage and their organizations institutionalized opportunities to enjoy and celebrate the iron horse, a parallel movement did much the same. This involved the preservation of railroad artifacts, ranging from steam locomotives to paper ephemera, and included much more than what enthusiast groups and individuals assembled. Some railroads preserved their own past, with the Baltimore & Ohio (B&O) being the foremost example. Having long been an innovator in motive power, the company saved representative locomotives and during its centennial year of 1927 showed them off at its highly acclaimed Fair of the Iron Horse. The B&O Museum in Baltimore came to feature an extensive exhibit of rolling stock and other large artifacts, but later fell on hard times. In 1964, due largely to Jervis Langdon Jr., the history-conscious B&O president, the museum took on new life. During a festive Fourth of July week, crowds came to view these transportation treasures. "In the first four days after the museum's reopening," reported *Railway Age,* "some 8,000 visitors filed past what B&O claims is the nation's largest collection of historic railroad equipment." The facility continued to be an important educational asset and tourist destination.

There would be other museums, some well established and some new, some large and some modest, that maintain the history of railroading. One is the Museum of Transportation, née National Museum of Transport, in Kirkwood, Missouri, founded in 1944. The original collection came from Purdue University, where several steam locomotives and an electric interurban car had once been used for the instruction of engineering students. After the museum opened, St. Louis–area carriers made donations, including historically significant pieces of rolling stock from the Illinois Terminal, St. Louis–San Francisco (Frisco), and Wabash. Although established as a privately operated museum, it acquired better financing when the St. Louis County Parks Department took control. And with the end of steam a variety of other privately funded museums and steam-powered tourist lines appeared. Some of the best known are the Colorado Railroad Museum in Golden, Illinois Railway Museum in Union, and Strasburg Rail Road in Strasburg, Pennsylvania. Then there are several publically sponsored museums, with the largest (and best) being the California State Railroad Museum in Sacramento (1981), Railroad Museum of Pennsylvania, Strasburg (1975), and Steamtown National Historic Site in Scranton, Pennsylvania (1995). While these institutions contain an assortment of equipment – locomotives, freight and passenger cars, and specialty pieces – railway preservation, directed by professionals, has reduced an emphasis on rolling stock to more sophisticated interpretations of the railroad legacy, adding roles played by workers, minorities, and women.

RAILS-TO-TRAILS

A not-so-distant cousin of railroad preservation is the national rails-to-trails movement, more accurately the Rails-to-Trails Conservancy. This nonprofit advocacy organization traces its origins to an event in the 1960s. In September 1963 May Theilgaard Watts, a naturalist at the Morton Arboretum in Lisle, Illinois, near Chicago, proposed in a letter to the editor of the *Chicago Tribune* a constructive use for the abandoned right-of-way of the Chicago, Aurora & Elgin Railway, an interurban that had shut down a few years earlier. "We are human beings. We are able to walk upright on two feet. We need a footpath. Right now there is a chance for Chicago and its suburbs to have a footpath, a long one." Likely the network of public walkways in Great Britain and the Appalachian Trail between Georgia and Maine inspired her suggestion. Watts's arguments spawned an active grassroots movement to convert portions of the weed- and brush-choked right-of-way in Du Page County into what became the popular Illinois Prairie Path, a 55-mile network of crushed stone and dirt trails between Maywood and Wheaton with spurs to Aurora, Batavia, Elgin, and Geneva. The formation in 1965 of the Illinois Prairie Path Corporation, a landmark organization in the rails-to-trails movement, did much to ensure success of Watts's proposal.

Today the West Virginia State Parks system extols its North Bend Rail Trail. This rails-to-trails unit is on a former Baltimore & Ohio main line, stretching 72 miles between Parkersburg and Wolf Summit and featuring twelve tunnels and thirty-two bridges. "The many points of interest," according to the flyer, "include sites of train robberies and legends of tunnel ghosts."

Author's coll.

The rails-to-trails movement, with its Washington, D.C.–based national coordinating organization and separate state units, happened at an opportune time. It would be in the 1960s and in subsequent decades when thousands of miles of branch, secondary, and even main lines were abandoned, as the nation's railroad network contracted dramatically, dropping from 217,552 miles in 1960 to 119,056 in 1990. By 2010 more than 15,000 miles of rails-to-trails (nearly equal to the total mileage of electric interurbans) served the public, and potentially railroad company, needs. Coinciding with the availability of possible trails was the growing interest in exercise and out-of-doors activities. Hikers, cyclists, equestrians, and snowmobilers wanted public-use corridors, especially if they were convenient to population centers. Railroads also came to be sympathetic to these reuse efforts. The Rails-to-Trails Act, passed by Congress in 1983, allowed carriers to preserve their easement rights when rail beds became recreational corridors. Since this would be an "abandonment suspended,"

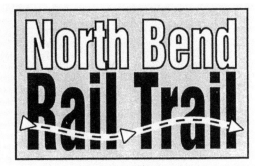

Rt. 1
Cairo, WV 26337
304/643-2391
1-800-CALL-WVA
http://wvweb.com/www/NORTH_BEND.html

Enjoy the
great outdoors...

not a traditional abandonment, railroads could donate, lease, or sell the
right-of-way to a trail group without the land reverting to adjacent land-
owners, thus "rail banking" the strip for a future need. At times landown-
ers howled; owners of reversionary right-of-way properties (land under
railroad right-of-way easements) had no voice in the rail-banking transactions. In a few instances rails-to-trails advocates also resented the measure

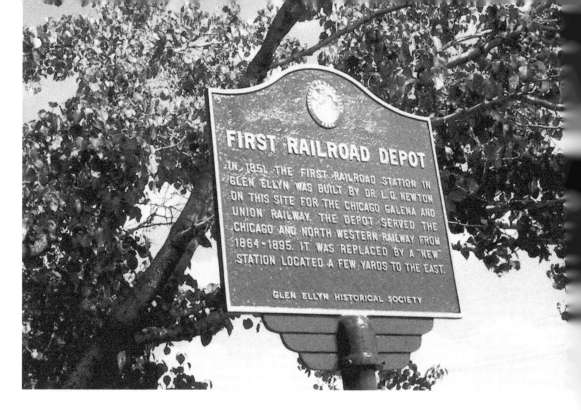

Historical markers dot the landscape, including those that denote railroad-related events, persons, and structures. The Glen Ellyn Historical Society located the site of the first depot building in this Illinois community. Unfortunately, the text writer misnamed the railroad; it's the Galena & Chicago Union Rail Road and not the "Chicago Galena and Union Railway."

David E. Kyvig photograph, Author's coll.

when a portion of a trail returned to being an operational railroad, something that has occurred on Norfolk Southern–controlled rights-of-way in Ohio and Pennsylvania.

These physical remains have spurred an interest in railroad history. "Who built this railroad? When did it open? What did the line carry? Were there many passenger trains? When did service end?" These are commonly asked questions, and trail groups make known basic facts through signs, brochures, and websites. The popular Virginia Creeper National Recreation Trail, which covers 34 miles of a former Norfolk & Western Railway branch line between the Virginia communities of Abington and White Top, trackage made famous by the carefully framed black-and-white photographs of the last days of steam by O. Winston Link, prompted these observations by a frequent visitor: "I always liked trains, but when I biked the Virginia Creeper, I became fascinated with the past operations of the N&W. I wanted to know more about the railroad and the people who worked and lived along this old branch."

The establishment of improved trails, which are no longer engulfed by nature, has encouraged preservation of railroad and railroad-related structures. It might be a depot, hotel, or boarding house (perhaps converted into a bed-and-breakfast business) that catered to passengers and railroad employees or something as mundane as a tool house or privy. Old metal bridges, whistle posts, mile markers, and other railroad artifacts might also be maintained. Protection of the former railroad corridor has become part of this national movement.

Preservation of structures, especially depots, already had gained strength before the rails-to-trails movement took hold, encouraged by the Great Society's creation of the National Register of Historic Places as part of the National Historical Preservation Act of 1966, and a growing wave of nostalgia, found especially in smaller communities. But not all depots have become museums (a common adoptive use); many of these surviving buildings have been recycled into offices, restaurants, and other public places. Some depots have become private homes or been adopted for personal use as farm or storage structures. Former office buildings also have taken on new life, being transformed into condominiums, hotels, educational centers, and government facilities.

Preservation has included names. Two examples are the dozen-mile Swamp Rabbit Trail, which links Greenville and Travelers Rest, South Carolina, and perpetuates the nickname given to the abandoned Greenville & Northern Railroad, and the 83-mile Wabash Trace Nature Trail, stretching between Council Bluffs and Blanchard, Iowa, that memorializes the Wabash Railroad, owner of this once busy line.

MARKERS AND MONUMENTS

Most Americans understand, even appreciate, memorial markers and monuments, whether they are dedicated to explorers, politicians, soldiers, or other individuals or events that shaped the past. People find value in these objects. Although in recent years such memorials have fallen out of favor, except for those that honor war heroes and remember national conflicts and the horrors of 9/11, scores of them that recognize the accomplishments of those with a railroad connection or a railroad happening dot the landscape, at times along abandoned rights-of-way. There is the stone marker in Jackson, Tennessee, that recalls the heroism of Illinois Central engineer John Luther "Casey" Jones, who died tragically outside Vaughan, Mississippi, on April 30, 1900. Better known are artifacts in the visitor's center and outdoor objects, including the Golden Spike Monument and two replica steam locomotives, that commemorate the "Wedding of the Rails" at Promontory, Utah, proclaimed in 1969 as a National Historic Site and administered by the National Park Service. Likely the oldest railroad memorial is known to more than a few: an obelisk at Relay, Maryland, designed by bridge builder Benjamin Latrobe Jr. This handsome piece of lightly colored granite, quarried at nearby Ellicott Mills, honors the men behind the B&O's Thomas Viaduct over the Patapsco River. The monument lists the date construction began, July 4, 1833; date of completion, July 4, 1835; the names of principals involved and the B&O directors. Formally dedicated on August 25, 1835, the stately stone

Occasionally a cemetery features a spectacular grave maker. Few can rival this Victorian monstrosity, located in Roseville Cemetery in Chicago, that marks the burial site of Colonel George S. Bangs, an architect of the highly successful U.S. Railway Mail Service. The inscription beneath the ornate carved-stone monument reads: HIS CROWNING EFFORT THE FAST MAIL.

David M. Habben photograph

remains at its original location, and CSX freight trains and Maryland Area Regional Commuter (MARC) passenger trains pass it daily.

A few monuments are much grander than the Thomas Viaduct obelisk, and they are mostly found in the West. The largest commemorates Oakes and Oliver Ames, two Massachusetts brothers who were instrumental in building the Union Pacific. These makers of shovels and other tools became intimately involved with the railroad and its construction affiliate, Credit Mobilier. While there was that spectacular railroad triumph, Oakes Ames, a member of the U. S. Congress, would in 1873 be condemned by fellow lawmakers for unethical dealings with the construction

firm. Credit Mobilier excessively overcharged the Union Pacific and thus was itself enormously profitable. To make matters worse, Ames handed out stock to twenty members of Congress and the vice president of the United States to prevent a congressional investigation. Although their reputations suffered (as did that of the U. S. House of Representatives), the "Hoax Ameses" would receive lasting recognition that was strikingly visible.

In 1875 Union Pacific board members voted for an Ames monument, and expense would not deter them. After a knoll on the barren Wyoming plateau near the Sherman station and adjacent to the highest point on this first transcontinental railroad was selected, work progressed. The renowned architect H. H. Richardson designed a four-sided pyramid that could easily be seen by travelers as passenger trains passed Sherman Hill. Laborers acquired rough-hewn pink granite boulders from nearby out-croppings and placed them on a thirty-three-degree slope to a height of sixty feet. There was more. The sculptor Augustus Saint-Gaudens created nine-foot-high bas-relief medallions of the brothers, which were installed near the apex of the pyramid. The bust of Oakes faced east and the bust of Oliver faced west. Grand indeed, the memorial, completed in 1882, cost a hefty $64,773 ($1.3 million in 2010 dollars).

The memorial to the Ames brothers remains, but not as the Union Pacific board had intended. Sixteen years after the pyramid was completed, a line relocation left these stones less visible to train riders. Then in 1916 directors voted to move the monument to a point along the relocated trackage, but that action never occurred. Corporate interest in the pyramid waned, weather caused damage, and vandals destroyed portions of the bas-reliefs. The monument, which the Union Pacific donated to the State of Wyoming in 1983, remains a curious relic to two men who shaped history.

While it proved impractical to relocate the Ames pyramid, smaller memorials have been preserved away from their initial locations. One is the multi-ton, twenty-foot statute of Commodore Cornelius Vanderbilt that once was centered in a bronze relief that depicted the icons of his long and successful career: sailing boats, steamships, and trains. This self-aggrandizing memorial, dedicated on November 10, 1869, cost an astonishing $0.5 million ($8 million in 2010 dollars) and adorned the newly completed New York Central & Hudson River freight depot in lower Manhattan. Another is the less grand and costly bronze statute of Samuel Spencer, cast by Daniel Chester French, which after being dedicated on May 21, 1910, graced the public plaza opposite the Southern Railway Terminal in Atlanta, Georgia. Vanderbilt, the architect of the Central, lived a long life, passing in 1877, but Spencer, president of the Southern since 1894, was killed in a railroad accident on November 26, 1906. Because of building changes the Vanderbilt statue presently rests outside Grand Central Terminal and faces Park Avenue South, and the Spencer bronze, having been relocated several times, stands in front of Norfolk Southern's Peachtree Street office tower.

While thousands of individuals pass daily the memorials to Vanderbilt and Spencer (likely ignoring them), more obscure tributes to people and events of the Railway Age may go largely unseen. There are widely scattered gravestones with railroad motifs, often carvings depicting a locomotive, car, or train. A most unusual monument, located in Chicago's largest burial ground, Rosehill Cemetery, honors George S. Bangs

IN MEMORY OF
JOHN J. KEISTER
SEPT. 2, 1886
JAN. 13, 1911
KILLED IN WRECK ON GREAT NORTHERN R.R., IDAHO, WHEN THE ENGINE ON WHICH HE WAS FIREMAN JUMPED THE TRACK AND PLUNGED INTO THE PEND D' OREILLE RIVER, WHERE HE SLEEPS BENEATH SEVENTY-FOUR FEET OF WATER.

(1826–1877), who shaped the U. S. Railway Mail Service. Underneath a stone tree, which is wrapped partially in foliage, rests a model of a Railway Post Office car poised at a tunnel, also fabricated out of stone. Another tombstone, which is also much different from traditional ones, is found in a small cemetery near Compton, Virginia. It features a mounted brass whistle from the locomotive that in 1906 caused the death of this railroad engineer. Some objects memorialize individuals who led uneventful careers in railroading, yet were proud of their occupations, usually engineers or conductors. Other headstones recognize victims of railroad accidents.

Representative of memorials dedicated to causalities of train wrecks are those that honor several victims of a disastrous railroad wreck that occurred near Eden, Colorado. It is not known how many people perished when a flash flood along Hogan's Gulch on the night of August 7, 1904, overturned a Denver & Rio Grande passenger train. The fatality count exceeded ninety, making this one of the deadliest accidents in American railroad history. In one Colorado cemetery stands the large Gartland family monument, which contains the inscription LOST THEIR LIVES IN THE EDEN WRECK, AUG. 7, 1904, and commemorates the death of mother Gartland and her four children. In another graveyard, Roselawn

A somewhat sedate headstone stands on the empty grave of John J. Keister in his hometown of Sumerset, Pennsylvania. The inscription tells of his tragic death in a railroad accident in distant Idaho.

Author coll.

Cemetery in Pueblo, is a more modest headstone that reads: HERE LIES THE BODY OF RALPH A. SCHWARZKOFF WHO WAS KILLED IN THE EDEN WRECK AUG. 7, 1904.

There are other lasting symbols of the heyday of railroads. This genre is represented by a large stained glass window that in early 1890s graced the new Methodist Episcopal Church in Stevens Point, Wisconsin. John Lennon, a locomotive engineer for the Wisconsin Central Railroad and a devout Methodist, solicited fellow enginemen to join him in contributing to a window, and they did. The result was a "leaded, stained glass replica of the 28 [Wisconsin Central America Standard 4-4-0], complete with long, rakish pilot, Yankee diamond stack and a purple glass black smoke plume floating away in the background." The window contained this simple inscription: PRESENTED BY RR ENGINEERS.

A church window is rare, but it became more common to have the image of a locomotive used as a decorative adornment, representing graphically the importance of the railroad. When the Crawford County, Ohio, courthouse, built in 1857 in Bucyrus, was remodeled about 1910, the courtroom received several plaster motifs, including one, INDUSTRY AND COMMERCE, that prominently featured the front of a steam engine. The inspiration may have come from the main lines of the Pennsylvania and Toledo & Ohio Central railroads that served this community.

RAILROAD HUMOR

During the golden age of railroads American often joked about trains. Humor based on exceedingly slow or late passenger runs became common. While this legacy has mostly disappeared in the era of the automobile and airplane, remnants remain.

As vaudeville acts grew in popularity after 1900, comedians loved to single out railroads. After all, everyone in the audience had had some sort of experience with passenger trains, depots, railroad employees, and the like. The Erie Railroad, the longest of the several trunk lines between New York City and Chicago, received more than its fair share of derision. The old vaudevillian wheeze – "I want to go to Chicago in the worst way." "Take the Erie!" – always drew a chuckle. And this joke elicited smiles: "A patriarch who presented a half ticket for a ride on the Erie between Suffern and Jersey City was informed that he must pay full fare. He replied: 'When I purchased that ticket before boarding this train, I was entitled to the half-fare rate'" (that is, the child's fare). Even composer Irving Berlin exploited the Erie's not-so-stellar on-time performance. He included the lines: "I know that he looks as slow as the Erie. But you don't know half of it dearie" in his hit song "You'd Be Surprised." The laughable image of the Erie prompted an editorial writer for the *Akron* (Ohio) *Beacon Journal* in

Elmer Peters has invented a new gate for railroad crossings. Elmer says: "Even when it's up the motorist stops to look at it."

1907 to comment: "During the last few years the Erie railroad has been made the butt of so many jokes that the average citizen has been almost made to believe that only behind-time trains are run over the Erie."

Then there was the printed humor that poked fun at railroads, materials that likely have survived. Admittedly they are badly dated and frequently politically incorrect, but readers might still be tickled. There were various books and pamphlets that focused on or contained railroad humor, including *Brother Jonathan's Jokes, Funny Stories, and Laughable Sketches* compiled by Thomas Carey and published in 1885, but the most renowned producer was Thomas William Jackson (1867–1934). In 1903 he self-published *On a Slow Train through Arkansaw: Funny Railroad Stories – Sayings of the Southern Darkies – All the Latest and Best Minstrel Jokes of the Day.* This railroad brakeman turned compiler and publisher took a financial gamble with his collection of humor. To his delight a strong market existed for such a work. Buyers of this ninety-six-page paperback, which cost twenty-five cents, were mostly passengers; train butchers sold thousands of copies. By 1950 the total press run had reached an astounding 7 million. A popular piece in the original version went this way:

The drawings that illustrate the 1938 humor book, *On a Fast Streamliner: Fun from New York to Frisco, A Trainload of Loud Laughs,* by Harry Jackson, once likely caused a chuckle or two, but less so in the twenty-first century.

Author's coll.

> You are not the only pebble on the beach for there is a little rock in Arkansaw. It was down in the state of Arkansaw I rode on this slowest train I ever saw. It stopped at every house. When it came to a double house it stopped twice. They made so many stops I said, "Conductor, what have we stopped for now?" He said, "There are some cattle on the tracks." We ran a little ways further and stopped

again. I said, "What is the matter now?" He said, "We have caught up with those cattle again." We made pretty good time for about two miles. One old cow got her trail caught in the cow-catcher and she ran off down the track with the train. The cattle bothered us so much they had to take the cow-catcher off the engine and put it on the hind end of the train to keep the cattle from jumping up in the sleeper.

Later Harry Jackson, Jackson's son, continued the family publishing business. (The backlist included a dozen popular collections of humor.) And he made his own contribution, writing in 1938 the less favored *On a Fast Streamliner, Fun from New York to Frisco, A Trainload of Loud Laughs.* The jokes and drawings, often racist and sexist, contained the same corny, even super-cornball humor, as this example attests: "Yes, everything is union in Chicago. We landed at a Union Depot. We left by a Union Depot. I went to a store to buy some under-clothes. They tried to sell me a union suit. I went into a Union Ticket Office; they tried to sell me a ticket over the Union Pacific."

By the mid-twentieth century the Jackson publishing business had declined markedly. Observed the younger Jackson, "Too many people are listening to radio and looking at movies and television instead of reading joke books." That may not have been correct, but it remained mostly so for railroad-related humor. Rail enthusiasts likely became the principal buyers of reprinted railroad humor; more than others they could relate to these jokes and stories.

CELEBRATIONS

Scores of communities have kept their railroad heritage alive. Whether big or small, these public-spirited boosters annually hold their "Railroad Days." It might be the grand celebration that takes place in conjunction with welcoming inductees into the National Railroad Hall of Fame in Galesburg, Illinois, or the more casual gathering of enthusiasts in Manchester, Georgia. No part of America lacks railroad-inspired celebrations: Brunswick, Maryland; Durand, Michigan; Portola, California; Snoqualmie, Washington; West Chicago, Illinois; and Yulee, Florida, hold such events.

Another place that remembers its railroad past is Central, South Carolina, a town of several thousand residents that straddles the busy main line of the former Southern Railway between Washington, D.C., and New Orleans, present-day Norfolk Southern. In recent years activities have centered around a house, located a block from the tracks, that has been converted into a small museum, highlighted by model train displays and signage that explains local railroad history. In the early 1870s the Atlanta & Charlotte Air Line Railroad, a predecessor of the Southern, gave birth to Central. Being centrally located (hence its name) between Atlanta and Charlotte, the town expected to become a division point and site of a repair facility. These hopes never materialized, although for years the railroad made meal stops at the Central station.

Some celebrations do more than remember the railroad in a community, but still have a railroad connection. An enduring event, "Hobo Days," takes place in Britt, Iowa, a town in the north-central section of the Hawkeye State. Unlike activities in a Galesburg or Central, the internationally known Britt affair dates back more than a century to August 22, 1900, and has continued every year since, even with the dramatically diminished number of true "boes."

Britt boosters sought to put their community on the map. "We wanted to do something different to show the world that Britt was a lively little town capable of doing anything that larger cities could do." Residents demanded growth, and they hoped to wrestle the Hancock County seat away from nearby Garner. Learning that the recently organized National Tourists Union, a hobo organization, wished to relocate its annual convention, Britt representatives contacted Charles Noe, who held the odd title of "Grand Head Pipe." Noe and his group, which consisted of an expanding membership, liked the offer, believing that if their gatherings were well publicized, there would be more than pleasurable experiences for participants. The union sought to improve relations with railroad workers and local law-enforcement officers. And it sought to modify stringent anti-vagrancy laws. The Britt event might advance its agenda.

The first of these hobo conventions went well. Hundreds of boes flocked to Britt on freights that traveled the rails of the Milwaukee Road and M&STL. The convention offered food, music, competitive events, and additional entertainment. Significantly, the national press took notice, with Chicago newspapers providing extensive coverage. "The hobo convention has come and gone," reported the *Britt News* about the inaugural event. "Nobody was killed, the town was not burned, nobody robbed." Crowed the paper, "Britt is the best advertised town in the United States. If everybody did not have a good time, it was their own fault as there was all colors of fun afloat."

Although Garner retained the county seat, the Britt hobo/railroad tradition flourished, providing the town with positive notoriety. Even though the bo population has plummeted since the Great Depression, those remaining knights of the road have not be forgotten. "Hobo Days are supposed to be about hoboes," as the events coordinator told the *Mason City Globe-Gazette* in August 2009. "We don't want to get away from what it's supposed to be about." And the traditional individual activities remain popular: hobo kiddie parade, hobo jungle entertainment, hobo king and queen coronation, and, most of all, free mulligan stew.

As the historical profession in America emerged in the last quarter of the nineteenth century, academically trained scholars began to consider the impact of railroads on the shaping of the nation. Those who studied the process of westward expansion revealed how the iron horse stimulated the farming, ranching, mining, and lumbering frontiers. However, it would not be until the formative decades of the twentieth century that historians looked closely at railroad subjects. Ulrich Bonnell Phillips (1877–1934) blazed the way. In 1908 his extensively researched book, *A History of Transportation in the Eastern Cotton Belt to 1860,* described and analyzed how transport forms, particularly railroads, contributed to the prosperity and expansion of the cotton culture in the Old South. The success of planters and their business associates in constructing railroads, Phillips concluded, led to the disastrous, one-sided staple-crop economy and a strong commitment to slavery. By the 1940s scores of scholarly volumes on a variety of railroad-related topics had appeared, although their thrust was heavily economic and political.

The process of studying the nation's railroad heritage continued. Just a rail enthusiasts launched their various groups in the 1930s and 1940s, so, too, did professional historians. The driving force behind what became the central organization for railroad scholars, the Lexington Group in Transportation History, was Richard "Dick" Cleghorn Overton (1907–1988). This Harvard-trained business historian wrote several well-received studies, including his first book, *Burlington West: A Colonization History of the Burlington Railroad,* published in 1941. On May 7, 1942, at a meeting of the Mississippi Valley Historical Association (today's Organization of American Historians), Overton and eight other men who were interested in railroad history gathered informally in the taproom of the Hotel Lafayette in Lexington, Kentucky, to discuss matters of common interest. "Our job, as we see it, is to exchange information on the availability of records, subjects that are worth exploring, and information that will help persons doing serious research," related Overton. After that impromptu meeting, Overton, a faculty member at Northwestern University, served as informal secretary. "We had no other 'officers.'" The Lexington Group grew, claiming more than two hundred members by the mid-1950s and becoming more structured.

After having played a pivotal role in creating the Lexington Group, Overton stepped down as secretary in 1954. Another scholar, Howard Bennett, also at Northwestern University, became secretary, and he was succeeded in 1969 by still another Northwestern faculty member, Richard Barsness. Under Barsness a major change occurred: the Lexington Group expanded to scholars and others interested in all forms of transportation – air, rail, truck, and water. Then in 1975 a prolific railroad historian, Don L. Hofsommer, took the throttle. He expanded the existing *Newsletter,* which became the *Lexington Quarterly,* to include book reviews and, as with earlier issues, news about Lexingtonians, bibliographies, and related information. Much later this informal organization incorporated, becoming the Lexington Group, Inc., but still seeking to nurture the study of America's railroad and transportation past.

It is understandable that most academics who write railroad history have ties to the Lexington Group and that it would be informally involved with several railroad research centers, most notably the John W. Barriger III National Railroad Library in St. Louis, Missouri. Other subsets of the historical profession also have encouraged the study of railroads, including the Business History Association. Alexis de Tocqueville was correct – America is a nation of joiners, whether railroad enthusiasts or railroad scholars.

MORE LEGACY

For many Americans the railroad legacy involves the visual. Aspects of the railroad experience, especially the historical, have become an integral part of the nation's cultural life. There are thousands of paintings and prints; libraries, museums, and private collections abound with railroad images. Well known (and widely reproduced) is *Lackawanna Valley* (originally titled *The First Roundhouse of the D. L. & W. Railroad at Scranton*) by the Hudson River School artist George Inness (1825–1894), depicting the Delaware, Lackawanna & Western Railroad roundhouse in Scranton, Pennsylvania. This oil canvas, painted in 1855 and hanging in the National Gallery of Art in Washington, D.C., may be the earliest work commissioned by a railroad from a recognized American painter, and it is a superb example of what American studies scholar Leo Marx calls "the machine in the garden." Another recognized oil painting, *The 9:45 AM Accommodation, Stamford, Connecticut, 1867* (reproduced in several mediums, especially holiday cards) by Edward Lamson Henry (1841–1919), is part of the permanent collection of the Metropolitan Museum of Art in New York City. The busy station scene, with its early American-standard locomotive, is realistic, an outstanding example of pure Americana.

The public is more familiar with the works of nineteenth-century lithographers Nathaniel Currier (1813–1888) and James Ives (1824–1895), particularly *The Express Train.* The Currier & Ives company offered a rich variety of colored lithographs that depicted railroad scenes. Usually the images were accurately portrayed, and they sold well and at reasonable

prices. Easy access to these Currier & Ives offerings gave the "democratic man" an opportunity to enjoy visually the Railway Age. And to this day they remain popular.

Later artists and illustrators also incorporated the railroad into their works. When the Ash Can School burst upon the American art scene before World War I, urban realist painters, including William Glackens (1870–1938), Robert Henri (1865–1929), and Everett Shinn (1876–1953), found railroads irresistible. They sought to portray "real life," and the smoking locomotive and the gritty rail yard fit their needs. This desire for realism continued into the maturing century. Edward Hopper (1882–1967), for one, received much acclaim for *Approaching a City* (1946), a painting depicting a stark concrete underpass with multiple sets of tracks. Hopper explained that he wanted to express the emotions of a train rider who is about to enter a strange city: "interest, curiosity, fear."

While lacking the prestige of members of the Ash Can School or an Edward Hopper, commercial artists have helped to create a popular vision of the railroad. Over time their works have become collectible and frequently reproduced. A number of carriers, including the New York Central, Pennsylvania, and Atchison, Topeka & Santa Fe, commissioned art for covers of their calendars, annual reports, and other publications. Some of the most admired creations were the colorful oils painted by Griffith (Grif) Teller (1899–1993). Between 1925 and 1958 Teller's talents adorned Pennsylvania Railroad calendars, and they were printed by his employer, the Osborne Company, a large New Jersey art-calendar firm. After its inception in 1971 Amtrak kept this tradition alive with original art on its yearly poster-size calendars.

Artists emerged who focused almost exclusively on railroad subjects. In recent decades affluent railfans became a steady market for their works, usually watercolors rather than oils, depicting trains, railroaders, and corridors. As steam vanished, there was a desire to capture the romance of the iron horse. Nostalgia also grew for "first generation" diesel-electric locomotives and other pieces of post–World War II passenger equipment. Skilled artists such as Howard Fogg (1917–1996), Gilmore "Gil" Reid (1918–2007), and Theodore "Ted" Rose (1940–2002) relied on private commissions, gallery sales, and revenues generated from seasonal calendars, holiday cards, and stationery to sustain their artistic endeavors. Always the entrepreneur, Rose also turned to the book format: Clarion Press in 1995 released his illustrated children's book, *The Banshee Train*, and five years later Indiana University Press published his *In the Traces: Railroad Paintings of Ted Rose*. The works of these contemporary railroad artists have been exhibited widely, including "Life Imitates Art: A Salute to Ted Rose" that in 2006 attracted receptive crowds to the California State Railroad Museum.

These railroad artists loved trains. Wrote famed war correspondent Ernie Pyle about Gil Reid in his 1944 book, *Brave Men*, "Young [Lieutenant] Reid was an artist and also a railroad hobbyist. He studied railroads with the same verve that some people show in collecting stamps. He once did a painting of a freight train at a small midwestern station, and when he got word overseas that it had been printed in color in a railroad magazine he felt he'd practically reached the zenith of his heart's desire." No wonder Reid, with this feeling, conveyed the power and excitement of the rails.

Although generally not as famous as the works of Currier & Ives, this H. Schile & Company color lithograph depicts an American standard 4-4-0 passenger train crossing the Humboldt River in Nevada, and operating over the Central Pacific, the western portion of the nation's first transcontinental railroad. As might be expected, the train brings out onlookers as it nears this frontier settlement.

Author's coll.

Entrepreneurial
photographers knew
that scenes along the
Union Pacific would
sell, even years after
the Promontory cel-
ebration. In the 1880s
Charles Witfle, who
owned a graphoscope
and stereoscopic
shop in Central City,
Colorado, sold a series
of views, including
this image of a passen-
ger on the Dale Creek
Bridge near Sherman,
Wyoming Territory.

Author's coll.

Photography and railroads developed about the same time. From the
1850s onward photographers pointed their cameras at railroad subjects.
Some of the most historically important photographs in American history came in 1869 when Andrew Joseph Russell (1830–1902) captured on
glass-plate negatives the golden spike ceremony at Promontory. These
iconic images, however, were staged; few Chinese track laborers are seen
in Russell's handiwork. Not long after this epic event Russell's *Great West
Illustrated* appeared, containing views of the region with ample railroad
representation. And for decades railroads hired commercial photographers, including F. Jay Haynes (1853–1921), William Henry Jackson (1843–
1942), and William H. Rau (1855–1920), to capture scenes along their lines
and physical properties, especially betterments – bridges, tunnels, and
stations. These companies used photographs for a variety of eye-catching
purposes, including large prints that were hung in depot waiting rooms
and city ticket offices and illustrations for timetables and promotional
brochures. Many of these images have been preserved, becoming part of
museum collections, illustrating books and articles, and being themselves
the subject of academic and enthusiast studies.

Long after the works of Haynes and others appeared, railroads continued to tap talented photographers. O. Winston Link (1914–2001) illustrates this tradition. In the mid-1950s this commercial photographer from
New York City received an assignment from the Norfolk & Western Railway to capture the final days of steam on this predominantly coal-hauling

road. A perfectionist, he worked for days at a trackside location arranging flash bulbs for a single photograph, gaining fame for his striking night-time scenes. Repeatedly Link demonstrated his skills by juxtaposing the railroad with the built environment. As a testimony to his talents, the O. Winston Link Museum in Roanoke, Virginia, opened in 2004 in the former Norfolk & Western passenger depot to display his works and to exhibit the railroad photography of others.

The silver screen became another visual medium for depicting the impact railroads have had on Americans. This has been a long-standing connection; the first movie designed for entertainment was *The Great Train Robbery*, which Edison Films released in 1903. This ten-minute "one reeler" was a milestone in motion-picture history, and demonstrated that a movie could be commercially viable. Moreover, *The Great Train Robbery* employed innovative techniques, including location shooting. Since trains were exciting and readily available and part of daily life, film makers exploited them. By the twenty-first century hundreds of movies have depended upon railroads for their story lines, ranging from *Union Pacific* (1939) and *North by Northwest* (1959) to *Planes, Trains and Automobiles* (1987) and *Unstoppable* (2010). Not to be overlooked were the "serials," which appeared in movie theaters, large and small, during the 1930s before special film "shorts" and radio made them less popular and then gone altogether. In 1932 a young John Wayne starred in the fast-moving twelve-part serial *The Hurricane Express*, featuring a mad saboteur known as "The Wrecker" who sought to ruin the mythical L&R Railroad.

For the non–visually oriented, there is an array of railroad-inspired music, a rich and diverse legacy. Americans have been exposed to this musical theme more than to any other art form. Virtually every camp song-book contains the music and lyrics of "I've Been Workin' on the Railroad," and it may be one of the first songs that a child learns. For generations "Little Red Caboose Behind the Train" probably ranked as a close second, although this piece of nearly vanished rolling stock may need to be explained to the youth of the present day. Many of the most remembered tunes have no known authors, for example, "New River Train," "Nine Hundred Miles," and the "Wabash Cannonball," the latter having a variety of lyrics. The origins of some songs can be traced to Irish immigrants who constructed and maintained track. "Paddy on the Railway" is one. Scores of others came from Tin Pan Alley songsmiths, including "Casey Jones" and "The Lightning Express." Another illustration is "The L&N Rag," which reflects the ragtime musical craze that swept the country between the Spanish American War and World War I. Even more songs are part of the blues, bluegrass, and country and western traditions, including such well-remembered ones as "John Henry," "Brakeman's Blues," "Train Whistle Blues," and "The Wreck of Old 97." The acknowledged "father" of

For decades reams of piano sheet music featured railroad themes. "I'm Going Back to Carolina," published in 1918, is a representative piece.

Author's coll.

country music, Jimmie Rodgers (1897–1933), had a personal connection to railroading. This native of Meridian, Mississippi, dubbed the "Singing Brakeman," worked in train service for the New Orleans & Northeastern and later as a switchman for the Southern Pacific.

More musical types have railroad ties. The twentieth-century pop music field has made lasting contributions, such as "On the Atchison, Topeka and the Santa Fe," "Chattanooga Choo Choo," and more recently "Midnight Train to Georgia," "The City of New Orleans," and "Runaway Train." Railroads also inspired scores of mostly forgotten religious tunes. The published format of one nineteenth-century song, "The Railway to Heaven," indicates that "This Line runs from Calvary through this vain world and the Valley of the Shadow of Death, until it lands in the Kingdom of Heaven." Later "The Gospel Train Is Coming/Get on Board" gained popularity, particularly among people of color in the South.

The railroad legacy remains a distinct part of the American heritage. "Railroads have really touched our lives," opined Chicago architect and passenger train historian Arthur Dubin. "I see it in the urban landscape, graphic arts, music and so much more. It really is astounding, even to someone like me who has collected and written about the past [of railroading]." Dubin is correct; railroads and the American people are strongly entwined. While it is still true today – and there is reason to believe that railroads will continue to be relevant in national life and not fade into the sepia-toned past – this connection was keenly pronounced during that long-lasting Railway Age.

SOURCES AND SUGGESTIONS FOR FURTHER READING

Aldrich, Mark. *Death Rode the Rails: American Railroad Accidents and Safety, 1828–1965.* Baltimore: Johns Hopkins University Press, 2006.

Alverez, Eugene. *Travel on Southern Antebellum Railroads, 1828–1860.* Tuscaloosa: University of Alabama Press, 1974.

Anderson, Nels. *The Hobo: The Sociology of the Homeless Man.* Chicago: University of Chicago Press, 1925.

Arnesen, Eric. *Brotherhoods of Color: Black Railroad Workers and the Struggle for Equality.* Cambridge, Mass.: Harvard University Press, 2001.

Athearn, Robert E. *Union Pacific Country.* Chicago: Rand McNally, 1971.

Bailey, Barbara Ruth. *Main Street Northeastern Oregon: The Founding and Development of Small Towns.* Portland: Oregon Historical Society, 1982.

Bain, David H. *Empire Express: Building the First Transcontinental Railroad.* New York: Viking, 1999.

Bartly, Ian R. *Selling the True Time: Nineteenth-Century Timekeeping in America.* Stanford, Calif.: Stanford University Press, 2000.

Bedwell, Harry. *The Boomer: A Story of the Rails.* New York: Farrar and Rinehart, 1942.

Beebe, Lucius. *Mixed Train Daily: A Book of Short-Line Railroads.* New York: Dutton, 1947.

Black, Robert C. *The Railroads of the Confederacy.* Chapel Hill: University of North Carolina Press, 1952.

Borkin, B. A., and Alvin F. Harlow, eds. *A Treasury of Railroad Folklore.* New York: Crown Publishers, 1953.

Bromley, Joseph. *Clear the Tracks! The Story of an Old-Time Locomotive Engineer.* New York: Whittlesey House, 1943.

Brown, Isaac Morris. *Boomer Bill: His Book.* St. Louis: n.p., 1930.

Brown, Walter Rollo. *I Travel by Train.* New York: Appleton, 1939.

Bryan, William J. *The First Battle: A Story of the Campaign of 1896.* Chicago: W. B. Conkey, 1896.

Bryant, Keith L., Jr. *Arthur E. Stilwell: Promoter with a Hunch.* Nashville, Tenn.: Vanderbilt University Press, 1971.

———. *History of the Atchison, Topeka & Santa Fe Railway.* New York: Macmillan, 1974.

Burns, Roger. *Knights of the Road: A Hobo History.* New York: Methuen, 1980.

Caldwell, Wilber W. *The Courthouse and the Depot: A Narrative Guide to Railroad Expansion and Its Impact on Public Architecture in Georgia, 1833–1910.* Macon, Ga.: Mercer University Press, 2001.

Call, Frank Wendell. *Gandydancer's Children: A Railroad Memoir.* Reno: University of Nevada Press, 2000.

Catton, Bruce. *Waiting for the Morning Train.* New York: Doubleday, 1972.

Chambers, William. *Things As They Are in America.* London: William and Robert Chambers, 1854.

Clark, John. *Railroads in the Civil War: The Impact of Management on Victory and Defeat.* Baton Rouge: Louisiana State University, 2001.

Clarke, Thomas Curtis, et al. *The American Railway: Its Construction, Development, Management and Appliances.* Secaucus, N.J.: 1988; reprint.

Cohen, Norm. *Long Steel Rail: The Railroad in American Folksong.* Urbana: University of Illinois Press, 1981.

Condit, Carl W. *The Railroad and the City.* Columbus: Ohio State University Press, 1971.

Danby, Susan, and Leo Marx, eds. *The Railroad in American Art.* Cambridge, Mass.: MIT Press, 1988.

Davis, Colin J. *Power at Odds: The 1922 National Railroad Shopmen's Strike.* Urbana: University of Illinois Press, 1997.

Deverell, William. *Railroad Crossing: Californians and the Railroad, 1850–1910.* Berkeley: University of California Press, 1994.

Dickens, Laurie C. *Wreck on the Wabash.* Blissfield, Mich.: Made for Ewe, 2001.

Dilts, James D. *The Great Road: The Building of the Baltimore and Ohio, The Nation's First Railroad, 1828–1853.* Stanford, Calif.: Stanford University Press, 1993.

Donovan, Frank P., Jr. *Harry Bedwell: Last of the Great Railroad Storytellers.* Minneapolis: Ross and Haines, 1959.

Douglas, George H. *All Aboard! The Railroad in American Life*. New York: Paragon House, 1992.

Droege, John A. *Passenger Terminals and Trains*. New York: McGraw-Hill, 1916.

Drucker, James H. *Men of the Steel Rails: Workers on the Atchison, Topeka & Santa Fe Railroad, 1869–1900*. Lincoln: University of Nebraska Press, 1983.

Dubin, Arthur D. *More Classic Trains*. Milwaukee: Kalmbach, 1974.

————. *Some Classic Trains*. Milwaukee: Kalmbach, 1964.

Dunbar, Seymour. *A History of Travel in America*. New York: Tudor Publishing, 1937.

Ely, James W., Jr. *Railroads and American Law*. Lawrence: University Press of Kansas, 2001.

Fant, David J., Jr. *Ambassador on Rails: David J. Fant, Engineer Evangelist*. Harrisburg, Pa.: Christian Publications, 1948.

Ferguson, E. A. *Founding of the Cincinnati Southern Railway*. Cincinnati: Robert Clark, 1905.

Fox, Charles Elmer. *Tales of an American Hobo*. Iowa City: University of Iowa Press, 1989.

Frailey, Fred W. *Twilight of the Great Trains*. Waukesha, Wisc.: Kalmbach Books, 1998.

Franklin, John Hope. *Mirror to America: The Autobiography of John Hope Franklin*. New York: Farrar, Straus, and Giroux, 2005.

Fried, Stephen. *Appetite for America: How Visionary Businessman Fred Harvey Built a Railroad Hospitality Empire That Civilized the Wild West*. New York: Bantam Books, 2010.

Gabler, Edwin. *The American Telegrapher: A Social History*. New Brunswick, N.J.: Rutgers University Press, 1988.

Gamst, Frederick C., ed. *Early American Railroads: Franz Anton Ritter von Gerstner's 'Die innern Communicationen' (1842–1843)*. Stanford, Calif.: Stanford University Press, 1997.

Gjevre, John A. *Chili Line: The Narrow Gauge Rail Trail to Santa Fe*. 3rd ed. Espanola, N.M.: Las Trampas Press, 1984.

Goddard, Stephen B. *Getting There: The Epic Struggle between Road and Rail in the American Century*. New York: Basic Books, 1994.

Gordon, Sarah H. *Passage to Union: How Railroads Transformed American Life, 1829–1929*. Chicago: Ivan R. Dee, 1997.

Grant, H. Roger. *"Follow the Flag": A History of the Wabash Railroad Company*. DeKalb: Northern Illinois University Press, 2004.

————. *North Western: A History of the Chicago & North Western Railway System*. DeKalb: Northern Illinois University Press, 1996.

————. *Rails through the Wiregrass: A History of the Georgia & Florida Railroad*. DeKalb: Northern Illinois University Press, 2006

————. *Twilight Rails: The Final Era of Railroad Building in the Midwest*. Minneapolis: University of Minnesota Press, 2010.

————, ed. *Brownie the Boomer: The Life of Charles P. Brown, an American Railroader*. DeKalb: Northern Illinois University Press, 1991.

Grant, H. Roger, and Charles W. Bohi. *The Country Railroad Station in America*. Boulder, Colo.: Pruett Publishing, 1978.

Grant, H. Roger, Don L. Hofsommer, and Osmund Overby. *St. Louis Union Station: A Place for People, A Place for Trains*. St. Louis: St. Louis Mercantile Library, 1994.

Greenberg, William T., et al. *The Handsomest Trains in the World: Passenger Service on the Lehigh Valley Railroad*. Westfield, N.J.: Bells & Whistles, 1978.

Handlin, David P. *The American Home: Architecture and Society, 1815–1915*. Boston: Little, Brown, 1979.

Harlow, Alvin F. *Old Waybills*. New York: D. Appleton-Century, 1934.

Harwood, Herbert H., Jr. *Invisible Giants: The Empires of Cleveland's Van Sweringen Brothers*. Bloomington: Indiana University Press, 2003.

Hawkins, Hugh. *Railwayman's Son: A Plains Family Memoir*. Lubbock: Texas Tech University Press, 2006.

Hayes, William Edward. *Iron Road to Empire: The History of the Rock Island Lines*. New York: Simmons-Boardman, 1953.

Hedin, Robert, ed. *The Great Machines: Poems and Songs of the American Railroad*. Iowa City: University of Iowa Press, 1996.

Helmers, Dow. *Tragedy at Eden*. Chicago: Swallow, 1971.

Henry, Robert Selph. *Railroad Business*. Indianapolis: Bobbs-Merrill, 1942.

————. *Trains*. Indianapolis: Bobbs-Merrill, 1934.

Hilton, George W. *American Narrow Gauge Railroads*. Stanford, Calif.: Stanford University Press, 1990.

Hilton, George W., and John F. Due. *The Electric Interurban Railways in America*. Stanford, Calif.: Stanford University Press, 1960.

Hofsommer, Don L. *The Quanah Route: A History of the Quanah, Acme & Pacific Railway*. College Station: Texas A&M University Press, 1991.

————. *The Southern Pacific, 1901–1985*. College Station: Texas A&M University Press, 1985.

————. *The Tootin' Louie: A History of the Minneapolis & St. Louis Railway*. Minneapolis: University of Minnesota Press, 2005.

Holbrook, Stewart H. *The Story of American Railroads*. New York: Crown Publishers, 1947.

Holt, Marilyn Irvin. *The Orphan Trains: Placing Out in America*. Lincoln: University of Nebraska Press, 1992.

Hubbard, Freeman H. *Railroad Avenue: Great Stories and Legends of American Railroading*. New York: McGraw-Hill, 1945.

Hudson, John C. *Plains Country Towns*. Minneapolis: University of Minnesota Press, 1985.

Hungerford, Edward. *Men of Erie: A Story of Human Development*. New York: Random House, 1946.

Itzkoff, Donald M. *Off the Track: The Decline of the Intercity Passenger Train in the United States*. Westport, Conn.: Greenwood, 1985.

Jensen, Oliver. *The American Heritage History of Railroads in America*. New York: American Heritage, 1975.

Johnson, Rob. *Short Lines: A Collection of Classic American Railroad Stories*. New York: St. Martin's Press, 1996.

Johnson, Stanley W. *The Milwaukee Road Revisited*. Moscow: University of Idaho Press, 1997.

Kennedy, William Sloane. *Wonders and Curiosities of the Railway*. New York: S. C. Griggs, 1884.

Kirkland, Edward Chase. *Men, Cities and Transportation: A Study in New England History, 1820–1900*. 2 vols. Cambridge, Mass.: Harvard University Press, 1948.

Klara, Robert. *FDR's Funeral Train*. New York: Palgrave Macmillan, 2010.

Kornweibel, Theodore Jr. *Railroads in the African American Experience: A Photographic Journey*. Baltimore: Johns Hopkins University Press, 2010.

Kromer, Tom. *Waiting for Nothing*. New York: Alfred A. Knopf, 1935.

Licht, Walter. *Working for the Railroad: The Organization of Work in the Nineteenth Century*. Princeton, N.J.: Princeton University Press, 1983.

Littlejohn, Douglas (Duffy) C. *Hopping Freight Trains in America*. Los Osos, Calif.: Sand River Press, 1993.

London, Jack. *The Road*. Santa Barbara, Calif.: Peregrine Publishers, 1970, reprint.

Lord, Robert F. *Country Depots in the Connecticut Hills*. Hartford, Conn.: Goulet Printery, 1996.

Lorenzsonn, Alex S. *The Advent of Railroads in Wisconsin, 1831–1861*. Madison: Wisconsin Historical Society Press, 2009.

Lyle, Katie L. *Scalded to Death by the Steam: Authentic Stories of Railroad Disasters and the Ballards That Were Written about Them*. Chapel Hill, N.C.: Algonquin Books, 1988.

Lyon, Peter. *To Hell in a Day Coach*. Philadelphia: J. B. Lippincott, 1968.

McCommons, James. *Waiting on a Train: The Embattled Future of Passenger Rail Service – A Year Spent Riding Across America*. White River Junction, Vt.: Chelsea Green Publishing, 2009.

McCrossen, Alexis. *Holy Day, Holiday: The American Sunday*. Ithaca, N.Y.: Cornell University Press, 2000.

MacGill, Caroline E., et al. *History of Transportation in the United States before 1860*. Gloucester, Mass.: Peter Smith, 1948.

McKissack, Patricia, and Frederick McKissack. *A Long Hard Journey: The Story of the Pullman Porter*. New York: Walker, 1989.

Maiken, Peter. *Night Train*. Chicago: Lakme Press, 1988.

Marrs, Aaron W. *Railroads in the Old South: Pursuing Progress in a Slave Society*. Baltimore: Johns Hopkins University Press, 2009.

Marshall, James. *Santa Fe: The Railroad That Built an Empire*. New York: Random House, 1945.

Martin, Albro. *Enterprise Denied: Origins of the Decline of American Railroads, 1897–1917*. New York: Columbia University Press, 1971.

———. *James J. Hill and the Opening of the Northwest*. New York: Oxford University Press, 1976.

———. *Railroads Triumphant: The Growth, Rejection and Rebirth of a Vital American Force*. New York: Oxford University Press, 1992.

Marx, Leo. *The Machine in the Garden: Technology and the Pastoral Ideal in America*. New York: Oxford University Press, 1967.

Mathers, Michael. *Riding the Rails*. Boston: Gambit, 1973.

Masterson, V. V. *The Katy Railroad and the Last Frontier*. Norman: University of Oklahoma Press, 1952.

Meeks, Carroll L. V. *The Railroad Station: An Architectural History*. New Haven, Conn.: Yale University Press, 1956.

Meyer, Balthasar H. *History of Transportation in the United States before 1860*. New York: Peter Smith, 1948; reprint.

Middleton, William D., George M. Smerk, and Roberta L. Diehl, eds. *Encyclopedia of North American Railroads*. Bloomington: Indiana University Press, 2007.

Miller, Merle. *On Being Different: What It Means To Be a Homosexual*. New York: Random House, 1971.

Miner, H. Craig. *A Most Magnificent Machine: America Adopts the Railroad, 1825–1862*. Lawrence: University Press of Kansas, 2010.

Moody, Linwood W. *The Maine Two-Footers*. Berkeley, Calif.: Howell-North, 1959.

Moore, John F. *The Story of the Railroad "Y."* New York: Association Press, 1930.

Moore, Truman E. *The Traveling Man: The Story of the American Traveling Salesman*. Garden City, N.Y.: Doubleday, 1972.

Morris, Juddi. *The Harvey Girls: The Women Who Civilized the West*. New York: Walker, 1997.

Morrison, David D., and Valerie Pakaluk. *Images of Rail: Long Island Rail Road Stations*. Charleston, S.C.: Arcadia Publishing, 2003.

Neil, R. M. *High Green and the Bark Peelers: The Story of Enginman Henry A. Beaulieu and His Boston and Maine Railroad*. New York: Duell, Sloan, and Pearce, 1950.

Newton, Louis M. *Rails Remembered*. Vol. 1. Roanoke, Va.: Progress Press, 1992.

Nolen, Edward W. *Northern Pacific Views: The Railroad Photography of F. Jay Hayes, 1876–1905*. Helena: Montana Historical Society, 1983.

O'Malley, Michael. *Keeping Watch: A History of American Time*. New York: Viking Penguin, 1990.

Orr, John W. *Set Up Running: The Life of Pennsylvania Railroad Engineman, 1904–1949*. University Park: Pennsylvania State University Press, 2001.

Orsi, Richard J. *Sunset Limited: The Southern Pacific Railroad and the Development of the American West, 1850–1930*. Berkeley: University of California Press, 2005.

Ovenden, Mark. *Railway Maps of the World*. New York: Viking, 2011.

Overton, Richard C. *Burlington Route: A History of the Burlington Lines*. New York: Knopf, 1965.

———. *Burlington West: A Colonization History of the Burlington Railroad*. Cambridge, Mass.: Harvard University Press, 1941.

Phillips, Ulrich B. *A History of Transportation in the Eastern Cotton Belt to 1860*. New York: Columbia University Press, 1908.

Potter, Janet Greenstein. *Great American Railroad Stations*. New York: John Wiley & Sons, 1996.

Prescott, D.C. *Early Day Railroading from Chicago*. Chicago: David B. Clarkson, 1910.

Reinhardt, Richard. *Workin' on the Railroad: Reminiscences from the Age of Steam*. Palo Alto, Calif.: American West Publishing, 1970.

Reisdorff, James J. *The Man Who Wrecked 146 Locomotives: The Story of "Head-On Joe" Connolly*. David City, Neb.: South Platte Press, 2009.

Reitman, Ben L. *Sister of the Road: The Autobiography of Box-Car Bertha as Told to Dr. Ben L. Reitman*. New York: Macaulay, 1937.

Repp, Stan. *The Super Chief: Train of the Stars*. San Marino, Calif.: Golden West Books, 1980.

Rhodes, Joel P. *A Missouri Railroad Pioneer: The Life of Louis Houck*. Columbia: University of Missouri Press, 2008.

Richards, Jeffrey, and John M. MacKenzie. *The Railway Station: A Social History*. New York: Oxford University Press, 1986.

Richardson, Frederick H., and F. Nelson Blount. *Along the Iron Trail*. Rutland, Vt.: Tuttle Publishing, 1938.

Richter, Amy G. *Home on the Rails: Women, the Railroad, and the Rise of Public Domesticity*. Chapel Hill: University of North Carolina Press, 2005.

Riegel, Robert F. *The Story of Western Railroads*. New York: Macmillan, 1926.

Robertson, Archibald Thomas. *Slow Train to Yesterday: A Last Glance at the Local*. Boston: Houghton Mifflin, 1945.

Robinson, Doane. *A Brief History of South Dakota*. New York: American Book, 1905.

Rose, Joseph R. *American Wartime Transportation*. New York: Thomas Y. Crowell, 1953.

Runte, Alfred. *Allies of the Earth: Railroads and the Soul of Preservation*. Kirksville, Mo.: Truman State University Press, 2006.

———. *Trains of Discovery: Western Railroads and the National Parks*. Flagstaff, Ariz.: Northland Press, 1984.

Sanders, D. G. *The Brasspounder*. New York: Hawthorn Books, 1978.

Schwantes, Carlos Arnaldo. *Going Places: Transportation Redefines the Twentieth-Century West*. Bloomington: Indiana University Press, 2003.

———. *Railroad Signatures Across the Pacific Northwest*. Seattle: University of Washington Press, 1993.

Schwantes, Carlos Arnaldo, and James P. Ronda. *The West the Railroads Made*. Seattle: University of Washington Press, 2008.

Schwieterman, Joseph P. *When the Railroad Leaves Town: American Communities in the Age of Rail Line Abandonment*. [Vol. 1:] *Eastern United States*. Kirksville, Mo.: Truman State University Press, 2001.

———. *When the Railroad Leaves Town: American Communities in the Age of Rail Line Abandonment*. [Vol. 2:] *Western United States*. Kirksville, Mo.: Truman State University Press, 2004.

Scott, Roy V. *Railroad Development in the Twentieth Century*. Ames: Iowa State University Press, 1985.

Shaw, Robert B. *A History of Railroad Accidents, Safety Precautions and Operating Practices*. Potsdam, N.Y.: Clarkson College of Technology, 1978.

Shippee, Lester B., ed. *Bishop Whipple's Southern Diary, 1843–1844*. New York: De Capo Press, 1968.

Southern Railway Company. *The Floods of July, 1916: How the Southern Railway Organization Met an Emergency*. Washington, D.C.: Southern Railway, 1917.

Speas, Stan, as told to Margaret Coel. *Goin' Railroading: A Century on the Colorado High Iron*. Boulder, Colo.: Pruett Publishing, 1985.

Stevenson, Robert Louis. *Across the Plains with Other Memories and Essays*. New York: Charles Scribner's Sons, 1892.

Stiles, T. J. *The First Tycoon: The Epic Life of Cornelius Vanderbilt*. New York: Knopf, 2009.

Stilgoe, John R. *Metropolitan Corridor: Railroads and the American Scene*. New Haven, Conn.: Yale University Press, 1983.

Stimson, H. A. *Depot Days*. Boynton Beach, Fla.: Star Publishing, 1972.

Stover, John F. *American Railroads*. 2nd ed. Chicago: University of Chicago Press, 1997.

———. *Iron Road to the West*. New York: Columbia University Press, 1978.

Stromquist, Shelton. *A Generation of Boomers: The Pattern of Railroad Labor Conflict in Nineteenth Century America*. Urbana: University of Illinois Press, 1987.

Swank, Walbrook D., ed. *Train Running for the Confederacy, 1861–1865: An Eye-witness Memoir.* Mineral, Va.: Privately printed, 1990.

Taibi, John. *Remembering the New York, Ontario & Western Railway: Oswego to Sidney and Branches.* Fleischmanns, N.Y.: Purple Mountain Press, 2005.

Taylor, George Rogers. *The Transportation Revolution, 1815–1860.* New York: Rinehart and Winston, 1951.

Taylor, Joseph. *A Fast Life on the Modern Highway, Being a Glance into the Railroad World from a New Point of View.* New York: Harper & Brothers, 1974.

Taylor, Wilma Rugh. *Gospel Tracks through Texas: The Mission Car Good Will.* College Station: Texas A&M University Press, 2005.

Thomas, Evan. *Robert Kennedy: His Life.* New York: Simon & Schuster, 2000.

Thomas, William. *The Iron Way: Railroads, the Civil War and the Making of Modern America.* New Haven, Conn.: Yale University Press, 2011.

Trent, Logan Douglas. *The Credit Mobilier.* New York: Arno Press, 1981.

Trostel, Scott D. *Angels at the Station.* Fletcher, Ohio: Cam-Tech Publishing, 2008.

———. *Bradford, the Railroad Town: A Railroad Town History of Bradford, Ohio, A Pennsylvania Railroad Town.* Fletcher, Ohio: Cam-Tech Publishing, 1987.

Tully, Jim. *Beggars of Life.* New York: Albert & Charles Boni, 1926.

Van Horne, John C., ed. *Traveling the Pennsylvania Railroad: The Photographs of William H. Rau.* Philadelphia: University of Pennsylvania Press, 2002.

Veenendaal, Augustus J. *American Railroads in the Nineteenth Century.* Westport, Conn.: Greenwood Press, 2003.

Ward, James A. *Railroads and the Character of America, 1820–1887.* Knoxville: University of Tennessee Press, 1986.

———, ed. *Southern Railroad Man: Conductor N. J. Bell's Recollections of the Civil War.* DeKalb: Northern Illinois University Press, 1994.

Watson, William E., et al. *The Ghosts of Duffy's Cut: The Irish Who Died Building America's Most Dangerous Stretch of Railroad.* New York: Praeger Publishers, 2006.

Weber, Thomas. *The Northern Railroads in the Civil War, 1861–1865.* New York: King's Crown Press, 1952.

Whitaker, Rogers E. M., and Anthony Hiss. *All Aboard with E. M. Frimbo: World's Greatest Railroad Buff.* New York: Grossman, 1974.

White, E. B. *One Man's Meat.* New York: Harper & Brothers, 1944.

White, John H., Jr. *The American Railroad Passenger Car.* Baltimore: Johns Hopkins University Press, 1978.

White, Richard. *Railroaded: The Transcontinentals and the Making of Modern America.* New York: W. W. Norton, 2011.

Williamson, Ellen. *When We Went First Class.* Garden City, N.Y.: Doubleday, 1977.

Winks, Robin W. *Frederick Billings: A Life.* New York: Oxford University Press, 1991.

Winter, Oscar Osburn. *The Transportation Frontier: Trans-Mississippi West, 1865–1890.* New York: Holt, 1964.

Winter, Thomas. *Making Men, Making Class: The YMCA and Workingmen, 1877–1920.* Chicago: University of Chicago Press, 2002.

Withers, Bob. *The President Travels by Train: Politics and Pullmans.* Lynchburg, Va.: TLC Publishing, 1996.

Wright, Helen R., ed. *Social Service in Wartime.* Chicago: University of Chicago Press, 1944.

Young, David M. *The Iron Horse and the Windy City.* DeKalb: Northern Illinois University Press, 2005.

INDEX

Page numbers in *italics* indicate presence of illustrations

Abbott, Rev. Edward, 155
Acela Express (passenger train), 92–93, 94
Adrian, Mich., 239–40
African-Americans, 4, 7, 8–9, 11, 13, 28–29, 30–31, 32, 53, 98, 124–25, 136, 208, 210, 221, 288. *See also* Jim Crow codes
Akron, Canton & Youngstown Railroad, 21. *See also* Northern Ohio Railway
Akron, Ohio, 206–207, 258
Alabama & Tennessee Railroad, 168
Alaska Railroad, xi
Albany, N.Y., 176
Albia, Iowa, 178, 215, 233, 259
Albion, Maine, 118
All Aboard with E. M. Frimbo, World's Greatest Railroad Buff (book), 269
Allen, William F., 239
Alliance, Nebr., 201
Along the Iron Trail (book), 262
Alstrom Company, 93
Alton Railroad. *See* Chicago & Alton Railroad
Amana (Iowa) Colonies, 6
American Baptist Church, 155
American Red Cross, 67
Ames, Oaks, 274–75
Ames, Oliver, 274
Amity College, 171
Amtrak, 1, 11, 20, 92–93, 139, 284
Ancient Order of United Workmen, 223
Anderson, William "Bloody Bill," 65–66

Angell, Roger, 76
Ann Arbor Railroad, 52
Appalachian Lumber Company, 20
Appanoose County Community Railroad, 235
Approaching the City (painting), 284
Ash Can School, 284
Ashburn, Ill., 69
Atchison, Topeka & Santa Fe Railway, 9, 38, 42, 50, 59, 87, 92, 99, 123–24, 153–54, 208, 221, 224, 252–53, 284. *See also* Chicago, Kansas & Western Railroad; Fred Harvey Company; *Super Chief;* Walnut Valley & Colorado Railroad
Atlanta, Ga., 102–103, 206, 276
Atlanta & Charlotte Air Line Railroad, 203, 280
Atlantic, Iowa, 183, 217
Atlantic & Great Western Railway, 108
Atlantic Coast Line Railroad, 138, 156
Atlantic Northern & Southern Railway, 183–84, 217
Atlantic Southern Railway, 183–84
Auburn & Rochester Railroad, 15
Augusta, Ga., 47
Aurora, Ill., 214, 222
Ava, Mo., xii

Balkan, Ky., 246
Baltimore, Md., 95, 127, 217–18, 232
Baltimore & Ohio Historical Society, 260
Baltimore & Ohio Museum, 269
Baltimore & Ohio Railroad, 7, 11–12, 13, 14, 18, 23, 38, 88–89, 91–92, 91, 95, 122, 127, 148, 151,

186, 188, 207, 212, 217–218, 218, 225, 232, 246, 252, 269–70, 273. *See also* Baltimore & Potomac Railroad; *Capitol Limited;* Cincinnati, Hamilton & Dayton Railroad; Coal & Coke Railway
Baltimore & Potomac Railroad, 162
Bangor & Aroostook Railroad, 129
Bangs, George S., 274–77
Banks, Joe, 127
Banner Blue (passenger train), 234
Banshee Train, The (book), 285
Barsness, Richard, 282
Batavia, Iowa, 175
Bay City, Mich., 217
Beach, Iowa, 194
Beebe, Lucius, 262–63
Belfast, Maine, 235
Belfast & Moosehead Lake Railroad, 235
Bennett, Howard, 282
Berkeley, Calif., 140
Berlin, Irving, 278
Berwyn, Nebr., 160
Big Four Railroad. *See* Cleveland, Cincinnati, Chicago & St. Louis Railroad
Billings, Frederick, 250
Billings, Mont., 250
Birmingham, Sheffield & Tennessee River Railroad, 250
Bismarck, N.Dak., 202, 204
Black Diamond (passenger train), 85
Blair, John I., 173–74, 250
Blanchard, Iowa, 171
Blood, Hiram, 185
Bloomington, Ill., 216–17
Blount, F. Nelson, 262
Blue Bird (passenger train), 234
Blue Ridge Railway, 225

Bob Hunting's Great Show, 142
Bombardier Transportation, 93
Bond, Colo., 184
Boone, Iowa, 66, 151, 173
Boonesboro, Iowa, 173–74
Boston, Mass., 176
Boston & Lowell Railroad, 15–16, 215
Boston & Maine Railroad,
    36, 116, 158, 252. *See also*
    Fitchburg Railroad; Portland
    & Ogdensburg Railroad
Boston & Providence
    Rail Road, 14–15
Boston & Worcester Rail Road, 1, 44
Boxcar camps, 213, 214
Boyd, Dallas, 191
Bozeman, Mont., 132
Bragg, Braxton, 64
"Brakeman's Blues" (song), 287
Branchville, S.C., 249
Bristol, Va., 65
Britt, Iowa, 281
Broadway Limited (passenger
    train), 10, 24
Brooks, Maine, 235
*Brother Jonathan's Jokes, Funny
    Stories, and Laughable
    Sketches* (book), 279
Brotherhood of Locomotive
    Engineers, 222
Brown, Charles P., 56
*Brown v. Board of Education
    of Topeka* (1954), 29
Brunswick, Ga., 40
Brunswick, Md., 280
Brush Creek, Tenn., 96–97
Bryan, William Jennings,
    139–40, 141
Bucklen, Herbert, 81
Bucyrus, Ohio, 278
Budd, Ralph, 158
Buffalo, N.Y., 150
*Bulletin of the Railway & Locomotive
    Historical Society* (periodical), 257
Burke, Tex., 133
Burlington, Cedar Rapids &
    Northern Railway, 153
Burlington, Iowa, 194
Burlington, Vt., 211
Burlington & Missouri River
    Railroad of Iowa, 175, 178
Burlington & Missouri River
    Railroad of Nebraska, 249, 250
Burlington Northern Santa
    Fe Railway, 252, 259–60

Burlington Railroad. *See* Chicago,
    Burlington & Quincy Railroad
Burnham, Daniel, 105
Business History Association, 283

C. A. Elmen & Company, 63
Calhoun, John C., 60
California High-Speed
    Rail Authority, 94
California State Fair, 242
California State Railroad
    Museum, 259, 269, 285
Camak, Ga., 250
Camp Dodge, Iowa, 67
Canaan, Conn., 122–23
Caney Fork & Western Railroad, 235
Canistota, S.Dak., 130
Canton, Ohio, 141, 185
Capitol Limited (passenger
    train), 7, 10, 88, 91
Carey, Thomas, 279
Carmel, Ind., 236
Carrington, N.Dak., 97
Carroll, Iowa, 116, 205
Carson City, Nev., 138
"Casey Jones" (song), 287
Cedar Rapids, Iowa, 151
Cedar Rapids & Missouri
    River Rail Road, 173
Centenary Exhibition and
    Pageant of the Baltimore &
    Ohio Railroad, 186, 269
Centerville, Iowa, 236
Central, S.C., 280–81
Central New England Railway, 122
Central Pacific Railroad, 21–22,
    154, 178–79, 220, 285
Central Rail Road & Banking
    Company of Georgia (Central
    of Georgia Railroad), 17, 29–30
Central Railroad of New Jersey,
    32, 258. *See also* Elizabethtown
    & Somerville Railroad
Centralia, Mo., 65–66
Century of Progress Fair
    (Chicago), 159
Chafin, Donald, 216
Chama, N.Mex., 265
Chamberlain, S.Dak., 202
Chambers, William "Big Bill," 81
Chariton, Iowa, 215
Charlotte & South Carolina
    Railroad, 65
"Chattanooga Choo
    Choo" (song), 288

Chautauqua Institution, 199
Chesapeake & Ohio Railroad, 7, 152
Chessie Steam Special
    (passenger train), 261
Chessie System Railroad, 261
Cheyenne, Wyo., 204
Chicago, Aurora & Elgin
    Railway, 270
Chicago, Burlington & Quincy
    Railroad, 62, 87–88, 102, 111,
    116, 118, 123, 131, 143, 158–60.
    171, 181, 183, 193, 194–95, 201,
    214–16, 222, 229, 232, 236, 251,
    259. *See also* Burlington &
    Missouri River Railroad of
    Iowa; Burlington & Missouri
    River Railroad of Nebraska
Chicago, Ill., 50, 103, 150–51,
    159, 188, 210, 213, 274–75
Chicago, Indianapolis &
    Louisville Railway, 38
Chicago, Kansas & Western
    Railroad, 229
Chicago, Milwaukee &
    Gary Railway, 194
Chicago, Milwaukee & Puget
    Sound Railway, 180–81
Chicago, Milwaukee & St. Paul
    Railway, 6, 38, 55–56, 97, 112,
    154, 158, 179–81, 198, 202, 208,
    227, 251, 281. *See also* Chicago,
    Milwaukee & Gary Railway;
    Chicago, Milwaukee & Puget
    Sound Railway; Chicago,
    Milwaukee & St. Paul
    Women's Club; Milwaukee
    & Mississippi Railroad
Chicago, Milwaukee & St.
    Paul Women's Club, 222
Chicago, Rock Island & Pacific
    Railroad, 51, 78, 89–90, 117–18,
    183, 194, 227–28, 232, 236, 252.
    See also Burlington, Cedar
    Rapids & Northern Railway
Chicago, St. Paul, Minneapolis
    & Omaha Railway, 25, 227
Chicago & Alton Railroad,
    26, 80, 216–17
Chicago & Eastern Illinois
    Railroad, 135
Chicago & North Western
    Historical Society, 260
Chicago & North Western Railway,
    49, 58, 64, 74, 75, 76, 81, 82, 94,
    101, 103, 104, 116, 125, 126, 130, 134,

136, *151*, 156, 161, *175*, 186, *188*, 194,
202, 205, 207–208, 214, 215, 222,
240, 241, 245, 254–55. See also
Cedar Rapids & Missouri River
Rail Road; Chicago, St. Paul,
Minneapolis & Omaha Railway;
Dixon Air Line Railroad; Galena
& Chicago Union Rail Road
Chicago Great Western
Railroad, *41*, 78, 101, 115, 118,
194, 252. *See also* Minnesota
& Northwestern Railroad
Chicago Railroad Fair, 186, *188–89*
Chinese, 211
Christian College, 20
Cincinnati, Hamilton &
Dayton Railroad, 110
Cincinnati, Ohio, 182–83, *212*
Cincinnati, Wabash &
Michigan Railway, 229
Cincinnati Southern
Railway, 173, 182–83
Cincinnati Union Station,
135, 148, *149*
"City of New Orleans,
The" (song), 288
City of San Francisco
(passenger train), 79
Clarinda, Iowa, 170
Clarkesville, Ga., 201
Clear Lake, Iowa, *41*, 208
Clegg, Charles (Chuck), Jr., 263
Clemson, Anna Calhoun, 5, 27
Clemson, Floride, 27
Clemson, S.C., 151–52, 203
Clemson College, 51, 52, 143, *146*, 151
Cleveland, Cincinnati, Chicago
& St. Louis Railroad, 107, 148,
225, 252. *See also* Cincinnati,
Wabash & Michigan Railway
Cleveland, Ohio, 123,
150, 185, 210, 217
Cleveland, Wisc., 245
Cleveland & Canton Railroad, 185
Cleveland & Mahoning
Railroad, 133
Clinchfield Railroad, 157, 221
Clyde, Ohio, 237
Coal & Coke Railway, 193
College Springs, Iowa, 170–71
Colo, Iowa, 250
Colorado Midland
Railway, 39, 42, 50
Colorado Railroad
Museum, 264, 269

Columbia, Mo., 20–21, 235
Columbia, S.C., *53*, 174–76
Columbia Terminal Railroad, 235
Columbian (passenger train), 23
Connecticut National Guard, 147
Connecticut Railroad
Commission, 229
Connolly, Joseph
"Head-On Joe," 241
Connotton Valley Railroad. *See*
Cleveland & Canton Railroad
Continental Limited
(passenger train), 239
Copley Plaza Hotel (Boston), 94
Cosmos, Minn., 196–97
Cosmos News (newspaper), 197
County Seat Removal Advocate
(newspaper), 200
Coyote, Kans., 197–98
Credit Mobilier, 274–75
Crestline, Ohio, 107
Creston, Iowa, 216–17, 222, 251
Creston, Winterset & Des
Moines Railroad, 217, 252
Crete, Nebr., 249
Crocker, Mo., 200
Crompton, Va., 277
Crosby, Minn., 232
Crush, W. G., 241
CSX Railroad, 236, 252
Cumbres & Toltec Scenic
Railroad, 265
Cumming (Burnett), Ga., 250
Cupper, Dan, 263
Currier, Nathaniel, 283
Currier & Ives, 283, 284

Dakota, Minnesota &
Eastern Railroad, 236
Dale Creek Bridge, *286*
Danville, Ill., 220
Danville, Ky., 173
Davis, Henry Gassaway, 193
Davis, William W., 177
Dayton, Ohio, 211
De Funiak, Fred, 199
De Funiak Springs, Fla., 199
Dearborn Station (Chicago), 103
Dearing, Ga., 250
"Death Valley Scotty."
See Scott, Walter
Decatur, Ill., 220, 234
Defense Plant Corporation, 74
DeKalb, Ill., 194–95

Delaware, Lackawanna & Western
Railroad, 43, 193–94, 283
Delphos, Ohio, 141
Delray, Fla., 134
Denver, Northwestern &
Pacific Railroad, *48*
Denver, South Park &
Pacific Railroad, 260
Denver & Rio Grande Western
Railroad, 50, 89, 121, 184–85,
223, 252, 264, 277
Depew, Chauncey, 150
Depots. *See* Railroad Stations
Detroit, Bay City & Western
Railroad, 217
Dewey, Thomas, 139
Dickens, Charles, 15–16
Dickinson, N.Dak., 249
Disney, Roy, 7
Dixon, Mo., 200, 209
Dixon Air Line Railroad, 177
Dodge, Grenville, 195
Dorchester, Nebr., 249
Douglas, Ariz., 68
Douglas, Ga., 47, 125
Douglas, Stephen A., 177
"Drummers." *See*
Traveling salesmen
Dubin, Arthur, 289
Duke, Donald, 264
Duluth, South Shore &
Atlantic Railway, 156
Dunkirk, N.Y., 188–89
Durand, Mich., 280
Durant, Dr. Thomas Clark, 178

East Tennessee, Virginia &
Georgia Railroad, 84
East Tennessee & Virginia
Railroad, 96–97, 114
Eastern Division, Union
Pacific Railroad. *See*
Kansas Pacific Railway
Eastern Ohio Chapter, National
Railway Historical Society, 258
Eastern Rail Road, 167
Eden, Colo., 277
Edgefield, S.C., 169–70
Edgefield, Trenton &
Aiken Railroad, 170
Edison Films, 287
Edna, Tex., 250
Edward G. Budd Manufacturing
Company, 87, 90, 158
Egan, William, 129–30

Egyptian Zipper (passenger train), 135
Eisenhower, Dwight D., 152
Elburn, Ill., *136*
Electric Short Line Railway, 195–97
Elizabeth, N.J., 138
Elizabethtown & Somerville Railroad, 138
Ellicott's Mills, Md., 95
Elmira, N.Y., 187–88
Elrod, S.Dak., 81
Emmitsburg, Md., 172–73
Emmitsburg Railroad, 172–73
Emporia, Kans., 221
Endicott, Wash., 249
Endicott, William, 249
Ephrata, Washington, *145*
Erie Lackawanna Railroad, 267
Erie Railroad, 108, 148, 151, 187–89, *190–191*, 212, 217, 224, 264, 278–79. *See also* Atlantic & Great Western Railway; Cleveland & Mahoning Railroad; New-York & Erie Railroad; New York, Pennsylvania & Ohio Railroad
Erwin, Tenn., 221
Espanola, N.Mex., 121
Exeter, Nebr., 249
Express companies, 11, 120, 129

Fair of the Iron Horse. *See* Centenary Exhibition and Pageant of the Baltimore & Ohio Railroad
Fairfield, Iowa, 215
Fairmont, Nebr., 249
Ferguson, E. A., 183
Fisher, Charles, 256–57
Fisk, Elizabeth Chester, 22–23
Fitchburg Railroad, 256
Florida East Coast Railway, *30*, 86, 115, 118
Florida Special (passenger train), 86
Florissant, Colo., fossil deposits, 42
Fogg, Howard, 263, 285
Fond du Lac, Wisc., 169
Forest Hill, N.J., 212
Fort Worth & Denver City Railway, xiii
Fort Worth & Denver South Plains Railroad, *184*
*400*s (passenger trains), 94
Frailey, Fred, 263
Frank Munsey Company, 264
Frank Parmelee Company, 108

Frankfort, Ind., 209
Franklin, John Hope, 29
Fred Harvey Company, *9*, 50, 123–25
French, Daniel Chester, 276
Frisco Railway. *See* St. Louis– San Francisco Railway
Fulton County Narrow Gauge Railway, 137

G&F Café (Douglas, Georgia), 125
Gadsden, James, 60
Gaithersburg, Md., 38
Galena & Chicago Union Rail Road, 186, 272
Galesburg, Ill., 222, 280
Garfield, James A., 162
Garrison, Mont., 179
Gary, Ind., 213
Gary Land Company, 213
Gassaway, W.Va., 193
General Motors Corporation, 158
Georgia & Florida Railroad, 47–48, 114–15, 125, 170
Georgia Railroad, 147, 250
Georgia Southern & Florida Railroad, 172
German-Russians, 154
Glackens, William, 284
Glasgow, Mont., *145*
Glen Ellyn Historical Society, 272
Golden Spike Monument, 273
Goleta, Calif., 161
Golf courses, 214–15
"Gospel Train Is Coming, The" (song), 288
Gould, Okla., *109*
Grafton, Nebr., 249
Grafton, W.Va., 246
Grand Central Station (Chicago), *7*, 103
Grand Central Terminal (New York), 102, 158
Grand Trunk Railway, 285
Grand Trunk Western Railway, *69*
Granger movement, 230
Grano, N.Dak., *203*
Grant, Iowa, 183
Graves at trackside, 81–82
Great Depression (1930s), 244
Great Northern Railway, 38, 76, 142–43, 180, *181*
Great Train Robbery, The (film), 287
Great West Illustrated, The (book), 286
Green Bay & Western Railroad, 252

Green Mountain, Iowa, 78
Greenville & Columbia Rail Road, 120
Greenville & Northern Railroad, 273
Greenville & Western Railway, 157
Greenwich, Ohio, 225–27
Guiteau, Charles, 162
Guthrie, Okla., 175
Gutman, Herbert, 242

H. Schile & Company, 285
Hackthorn, Henry, 147
Haileyville, Okla., 221
Hamburg & Edgefield Plank Road Company, 169–70
Harding, Florence, 151
Harding, Warren G., xi, 150, *151*
Harlow, Alvin F., 122, 268
Harvard, Nebr., 249
Harvard University (Baker Library), 257
Harvey, Frederick (Fred) H., 123–24
"Harvey Girls," 124
Hastings, Nebr., 249
Hauck, Cornelius W., 264, *265*
Havana, Ill., 37
Hawley, Glover, 251
Hawleyville, Conn., 251
Hawthorne, Nathaniel, xi
Hayne, Robert Y., 174
Haynes, F. Joy, 286
Hays, Kans., 157
Hazard, Ky., *130*
Hecla, S.Dak., *54*
Heinz, H. J., 37
Helena, Mont., 133
Hemmingford, Nebr., *201*
Henderson v. United States (1950), 29
Henri, Robert, 284
Henry, Edward Lamson, 283
Henry, Ralph Selph, 262
Hepburn Act (1906), 231
High Iron: A Book of Trains (book), 262
High Speed Ground Transportation Act (1965), 90
Highball: A Pageant of Trains (book), 263
Highliners (book), 263
Hill, James J., 80–81, 143
Hiss, Tony, 269
History of Transportation in the Eastern Cotton Belt to 1860, A (book), 282

Hitchcock, Alfred, 256
Hite, Clarence, 80
Hobo Days (Britt, Iowa), 281
Hobo "jungles," 213
Hoboes, 52–60
Hofsommer, Don L., 283
Holden, P. G., 143
Hooppole, Ill., 181
Hooppole, Yorktown &
    Tampico, 181–82
Hopper, Edward, 284
*Hopping Freight Trains in
    America* (book), 60
Horlick, Wash., 251
Horry, Elias, xi–xii
Hot Springs Railroad, 62
Housatonic Railroad, 95–96, 122, 251
House of Seven Gables, The (book), xi
Houston East & West
    Texas Railroad, 252
Hubbard, Elbert, 124
Hubbard, Freeman, 264
Hudson, John, 203, 204
Humeston, Iowa, 192–93
Hunt, Freeman, 12
Huntington, Ind., 224
Huntly, N.J., 194
Huron, S.Dak., 202, 222–23
Hurricane Express, The (film), 287

Illinois, Iowa & Minnesota
    Railroad, 194
Illinois Central Historical
    Society, 260
Illinois Central Railroad, 59,
    103, 146, 203, 213, 250, 273.
    See also New Orleans &
    Northeastern Railroad
Illinois Prairie Path, 270
Illinois Railway Museum, 269
Illinois Terminal Railroad, 269
*In the Traces: Railroad Paintings
    of Ted Rose* (book), 285
Indiana Hi-Rail Corporation, 236
Indiana Rail Road, 157
Indianapolis, Ind., 104–105, 150
Indianapolis University
    Station, 104–105
Inez, Tex., 250
Inland, Nebr., 249
Inness, George, 283
International Engine
    Picture Club, 257
International Locomotive
    Association, 257

International Order of
    Oddfellows, 223
Interstate Commerce Act (1887), 230
Interstate Commerce
    Commission, 231
Interstate Trolley Club, 257–58
Interurban Development
    Company, 196
Interurbans, 171
Iowa & Southwestern
    Railway, 171, 252
Iowa Central Railway, 62
Iowa Chapter, National Railway
    Historical Society, 259
Iowa State Agricultural College, 143
Ismay, Mont., 154
"I've Been Workin' on the
    Railroad" (song), 287
Ives, James, 283

J. B. O'Connor's Beanery, 125
Jackson, Henry, 279–80
Jackson, Tenn., 273
Jackson, Thomas William, 279
Jackson, William Henry, 286
Jacobs, S. D., 169
James, Frank, 80
James, Jesse, 80
James gang, 79–80
Jamestown, Westfield & North
    Western Railroad, 252
Jersey City, N.J., 258
Jet Rocket (passenger train), 89–90
Jewell, Iowa, 125
Jim Crow codes, 20, 28–30
"John Henry" (song), 287
John W. Barriger III National
    Railroad Library, 283
Johnson, Andrew, 165
Johnson, Tom L., 6–7
Jones, John Luther "Casey," 273
Junction City, La., 251
Junction City, Ohio, 251
Junction City, Wisc., 208

Kalmbach, Al C., 264, 266
Kalmbach Publishing
    Company, 266
Kansas & Colorado Railroad, 200
Kansas Board of Railroad
    Commissioners, 229
Kansas City, Mexico &
    Orient Railway, 195
Kansas City, Ozark &
    Southern Railway, xii

Kansas City Southern
    Railway, 195, 252
Kansas Pacific Railway, 83, 197
Katy Railway. *See* Missouri-
    Kansas-Texas Railway
Kenesaw, Nebr., 249
Kennedy, Robert F., 152
Kent, Ohio, 217
Keokuk Junction Railway, 157
"Kid in Upper 4, The"
    (advertisement), 71–72
Kingsport, Tenn., 157
Knox Clay Products Company, 231
Knoxville, Iowa, 231–32
Knoxville, Tenn., 114
Ku Klux Klan, 47, 156
Kyle Railroad, 237

"L&N Rag, The" (song), 287
La Crosse, Kans., 199–200
La Grange, Ind., 81
La Salle Street Station
    (Chicago), 103
Lackawanna Railroad. *See*
    Delaware, Lackawanna
    & Western Railroad
Lackawanna Valley (painting), 283
Lake Erie & Western
    Railroad, 97, 252
Lake Lillian, Minn., 197
Lake Lillian Echo (newspaper), 197
Lake Shore & Michigan
    Southern Railroad, 210
Lancaster Railway & Locomotive
    Historical Society, 257–58
Lander, Wyo., 133–34, 175
Landrum, S.C., 120
Langdon, Jervis, Jr., 269
Lark (passenger train), 91–92
Las Vegas, N.Mex., 208
Latrobe, Benjamin, Jr., 273
Lehigh Valley Railroad, 85
Leipsic Junction, Ohio, 110
Leslie, Florence, 24
Lewis, Sinclair, 237
Lewistown, Ill., 37, 137
Lexington & Eastern Railway, 130
Lexington & Frankfort
    Rail Road, 25
Lexington & Ohio Railroad, 232–33
Lexington Group in Transportation
    History, 282–83
Lexington Quarterly
    (periodical), 283
Libby, Montana, 196

"Lightning Express,
The" (song), 287
Lima, Ohio, 148
Lincoln, Abraham, 150
Lincoln, Nebr., 204, 222
Link, O. Winston, 272, 286–87
Link, Theodore, 105–106
Litchfield (Depot), Conn., 101
"Little Fellow," 82, 82–83
"Little Red Caboose Behind
the Train" (song), 287
Littlejohn, Duffy, 60
Live Oak, Perry & Gulf
Railroad, 256
Locomotives, 1, 166–67
Logan, Iowa, 240
Logan, Mont., 131, 133
Logan County, W.Va., 216
London, Jack, 57
Long Island City, N.Y., 162
Long Island Railroad, 43,
129, 162–63, 233
Lorillard, Pierre, 6
Los Angeles, Calif., 50–51, 182
Los Angeles & San Pedro
Railroad, 182
Louise, Tex., 250
Louisiana Purchase Exhibition
(St. Louis), 110
Louisville, Cincinnati & Charleston
Rail Road, 174–75, 249
Louisville, Ky., 182, 232–33
Louisville & Nashville Railroad,
173, 199, 246. See also
Lexington & Eastern Railway;
Lexington & Ohio Railroad
Lowell, Charles, 195
Lowell, Nebr., 249
Luce Lines. See Electric
Short Line Railway

Mackay, Charles, 18, 20
Macksburg, Iowa, 217
Madison, Ind., 167
Madison, Minn., 160
Madison, Wisc., 176–77
Main Street (book), 237
Maine Central Railroad, 235, 251
Malvern, Iowa, 5
Malvern, Pa., 82–83
Manchester, Ga., 280
Manchester (Depot), Vt., 101
Mann Boudoir Car Company, 84
Mann-Elkins Act (1910), 231

Marion, Iowa, 198
Marion, Ohio 151
Marshalltown, Iowa, 78–79, 244
Marshfield, Mo., 67
Martin, Albro, 253–54
Maryland & Pennsylvania
Railroad, 252
Mason & Oceana Railroad, 43
Masonic Order, 223
Mayo Clinic, 74
Maysville, Ky., 152
McBride, S. S., 121
McCook, Nebr., 222
McKinley, William, 80, 139, 141
McMinnville, Tenn., 235
Meadville, Pa., 108
Melville, N.Dak., 171
Memphis, Tenn., 114
Memphis & Charleston
Rail Road, 113–14
Meridian, Miss., 106–107
Meridian Terminal Company, 106
Merrick, N.Y., 163
Merwinsville (Gaylordsville),
Conn., 95–96
Metcalfe, Nelson, Jr., 71–72
Methodist Episcopal
Church, 155, 224, 278
Metroliner (passenger train), 90–91
Metropolitan Museum of Art, 283
Mexicans, 214
Meyerdale, Pa., 261
Midland Continental Historical
& Technical Society, 260
Midnight, The (passenger train), 234
"Midnight Train to
Georgia" (song), 288
Mill City, Nev., 154
Miller, Merle, 244–45
Milles, Carl, 106
Milwaukee, Wisc., 177
Milwaukee & Fond du
Lac Railroad, 169
Milwaukee & Mississippi
Railroad, 176
Milwaukee Road. See Chicago,
Milwaukee & St. Paul Railway
Milwaukee Road Historical
Association, 260
Mingo Junction, Ohio, 67
Minneapolis, Minn., 76, 196
Minneapolis, St. Paul & Sault Ste.
Marie Railroad (Soo Line), 97,
99, 110, 159, 203, 232, 249. See also
Wisconsin Central Railway

Minneapolis & St. Louis Railroad,
45, 46, 122, 160, 252, 281
Minnesota & Northwestern
Railroad, 82
Mississippi & Tennessee
Railroad, 61
Mississippi Central Railroad, 153
Mississippi Valley Historical
Association, 282
Missoula, Mont., 181
Missouri & North Arkansas
Railroad, 252
Missouri-Kansas-Texas Railway,
21, 29, 98, 109, 187, 241, 252
Missouri Pacific Railway, 57, 84,
200, 217–19, 246–47. See also
Kansas & Colorado Railroad;
St. Louis, Iron Mountain
& Southern Railway
Mitchell, S.Dak., 202
Mixed Train Daily: A Book of Short
Line Railroads (book), 263
Moberly, Mo., 216, 220, 243
Mobile & Ohio Railroad, 106, 158
Mobridge, S.Dak., 250–51
Model Railroader
(periodical), 264, 266
Monon Route. See
Chicago, Indianapolis &
Louisville Railway
Montgomery, Pa., 34
Morley, Christopher, 32–33
Morris, Thomas Armstrong, 104
Mosquito, Maine, 251
Mount Pleasant, Iowa, 215
Mount Royal Station
(Baltimore), 127
Mount Saint Mary's College, 172
Muir, John, 42
Mulino, Oreg., 171
Muncy, Pa., 34
Museum of Transportation
(St. Louis), 269

Nashville, Chattanooga & St.
Louis Railway, 77–78
Nashville, Tenn., 78
National Gallery of Art, 283
National Historic Preservation
Act (1966), 273
National Railroad Passenger
Corporation. See Amtrak
National Railway Historical
Society, 192, 257–60

National Railway Historical Society Bulletin (periodical), 259
National Register of Historic Places, 273
National Road, 166
National Tourists Union, 281
National Train Day, 92
Naugatuck Railroad, 229–30
Neola, Iowa, 117
New Castle & Frenchtown Rail Road, 11
New Haven Railroad. *See* New York, New Haven & Hartford Railroad
New Jersey Central. *See* Central Railroad of New Jersey
New London, Ohio, 21
New Orleans, La., 138, 146
New Orleans & Northeastern Railroad, 288
"New River Train" (song), 287
New York, Chicago & St. Louis Railroad, 110, 251, 254
New York, New Haven & Hartford Railroad, *31,* 71–72, 89, 120–22, 138. *See also* Boston & Providence Rail Road; Housatonic Railroad; Naugatuck Railroad
New York, N.Y., 158, 177–78, 217, 267, 276
New York, Ontario & Western Railroad, 45, 160, 260
New York, Pennsylvania & Ohio Railroad, 252
New York, Texas & Mexican Railway, 250
New-York & Erie Railroad, 97
New York & Harlem Railroad, 177–78
New York Central & Hudson River Railroad, 38, 276
New York Central Historical Society, 260
New York Central Railroad, 2, 10, 32–33, 39, 89, 91, 252–54, 284. *See also* Boston & Worcester Rail Road; Cleveland, Cincinnati, Chicago & St. Louis Railroad; Lake Erie & Western Railroad; Lake Shore & Michigan Southern Railroad; New York Central & Hudson River Railroad; Penn Central Railroad; Toledo & Ohio Central Railroad; *Twentieth Century Limited* (passenger train)
New York Children's Aid Society, 156

Newburg, Mo., 209
Newport, N.Dak., 171
Nickel Plate Road. *See* New York, Chicago & St. Louis Railroad
9:45 AM Accommodation, Stamford, Connecticut, 1867, The (painting), 283
"Nine Hundred Miles" (song), 287
Noe, Charles, 281
Norfolk, Va., 138–39
Norfolk & Virginia Beach Railroad, 138
Norfolk & Western Railway, 138, 152, 272, 286–87
Norfolk Southern Railroad, 183, 235–36, 252, 272, 280
North Bend Rail Trail, *271*
North by Northwest (film), 287
North Carolina Rail Road, 147
North Conway, N.H., 101
North Enid, Okla., 227
North Little Rock, Ark., 246–47
North Little Rock Shops Booster Club, 246
North Missouri Railroad, 65–66
North Platte, Nebr., 148
North Vernon, Ind., 122, *153*
North Western Railway. *See* Chicago & North Western Railway
Northampton, Mass., 165
Northern Cross Rail Road of Illinois, 13–14
Northern Ohio Railway, 225–26
Northern Pacific Railroad, 38–39, 55, 80, 110, 131, *132,* 133, 171, 180, *196, 202,* 249–50

O. Henry (William Sydney Porter), 79
O. Winston Link Museum (Roanoke, Va.), 287
Oakes, Thomas F., 249
Oakesdale, Wash., 249
Oakfield, Maine, *129*
Obama, Barak, 139
Oelwein, Iowa, 244
Official Guide to the Railways, 127–28, 256
Ohio & Erie Canal, 193
Ohio & Mississippi Railway, 79
Ohio Railroad Commission, 226
Old Fort, N.C., 247
Omaha, Nebr., 217
Omaha Road. *See* Chicago, St. Paul, Minneapolis & Omaha Railway

On a Fast Streamliner: Fun from New York to Frisco (book), 279, 280
On a Slow Train through Arksansaw: Funny Railroad Stories – Sayings of the Southern Darkies – All the Latest and Best Minstrel Jokes of the Day (book), 279–80
"On the Atchison, Topeka and the Santa Fe" (song), 288
Order of Railway Telegraphers, 112
Order of the Knights of Phythias, 223
Oregon River & Navigation Company, 250
Oskaloosa, Iowa, 20
Overton, Richard C., 282
Owl (passenger train), 70

Packard, Frank, 264
"Paddy on the Railway" (song), 287
Paducah & Louisville Railroad, 237
Palmer, Potter, 24
Parcel Post Act (1913), 129
Parkersburg, W.Va., 246
Parsons, Kans., *187*
Penn Central Railroad, 90, 152
Pennington, Edmund, 249
Pennington County, Minnesota, 249
Pennsylvania Limited (passenger train), 253
Pennsylvania Railroad, 4, 6, 10, 23–24, 33–36, 47, 56, 67, 122, 129, 141, 148, 151, 243–44, 253–54, 284. *See also* Long Island Railroad; Penn Central Railroad; Philadelphia, Washington & Baltimore Railroad; Philadelphia & Columbia Rail Road; Pittsburgh, Fort Wayne & Chicago Railroad
Pennsylvania Station (New York), 129, 158
Peoria, Ill., 208
Peru, Ind., 220
Phil Campbell, Ala., 250
Philadelphia, Pa., 150
Philadelphia, Washington & Baltimore Railroad, 150
Philadelphia & Columbia Rail Road, 82–83
Philip, S.Dak., *241*
Phillips, Ulrich Bonnell, 282
Phillips & Rangeley Railroad, 39
Pickens Railroad, 20
Piermont, N.Y., 187

Pierre, Rapid City & North
    Western Railway, 252
Pierre, S.Dak., 202
Pittsburgh, Akron &
    Western Railroad, 222
Pittsburgh, Fort Wayne &
    Chicago Railroad, 107
Plainview, Texas, *184*
Planes, Trains and Automobiles
    (film), 287
Plessy v. Ferguson (1896), 28–30
Plymouth, N.C., 156
Pond Creek, Okla., 227–28
Pond Creek Station, Okla., 227
Porter, William Sydney
    (pseud. O. Henry), 79
Portland & Ogdensburg
    Railroad, 101
Portola, Calif., 280
Posner, Henry, III, *268*
Postal Telegraph Company, 112
Potatoland Special
    (passenger train), *129*
Potin, Horace, 257
Potter Act (1874), 230
Poussin, Guillaume, 1
Presbyterian Church, 224
Prescott, C. H., 249
Prescott, Wash., 249
Primghar, Iowa, 250
Promontory, Utah, 273, 386.
    See also Railroads: Golden
    spike ceremonies
Protestant Episcopal Church, 155–56
"Public be damned," 253–55
Puddleville, Ga., 172
Pueblo, Colo., 278
Pulaski County, Mo., 200
Pullman, George, 24
Pullman Company, 7, 9, 23–24,
    72, 73, 74, 83–84, 86
Purdue University, 269
Putnam, Robert, 261
Pyle, Ernie, 285

Quakers. *See* Society of Friends
Quanah, Acme & Pacific
    Railroad, *204, 205*
Quigley, J. B., xii

Railroad Division, Young Men's
    Christian Association, 210–11
Railroad Enthusiasts,
    255–69, 280, 285
Railroad History (periodical), 257

Railroad Magazine
    (periodical), 264, 266
Railroad Men's Magazine
    (periodical), 264
Railroad Museum of
    Pennsylvania, 269
Railroad reform legislation, 230–31
Railroad Station Historical
    Society, 260
Railroad Stations
    Agents, xiii, 99–122
    Agents' housing, 99–101, 159–61
    Architectural structures
        and styles, 95–109
    Boomer agents, 114–15
    Complaints about,
        109–10, 229–34
    Depot district, 207–14
    Depot hotels, 108
    Depot parks, 106–107
    Events and experiences at, xiii,
        139–43, 158–59, 161–64
    Location of, 101
    Public space, 130–31, 133–39
    Quest for better depots, 225–229
    Specific events at: Agricultural/
        Educational trains, 142–46;
        Chapel cars, 155–56; Circus
        trains, 142; Funeral trains,
        150–52; Immigrant trains,
        152–55; Orphan trains,
        156–57; "Santa trains," 157–58;
        Troop trains, 147–50
    Union stations, 104–108
    Weather information, 137–38
    Workers: Food service,
        122–25; Red Caps, 125–27;
        Urban station staff and
        personnel, 127–30. *See also*
        Railroad Stations: Agents
Railroad Stories (periodical), 264
Railroads
    Accidents, wrecks, and staged
        wrecks, 215, 239–43
    Art, 283–85
    Celebrations, 174–85,
        280–81, 186–87
    Children, 244–45
    Community carriers, 235–36
    Film, 287
    Free passage, 60–64
    Golden spike ceremonies, 178–82
    Headquarters, 217–19
    Historic preservation and
        museums, 269–70, 272–73
    Historical profession, 282–83

Hospitals, 219–20
Housing patterns, 221
Humor, 278–80
Line abandonments, 234–36
Markers and monuments, 273–78
Mileage, xi, 270
Music, 287–88
Naming impact, 248–51
Nicknames, phrases,
    and words, 251–55
Opposition to, 165–66
Passenger train experiences,
    xii, 1–5, 11–18, 20–25, 27–31,
    33–52, 77–82, 83–94
Passenger train "take offs" and
    last runs, 189, 192, 234
Photography, 286
Public aid and assistance, 245–47
Publications, 261–64, 266
Quest for and value of, xii, 167–73
Rhythms of community
    life, 237–38
Rolling stock, 1, 13–15, 18,
    20–27, 33, 43, 86, 88–93
Shortline and regional
    carriers, 236–37
Speech patterns, 255
Strikes, 216, 242–44
Sunday operations, 34–38
Telegraphy, 111–13
Time, 238–39
Town creation, 171–74, 193–98
Town designs, 202–206
Travel amenities, 8–10
Troop trains, 64–73
Urban development, xiii, 216–17
Urban rivalries, 199–202
Women travelers, 24–28
Workers, 2–11, 13, 27, 30, 57,
    221–25. *See also* Railroad
    Stations: Agents
Workers' wives, 222–23
World War II, 70–74
Rails-to-trails, 270–73
Rails-to-Trails Act (1983), 270–72
Railway & Locomotive
    Historical Society, 256, 260
Railway Employees'
    Department, American
    Federation of Labor, 242
"Railway to Heaven,
    The" (song), 288
Ramsey, Margaret Crozier, 65
Rangeley Lake, Maine, 39
Rapid City, S.Dak., 202
Rau, William H., 286

Rauls, Lou, 1
Raymond & Whitcomb
    Company, 49
Reading Railroad, 33–34
Red Oak, Iowa, 102, 116, *123*, 215
Redfield, S.Dak., 208
Reevy, Tony, 263
Reid, Gilmore (Gil), 285
Relay, Md., 273–74
Relief, sigh of, 289
Rensselaer & Saratoga
    Rail Road, 12–13
Republican, Nebr., *131*
Reynolds, Jonathan, 62
Richardson, Frederick, 262
Richardson, H. H., 276
Richland, Mo., 200
Riddle, Oreg., *144*
Rio Grande Southern Railroad, 260
Rio Grande Western Railway, *61*
Roaring Springs, Tex., *204–205, 206*
Roaring Springs Townsite
    Company, 205
Robbins, Oreg., 171
Robertsville, Ohio, *113*
Robinson, Archie, 256, 263
Rochester Special (passenger
    train), 75
Rock Island Railroad. *See* Chicago,
    Rock Island & Pacific Railroad
Rocky Ridge, Md., 172
Rodgers, Jimmie, 287–88
Roebling, John Augustus, 285
Rogers, Will, 124–25
Roman Catholic Church,
    155–56, 214, 224
Roosevelt, Franklin D., 151–52
Rose, Theodore (Ted), 285
Rosehill Cemetery
    (Chicago), 274–75, 276
Ross, C. A., 183
"Roxie," the railroad dog, 162–63
"Runaway Train" (song), 288
Rush County, Kans., 199–200
Russell, Andrew Joseph, 178, 286
Russell, Iowa, *111*
Russian Orthodox Church, 155
Rutland & Washington
    Rail Road, *19*

Sabetha, Kans., 137
Sacramento, Calif., 138, 220, 242
Safety Appliance Act (1893), 20
Saint-Gaudens, Augustus, 276
Salamanca, N.Y., 188, *190*
Salida, Colo., 223

San Francisco, Calif., 217, 219
San Joaquin Valley Railroad, 237
Sand Creek, Mich., 240
Santa Fe Railway. *See* Atchison,
    Topeka & Santa Fe Railway
*Sarah Keys v. Carolina Coach
    Company* (1955), 29
Scott, Thomas (Tom), 253
Scott, Walter, 50
Scranton, Pa., 283. *See also*
    Steamtown National
    Historic Site
Seaboard System, 235
Seneca, Mich., 239–40
Seward, William, 176
Shaw, M. M., 49–50
Sheldon, Iowa, 227
Shinn, Everett, 284
Shopmen's Strike (1922–23), 242–44
Simpson College, 51
Sioux Falls, S.Dak., 112, 202
*Slow Trains to Yesterday: A Last
    Glance at the Local* (book), 263
Snoqualmie, Wash., 280
Snyder, Nebr., 161
Society of Friends, 20
Soo Line. *See* Minneapolis,
    St. Paul & Sault Ste. Marie
    Railroad (Soo Line)
South Acton, Mass., 256
South-Carolina Canal & Rail-Road,
    xi, 34, 60, 62, 169, 174, 249
South Carolina Rail Road, 5, 17
South Enid, Okla., 227–28
South Pekin, Ill., 214
Southern Pacific Historical &
    Technical Society, 260
Southern Pacific Railroad, 62, *70*,
    71, 72, 74, *79, 84, 85*, 91–92, 133,
    138, *140, 144*, 151, 160–61, *180*,
    217, 219–20, 252–53, 288. *See also*
    Central Pacific Railroad; New
    York, Texas & Mexican Railway
Southern Railway, 47, 52, *53*, 92, 106,
    120, 138, 151, 201, 247, 276, 280.
    See also Atlanta & Charlotte Air
    Line Railroad; Birmingham,
    Sheffield & Tennessee River
    Railroad; Blue Ridge Railway;
    Edgefield, Trenton & Aiken
    Railroad; Georgia Southern
    & Florida Railroad
Southern Railway Historical
    Society, 260
Spearman, Frank, 264
Spencer, Iowa, *158*

Spencer, Samuel, 276
Spokane & Inland Empire
    Railroad, 144
Springfield, Ill., 220
St. Joseph & Grand Island
    Railway, 137
St. Joseph Valley Railway, 81
St. Louis, Iron Mountain &
    Southern Railway, 38
St. Louis, Mo., 74, 76,
    105, 106, 110, 218
St. Louis County (Missouri)
    Parks Department, 269
St. Louis–San Francisco
    Railway, 72, 200, 209, 269
St. Louis Union Station, 105–106,
    108, 125, 127–28, *162–64*
Staggers Act (1980), 231
Standiford, E. D., 173
Stanford, Leland, 178–79
Stanton, Iowa, 229
Starbuck, W. H., 250
Starbuck, Wash., 249
Staunton, Va., 7
Steamtown National
    Historic Site, 262, 269
Stearns, Isaac Ingalls, 249
Stearns County, Minn., 249
Stephens College, 20
Sterling, Ill., 177
Stevens Point, Wisc., 278
Stevenson, Robert Louis, 6, 21–22
Stickney, A. B., 101
Stilwell, Arthur, 195
Stroeh, E. F., 246
Strong, Joseph, 152–53
Studebaker, J. M., 37
Sunshine Special (passenger
    train), 84
Super Chief (passenger
    train), 9, 87–88
Susquehanna, Penn., 97, 108, 224
Swamp Rabbit Trail, 273
Syracuse, N.Y., 150

Taber, Thomas T., 266, 267
Tabor & Northern Railroad, 5
Taft, William Howard, 139
Talgo (passenger train), 89
Tallulah Falls Railway, 138
Tampico, Ill., 181
Tanner, William, xii–xiii
Taunton, Mass., 138
Telegraphy schools, 112–13
Telfener, Count Joseph, 250
Teller, Griffith (Grif), 212, 284

Terminal Railroad Association
  of St. Louis, 105–106
Texarkana, Ark., 208
Thatcher Perkins (locomotive),
  186–87, *191*
Thomas Viaduct, 273–74
Thompson, "Boxcar" Bertha, 59–60
Thorpe, Minn., 197
Timken, Kans., 229
"To a Locomotive in
  Winter" (poem), 1
Toccoa, Ga., 201
Toledo, Peoria & Western
  Railway, 252
Toledo & Ohio Central
  Railroad, 278
Tom Taber Express
  (commuter train), 267
Topeka, Kans., 221
Torrington, Conn., 147
Train a Grande Vitesse (TGV)
  (passenger train), 94
"Train Whistle Blues" (song), 287
Train X (passenger train), 89
Trains (book), 262
Trains (periodical), 264, 266
Trains in Transition (book), 263
Transportation Act (1958), 234
Travel in pre–Railway Age, 166
Travelers Aid Society, 128, 148
Traveling salesmen, 133
Tri-County (Tennessee)
  Railroad Authority, 235
Tripoli, Iowa, 115
Trollope, Anthony, 195
Troutdale, Maine, 251
Truman, Harry, 139, *140*, 256
Turner, Frederick Jackson, 195
Turtle Lake, N.Dak., 171
Twentieth Century Limited
  (passenger train), 10, 32–33, 87
Twin Zephyr (passenger train), 89

Union Pacific (film), 287
Union Pacific Railroad, 16, 21, 22,
  67, 89, *100*, 148, 151–52, 157–58,
  178–79, 195, 207, 217, 252–53,
  274–76, *286*. *See also* Kansas
  Pacific Railway; Oregon River
  & Navigation Company; St.
  Joseph & Grand Island Railway
Union Passenger Station
  (Chicago), 103
Unionville, Conn., 120–21
United Service Organization
  (USO), 148, *149*, 150

University of Idaho, 144
University of Missouri, 20, 143
University of South
  Carolina, 51–52, 174
Unstoppable (film), 287
Urbana, Ind., 228–29
U.S. Office of Defense
  Transportation, 68, 70
U.S. Post Office Department,
  92, 129, 251
U.S. Railroad Administration, 68
U.S. Railway Mail Service,
  11, 134, 274, 277
U.S. Signal Corps, 137
U.S. War Relocation
  Authority, 69–70

Valley Junction (West Des
  Moines), Iowa, 251
Valley Railway, 141
Van Horne, Iowa, 198
Van Horne, William, 198
Van Voy News Service, 7
Van Wert, Iowa, *192*
Vanderbilt, Cornelius, 276
Vanderbilt, William Henry, 253–55
Vanderbilt, William K., 245
Vassar, Wash., 251
Villa Grove, Ill., 135
Villard, Henry, 180, 249
Villisca, Iowa, 183
Virginia & Truckee Railway, 138
Virginia Creeper National
  Recreation Trail, 272
Virginia-Harlow Coal
  Corporation, 246
Von Gerstner, Franz Anton, 28

Wabash, St. Louis &
  Pacific Railway, 216
"Wabash Cannonball," (song), 287
Wabash Railroad, 33, *62*, 74,
  76, 80, 110, *141*, 143–44, 220,
  234, 239–40, 243–44, *259*,
  269, 273. *See also* Ann Arbor
  Railroad; Northern Cross
  Rail Road of Illinois; Wabash,
  St. Louis & Pacific Railway
Wabash Trace Nature Trail, 273
Waco, Beaumont, Trinity &
  Sabine Railway, 252, 256
Walhalla, S.C., 225
Walker, W. W., 173–74
Walnut City, Kans., 199–200
Walnut Valley & Colorado
  Railroad, 199–200

Warman, Cy, 264
Washington, Baltimore &
  Annapolis Electric Railway, 258
Washington, D.C., 105, 162
Washington (Depot), Conn., 101
Washington State Agricultural
  College, 144
Washington Union Station, 152
Watertown, S.Dak., 202
Watts, May Theilgaard, 270
Wausau, Wisc., 222
Wayne, John, 287
Waynesville, Mo., 200
Webster, Daniel, 187
"Welcome Travelers"
  (radio program), 135
Weldon, Iowa, *193*
Wellsville, N.Y., 187, *190*
West, Tex., 241
West Burlington, Iowa, 194
West Burlington Land
  Company, 194
*West Chester and Philadelphia
  Railroad Company v.
  Miles* (1867), 28
West Chicago, Ill., 280
West Eola, Ill., 214
West Virginia State Parks, 271
Western & Atlantic Rail Road, *61*
Western Maryland Railway, 172–73
Western Pacific Railroad, 79
Western Rail Road of
  Massachusetts, 176
Western Union Telegraph
  Company, 112, 120, 179
Wheeling, W.Va., 18, 20
Wheeling & Lake Erie Railroad,
  113, 141. *See also* Cleveland
  & Canton Railroad
Whipple, Henry Benjamin, 17
Whitaker, Rogers E. M. ("E.M.
  Frimbo"), 266–67, *268*, 269
White, E. B., 86
White, John H., Jr., 257
Whitman, Walt, 1
Willamette Valley Southern
  Railway, 171
William Penn College, 20
Williams, H. R., 251
Williamsport, Pa., 34
Wilmington, N.C., 138
Wilmington & Susquehanna
  Railroad, 12
Wilson, Lena, 59
Winona Assembly and
  Summer Assembly, 37

Winona Inter-Urban Railway, 37
Winsted, Conn., 229–30
Wiscasset, Waterville &
    Farmington Railway, 117–18
Wisconsin Central Railway, 208, 278
Witfle, Charles, 286
Woolman, John, 20

"Wreck of Old 97, The" (song), 287
Wyndemere, N.Dak., 110

Xplorer (passenger train), 89

Yankton, S.Dak., 202
YMCA. *See* Railroad
    Division, Young Men's
    Christian Association

Yorktown, Ill., 181
Young Women's Christian
    Association, 128
Youngstown, Ohio, 133
Yulee, Fla., 280

Zephyr (passenger train),
    87, 158–59, 184

BOOKS IN THE RAILROADS PAST AND PRESENT SERIES

Landmarks on the Iron Road:
Two Centuries of North American
Railroad Engineering
William D. Middleton

South Shore: The Last Interurban
(revised second edition)
William D. Middleton

Katy Northwest:
The Story of a Branch Line Railroad
Donovan L. Hofsommer

"Yet there isn't a train I wouldn't
take": Railway Journeys
William D. Middleton

The Pennsylvania
Railroad in Indiana
William J. Watt

In the Traces:
Railroad Paintings of Ted Rose
Ted Rose

A Sampling of Penn Central:
Southern Region on Display
Jerry Taylor

The Lake Shore
Electric Railway Story
Herbert H. Harwood Jr. &
Robert S. Korach

The Pennsylvania Railroad at Bay:
William Riley McKeen and the
Terre Haute & Indianapolis
Railroad
Richard T. Wallis

The Bridge at Québec
William D. Middleton

History of the J. G. Brill Company
Debra Brill

Uncle Sam's Locomotives: The
USRA and the Nation's Railroads
Eugene L. Huddleston

Metropolitan Railways:
Rapid Transit in America
William D. Middleton

Perfecting the American
Steam Locomotive
J. Parker Lamb

From Small Town to Downtown:
A History of the Jewett Car
Company, 1893–1919
Lawrence A. Brough &
James H. Graebner

Limiteds, Locals, and Expresses in
Indiana, 1838-1971
Craig Sanders

Steel Trails of Hawkeyeland:
Iowa's Railroad Experience
Don L. Hofsommer

Amtrak in the Heartland
Craig Sanders

When the Steam
Railroads Electrified
(revised second edition)
William D. Middleton

The GrandLuxe Express:
Traveling in High Style
Karl Zimmermann

Still Standing: A Century of
Urban Train Station Design
Christopher Brown

The Indiana Rail Road Company:
America's New Regional Railroad
Christopher Rund

Evolution of the American
Diesel Locomotive
J. Parker Lamb

The Men Who Loved Trains:
The Story of Men Who Battled
Greed to Save an Ailing Industry
Rush Loving Jr.

The Train of Tomorrow
Ric Morgan

Built to Move Millions:
Streetcar Building in Ohio
Craig R. Semsel

The CSX Clinchfield Route
in the 21st Century
Jerry Taylor & Ray Poteat

The New York, Westchester &
Boston Railway: J. P. Morgan's
Magnificent Mistake
Herbert H. Harwood Jr.

Iron Rails in the Garden State:
Tales of New Jersey Railroading
Anthony J. Bianculli

Visionary Railroader:
Jervis Langdon Jr. and the
Transportation Revolution
H. Roger Grant

The Duluth South Shore &
Atlantic Railway: A History
of the Lake Superior District's
Pioneer Iron Ore Hauler
John Gaertner

Iowa's Railroads: An Album
H. Roger Grant &
Donovan Hofsommer

Frank Julian Sprague:
Electrical Inventor and Engineer
William D. Middleton &
William D. Middleton III

Twilight of the Great Trains
(expanded edition)
Fred W. Frailey

Little Trains to Faraway Places
Karl Zimmermann

Railroad Noir:
The American West at the End
of the Twentieth Century
Linda Grant Niemann

From Telegrapher to Titan:
The Life of William C. Van Horne
Valerie Knowles

The Railroad That Never Was:
Vanderbilt, Morgan, and the
South Pennsylvania Railroad
Herbert H. Harwood Jr.

Boomer: Railroad Memoirs
Linda Grant Niemann

Indiana Railroad Lines
Graydon M. Meints

The Indiana Rail Road Company:
America's New Regional Railroad
(revised and expanded edition)
Christopher Rund,
Fred W. Frailey, & Eric Powell

The CSX Clinchfield Route
in the 21st Century
(now in paperback)
Jerry Taylor & Ray Poteat

Wet Britches and Muddy Boots:
A History of Travel in Victorian
America
John H. White Jr.

Landmarks on the Iron Road:
Two Centuries of North American
Railroad Engineering
(now in paperback)
William D. Middleton

On Railways Far Away
William D. Middleton

Railroads of Meridian
J. Parker Lamb, with
contributions by David H.
Bridges & David S. Price

H. ROGER GRANT is Kathryn and Calhoun Lemon Professor of History at Clemson University. He is author of more than 30 books, including *Electric Interurbans and the American People* (IUP, 2016), *Railroaders without Borders: A History of the Railroad Development Corporation* (IUP, 2015) and *The Louisville, Cincinnati & Charleston Rail Road: Dreams of Linking North and South* (IUP, 2014).

CPSIA information can be obtained
at www.ICGtesting.com
Printed in the USA
LVHW071116051219
639428LV00007B/6/P